UNHAPPY THE LAND

This book is dedicated to two friends, historians both: Ruth Dudley Edwards and David A. Wilson.

UNHAPPY THE LAND

The Most Oppressed People Ever, the Irish?

LIAM KENNEDY

MERRION
PRESS

First published in 2016 by
Merrion Press
8 Chapel Lane
Sallins
Co. Kildare

British Library Cataloguing in Publication Data
An entry can be found on request

978-1-78537-028-1 (Paper)
978-1-78537-029-8 (Cloth)
978-1-78537-030-4 (PDF)
978-1-78537-047-2 (Epub)
978-1-78537-048-9 (Mobi)

Library of Congress Cataloging in Publication Data.
An entry can be found on request

Contents

PREFACE AND ACKNOWLEDGEMENTS   VI

LIST OF TABLES   IX

INTRODUCTION   1

Part 1: The Long View

CHAPTER ONE   A Most Oppressed People?   11

CHAPTER TWO   The Planter and the Gael   42

CHAPTER THREE   Nationalism and Unionism in Ireland   53

Part 2: Famine in Ireland

CHAPTER FOUR   Cry Holocaust: The Great Irish Famine and the Jewish Holocaust   81

CHAPTER FIVE   Ireland, Irish-America and the Man who 'Invented' Genocide   105

Part 3: The Revolutionary Decade

CHAPTER SIX   Harbinger of Reaction: The Ulster Covenant   127

CHAPTER SEVEN   Bad Blood: The Proclamation of the Irish Republic   146

CHAPTER EIGHT   Texting Terror: 1912 and 1916   168

CHAPTER NINE   Was There an Irish War of Independence?   187

ENDNOTES   218

BIBLIOGRAPHY   267

INDEX   285

Preface and Acknowledgements

These essays were so long in the making, assisted by long periods of neglect it has to be acknowledged, that my inventory of intellectual and other debts is more than usually long. Many will disagree with my arguments, including some or possibly all of those given mention below. In the beginning I suppose there are the historians. These, but not only these, caused me to *think* (or make my brain hurt, as one colleague puts it). I have benefited in many ways from reading and talking to a gifted generation of historians of Ireland. These include, and I am sure to omit some dear colleagues and friends: Jonathan Bardon, Paul Bew, Andy Bielenberg, Marie Coleman, Vincent Comerford, Sean Connolly, Louis Cullen, Mary Daly, Alun Davies, Enda Delaney, David Dickson, Richard English, Sean Farrell, Diarmaid Ferriter, David Fitzpatrick, Roy Foster, George Gandy, Peter Gray, Brian Gurrin, David Johnson, Christine Kinealy, Michael Laffan, Joe Lee, Breandán Mac Suibhne, Patrick Maume, Fearghal McGarry, James McGuire, Don MacRaild, Bob Morris, John A. Murphy, Willie Nolan, Gearóid Ó Tuathaigh, Mary O'Dowd, Sean O'Connell, Alan O'Day, Philip Ollerenshaw, Henry Patterson, Seamus Smyth, Willie Smyth, Brian Walker, Irene Whelan, Karin White. And there is always Cormac Ó Gráda, *saoi is duine sár-léannta ar fad*.

Then there are the historians of Ireland from farther afield in North America who have done so much to enrich our understanding of our own wee country (as I have learned to say after years of northern domicile): the inspirational Don Akenson and the rest of that coterie of brilliant scholars which includes Jim Donnelly, the late Peter Hart, David W. Miller and Kerby A. Miller. It has been my privilege to welcome them to my home in Belfast. Some said they enjoyed the accommodation, despite a certain lack of facilities that are common, apparently, in the New World.

Having one foot in the social sciences, I must, of course, pay tribute to the historically-minded social scientists, on both sides of the Atlantic. Among these are: Graham Brownlow, Dominic Bryan, Brice Dickson, Graham Gudgin, Joel Mokyr, Lucia Pozzi, Katy Radford, Joe Ruane, Peter Solar, Jennifer Todd. I owe an indirect debt to writers of various kinds. Their influence seeped into the writing in sometimes unlikely places. There are many and I will only mention Paul Durcan, Michael Longley, Fintan O'Toole and Stewart Parker.

Literary and cultural historians have sometimes spoken to me. John Wilson Foster was good enough to read through the entire text and make incisive observations. I want also to mention Eamonn Hughes and Edna Longley, both of this parish, and one of my oldest school friends, Denis Sampson, the biographer of John McGahern. Irene Boada Montagut, the author of a feminist study of Irish and Catalan short stories, was hugely warm and supportive. As George Bernard Shaw might have had it (*Man and Superman*), in more recent times, and after much prevarication, she was good enough to encourage me to propose that I marry her.

Three of these essays have been previously published. Chapter One appeared many years ago in my *Colonialism, Religion and Nationalism in Ireland* under the title 'Out of History: Ireland, "That Most Distressful Country"'. Chapter Two, 'The Planter and the Gael: Explorations in Irish Ethnic History' was co-written with Kerby A. Miller, Brian Gurrin and Gareth Davies and was published in *The Imaginary of the Stranger: Encountering the Other* edited by Karin White and Julie Costello. Kerby Miller and I would like to acknowledge with gratitude the financial assistance of the National Endowment for the Humanities and the Guggenheim Foundation towards the research on which this chapter was based. I hope to develop some of these themes further in the future. Chapter Nine appeared in a collection of essays edited by Bruce Stewart, *Hearts and Minds: Irish Culture and Society under the Act of Union*. On the whole, I have left the texts as they were, apart from some minor alterations, including stylistic changes. I might add, though it is probably of only autobiographical interest at this stage, that the bulk of Chapter Four, 'Cry Holocaust: The Great Irish Famine and the Jewish Holocaust' comes from my inaugural lecture at Queen's University, Belfast in 2004. I had intended publishing it then but life got in the way.

These pages might never have been rescued from the obscurity of my filing cabinet but for the persistent encouragement of my editor, Lisa Hyde. I must have set a record for broken deadlines and, indeed, for a year or two I had forgotten completely that I was supposed to be working on this volume. Lisa got me back on track, with tact and creative suggestions. Conor Graham was a supportive publisher, despite the many ups and downs, and was equally keen to see the project through to a conclusion. To both, thanks a million, as my daughter says (though not very often).

The volume itself is dedicated to two remarkable historians and friends of mine, Ruth Dudley Edwards and David A. Wilson. Each has stayed with me in Rugby Road, Belfast; each has talked late into the night; each has helped put the world to rights. I have spent time with them, in London and Toronto respectively, and look forward to continuing the conversation. But for their wise words I would still be floundering in a lake of alternative possibilities. May they long continue to light up the firmament of Irish and trans-Atlantic studies.

Liam Kennedy
Institute of Irish Studies,
Queen's University, Belfast
May Day, 2015

List of Tables

TABLE 1.1 Violent deaths: the First World War, 1914–18

TABLE 1.2 Language Survival and State Structure in Western Europe

TABLE 1.3 Deaths of Infants under One Year Old per 1,000 Live Births (Ireland=100)

TABLE 2.1 Protestant British surnames from the 1600s, and the proportion (%) who had been absorbed into the Catholic ethno-religious bloc by 1911

TABLE 2.2 The Bells of County Dublin in 1911: a comparison of selected occupations by religion

TABLE 3.1 Five Indicators of Economic Progress or Non-Progress in Ireland, North and South, 1800–1914

TABLE 8.1 Comparing the texts of the Ulster Solemn League and Covenant and the Proclamation of the Irish Republic

TABLE 9.1 Conceptualising the Conflicts in Ireland, 1919–23

Introduction

As a new year beckons, I am confident that Irish people will draw on the character and resilience they have so often shown to craft a vision of our shared Irishness that is defined by the values of care, solidarity, trust and responsibility.

New Year's message of President Michael D. Higgins
to Irish people at home and abroad for the year 2014

In my more pretentious moments I think of these essays as distilling the essence of decades of reflection on the course of modern Irish history. But not really. It might be a bit more accurate to say they have been shaped by discussions with friends, colleagues and opponents – an inter-changeable set of roles – as well as conversations that rolled on through the magical medium of electronic communication. They were also completed at different moments in time. The themes are a selection from a larger bundle of writings scattered round my study. Each, I suspect, carries the imprint of the economic and demographic historian, even if sometimes subliminally. For better or worse, the subjects chosen happen to be controversial, as they engage with some of the big questions in the making of modern Irish society. Some of these themes may speak to a wider audience in that famine, Holocaust studies, nationalism and insurgency transcend the field of Irish studies.

The opening chapter in Part 1 plunges into the 'cup of Ireland's misery [that] has been overflowing for centuries, and is not yet half full'.[1] This claim, which dates from the later eighteenth century, has been expressed more ably by others and has been elaborated down the generations. The acronym MOPE (Most Oppressed People Ever) may be said to sum up this understanding of Irish history. The term has enjoyed some currency of late but I'm not sure that all that many people read the original essay in which it was introduced. Well, that's easy to understand, says my friend and sometimes ideological opponent, Ruth Dudley Edwards. 'But you hid away a good essay at the very end of a book containing lots of boring economic history.'[2] While I would challenge the assumption as well as the presumption of the speaker – economic life is full of quiet drama that sometimes boils over in times of famine, revolution or financial collapse – it does seem that the essay has been less than easily accessible. It is reproduced here without change, apart from a new title and some tiny corrections. It was an attempt, successful or otherwise, to place Irish experience in a wider European comparative setting.[3]

The motif of victimhood bulks large in Irish national self-consciousness and, surprisingly perhaps, there are parallel images to be found in loyalist circles in Northern Ireland in more recent times. These syndromes are not unique to Ireland. Other nations have laid claim to victimhood as a defining characteristic of their histories. It is a commonplace of submerged or subordinated nationalisms. Polish ultra-nationalists (self-styled 'patriots') have long celebrated Poland as the 'martyr nation' and a sense of 'national martyrology' pervades much traditional writing on its history. This, of course, conveniently skips over anti-Semitic pogroms and discrimination against ethnic minorities once Poland achieved independence after the First World War. A recent revisionist account of Polish history has the controversial sub-title 'Beyond Martyrdom'.[4] At the southern end of Europe, and moving forward to the 1990s, one has only to recall the self-pitying rhetoric of Serbian nationalists which played alongside the merciless treatment of Muslim neighbours during the break-up of Yugoslavia. The siege of Sarajevo and the gender-specific massacre of some 8,000 Bosnian Muslims at Srebrenica came, in part, out of a hate-filled history of victimhood. The sadism of the moment was clouded by the rhetoric of the centuries. Maybe Susan Sontag was right: 'Perhaps too much value is assigned to memory, not enough to thinking.'[5] In any case, these master narratives, in Irish and in other national histories, should at least be open to challenge.

Those of us of a certain age were schooled, aye steeped in the verities, then seemingly eternal, relating to the *fíor-Ghael*, the *Gall* and the *Sasanach*. But the past isn't that simple, at least for the jobbing historian. Genes as well as blood were spilled in the making of the peoples of Ireland. The seventeenth century was a period of great flux as people moved hither and thither across the four-way ethnic divide separating Scottish Presbyterians, New English Protestants, Old English Catholics and Catholics of Gaelic stock. Intermarriage down the generations further complicated the ethnic mix. It may come as a surprise that one in three of the Dohertys in County Antrim, presumably descended from true-blue Gaelic stock, had converted or perverted (to use a Victorian term) to a Protestant religion of one sort or another by 1911. On the other hand, almost one half of the New English families named Anderson living in the provinces of Connacht and Munster in the same year had forsaken the faith of their forefathers, to become adherents of Catholicism and, in all probability, nationalists to boot. Not that these migrations across religious and ethnic divides seem to have done much to mollify communal animosities. During the revolutionary period of the early twentieth century, political activists from split ethnic backgrounds seem, if anything, to have been disproportionately represented among the leading advocates of political violence. These included Patrick Pearse (Pádraig Mac Piarais), Edward de Valera (Éamon de Valera), Mary MacSwiney (Máire Nic Suibhne) and Charles Burgess (Cathal Brugha).

The political landscape of nineteenth- and twentieth-century Ireland is dominated by the struggling giants of unionism and nationalism. Those of us who do not define ourselves primarily in terms of an Irish, English or British nationalism sometimes struggle to understand the bewitching voices of nationalist ideology, more especially when the ideas float free of material considerations. Think of phrases like 'the spirit of the nation' or the dirge-like 'patriotic' ballad, 'Kevin Barry'. But this is not only in Ireland. These apparently captivating melodies rise as insistently on the banks of the Rhine, the Lagan, the Clyde and the Volga, as in the hinterlands of the Liffey, the Shannon and the Suir. Nationalisms span the twenty-first-century globe, though sometimes (and, let it be said, with progressive potential) competing with more theologically-based systems of belief as reflected in the recent rise of Islamist movements. My own, possibly simplified resolution of this dilemma, is to suggest that nationalism appeals to the whole person – the imagination, the emotions and the cognitive faculties. Moreover, at the group level, it supplies a mythological system that confers meaning and coherence on the lives of its adherents. Hence its powerful appeal and its motivational power in the modern era.

Ireland's political and constitutional dilemma is that two competing nationalisms emerged in the nineteenth century on the one small island. One was Irish nationalism which harked back to an ancient Gaelic civilisation and was infused with Catholic culture and Anglophobic sentiment. The other was a regional dialect of British nationalism which took on a distinctly confessional character in Ulster. Its relationship with the British political system and changing currents in British culture was sometimes fractious, but only the self-deceived, and there were many, could fail to see that Ulster unionism's attitudes and feelings towards an emerging Irish nationalism were devoid of ambiguity, being resolutely opposed to the idea of an All-Ireland state. In the political arena the 'other' faced its 'other' in a mutually deforming embrace.

Neither ideology was or is capable of subjugating the other but the interplay of the two has dogged the past and threatens to hold the future in hock. Deconstructing this malign dialectic requires a critical understanding of the structural bases of these discontents. Part of the story relates to deep economic structures and temporally-bounded and changing economic forces, as well as the more conventional narratives that run in terms of political action and reaction. A surprising conclusion to the chapter on nationalism and unionism is that what really mattered in the late nineteenth and early twentieth century was not the presence of ethnic groups of English or Scottish descent but rather industrialisation. The argument is not developed here – a separate chapter detailing it had to be dropped because of pressures of time and space – but, in a nutshell, the case would run as follows: industrialisation created tens of thousands of economic niches in east Ulster, thereby staunching the long-established outflow of Protestants from Ulster.[6] Without industrialisation there would not have been the critical mass of Protestants in a compact area capable of defying both the British government and Irish nationalists.[7] In other words, the influx of English and Scottish newcomers to Ulster in the seventeenth century was not the defining moment it is sometimes held to be. Partition not only was not inevitable, it was a quite unlikely political outcome if one reads history forwards rather than backwards. But that's history for you, in Ireland as elsewhere. Contingencies and unexpected conjunctures happen.

These are the longer-term perspectives. Later parts of the volume address more specific subjects. Though short-lived in the great sweep of time, the Great Famine of the 1840s (to distinguish it from the other great famine of the preceding century, that of 1740–41) gave rise to a flood of consequences. Arguably the Great Famine or the Great Hunger, or *An Gorta Mór*, has a stronger presence in Irish national consciousness today than at any time since the dying out of the generation of post-Famine survivors. At a scholarly level this has to do with a huge investment of research time in recent decades and, at a more popular level, the ease of communication and comment-making in the digital age.

The Famine section of the volume deals, *inter alia*, with popular memory (to use that modish term), though how popular and how skilfully contrived are these 'memories' or representations of the past is another matter. It is noteworthy that unionists in Northern Ireland have begun belatedly to incorporate the island-wide tragedy into their historical narratives.[8] The Famine had such devastating consequences for the population that it is difficult to know how to represent the deep trauma of a society unhinged by the catastrophe and also carry forward a coherent analytical account. The two are not mutually exclusive but the optimal degree of emotion to be infused into Famine writings, or writings on any catastrophe, is a difficult one. One leading historian is of the opinion that 'only a blend of analysis and emotion, an account of the Famine which takes stock of its legacy in economics, politics, folklore, and poetry will meet the needs of scholarship and popular memory alike'.[9] As with story-telling, there is no blueprint or easy resolution of the dilemma and each writer is obliged to strike her or his own balance, in the sure knowledge that later commentators, or even contemporaries, may well favour a different register. In recent times historians have become interested in the history of emotions *per se*. I would argue that emotions such as anger, hate, shame and vengeance have been among the most powerful if under-recognised forces shaping Anglo-Irish relations. As with discussions of the Great Famine, emotional currents have to be handled by historians as data in their own right. Less obvious is the issue of how historians handle their own emotions in the act and art of producing history.[10]

Politicians and some political tendencies have ransacked the graves of the 1840s for ideological advantage in the twenty-first century. In some accounts, the Great Famine was the Irish Holocaust. This perspective is particularly noticeable on the wilder fringes of Irish-America, but it is also apparent in some quarters in Ireland itself. Assertions of this nature are subjected to critical attention in Part 2 of the book. The more bizarre psychological claim that forms of trauma have been transmitted from the 1840s down to the present day also falls within the bailiwick of current political posturing. The wry comment of an Irish literary critic – 'so that explains why I've never liked potatoes' – is perhaps a sufficient antidote to such psychologising.[11]

An intriguing, almost accidental find in my work on famines was the discovery that the originator of the term 'genocide', Raphael Lemkin, had once referred to the Irish Famine as a probable case of genocide. This may offer some comfort to proponents of the thesis that the Irish Famine, like that of the Ukraine in the 1930s, was indeed an egregious instance of genocide. After all, Lemkin was the towering intellect who shaped all subsequent attempts to write the crime of genocide into world consciousness. On closer inspection, however, this seems to have been little more than a throwaway remark by Lemkin based on little knowledge. Still, because comparisons of the Irish Famine and the Jewish Holocaust are rife on the internet and in other public fora where popular historical knowledge is being forged, in more senses than one, there is a need for a systematic analysis of these contentions. The exploration also casts a sidelight on subjects that have been confined to the shadows, such as racism in Ireland and, in more manifest form, within the Irish diaspora.

This being the 'decade of commemorations' or the 'decade of centenaries', there is no avoiding the turmoil of thought and action that inspired a generation of nationalists and unionists to come into militant confrontation with each other and with the sovereign power at Westminster. First into the field were the Ulster unionists with massive demonstrations against Home Rule for all-Ireland. Summoning its people to its flag, the Solemn League and Covenant became the sacred writ of Ulster unionist opposition to the 'conspiracy' that was Home Rule. The irony, in retrospect, is that a far more threatening conspiracy was afoot which culminated not only in the Rising of 1916 but in a sea-change in nationalist attitudes to the Union.

I have to confess that I had never read the Ulster Covenant and my introduction was a rather unusual one. On a late afternoon sometime in 2012 I looked in my diary and noticed I was due to attend a banquet at Belfast

City Hall. The entry did not indicate the purpose of the occasion. I duly turned up, unmindful of the economists' nostrum that there is no such thing as a free meal, and mingled with the hundreds of others. As the evening wore on I became aware that we were marking the hundredth anniversary of the signing of the Covenant. Some of the speeches increased my sense of unease, so I resolved to read the text of the Covenant line by line, and word by word. This resulted in the critique of the document that kicks off Part 3 of the book. No doubt, my unionist friends will find the conclusions disquieting, possibly even offensive, but my current view is that the document was, in effect, 'texting terror'.

There was no escaping the text of the Proclamation of the Irish Republic. My schoolmaster in Ileigh National School in County Tipperary in the 1950s read it to us with reverence and, since then, it has been regularly read or reprinted on public occasions that touched on the matter of the nation (the Irish nation). Yet, until fairly recently, I had never really read it with any attention, other than regarding it as a fine manifesto for a state-in-the-making. It was more icon than argument and some might prefer to leave it there. That is not an option for the historian and my critique of the text is unlikely to find favour with my nationalist friends. Some friends and colleagues on the left, though by no means all, will be unhappy with my characterisation of the anti-Home Rule agitation of 1912–14, the arming of the Ulster Volunteer Force, and the events of Easter 1916 in Dublin as representing giant lurches to the right in Irish politics.

I wrote on the 'Irish War of Independence' many years ago after a sumptuous conference hosted by the Princess Grace Irish Library in Monaco.[12] Ever so fleetingly I had a sense of what life must be like in the principality for Irish and other multi-millionaire tax 'exiles'. Was there an Irish War of Independence was my question. For those who want the appellation, so be it. The term itself is a later invention.[13] The substantive historical point, however, is that the episode was not only brutal, on all sides, but that the people's allegiances were more complex and in a state of greater flux during the course of the ordeal than is sometimes represented. For unionists in Ireland, North and South, it was hardly a war of independence. Nor was it so for Catholic unionists, nor for some Redmondite nationalists who still accounted for a large minority of nationalists at the famous General Election of 1918 (when Sinn Féin won a huge majority of the Irish parliamentary seats but a less impressive share of the popular vote). It is easy to forget the complications, the cross currents, the discordant voices but, as the Belfast playwright, Stewart Parker, once wrote: 'History's a whore. She rides the winners.'[14]

The literature on the revolutionary decade (1912–22) is now vast. I would have benefited greatly from the later work of historians such as Fearghal McGarry, Marie Coleman, David Fitzpatrick, Charles Townshend, Roy Foster and Diarmaid Ferriter had their superb studies been available to me at the time of writing. My other reflection is that I was a little too mellow in my treatment of attacks on Protestants in County Tipperary. I do not wish to generalise beyond my native county but it is now more apparent to me that 'community terror', inflicted by local volunteers, was more widespread than I had once realised.[15] Some Irish Republican Army (IRA) men acted as badly as the blackest of Black and Tans and, overall, the scale of terrorisation of civilians in Ireland by the IRA during the 'Troubles' of 1919–23 probably exceeded that of the Crown forces.

Some speak of a war in defence of the 'Republic' after 1921, the assumption being that counter-revolutionaries had triumphed with the acceptance of the Anglo-Irish Treaty in 1922. I recall this language from a dedication ceremony in Ileigh churchyard in the 1950s to the memory of three (Anti-Treaty) IRA men who were executed by Free State soldiers at Roscrea, also in County Tipperary, in January 1923. But this apologetic reasoning – 'do not call it a civil war', we were enjoined – was to miss the point: paradoxical as it may seem, the revolution *was* the counter revolution. The ethnic blood was up; discourses of faith and fatherland assumed hegemonic proportions; alternative discourses were crowded out. Similarly, the threatened rebellion in Ulster, backed up by the force of the Ulster Volunteer Force (UVF), also signified a descent into reaction. Those who sought to advance the causes of labour, pacifism, women, agricultural co-operation and social reform more generally – minority movements that had made significant advances since the late nineteenth century – were given short shrift, if not the back of the hand, by the zealots of nationalism and unionism. Much rhetoric was needed to plaster over the less pleasant social realities.

So often in Irish history, as Joe Lee has remarked, it is the sequel that matters.[16] The convulsions of the early twentieth century resulted in two states on the island of Ireland, broadly if imperfectly reflecting long-standing ethnic divisions on the island. Partition, when it came, was viewed as a national calamity, particularly by those Irish republicans whose actions had made any alternative to partition virtually impossible. Though they were loath to say so, even to themselves, the only pathway to a 'United Ireland', once the sword had been unsheathed, would have involved massive repression and almost certainly widespread ethnic cleansing. The IRA hero, Ernie O'Malley recognised as much.[17]

Fortunately, the political and ideological bankruptcy of nationalist and unionist zealots was never put to the ultimate military test, as this would have entailed massive civilian deaths in a variant of civil war. In a curious sort of way, partition allowed each of the major ethno-national formations on the island to fashion states and policies that were broadly congenial to each, in view of the mutually exclusive political, constitutional and symbolic preferences of nationalists and unionists. This was not good for the ethnic *minorities* in either of the Irish states, but it might also be acknowledged that their fates were only mildly oppressive by comparison with the experiences of ethnic minorities in many other parts of Europe during the course of the twentieth century.

PART 1
THE LONG VIEW

CHAPTER ONE

A Most Oppressed People?[1]

Introduction

Ireland's past is not a foreign country. For the plain people, unionist as well as nationalist, it is familiar, static and reassuring. It sometimes seems, as Theodore Hoppen says, 'as if time itself has lost the power to separate the centuries'.[2] For unionists and Protestants, even at the end of the twentieth century, images of massacre, of siege, of insecure victory still carry a powerful charge. For Catholics and nationalists, there are the 700 years of oppression at the hands of the English and, for some, the unfinished business of the British presence in Ireland. For all the emphasis by historians on complexities and discontinuities, there is a popular sense of deep continuities, of enduring patterns which stand outside of historical time.

The contemporary use to which workings and re-workings of the past have been put, from at least the time of the Union onwards, is perhaps the primary reason for this. But there are deeper reasons. Embedded in the Irish historical consciousness is an understanding, partaking almost of the status of an archetype, that the past in Ireland is uniquely painful. Once framed in terms of misery and catastrophe, as exemplified by repeated and unspeakable wrongs, history assumes a mythic continuity. This beguiling framework, which speaks as much to the emotions as to reason, has been enormously influential in shaping historical thought on Ireland, both at the level of folk history and of academic writing.

The Exceptionalism of Ireland

A nation with such a strange history must have some great work yet to do in the world. Except the Jews, no people has so suffered without dying.

A Popular History of Ireland[3]

Such traumatic conceptions of the past are most pronounced within Irish nationalism but have gained a degree of acceptance in some unionist writings also. It was a unionist, after all, fearful of the malign heritage of history, who remarked that 'Anglo-Irish history is for Englishmen to remember, for Irishmen to forget.'[4] Not that nationalist Irishmen, or women for that matter, were likely to forget, or be allowed to forget. The political and agrarian agitations of the late nineteenth and early twentieth centuries articulated a vast legacy of historic wrongs, ranging from conquest, confiscation and penal laws to forms of servitude unparalleled in the civilised world. The champion of home rule and land reform in Ireland, Charles Stewart Parnell, had little difficulty in convincing a meeting at Balla, in County Mayo, in late 1879 that they were challenging 'the most infamous system of land tenure that the world has ever seen (cheers)'.[5] To a more sceptical audience in the House of Commons a few years later, he affirmed that Ireland 'was the most miserable country on the face of the earth'.[6] Parnell could be less sweeping and more specific in his use of comparisons. Reports of the 'Bulgarian Atrocities' in the later 1870s had excited and troubled the sensibilities of liberal Britain. Throwing this concern back in the face of Gladstone and his fellow liberals, the emerging leader of the Home Rule movement pronounced that Ireland had suffered much more at the hands of the English than the Bulgarians at the hands of the Turks.[7]

The architect of conservative Home Rule, Isaac Butt, who had a particular interest in the agrarian question, repeatedly talked of the slavery of Irish tenants due to insecurity of tenure.[8] Wiggins' ostentatiously-titled *The 'Monster' Misery of Ireland* had a similar theme.[9] The enslaved status of the Irish people, both politically and culturally, was a veritable obsession with the Young Irelanders, a group of romantic nationalists associated with the *Nation* newspaper in the 1840s. John Mitchel, a Young Irelander who supported the southern confederate cause during the American civil war and hence had more than a passing acquaintance with slavery, raged not only against Irish slavery but also against the 'long agony' of Ireland, and its 'tale of incredible horror'. The case and the cause of Ireland was 'a horror and a scandal to the earth'.[10] Some of Mitchel's complaints, which have not found their way into the canon of grievances, were a little unusual. Writing of the reaction to his trial and conviction in 1848, he was convinced there were 'many thousands of men then in Ireland, who longed and burned... to earn an honourable death'. He continues that, alas:

> the British system disappointed them even of an honourable death... A man can die in Ireland of hunger, or of famine-typhus, or of a broken heart, or of *delirium tremens*; but to die for your country, – the death *dulce et decorum,* – to die on a fair field, fighting for freedom and honour, – to die the death even of a defeated soldier, as Hofer died: or so much as to mount the gallows like Robert Emmet, to pay the penalty of a glorious 'treason', – even this was an *euthanasia* which British policy could no longer afford to an Irish nationalist.[11]

Daniel O'Connell, who was rather more engaged with the possibilities of glorious living, was quick to invoke the sufferings of the Irish people to make a political point. His opposition to the extension of the English poor-law system to Ireland, for example, was predicated on the claim of a 'misery and destitution that are unequalled on the face of the globe'.[12] Nor was this all. A few years later in an *Address to the Inhabitants of the Countries subject to the British Crown*, he charged: 'England has inflicted more grievous calamities upon Ireland than any country on the face of the earth besides has done upon any other. In the history of mankind there is nothing to be compared with the atrocity of the crimes which England has perpetrated on the Irish people.'[13]

Protesting Ireland's misery goes deeper in historical time. A correspondent to the American paper, the *Shamrock*, in March 1812, contrasted the natural advantages of Ireland, in terms of climate and soil, with the misery of its inhabitants: 'yet with all these advantages, they are the most oppressed people on the face of the earth'.[14] Naturally, these protestations emanated from literary as well as political milieux. Thomas Moore, a contemporary of O'Connell, was one of those, to paraphrase Yeats, who sang to sweeten Ireland's wrong. Though a more complex figure than his status as national bard would imply, Moore's 'Irish Melodies' were replete with sweet melancholy: 'lov'd island of sorrow' (from 'She is Far From the Land'), 'the ruined isle' (from 'Weep On, Weep On'), 'ages of bondage and slaughter' (from 'The Song of O'Ruark'), 'the long night of bondage' (from 'Erin, Oh Erin'), 'hapless Erin', 'my lost Erin' (from ''Tis Gone and For Ever').[15] Sighing harps, the riveting of chains, Erin betrayed and enslaved by the Saxon: here were the soft-focused images that, with the superlatives of the politicians, would help fashion a *national rhetoric* to thrill the generations of newly English-speaking Irish people.

It may be tempting to regard, or disregard all this as the preserve of politicians, polemicists and minor poets. But, outside the economic sphere, Irish history is moved by little else. That is, if one includes British as well as Irish practitioners. Phrases coined, initially and self-consciously as hyperbole, could mutate over time into articles of faith and a call to action. 'In the evening I was in a whirl; my mind jumped from a snatch of song to a remembered page of economic history' (as the revolutionary Ernie O'Malley exclaimed at the start of the Easter Rising in 1916).[16] Moreover, these preconceptions, often unacknowledged and sometimes barely recognised, have infiltrated the writing of Irish history. Such classic works as K.H. Connell's *The Population History of Ireland* were conceived within this framework of ideas (though interestingly not his later *Irish Peasant Society*) while the mood of K.A. Miller's monumental history, *Emigrants and Exiles,* is burdened by gloom and pessimism.[17] The point is more explicit in Robert Kee's fine trilogy, *The Green Flag*, the first volume being entitled, *The Most Distressful Country*. In the words of Kee: 'For over seven centuries the history of the people who lived in Ireland had been a folk-trauma comparable in human experience perhaps only to that of the Jews.'[18] This would find a resonance on the walls of West Belfast today. On the 150th anniversary of the start of the Great Famine, that vast tragedy was being projected through a series of mural paintings as the Irish holocaust.[19] The film-maker Kenneth Griffith took as axiomatic 'the inherent tragedy of Irish history'.[20] Among Irish-Americans, Thomas Gallagher spoke no more than the accepted wisdom: Irish history was one of 'centuries of turmoil, conflict, and suffering'.[21] A compatriot of his went much further: in an unusual sequencing of ideas, Thomas Jackson believed that in Ireland 'genocide was… aided by the natural calamity of the Famine'.[22] A most scholarly, but also one of the most sweeping expressions of the catastrophic dimension to Irish history came from the pen of the Cambridge don, Brendan Bradshaw. Mentioning explicitly the problem of writing a history of the Jews – whose past, as is generally acknowledged, was marked by catastrophe – Bradshaw felt that a similar interpretative problem arises in the Irish case. 'That such a challenge is posed to the historian of Ireland will hardly be disputed, seared as the record is by successive waves of conquest and colonisation, by bloody wars and uprisings, by traumatic social dislocation, by lethal racial antagonisms, and, indeed, by its own nineteenth-century version of a holocaust.'[23]

Beyond Ireland

The folk-trauma of Irish history can of course be explored within its own spatial and temporal frame, as is the way with ethnocentric history. But there is an invitation, an implicit one at least, to go beyond Ireland, to look at other *folk*. How does this self-image of exceptional suffering and victimhood, which belongs primarily to the nationalist community in Ireland, look when viewed in comparative terms? This, of course, begs a number of further questions. What particular issues should be brought into the reckoning? What is the appropriate comparative frame of reference? What is the time period over which comparisons are being made?

The last is the easiest to settle: I have concentrated on the last three centuries, not wholly arbitrarily. It is the period for which our knowledge of the past is at its most robust. This is a lengthy, indeed barely manageable time span which allows us to abstract from short-lived influences and fluctuations. It may be objected that this excludes a particularly troubled century in Irish history, that of the seventeenth. I am not sure this is true in comparative terms, that is, if the Irish experience is viewed against the west European backdrop of power rivalries, religious wars and dynastic contests.[24] The Thirty-Years War devastated large parts of central Europe, the Franco-Spanish war ran from 1635–59, and also embraced the Netherlands. Indeed, the Netherlands had experienced an eighty-year war, though with some profit, up to the 1640s.[25]

After the battle of Kinsale in 1601, there were only two significant military disruptions to the course of social and economic life in Ireland: the long war of 1641–52 and the shorter campaign of 1689–91. The dramatisation of selected events from the seventeenth century by later generations – the 1641 massacres of Protestants, the 'curse of Cromwell', the fall of the Gaelic elite, the victory of William of Orange at the Boyne – all tended to obscure the more material realities as these affected the bulk of the people of the island.

The issue of relevant comparative frameworks for the study of Irish history is one which has been relatively neglected by Irish scholars. For present purposes, the British and Irish Isles and continental Europe are assumed to be most relevant, primarily because this was the historical and geographic milieu within which much of Irish history unfolded, though obviously there were influences from outside Europe also, in particular from the transplanted European societies of North America and Australasia. Finally, the issues I have chosen to highlight are those which seem to me to bear most directly on human welfare: the ecological setting, experiences of violent conflict, land and poverty, conditions for the expression of religious and cultural values and the position of women. While this is a substantial agenda, it is, needless to say, only a partial one. What follows is the beginnings of an intellectual enterprise, not its definitive expression.

Ecology

Of all kinds of reptiles only those that are not harmful are found in Ireland. It has no poisonous reptiles. It has no serpents or snakes, toads or frogs, tortoises or scorpions… This is the most temperate of all countries. Cancer does not here drive you to take shade from its burning heat: nor does the cold of Capricorn send you rushing to the fire… The air is so healthy that there is no disease-bearing cloud, or pestilential vapour, or corrupting breeze.

Giraldus Cambrensis[26]

A natural starting point, one might say, in considering the situation of Irish people historically is the physical and biological setting. Human activity takes place within an environmental framework which, in turn, can have profound implications for human welfare. The contemporary experience of world regions such as Sub-Sahelian Africa or disease- and flooding-prone Bangladesh reminds us of the horrors associated with a precarious ecological balance. In global terms, Ireland's situation within the northern temperate zone was clearly a favourable one, if not quite the enchanted western isle of Celtic mythology.[27] It was largely or wholly free of typhoons, tornadoes, volcanic eruptions, draughts and snow storms. In terms of malign biological forms, it was situated well beyond the range of the greatest killer in human history: the mosquito, with its lethal disease-carrying capacity.[28] Even in the context of Europe, it may be remarked that Ireland was relatively advantaged by its mild climatic conditions as compared to the Mediterranean zone. In southern Europe, by contrast, the hot, dry summers, arid conditions and an associated low-productivity agriculture, served to depress living conditions. The peasants of Carlo Levi's autobiographical account of life in Lucania, a backward province in southern Italy – thirsty, sweating, drained by the merciless sun, touched by malaria – inhabit a landscape even more cruel than Synge's Aran islanders.[29]

The ecological advantages of Ireland hardly need stressing. They were freely acknowledged and frequently embroidered, all the better to point up the misery of the inhabitants. O'Connell, in what was a standard refrain in the repertoire of public speakers in nineteenth-century Ireland, exclaimed: 'Ireland has a soil fertile to a proverb; capable of producing abundant sustenance for four times her present population. She has a genial climate, never parched into barrenness by the summer's sun; never chilled into sterility by the winter's cold. Her perennial greenness shows a perpetual impulse of vegetation. Nature and nature's God have bestowed on her many other good gifts.'[30]

These gifts included a favourable geographic location between Old and New Worlds, spacious bays and safe harbours, navigable rivers and estuaries, and water power 'capable of turning all the wheels of the machinery of the British empire'. Not surprisingly, in view of these natural endowments, the island yielded a wealth of produce, consisting of 'all the prime necessaries of life, and many of its luxuries'.[31] One does not, of course, have to take this at face value to accept that the island of Ireland, when viewed comparatively, was favourably circumstanced in terms of soil, climate and biological conditions.

First Rider of the Apocalypse

War and Welfare

But, to paraphrase O'Connell again, the blessing of heaven may be blighted by the curse of humankind.[32] Other than those who pine for a 'glorious death' on the scaffold or the battlefield, few will need convincing that the probability of a violent end is a major determinant of human welfare. Periodic wars characterised Europe during the eighteenth and the nineteenth centuries. Ireland contributed to these through Irish recruits to the French, Spanish and other continental monarchies, but the primary role of Irish fighters was overseas with the British army and navy.[33] Apart from tiny numbers press-ganged into service, this was by choice. In addition, Irishmen, and Ulstermen in particular, fought during the American war of independence. Irish volunteers also served in Italy in the 1850s in defence of the temporal power and wealth of the Papacy and, more importantly, played a significant part a few years later in the American Civil War.[34] But the typical Irish soldier in the nineteenth century served the Crown: in the Napoleonic wars and at Waterloo, in various colonial adventures, in the Crimean War at mid-century and in the Boer War at the end of the century.

Thus war, and its consequences, did not leave Irish society untouched. This was especially true of the poorer households, whose limited opportunities for wage earning and social recognition within Irish society made them responsive to the blandishments of the recruiting officer. But it is important not to lose sight of a fundamental point, one which does not apply to many areas of continental Europe. *No major war was fought on Irish soil after the seventeenth century.* With the exception of the bloodletting of the summer of 1798 – in Foster's words, 'probably the most concentrated episode of violence in Irish history',[35] when at least 30,000 were killed – there has been no significant confrontation on Irish territory for the last three centuries. Since the time of the War of the Three Kings at the end of the seventeenth century, no hostile armies rolled across the Irish countryside in the manner suffered by Flanders, Schleswig-Holstein, Alsace or Lorraine. The experience of Ireland is at the other end of the spectrum from that of submerged nations like the Poles or the Serbs who found themselves repeatedly in the eye of the military storm. Even civilians on the neighbouring island do not share this record of immunity. During the Second World War, British civilians had the unwelcome, but also unusual experience of being in the front line as German bombers rained down destruction from the skies. More than 60,000 children, women and men were killed and 80,000 were wounded. Tens of thousands of homes and workplaces were reduced to rubble.[36] With the exceptions of Switzerland and Iceland, and for some of the same reasons, it is difficult to think of any major European society which has enjoyed the degree of insulation Ireland enjoyed from the immediate depredations of war – the imposition of regimes based on terror, the sexual abuse of women and the destruction of land and capital assets – which marked European wars and occupations in recent centuries.

Tragically, the scale of terror in Europe, even in the last century, particularly in the last century, defies description. The statistical summary in Table 1.1 gives some indication in relation to the First World War, but the magnitudes involved – more than a million and a quarter Frenchmen killed (three and a half million wounded), for example, are almost beyond human comprehension.[37] In relation to Ireland, and at the risk of contributing to the historiographical blindness which has written the Irish soldiers of the Great War out of the national past,[38] it can be said that Ireland indeed contributed to the mountain of death but its share of casualties and the extent to which the population was mobilised for war were small by comparison with the major combatants. Going down the scale of death, Irish casualties during the 'war of independence', or secession, which commenced soon after European hostilities subsided, were smaller again.[39]

Table 1.1
Violent deaths: the First World War, 1914–18

COUNTRY	number mobilised (millions)	number mobilised as % of all males	number killed in the war (millions)	proportion of those mobilised killed (%)	death rate per 1,000 males in the population
Austria-Hungary	9.0	36	1.45	16	58
France	8.4	44	1.35	16	71
Germany	13.0	41	1.6	12	50
Italy	5.2	31	0.5	10	50
Russia	-	-	2.3	-	36
UK	8.0	37	0.95	12	43
Ireland	0.2	9	0.027	13	12

Source: see end note 37

Terrible as was the First World War, its toll of suffering was exceeded within a generation. According to one estimate, the period 1914–18 witnessed the deaths of over 9 million soldiers out of a total of some 60 million combatants.[40] During the Second World War some 110 million soldiers were thrown into combat. Twenty-seven million did not survive.[41] To this has to be added the output of the mass extermination campaigns which, with the exception of the war in the Far East, were conducted and perfected on the European mainland. Irish men and women, from North and South, fought in this war but in relatively small numbers, and experienced a much lower casualty rate than in the First World War.[42] As a state, *Eire* stood aloof. In official quarters this interlude (1939–45) was simply 'The Emergency', signifying psychological remoteness from the theatres of death.[43]

National Independence

Irishmen and Irishwomen. In the name of God and the dead generations from which she receives her old tradition of nationhood, Ireland, through us, summons her children to her flag and strikes for her freedom.

Proclamation of the Irish Republic, 1916

The Irish Revolution of 1919–21, has barely been mentioned. Did it, perhaps, transform the Four Green Fields into the killing fields of Europe? The main phase of the secessionist conflict, between the end of the First World War and the Truce of 1921, resulted in some 1,400 deaths, with nearly half of the victims being soldiers or policemen.[44] Deaths of Irish people due to violence in 1919–21 were less than 5 per cent of those of Irish soldiers during the World War, though the former conflict occupies a much larger dramatic space in the consciousness of nationalist Ireland.[45] This scale of conflict bears comparison with some secessionist struggles elsewhere in western Europe: the breakaway by the Belgians from the Kingdom of the Netherlands in 1830–31; Norway's switch from union with Denmark to union with Sweden in 1814, and full independence in 1905. But these were the exceptions. They pale by comparison with the nineteenth-century independence struggles in Poland, Greece, the states of northern Italy, Hungary, Bulgaria, Serbia, Croatia and Montenegro. Finland is an unusual case, and might appear to have echoes of the Irish experience. Forcibly joined to Russia eight years after the union of Britain and Ireland, it was accorded the status of a Grand Duchy within the Czarist empire. A fierce civil war in 1918–19 was followed by independence, but this was extinguished with heavy casualties after the twin wars of 1939–40 and 1941–44. Thereafter, it experienced a semi-independent existence, in the shadow of the Soviet Union, until it achieved full sovereignty after the implosion of the Soviet empire at the end of the 1980s. The contrasts with the Irish experience seem more pronounced than the similarities.

To round off this part of the discussion of war and violent death, if the Irish nationalist struggle for political independence is conceived in purely *colonial* terms, as it sometimes is, the contrasts are even more striking. The Algerian struggle against French rule, with the Ulster Protestants relegated to the position of *colons,* has, for instance, been a favourite reference point in polemical writings.[46] The unsatisfactory nature of any such comparison is apparent in many ways, not least in terms of the magnitude of the casualties and the responsibility for killings. In the eight years of war, 1955–62, the French forces lost 17,000 soldiers, a third of whom were killed 'accidentally'. The Muslims bore a much heavier penalty: *Le Front de Libération Nationale* (FLN) suffered 140,000 deaths at the hands of the French security forces, that is, an eight-fold disproportion in killing rates. The battle of Algiers in early 1957, to take one of the worst episodes within the war, was accompanied by the widespread use of torture and summary executions on the part of French paratroopers. In addition, the FLN killed in the region of 100,000 other Muslims. While not a society unhinged, in the way that Russia was after the Bolshevik revolution, it is plain that during the process of decolonisation the Algerian peoples underwent a trauma of terrible proportions.

A number of essential points, with a direct bearing on human welfare, emerge from this brief survey. During the last three centuries there have been no major invasions of Ireland, with all the malign consequences for civilian populations as well as soldiers these imply. Irish participation in European wars has been on a voluntary basis. So, unlike many European countries, the

Irish peoples have never experienced military conscription. This was true even in Northern Ireland after 1920, despite unionist support for the extension of conscription to the province during World War Two.[47] More generally, during the most brutal century that Europe has ever known – the twentieth – Ireland escaped relatively unscathed.

Civil War and Other Conflicts

Not all armed conflicts are national, imperial or anti-imperial. Insurrections, civil disorder and civil war have shaken the social foundations of a number of European states. France occupies the pre-eminent position, as the political shock waves released by the French Revolution had repercussions across Europe, including Ireland. While images of the Terror in France during the 1790s have captured the popular imagination, the real bloodletting came with the sequel: Napoleon's grand military adventures were at the cost of more than a million Frenchmen's lives.[48] The following century was punctuated by a variety of internal disturbances, of which the suppression of the Paris Commune in 1871 was especially vengeful. In the last century, in the aftermath of the Nazi occupation and the collapse of the Vichy regime, there was a veritable civil war in which tens of thousands of French men and women were put to death by their compatriots.[49]

Before exploring the Irish case, it may be instructive to look at some other instances from the European experience. The Russian civil war, 1917–20, achieved its most terrible impact off the battlefield. Estimates of the numbers of victims vary. While perhaps 800,000 combatants died from war and disease, some authorities claim civilian deaths may have exceeded 7 million as a result of mass executions, widespread chaos, hunger and infectious diseases.[50] 'The civil war unleashed by Lenin's revolution was the greatest national catastrophe Europe had yet seen.'[51] The Stalinist purges of the 1930s compounded the national tragedy.

Of closer interest to the Irish public, particularly that of Catholic Ireland, was the Spanish civil war. This concern arose out of religious identification with 'Catholic Spain': the rebel leader, General Franco, being presented as the champion of Catholic and national interests in the face of an atheistic and communistic threat. The fact that the Irish civil war had ended little over a decade earlier may have further enhanced its interest. Of more direct significance, small numbers of Irish people went to fight in Spain. (Blueshirt – or right-wing – sympathisers volunteered in support of the nationalists under General Franco, while more left-wing elements, Catholic and Protestant, fought for the republican cause.)[52] An indication of the severity of the Spanish civil war may be deduced from the number of deaths it occasioned. Earlier accounts suggested that one million Spanish, Catalan and Basque peoples lost their lives, either directly or indirectly. Revisionist scholarship has moved these estimates onto a lower plane, that is, in the region of 600,000 deaths.[53] This is the equivalent of one-in-every forty of the total population, still underlining the ferocity of the conflict. Tens of thousands of the defeated republicans were driven into exile in France and Latin America. When the Nazis occupied France a few years later, some of these refugees were handed back to the Madrid authorities for execution.[54] Moreover, the legacy of the civil war proved long-lived: the victory of the Francoist forces inaugurated four decades of internal repression and authoritarian rule.

Less easily categorised than civil wars are communal and ethnic conflicts deriving from fractures within society. The anti-Semitic pogroms of nineteenth- and twentieth-century central and eastern Europe, culminating in the Jewish holocaust, are all too well known to require rehearsal here.[55] Less well known are the periodic massacres of Armenian Christians carried out by the Turkish state between the end of the nineteenth century and 1922. In something very close to a 'final solution', perhaps 1.5 million, out of a population of about 2.5 million Armenians, died as a result of imprisonment, torture, forced labour, long marches and mass executions between 1915 and 1922. Half a million were refugees, driven from their lands, scattered in exile.[56] In more recent times, Europe has witnessed the genocidal passions unleashed following the end of the Cold War and the break-up of Yugoslavia.

In Ireland, it is conventional to regard the Anglo-Irish hostilities of 1919–21 simply in terms of a war of independence, but a more complex formulation would recognise the elements of a muted civil war contained therein. In a prelude to the nationalist civil war of 1922–23, militant nationalists purged the less militant within their ranks, including numbers of alleged informers. Irish loyalists in southern Ireland could also become the objects of local repression. More importantly, the other ethnic formation on the island – the northern Protestants – stood in direct opposition to the political aspirations of their Catholic neighbours.

As the conflict in Ireland gathered momentum, communal tensions in the Ulster counties boiled over into attacks, reprisals and killings.[57] Between June 1920 and June 1922 – the worst period of communal violence – more than 400 northerners, nationalist and unionist, lost their lives.[58] Thereafter, communal killings (though not hatreds) were brought under control, that is, until a new wave of terror broke a half-century later.

The nationalist civil war in Ireland began in earnest with the bombardment of the Four Courts, which had been occupied by anti-Treaty forces, in June 1922. By the time the civil war had ended, a year or so later, more volunteers had been killed than in the whole period 1916–21.[59] While the fighting left a residue of remarkable bitterness, the conflict was relatively well-contained in terms of its lethal effects, the impact on the death rate for society in the

Irish Free State being indistinguishable from normal years.[60] Moreover, by comparison with civil wars elsewhere in Europe, it was both absolutely and relatively minor. Ironically, the civil war of greatest quantitative significance for Irish men took place in that other Ireland, across the Atlantic.[61] The American civil war, in which Irish men fought on the side of the Union and of the Confederacy, claimed in excess of 620,000 soldiers' lives, including many Irish who fought with conspicuous bravery.[62]

The Land

Security is a basic human need. Even more fundamental is subsistence. Land was fundamental to economic welfare in all European societies, with the possible exception of the Dutch, before the transformations wrought by the Industrial Revolution. Inevitably, conflict surrounded control of this prime economic resource. The formation of landed ascendancies whose *apogee,* in many cases, was during the eighteenth century, can be traced back to the medieval and early-modern periods. Contrary to some theoretical developments in modern economic history, where relationships between lord and peasant are presented as voluntary arrangements in which the lord supplied public goods – defence and security – in return for the economic surplus of the land,[63] it is necessary to assert the historical reality that the origins of land ownership lay in the forcible expropriation of land, and sometimes of its inhabitants. Ireland was no exception, with property rights in land being written with the sword. The long march of the European peasantries involved gaining control of the land they worked from the lords and nobles.

The intensity of this struggle varied, and it was by no means continuous.[64] Notwithstanding the use of inflated terms such as the 'Land War' or the 'Fall of Feudalism in Ireland', it is surprising how peaceful the eviction of Irish landlords from their ancestral properties turned out to be.[65] It is true the Danes managed a non-violent revolution in land tenure almost a century before the Irish – by 1820 more than half of Danish farmers owned their land – but other rural societies fared less well.[66] The French peasants secured control of their landholdings in the 1790s but at a high price in terms of bloodshed. In nineteenth-century Russia there were periodic peasant risings, followed by fierce repression. That of 1905 was a bloody prelude to the October Revolution of 1917. War, revolution, civil war and famine accompanied the transition to peasant ownership. But the gains, if such they were, proved short-lived. The Red Terror of Stalin's collectivisation programme during the 1930s, involving mass executions, deportations, concentration camps and famine, expropriated land and rural labour even more thoroughly than had been the case under serfdom. In the process, millions of country people were driven to their deaths.[67]

Russia, it should be said at once, was an extreme case of oppression, both in terms of scale and intensity. But, in middle Europe, the semi-feudal status of landholders persisted into the nineteenth century, with the noble estate owners in Prussia, Hungary and Austria offering strong resistance to land reform. The uprisings in various parts of Europe during the year of revolution, that is, 1848, demonstrated widespread dissatisfaction in the countryside as well as the towns, leading to the emancipation of the peasantry on favourable conditions in Austria-Hungary.[68] In Italy and the Iberian Peninsula agrarian reform proceeded at a painfully slow pace, punctuated by frequent acts of violence.[69] Suffice to say that, in Ireland, on the eve of independence, land reform had proceeded, and on the whole relatively peacefully, to the point that virtually the entire farming population owned the land, or were in the process of becoming full owners. This contrasted with extensive rental arrangements and sharecropping in much of Europe.[70]

Living Standards

The countryman shows, in his every feature, the face of misery and woe: his eyes are uncertain, timid, his face expressionless, his gait slow and clumsy… animals with two feet, hardly resembling a man…

Eugen Weber[71]

Was Ireland far outside the European mainstream in terms of material living standards during the eighteenth and nineteenth centuries, as some contemporary and academic accounts would seem to suggest? In our current state of knowledge it is impossible to say how standards in Ireland compared with those of other regions of Europe in, say, 1700 or 1800. Certainly, we can say that Irish society was well within its productive capacity in the eighteenth century, as the remarkable population growth shows. Some held that population growth signified happiness.[72] If so, Ireland was a happy place indeed. But this is simplistic. The relationship between economic welfare and human reproduction is a contested one and is also likely to vary between historical epochs, depending on cultural values and opportunity costs, each in turn subject to change.

Scotland is near at hand, and has been the subject of some comparative historical work. Cullen and Smout suggest that the economic positions of Ireland and Scotland were roughly comparable during the first half of the eighteenth century.[73] Their growth trajectories diverged in the later eighteenth century, though both societies enjoyed expansionary trade and export conditions into the early years of the nineteenth century. Labourers' wage rates in agriculture, the dominant sector in both societies, were perhaps double the Irish level in Scotland in the 1790s,[74] though the gap in real incomes per capita was likely to have been much smaller (not least because of the low cost per calorie of the ubiquitous potato). The contrasts in economic structure and performance, if anything, became more pronounced during the following century. Lowland Scotland was in the forefront of the industrial revolution and, henceforth, is a distorting prism through which to look at comparative performance, not only for agrarian societies like Ireland (outside of Ulster) but also for regions such as northern Portugal, Galicia, Brittany, southern Italy and most of eastern and southern Europe.

Still, there is impressionistic evidence from a variety of visitors to Ireland in the pre-Famine period to suggest a process of immiseration and conditions of life that were low, not only by English and Scottish standards but by those of continental European regions also.[75] If Ireland ever was wretchedly poor between 1700 and 2000, comparatively speaking that is, then it was surely in the years between Waterloo and the end of the Great Famine. But even here there is a paradox to Irish poverty which has been well expressed by Joel Mokyr. As late as the eve of the Great Famine, the great mass of potato eaters was well-nourished, if condemned to a monotonous diet, and their fuel needs were met largely from the plentiful supplies of turf available in most districts.[76] One might add, there is also evidence of considerable cultural vitality, in terms of aspirations to literacy, the celebration of traditional feast days and the performance of rituals surrounding marriage, death and neighbourliness. Out of joint with this reassuring picture were the miserable cabins of the rural poor, the hungry season in the months before the new potatoes became available, high infant mortality and quickening emigration.[77]

The Great Famine seems like the culmination of an inexorable descent into absolute misery. This is to read history backwards. Few, if any countries in Europe experienced such a massive destruction of the main food crop in a single year. No country in Europe experienced a failure of its staple food supply, effectively for four seasons in succession. In terms of *duration* and *intensity,* this seems to have been an ecological disaster outside of European experience.[78] Because other societies were not exposed to the same terrible stresses, the calamity of the Great Hunger cannot be held to constitute a test of Ireland's relative backwardness.

We emerge from the statistical dark age in the second half of the nineteenth century and can place Ireland with somewhat greater confidence in a comparative setting. It is generally acknowledged that income per head grew as fast, probably faster, in Ireland between 1850 and 1914 than in the United Kingdom as a whole. This would place Ireland among the fastest growing economies in Europe at the time.[79] On the eve of the First World War, income per head in Ireland was above the European average.[80] Despite slow growth in particular sub-periods, most noticeably during the years 1932–38 and 1951–59, the growth performance of the Irish economy over the twentieth century *as a whole* has been at, or close to the west European average, and well ahead of that in eastern Europe.[81] Measured in terms of income per head of the population, the Irish Republic and Northern Ireland today rank among the rich regions of the world.

Emigration

In thousands we are driven from home which grieves our heart full sore.
We are fraught with famine and disease, we emigrated across the seas
From that sore oppressed island that they call the shamrock shore.

Paul Brady, 'Shamrock Shore'[82]

Some would argue that income per head is not a good indicator of economic welfare because Ireland, historically, has been a land of emigration. There is some substance to this view, though it might also be suggested that high rates of natural increase in the context of an economy with a propensity towards pastoral production are incompatible with high incomes and low outmigration. Intense industrialisation and urbanisation might have solved this dilemma, but this was achieved on a significant scale only in east Ulster during the nineteenth century.[83] Thus, decisions taken by Irish parents to feed the emigrant stream through high fertility accounted, in part, for the scale of the outflow.

Moreover, Irish emigrants in the last three centuries were overwhelmingly *economic* migrants, self-sorrowing images of expulsion and exile notwithstanding. Freedom of movement, internally and overseas, has always been part of the Irish experience.[84] Irish migrants to Britain enjoyed a privileged citizenship status even after the creation of an independent Irish state. The significance and value of this freedom, though sometimes drowned out by the 'loud communal whine' of Irish-American politics, are hard to exaggerate.[85] It was denied during the long era of serfdom elsewhere in Europe. One of the haunting images from eastern Europe is that of the runaway serf being hunted like an animal across vast plains which afforded little, if any cover.[86] In Russia, under the Czarist regime, there were limits on people's internal as well as external movements. The triumph of Lenin and the Bolsheviks in 1917 reinforced the use of passports to control personal mobility.[87] Mobility between occupations was also controlled, through Leon Trotsky's dream that labour should be subjected to military-style mobilisation and deployment was, mercifully, not realised.[88] The extension of Soviet rule westwards as far as Prague and Berlin after the Second World War meant that freedom of movement was denied to most people in eastern, central and parts of southern Europe. The Iron Curtain was no metaphor: with its barbed wire, minefields and border guards, it furnished a deadly barrier to emigration from the Soviet sphere of influence.

Not only did the Irish have unlimited freedom of exit, which was the tradition generally in western Europe, they also enjoyed access to two of the highest-wage economies in the world during much of the period: those of North America and Britain.[89] Freedom of exit, paradoxically, was only seriously threatened under conditions of independence: during the later 1940s there was Episcopal and civil service backing for curbs on the emigration of young women to Britain.[90] Women also participated in this freedom. In the later nineteenth century, and unusually among European emigrants to the New World, single Irish women were as likely to emigrate as single men.[91] Irish immigrants entered not just a labour market but a new society also. Like most outsiders, they experienced hostility and discrimination, before going on to refine their own systems of discrimination,[92] most notably in some of the east coast cities of the United States. Much has been made of the prejudice Irish people, especially Irish Catholics, encountered in the new societies. Prejudice there was, particularly in relation to each wave of new arrivals but declining in relation to the children and grandchildren of the immigrants. A white skin and a knowledge of English, the language of the host societies, smoothed the transition to acceptance and, in the case of the Catholic Irish in the United States, remarkable upward social mobility.[93] It is doubtful, though, if the hostility experienced by the Irish was as severe as that facing many other immigrant groups: Mexicans and Puerto Ricans in the United States, Turks in Germany, Albanians in Italy, or Jews in many parts of the world (including Ireland).[94]

Between the mother country and the receiving country, lay the sea passage, at least before the age of aviation. There is no doubt, during the panic-stricken famine exodus of the 1840s, that significant numbers of Irish emigrants suffered horribly on the transatlantic crossings. Disease, compounded by overcrowding, resulted in abnormally high death rates. It is important to recall these images of suffering. It is also important to remember that these conditions were untypical, even for the eighteenth and the nineteenth centuries. Moreover, unlike famine refugees in the twentieth century, receiving countries were open, and remained open to them.[95] Strikingly, this was despite the mass nature of the influx. There was no equivalent to the difficulties facing the Vietnamese 'boat people', for example, who took to their fragile crafts and cast themselves on the seas in the 1970s.[96] The risks were terrible, as they faced problems of exposure, piracy, drowning and murder. Some who reached 'safe lands' faced the risk of being repatriated. A less appalling case from late-twentieth-century Europe was the experience of the Albanian 'boat people' of the 1990s, fleeing to Italy in the first instance. They were turned back by the authorities and barriers to the mass immigration of Albanians to the labour markets of the European Union remained intact.[97]

Much more could be said. Migration and emigration have painful dimensions to them. But the extent to which this is true varies according to circumstances. It is far from apparent that the Irish have been particularly disadvantaged in the matter of emigration, in terms of its costs and its opportunities.

Language and Language Change

Taking away the language of a people might be considered the cultural analogue of material dispossession. Language is not simply a means of communication. It is a repository of cultural meanings which are vital to the wellbeing of the individual and the wider society. In the late sixteenth century, English had some claims to being the endangered language in Ireland, hence the coercive measures by the English administration to extend its sway. In 1700, despite war and colonisation, the vernacular language of some two-thirds of the peoples of Ireland was Gaelic.[98] A century later, half the population could still speak the indigenous language.[99] But by the time of the creation of an independent Irish state in 1922 hardly anyone was a monoglot Gaelic speaker outside of a few remote areas in the West of Ireland. Thus the major decline of Gaelic speaking was concentrated in the nineteenth century and the attrition of the Irish language continued apace during the course of the twentieth under conditions of political independence. Some would even speak of the death of the Irish (Gaelic) language.

It is tempting to blame this on the absence of state structures which might have been supportive of Gaelic, and no doubt there is some truth in this. Had a centralised Gaelic state emerged in Ireland in the twilight years of the reign of Elizabeth I, and had it maintained its independence, there is reason to believe Irish Gaelic would be spoken widely on the island today. In fact, if one looks at the twenty or so nation states of northern and western Europe (Table 1.2), one finds that the language of each state is that which was spoken by the core ethnic population in the seventeenth century.[100] With

Table 1.2
Language Survival and State Structure in Western Europe

	LANGUAGE SURVIVAL	LANGUAGE LOSS
NATION STATE	Danish, Dutch, English, Finnish, Flemish, French, German, Italian, Norwegian, Portuguese, Spanish, Swedish	Irish Gaelic
NO NATION STATE	Catalan	Basque, Breton, Corsican, Frisian, Faroese, Galician, Lap, Occitan, Sardinian, Scots, Scottish Gaelic, Welsh

the exception of the recently-created Irish Republic, there is no instance of a nation state which has lost the original language of its inhabitants during the course of the last three centuries. In this respect Ireland seems unique.[101] Is it the case then, that the Gaelic speakers of Ireland had their language wrenched from them in a particularly violent or coercive manner?

The processes which undermined the language of the Gael have been explored in both elegiac and analytical ways by a variety of writers.[102] These include: the changing ethnic composition of the population, with a quarter of those in 1700 being of recent Scottish or English colonial origin; the process of commercialisation affecting all aspects of economic life; the dominance of English in the legal, religious and political spheres; the growing significance of economic opportunities beyond Ireland, particularly in terms of migrant opportunities in Britain and North America; the demand by parents for a language which seemed to fit their sons and daughters better for survival in a changing world, expressed through the medium of the hedge schools and the national system of education from 1831 onwards. Finally, of course, there was the Great Famine, a tragic visitation which selected the poor, the illiterate, the westerly communities, in short, the Gaelic speakers of Ireland.

One can readily acknowledge that the structures of the state had the effect of limiting the use of Gaelic, particularly in the public sphere. What is noticeable, though, from this catalogue is that the role of state policy in discriminating against Gaelic is accorded no direct significance. The decline of Gaelic in Ireland seems to be part of a wider pattern of language change within the British and Irish Isles – a form of linguistic homogenisation driven by the forces of the market, by new literacy requirements, and by closer cultural contact between different localities. During the eighteenth and nineteenth centuries, Gaelic declined in the Scottish Highlands, as did Scots in the lowlands, while Cornish and Manx virtually disappeared from their peripheral locations on the edges of Britain. Of the Celtic languages, Welsh proved most resilient. Despite cohabiting within the same state, that of the United Kingdom, and despite being subject to much the same legislation, one out of every two Welsh people spoke the language in 1901 as compared to only 14 per cent in Ireland.[103] These very different rates of attrition suggest the complexity of language decline, which cannot for instance be summed up simply in terms of the changing power relationships within the British and Irish Isles.[104]

This policy of official neglect rather than persecution, which seems natural enough when viewed in terms of the historical experience of these islands, is quite striking when placed in a European context. There was active discrimination against the Catalan language by the Spanish authorities from at least the beginning of the eighteenth century, following the defeat of the Catalan cause in 1714.[105] In the twentieth century, despite being the language of the majority of the people of Catalonia, Catalan was banned from the school system. Relief came only after the death of General Franco in 1975. The resilience of Catalan language and culture – there are more speakers of Catalan in the 1990s than there were in the 1900s – has a further significance. It makes the less-than-obvious point that while a favourable state apparatus may be a sufficient condition for the survival of a language, it is not a necessary one.[106] The position of the other two major minority languages in Spain, that of *Galego* in Galicia and *Euskara* in the Basque Country, is less secure. Both have suffered at the hands of the Madrid authorities where, as in the case of Catalonia, there were determined efforts to impose Castilian speech and culture.[107]

The linguistic policies of the highly-centralised French state show a similar lack of tolerance for minority languages. Weber has made the controversial claim that, as late as 1870, French was a foreign language for half the people of France.[108] Exaggerated or not, France contained within its boundaries large minorities of speakers of Breton, Flemish, Basque, Catalan, Occitan (*la langue d'oc)*, Corsican, German and Italian. The French Revolution, far from extending the values of *liberté, égalité et fraternité* into the realm of linguistic politics, actually persecuted regional languages in the name of the Republic. To use the experience of Brittany as a test case: among the state measures used to destroy Breton during the nineteenth century were prohibitions, fines, imprisonments and the public humiliation of school children caught speaking Breton.[109] Being sent to clean out the school latrine was one of the favoured penalties for contaminating the school environment with Breton speech. As a group of teachers were reminded at a public meeting in 1845: 'remember above all, gentlemen, that you have been set up only in order to kill the Breton language'.[110] Almost a century later, in 1925, the French minister for education echoed these sentiments: 'for the unity of France, the Breton language must die'.[111] After the Second World War there was agreement in principle that the languages of Breton, Occitan, Basque and Catalan might be given a minor role in the school curriculum. In practice, obstacles were placed in the way of the implementation of these minimal reform measures. Not until the 1970s, and then only grudgingly, was Breton, for example, given a significant presence in the school examination system.

The repression of minority languages is closely related to the rise of European nationalisms, specifically the drive to produce linguistically-pure national societies. It hardly comes as a surprise, therefore, to find that the Prussian authorities became actively hostile towards minority languages, particularly Polish, from the later nineteenth century. Within the boundaries of the newly-united German state after 1870 only German was regarded as consistent with full loyalty to the state. But the process of linguistic intolerance had begun even earlier in Hungary. This is of particular interest from an Irish viewpoint because the national revival there drew admiring glances from Irish nationalists, and was celebrated by Arthur Griffith, the founder of Sinn Féin, in his work *The Resurrection of Hungary*.[112] From the mid-nineteenth century onwards, Hungary embarked on a policy of Magyarisation, deliberately seeking to marginalise the various ethnic minorities of Slovaks, Rumanians, Germans, Croats, Serbs and Slovenes.[113]

One could go on to explore the Italian fascist persecution of German speakers and their culture in the South Tyrol in the interwar period, but the point is surely made. Many of the nation states of western Europe were no models of tolerance in relation to minority languages. By contrast, the vicissitudes of the Gaelic language in Ireland owed little to active state policy. The experience of decline worked itself out against the backdrop of British traditions of linguistic *laissez faire*, not those of the more negatively interventionist states of mainland Europe.

Religious Freedoms

… the religion of the people was cruelly persecuted; the Catholic priesthood were sent into exile or dragged to the scaffold; and a code of penal laws was enacted, which in its cruel ingenuity, surpassed everything of the kind ever heard of in the world.

Cardinal Paul Cullen[114]

The introduction of the Penal Laws at the end of the seventeenth century has much the same resonance in Irish Catholic history as the Revocation of the Edict of Nantes in French Protestant history. Both are closely related in time, and each is a reflection of renewed religious intolerance during the final decades of a century marked by much bloodletting on the issue of religious and civil allegiances.[115] The English Catholic hymn, 'Faith of our Fathers', which, for a time, was virtually the Irish national anthem, tuned in to popular perceptions of religious repression, as perceived within the Catholic tradition in Ireland.[116] 'Faith of our fathers, living still/in spite of dungeon, fire and sword…' A later verse rejoices:

> *Our fathers, chained in prisons dark,*
> *were still in heart and conscience free:*
> *how sweet would be their children's fate,*
> *if they, like them, could die for thee!*

To these images one might add those of the fugitive priest tending his down-trodden flock, of the odious priest-hunters, of mass paths and mass rocks; in short, we see a church and virtually a whole society under persecution in some not-distant but ill-defined time in the past.[117] Cardinal Cullen, the dominant personality in the Irish Catholic Church during the second half of the nineteenth century, was of the opinion that the penal laws in Ireland were the worst the world had ever known.[118] The fact that the catholic faith was the faith of the majority was seen as a source of further grievance, though why the persecution of a *minority* should be taken as less objectionable is not clear. Indeed, one might think there was some consolation and less vulnerability in being part of a persecuted *majority*.

Presbyterians and other dissenters have their own stories of religious disabilities and grievances, with emigration from Ulster to the New World in the eighteenth century being presented as one response to the intolerance of the Anglican establishment.[119] Historians have a tendency to spoil good stories, indeed this may be one of their distinguishing characteristics. The Penal Laws after 1715, and particularly after 1760, were fiercer on the statute book than in practice. By the 1790s Catholics and dissenters in Ireland enjoyed freedom of worship, churches and chapels dotted the countryside, a state-subsidised national seminary for Catholic priests was coming into being, and there was a generous electoral franchise by the standards of the time.[120] For the neighbouring island, John Bossy is of the view that Catholics in England were generally untroubled by the state after 1688, though anti-popish mobs might occasionally go on the rampage.[121]

On the continent, however, the persecution of religious dissent, under the *ancien regimes* of Spain and France in particular, seems to have been more vigorous.[122] But where European histories really diverge from the Irish experience is in the treatment of religion and the religious following the popular challenges to established authority, set in motion from the time of the French Revolution onwards. Under 'The Terror' in France priests went to the guillotine, others were deported, churches were closed, convents and monasteries were ransacked, and public worship was prohibited.[123] Though the period of savage persecution was short-lived, as the revolution soon consumed the revolutionaries, the following century witnessed episodes of intense anti-clericalism and hostile legislation directed at the French Catholic Church and its followers.

In the German states the attack on church power reached a peak in the early 1870s, which contrasts with the reforming policy of the British government in Ireland where the minority Church of Ireland had just been disestablished and tithes finally abolished. In the united Germany the famous or infamous Falk laws, beginning in February 1872, made all schools subject to state inspection in relation to religious as well as non-religious subjects. Religious orders were banned from teaching, even from religious teaching. The Reichstag, under the leadership of Bismarck, insisted on a state role in the training of the clergy, that Jesuit priests be prohibited from saying mass, and that disciplinary powers over the clergy be transferred from the bishops to the state. The Kulturkampf took a new turn in 1875 when hundreds of priests were imprisoned or expelled. Monks and nuns followed into exile. In a German clerical equivalent of the 'coffin ship', the *Deutschland* ran aground in winter storms off the Thames estuary, with loss of life.[124] The Papacy, and the mainly-Catholic Centre Party, which drew some of its inspiration for church–state relations from Daniel O'Connell and his campaign for Catholic emancipation, effected a relaxation of these punitive measures in 1886. Nonetheless, the state had succeeded in the longer term in imposing a measure of control over church affairs which would have been unthinkable in Victorian Ireland.

In the other German state of Austria, and in part influenced by Prussian example, the Emperor Franz Joseph introduced a secular educational system, and state controls over marriage and divorce. The traditional spheres of influence of the Catholic Church were being squeezed. More so than in Germany or Austria, the Risorgimento in Italy carried with it measures of anti-clericalism and anti-Catholicism of a particularly sustained kind.[125] The city of Rome and the Papal States were seized, the pope becoming the 'prisoner in the Vatican'. In a piece of blind retaliation, the autocratic Pope Pius IX ordered that Italian Catholics should not participate in the political life of the new kingdom, a ban that was not lifted until after the First World War in 1919. In the united Italy, particularly after the Left won power in 1876, the assault on the privileges and powers of the Catholic Church was pressed home. Education was secularised. Displays of popular religious culture, such as religious processions and feast days, were suppressed. Groups of religious, monks and nuns, were persecuted. Priests were conscripted for the army. At one point (January 1877) a bill forbidding any criticism of the State by the clergy was mooted. How the authorities would have reacted to the clerical denunciations of the state and the social order which rained down from political and agrarian platforms across the length and breadth of Ireland in this period is not hard to imagine.[126]

On the Iberian Peninsula the strong cultural links between Portugal and France meant that the former was especially open to the anti-clericalism of the French Third Republic. By the eve of the First World War all of the religious orders in Portugal had been banned, the teaching of religion in the schools had been outlawed, and priests had been subjected to compulsory military service. Spain also had deep anti-clerical traditions, as in industrially-developed Catalonia for example, but the apotheosis of church–people relations was reached in the 1930s with the sacking of church property, the rape of nuns and the killing of priests *qua* priests.[127] One can find, in eighteenth-century Ireland, instances of Catholic priests and Presbyterian ministers being executed for their public roles. Best known are the priests and ministers executed during the 1798 rebellions and the rather different case of Father Sheehy of Tipperary, hanged for alleged Whiteboy activities during the 1760s.[128] But one has to go back to the late seventeenth century to find cases of men of the cloth being executed on essentially religious or anti-religious grounds.

There are several paradoxes to this overview of religious toleration and religious intolerance. While virtually all states and state churches in the late-seventeenth century persecuted religious minorities – the Netherlands stands out as a haven of relative toleration – the most intense conflict in the nineteenth century was between the forces of secularism and anti-clericalism, on the one side, and Christian churches on the other. The sharpest persecutions seem to have been within Catholic societies, whereas the anti-clericals in France, Italy, Spain and Portugal showed as much respect for religious freedoms as the alliance of church and state had bestowed on dissidents in earlier times. When the boot was on the other foot again, as under the dictatorial regimes of Franco and Salazar on the Iberian peninsula, there was little sign that anything much had been learned other than an appetite for vengeance.[129] Only with the liberating influence of Pope John XXIII and the Second Vatican Council in the 1960s did the Roman Catholic Church finally come to terms with the notion of complete freedom of religious worship.[130]

Strangely, before independence, it was Ireland's fortune to be closer to the experience of European Protestant states, and more specifically that of the Protestant state of the United Kingdom, where violent anti-clericalism and governments bent on the destruction of church interests were absent. The nineteenth century saw the virtually uninterrupted progress of the popular church in Ireland, the Roman Catholic Church, towards the creation of a vast infrastructure of churches, presbyteries, convents, monasteries and bishops' palaces.[131] The jewel in the papal crown was clerical control of the schooling system, with the aid of state funding. Furthermore, and unlike the position in continental Europe, clerical education and clerical appointments were independent of any state controls. Most fundamentally of all, freedom of worship, despite the lovingly-cultivated images of 'dungeon, fire and sword', had been effective from at least the 1740s, a position sealed by the disintegration of the Stuart cause following the defeat of the 1745 rising in Scotland.[132]

Women's Experiences

Though the point no longer has novelty, it is still important to remind ourselves that women made up a good half of Irish society. Any attempt to sketch their experiences, still less place these in a wider context, is beyond the scope of this chapter and also beyond the competence of the writer. A few small-scale borings into the evidence, nonetheless, might be of some interest. The earlier, more general arguments obviously related to women as well as men, either directly as in the case of religious freedoms or indirectly as in the case of land reform (though the latter directly affected a minority of female land occupiers too). Some have a specifically female dimension, which has not been brought out, as in the discussion of war and violence. The fact that

Ireland was not the scene of invasions and occupations after 1700 meant that the use of rape as a weapon of collective aggression was virtually absent.[133] The fate of German and Austrian women, as victorious Soviet troops poured eastwards in 1944–45, or of Bosnian Muslim women at the hands of Serb militiamen during the 1990s, is brutally revealing of some of the gender-specific dimensions of war.

A cluster of welfare indicators, admittedly for only a small segment of the time period under discussion, suggests that the position of women in Ireland compared fairly well with that of their European counterparts. Literacy is one such variable. It is difficult, of course, to get measures that are truly comparable across cultures and societies, though the ability to sign the marriage register is a minimal test that seems reasonably unambiguous. In 1900 the proportion of brides in Ireland who accomplished this task was 89 per cent; in Belgium it was 90 per cent; in France 94 per cent; and in England and Wales 97 per cent.[134] In Akenson's telling phrase, these are 'small differences'.[135] Not so small was the difference with Italy (and, one suspects, much of southern and eastern Europe), where the proportion who could sign the register was only one out of every two Italian brides.

Child mortality has an obvious bearing on welfare, on women more so than men, though its incidence is shaped by a host of factors from social attitudes to housing conditions and medical care. Table 1.3 presents some data for some European countries at two points in time. There is no suggestion of strict comparability across national boundaries. Neither should the magnitudes be taken as other than the roughest of guides to welfare issues. Still, it is

Table 1.3
Deaths of Infants under One Year Old per 1,000 Live Births
(Ireland=100)

	year 1900	year 1950
Austria	212	143
Hungary	205	187
Spain	187	139
Portugal	-	204
Belgium	158	115
France	147	113
England and Wales	141	65
Denmark	117	67
Ireland	100	100

difficult to avoid the conclusion that Ireland, and Irish women, were relatively comfortably situated within this particular European league.

Most people, most of the time, prefer longer rather than shorter lives. So, life expectancy can be a useful measure of human welfare. Some quick comparisons in relation to the life expectancy of females indicate that Irish women around 1900 could expect to live six years longer, on average, than Italian women; more than seven years longer than Bulgarian women; but two and a half years less than their English counterparts.[136] In 1992, the life expectancy of Irish women at birth was 98 per cent that of the European Union (12 countries).[137] So Irish women would appear to have been well within the mainstream of the European experience in this century.

There is an important exception to these favourable comparisons. On biological grounds, one would expect female life expectancy to exceed that of males by several years. This was true of women in advanced societies such as Britain and the United States early this century. It was not true of Irish women during the first half of the twentieth century. The demographic historian, R.E. Kennedy, attributes this intriguing problem to unequal access to food, shelter and other resources.[138] This may be true, though the evidence is impressionistic and indirect. Other possible explanations might focus on the high fertility of Irish women, pregnancies late in life (with the attendant risks of maternal mortality), perhaps other health care problems unrelated to male–female inequalities, and differences in the nature of the local economy. In relation to the last, it is interesting that life expectancy among females *relative to men* was worse in the North of Ireland as compared to rural Ireland during the quarter century before 1914. Does this mean that the relative status of women in the most industrialised and urbanised region on the island was actually lower than in the west of Ireland? Surely not. It seems more sensible to conclude that the male–female differential under discussion can sometimes be a misleading guide to status differences. In the Ulster case, an explanation in terms of industrial health hazards, particularly conditions in the female-dominated linen industry, must have some relevance.[139]

Irish women showed a high propensity to migrate out of Irish society. In some years in the later nineteenth century, for instance, more women than men emigrated.[140] This is unusual when viewed in a European context. The feminisation of emigration after the Great Famine might be read as evidence of the dismal prospects facing women within a male-dominated Irish society. Alternatively, it might be read as an indication of the freedom enjoyed by women within Irish families, in particular the scope afforded them to better their position through migration. This complex issue deserves further exploration, though the fact that, when abroad, many Irish women married Irish men, sometimes from the same locality, does not suggest an aversion to the world of the Irish male, its privileges and its presumptions.

The point at issue in this discussion of women's position in Irish society, it is worth emphasising, is not whether Irish women were badly treated. They were, compared to men. James Connolly's well-known utterance, of women being the slaves of the slaves, is not altogether guff.[141] What matters here is whether women in Ireland were treated in a worse fashion than in other, comparable societies. The evidence so far is scanty, but it does not lend easy support to notions of an exceptional oppression of women within Irish society.

Issues of gender operated at a metaphorical level as well. The personification of Ireland and the feminisation of that persona were, and still are, important manipulative devices in Irish national culture. Like the Irish Catholic nation, Mother Ireland was helpless, a victim of historical circumstances.[142] The position in relation to unionism seems different: sexual identity and ethnic identity were less intimately connected. Indeed in contemporary times, male rather than female imagery is more to the fore. The warrior figure, Cúchulainn, defender of Ulster, leaps into action on the walls and gable-ends of loyalist Belfast. The more traditional male hero for Ulster loyalists, King Billy – mounted on a white horse, forever destined to cross the Boyne – embodied a cause rather than a 'fatherland'.[143] Within Catholic Ireland, Cathleen Ni Houlihan did send out her sons to be shot, through with what benefit to Irish women is far from clear. Whether gendered representations of nationhood materially and adversely affected the status of women is, however, something which needs to be demonstrated rather than assumed.[144] Such representations were of course a commonplace: bare-breasted Marianne fired generations of young Frenchmen; mother Russia was a more potent symbol than the cult of Stalin; Spanish fascists killed for the love of *la madre patria*. There being no accounting for taste, Britannia may have done something similar for the virgin soldiers of the empire on which the sun never set.

The Making of Ireland

In one way or another, life was passing us by and we were suffering misery, sometimes having a potato and at other times having nothing in our mouths but sweet words of Gaelic… Certainly I suffered Gaelic hardship throughout my life – distress, need, ill-treatment, adversity, calamity, foul play, misery, famine and ill-luck.

Flann O'Brien[145]

There is an almost palpable sense of victimhood and exceptionalism in the presentation of the Irish national past, particularly as reconstructed and displayed for political purpose. It is a syndrome of attitudes that might be summed up by the acronym MOPE, that is, the most oppressed people ever. Less extravagantly stated, the claim is to being *one* of the most oppressed peoples in the history of world civilisation. But the burden of the story so far is that there was a large gap between images of singular oppression and the material and cultural conditions which were the lot of people in Ireland.[146] If so, there is a problem. How do we explain the emergence of this dominant set of images – of a history of incomparable oppression, of Ireland as Deirdre of the Sorrows, of its people as the bearers of unspeakable misery comparable only to that of the Jews?

The origins of this mind-set can hardly lie deep in the medieval Gaelic past. The *literati* of Gaelic society and of the Hibernicised Old English appear to have been self-confident, assertive, even harbouring traces of cultural supremacism.[147] The beginnings of an explanation might draw on at least four streams of cultural influence. Firstly, the political rhetoric of the eighteenth-century 'Irish Nation', especially those elements of the Protestant elite who were conscious of being inheritors of English traditions of rights and freedoms, and who chafed at Ireland's political subordination to Westminster. The line stretches from Swift and Flood to Tone. Secondly, there may well be a Gaelic contribution, mediated, sometimes distorted by translators of an antiquarian and romantic frame of mind, particularly as represented in oral tradition in reaction to the defeats of the Gaels and the Old English in the seventeenth century. Jacobite poetry of the *Aisling* variety, with its themes of oppression, dispossession and deliverance, has a place here.[148] These images commingled with a third set of influences, that of European romanticism, which deeply affected political and cultural discourses in the formative phase of Irish nationalism during the early decades of the nineteenth century. Moreover, as conflicts of class were subsumed in an overarching romantic nationalism – an act of appropriation made easier by the association between wealth and Protestantism in Ireland – the chalice of national suffering brimmed to overflowing. Finally, at a deeper, more diffuse level of consciousness, there was the image-world of Christianity and its symbolic representations of pain, sorrow and exile – universals of the human predicament – which could be exploited selectively to colour the Irish collective experience.[149]

The argument then is that the cultural processing of the past – the invention of 'Ireland' – drew on these sources.[150] But what of the raw materials of the past themselves? Though these might be selected and interpreted in a variety of ways, three interrelated features of Irish history seem to lend themselves to a heightened sense of victimhood. Firstly, the long engagement with 'England' stretching back to the twelfth century, when reconstructed retrospectively, gave the story of Ireland a poignancy and coherence that was less apparent in the case of countries whose encounters were of a multiple and changing character. 'Little Belgium' and the Belgians, for instance, on whose behalf Irish volunteers were exhorted to fight in the Great War, had been dominated variously by the Spanish, the Austrians, the French, the Dutch and the Germans at different times from the seventeenth to the mid-twentieth century.[151] Great powers, such as the states of France, Prussia, Spain, Austria and the United Kingdom were, almost inevitably, involved in complex alliances and enmities through time, as coalitions formed and fragmented, sometimes within the same campaign. This precluded fixation on a single 'other'. By contrast with such bewildering shifts both in the loci of threat and the foci of aggression, the Irish case had a stark simplicity. The reality of a unitary and consistent source of Ireland's political subordination was conducive to simple notions of oppression, at least as perceived by representatives of the Catholic community in Ireland.[152] Even with the creation of the Irish Free State at the end of 1922, there was a widespread perception that the state had been unjustly and unnaturally truncated by virtue of partition. That festering wound, the sense of 'unfinished' historical business between Britain and Ireland, was re-inflamed during the quarter century of communal violence in Northern Ireland after 1969. Thus, the 'Irish Question', now transmuted into the 'Ulster Question', was carried forward to the eve of the millennium.[153]

It is important, though, to add some perspective to this straightforward story. The general point about the longevity of the Irish question and its axis in Anglo-Irish relations is hardly open to dispute. But notions of Irish singularity can be easily over-done. Other regional or 'internal' nationalisms, such for example as those of Catalonia and the Basque Country, not only shared deep historic roots but also had their focus on a constant source of subordination, in these instances the metropolitan power centred in Madrid. Quebec, on the far side of the Atlantic, might also be a case in point.

Secondly, unlike other states in western Europe, the emergence of an Irish nation state came relatively late in historical time. This not only added to the sense of grievance, it meant that the articulation of the case for devolution or independence, and its timing, occurred during an era of nationalist ferment across Europe, one in which the scope for mass mobilisation and mass propagandising was of a kind unthinkable under the conditions of an *ancien-regime* Europe. Thus Irish independence was preceded by a century of popular politics – mass meetings, fiery platform rhetoric, widespread reportage in local newspapers – which did much to amplify notions of oppression and victimhood. Anglicisation, a progressively expanded franchise and mass literacy aided projection of the national saga.

Finally, the apparent consistency of patterns of oppression through time gave a cumulative character to the story of Ireland. Grievances from one period could be pitch-forked on top of grievances from a later period, with little sense of historical change. The Penal Laws, long after they had been repealed, still mattered. The timeless quality of the grievances, at least at a polemical level, and the ease with which they could be aggregated through time, facilitated representation of the whole historic Irish experience as one of monstrous proportions.

There is at least one further and related question. Why did so many commentators, including politicians, journalists, authors and poets, feel that the Irish past was especially sorrow-laden relative to the experience of peoples elsewhere? At one level, the answer is simple. The insularity of much Irish thought, an ignorance of conditions abroad (outside of Britain and North America), and a lack of interest in other cultures, meant that comparisons could be made with impunity. The life experiences of African Hottentots, American blacks, Russian serfs, or Turkey's Christian subjects could be raided and trivialised for purposes of domestic political advantage. Nonetheless, there *is* an authentic sense of *relative deprivation* to many of the utterances. Two points of reference stand out above all others in terms of their salience and their consistency through time: England and the Protestant community of Ireland. Adoption of these comparators fuelled a deep and abiding sense of disadvantage and deprivation. In relation to the first, England was the most developed country in the world during the nineteenth century, while the United Kingdom had succeeded in creating a multi-national empire of stupendous size and wealth. In the circumstances, and particularly by the late Victorian period, it was not difficult to feel relatively deprived in terms of economy, culture and self-esteem. It may even be that one of the sources feeding anxieties in relation to the Anglicisation of Irish society derived from cultural envy. Within Irish society itself, the Anglican establishment, the largely-Anglican landlord class, and the Protestant elites which dominated industry and the professions in Ireland, invited hostility and resentment. Irish Catholics *were* both absolutely and relatively deprived in terms of these claustrophobic comparisons. Beyond Britannia lay other societies which, in many respects, in most time periods, compared even more unfavourably. But these two rocks of comparison, fixed and perceived as hostile, experienced directly rather than in the abstract, go a long way towards explaining the intensity of the MOPE mentality in Ireland.

Conclusion

To see the Irish experience as an exemplar of misery and oppression among European peoples, still less against the backdrop of the wider world, is simply an expression of ignorance in relation to the histories of other nations. Whether it is location, climate, land occupancy, political and religious rights, economic welfare or violence, the Irish record is no worse than the modal European experience and is, in a variety of respects, more fortunate. Obviously Ireland's relative position on different indicators changed through time, and was clearly at its worst during the second quarter of the nineteenth century. Its position during the eighteenth century was frequently misunderstood in the more traditional accounts of the Irish past, while the relative position of the Irish, comprehended in the round, was probably at its best during the twentieth century.[154] Still, it is hard to overestimate the role of self-delusion in Irish history, whether as a force animating colonial 'reformers' in the seventeenth century or Sinn Féin activists in the early twentieth.

The MOPE world view has a variety of significances. At a political level, the self-conscious use of platform rhetoric, with the passage of time and by dint of repetition, could easily pass into orthodoxy, with powerful motivating consequences for constitutionalist and revolutionary alike. In terms of socio-political demands, be it seeking land reform in the 1880s or chasing a review of the land annuities paid to Britain in the 1930s, an invincible belief in Erin's wrongs could usefully underpin a negotiating stance.[155] In more recent times, a modernised variant, now expressed in terms of structural problems and peripheral location, may have emboldened Irish negotiators and impressed its European partners into channelling disproportionate economic assistance to the Irish Republic, to the disadvantage of the much poorer member states of Greece and Portugal.[156] There is, therefore, the paradox: the projection of a victim status could be both functional and empowering. It could, unfortunately, and to even greater effect, be dysfunctional too, especially when laced with aggressive self-righteousness. It undoubtedly contributed to the ethnic blindness which allowed nationalist leaders to dismiss the problem of ethnic diversity in Ireland, with tragic consequences during the course of the twentieth century. Ulster unionists matched that blindness, image for image. The result: a flourishing of the wilder forms of fanaticism, feeding off their mutual atavisms. For these traffickers in the past, history was a suppurating wound, beyond time and healing, regularly to hand in the service of the present.

At a historiographical level, the belief that Clio had turned *Roisin Dubh* out of her luxuriant acres and onto the hardest of hard roads has exercised a profound influence on the reconstruction of the Irish past and the making of collective portraits of the Irish experience. Most of the older histories of Ireland, some of a highly politicised nature, some not, were fashioned explicitly within this framework of assumptions. In recent times, this mode of thinking and writing seems to have passed over uncritically into historically-minded literary and cultural criticism.[157] Subliminal traces affect even the best of modern historical scholarship; it is visibly present in others.[158] In part, but only in part, this is because much Irish history writing lacks a comparative perspective. But such is the seductive power of the Irish saga of oppression, misery and victimhood, it is difficult to re-vision the Irish past independently of this paradigm of beliefs, ideas and sentiments. In challenging the MOPE world view we are engaging with the most influential frame through which Irish history is viewed.[159] It is the master template for writing modern Ireland.

In history we recall the women and men of the Irish past: not figments of pious recollection but real people who breathed, loved, hated, suffered, believed and died. It is unnecessary, and ultimately self-destructive, to compete for wider attention with claims to an ethnic trauma of singular scale and intensity. But it would be an act of denial of equal insensitivity to fail to acknowledge that Irish history is replete with instances of persecution, of evictions, of famines. These form part of a European historical experience that was, time out of mind, brutal, bloody and oppressive. One does not have to go all the way with Hobbes to conclude: the past is not a pleasant place.

CHAPTER TWO

The Planter and the Gael

Co-written with Kerby A. Miller, Brian Gurrin and Gareth Davies[1]

Introduction

The Belfast-born poet, John Hewitt (1907–1987), struck what was for some a paradoxical note when he wrote: 'I am by birth an Irishman of Planter stock.'[2] Could Planters be Irish, and could Irish people be of Planter stock? Though a less acute dilemma nowadays in the Ireland of the New Irish, where the children of Lithuanian, Polish, Nigerian and other nationalities are recognised as Irish, this was less true in times past. The cultural revival of the late nineteenth century in Ireland, as indeed elsewhere in Europe, placed a renewed value on ethnic and linguistic purity and on historical origins. Ulster unionism's threat of revolt on the eve of the Great War and the Irish revolution of 1916–21 gave a further urgency and intensity to these longings.

Yet, as a small island on the western edge of Europe, it is hardly surprising that Ireland historically had been open to waves of invaders, predators and settlers, riding in from western and northern Europe. Thus the notion of an original ethnic stock, Gaelic and Gaelic-speaking, was always bound to be a fiction, though one that infused, sometimes in more subtle form, nationalist discourses in twentieth-century Irish society.

In parallel fashion, a quest for ancient origins and contemporary legitimacy has animated sections of Ulster Unionism. The mythology surrounding the Cruithin – allegedly pre-historic Ulster tribes driven out of Ireland by the Gaelic tribes to the south, only to return from Scotland to their ancestral homelands during the Plantation of Ulster – is spun from the same kinds of yearnings.[3] A more fantastical take on an imagined past is the belief, held by few admittedly, that the Protestants of Ulster were descended from the lost ten tribes of Israel.

This would confer a biblical legitimacy on their latter-day descendants.[4]

The Long View

The early history of the formation of human society in Ireland, inevitably, is lost in the mists of time. Seemingly inevitably also, this calls forth imagination and invention. *The Book of Invasions* or *The Book of Conquests* (in Gaelic *Leabhar Gabhála Éireann*), compiled in the eleventh century, charts a succession of invasions, dating from a pre-Gaelic and even a biblical past, to the Gaelic colonisation of the island. Irrespective of the accuracy or otherwise of these stories of invasion, the image of an island open to periodic influxes of other peoples and racial intermingling is surely correct. The watery highways linking Ireland to Britain and Europe ensured this was and would continue to be the case, whether the newcomers were warlike or pacific, traders or invaders.

Within the period of recorded history there were the Viking raids, incursions and eventual settlements, touching four centuries: from 795 to the Battle of Clontarf in 1014. The influence of the Ostmen, and their urban settlements, continued long after their military power was broken. Then there were the Normans, the Anglo-Normans and the English who entered Ireland during the early to late Middle Ages, seizing power, land and people, and also fashioning new systems of governance, economy and culture. Many were assimilated into 'native' ways of life, as intercourse between the different ethnic groups assumed literal and metaphorical meanings. While these 'Old English' hardly became 'more Irish than the Irish', cultural exchanges were deep and pervasive. The flow was both ways, with regional nuances and variations. Intermarriage and the adoption of customs and laws, language, house types, technology (including military technology) and farming practices became part of the new cultural mix.

Only a narrow stretch of water, the North Channel, separates and indeed links the north of Ireland and the south-west of Scotland.[5] Irish–Scottish contact and exchanges were maintained down the centuries. During the Middle Ages the Scots supplied soldier-mercenaries to the northern chieftains, some of whom settled permanently in Ireland (the McSweeneys in the north-west being a case in point).[6] Scottish-born farmers and farm workers settled in places such as the Glens of Antrim, with the encouragement of local landlords. Sometimes, of course, this cultural contact could take a particularly destructive turn. Though short-lived, the intervention of the Scottish warlord, Edward Bruce ('the destroyer of Ireland'), produced wanton destruction on a grand scale. With remarkably bad timing, his attempts to grab the kingship of Ireland coincided with the great European famine of 1315–17, thereby magnifying the deaths due to war-related causes.[7]

Before turning to later external interventions and attempted conquests of Ireland, it is as well at this stage to underline a critical point: these various outsiders or foreigners shared, or, as in the case of the Viking marauders, were converted to a common cultural heritage in the form of Christianity. Thus ethnic divisions were more permeable than would later be the case by virtue of some fundamental commonalities of religious belief and practice.

Reformation

The Protestant Reformation affected Ireland later in time than in other parts of Europe but its political and social impact was to prove of enduring significance. Henceforth, divisions of ethnicity were reinforced by divisions of religion, as opposing religious beliefs and practices gave rise to ever more antagonistic group relations. In the process, ethnicity, which far from being a constant mutates over time, came to assume more complex and more divisive forms. The first state-planned plantation of Ireland, in Leix-Offaly in the 1550s, was inaugurated during the short-lived reign of the Catholic Queen Mary, but all subsequent English monarchs were Protestant (with the one exception of James II who was usurped by his son-in-law, William of Orange, after only a few years on the throne). The planting of loyal English and Protestant subjects in Ireland came to be seen as an essential element in the Tudor strategy of completing what for long had been only a partial conquest of the neighbouring island. In the 1580s the suppression of the rebellion of the Munster Geraldines, with its overtones of a Catholic 'holy war', was accompanied by the introduction of farmers, craftsmen and labourers from England to re-people the devastated countryside. The strategy was to implant elements of English civility, Protestantism and loyalty to the Tudor crown in the southern counties of Ireland.[8]

The plantation scheme that registered the greatest long-term impact was undoubtedly the Plantation of Ulster.[9] This involved not only the confiscation of Gaelic estates and new patterns of authority but also involved large inflows of people from Scotland and England. These transformative changes were initiated in 1609, in the wake of the flight of the Gaelic Earls, principally O'Neill and O'Donnell. Both were under pressure from the English administration in Dublin and, in turn, had been conspiring with the Spanish enemies of James I of England (James VI of Scotland). The British 'newcomers' arrived in their thousands and were Protestant in the main. They were also English- or Scots-speaking. Thus ethnic, religious and linguistic differences intertwined, strengthening the barriers that separated the newcomers from the Gaelic-speaking and Catholic inhabitants of Ulster whom they forcibly displaced. In counties Antrim and Down, private plantations and settlements had introduced large numbers of Scots even before the official Plantation of Ulster. Scottish settlers and migrants tended to be Presbyterian in religion while their English counterparts were generally Anglican. It is noteworthy that the patterns of settlement varied along ethnic lines.[10] The new Scots were to be found disproportionately in north Down, in south Antrim, the 'Route' area of north Antrim, in north-east Londonderry and in the Foyle basin between Tyrone and Donegal. The new English, by contrast, settled mainly in north Armagh, Tyrone, Fermanagh, Cavan and Monaghan. By the end of the century roughly a quarter of the population of Ireland was Protestant, with scatterings of Protestants in every county in Ireland, though the demographic heartland was still situated in Ulster.[11]

Other rivulets of Protestant immigration, such as the French Huguenots and the German Palatines who were fleeing religious persecution in Europe, arrived in Ireland in the late seventeenth and beginning of the eighteenth century.[12] These added to the religious and ethnic complexity of the island, while a trickle of Jewish immigrants from eastern Europe, also fleeing religious persecution, made their way to Ireland in the decades before the First World War. The more typical strangers in the two centuries after 1700, however, were English and Scots, whether entrepreneurs, craft workers, administrators, land agents, ministers of religion, soldiers, police, holders of other occupations or none. Much of Ireland's success in terms of modern industrialisation, such as it was, can be traced to these voluntary migrants.[13] This means not only entrepreneurs such as Edward Harland from England and Gustav Wolff from Germany but shipyard workers from the north of England and the west of Scotland whose skills were essential to the growth of shipbuilding and engineering in Belfast.[14]

An Ethnic Melting-Pot?

Having identified the distinctive ethnic strands that constituted the tapestry of Irish society in the early modern period, we may now turn to the question of the blending of these over time. Or to change the metaphor, was Irish society from the seventeenth century onwards a melting-pot for the diverse elements that went into the making of Irish society? The answer, at first glance, might seem to be overwhelmingly in the negative.

The ethno-religious divide, between Protestants of whatever denomination and Roman Catholics, has been enduring, as the Troubles of the early 1920s and of the late twentieth century amply testify. Riot, house burning, expulsions, intimidation, shootings and killings have marked the politics and the social life of twentieth-century Ulster and Ireland. This was true to a far greater extent than in the preceding century. Yet beneath the hard crust of mutually exclusive political and religious claims, there has been more traffic between the three major ethno-religious blocs – the Anglican, the Presbyterian and the Catholic – than is sometimes realised. Conversions from one faith to the other did happen, for a variety of motives. Marriage across ethnic and religious boundaries, or mixed marriages, occurred at the local and neighbourhood level. Such marriages were viewed with opprobrium within all three of the major ethno-religious groups, not least because the reproductive power of the union threatened to create new blood lines in which one identity was likely to be suppressed.

What is the evidence for this? One pointer is that some of the smaller Ulster Gaelic septs, such as the McGimpseys, appear in the 1911 census of Ireland as exclusively Protestant.[15] Thus of the 222 persons with this spelling of the surname, 181 were Presbyterian, and the rest non-Catholics of one kind or another, even though their ancestors before 1600 were most likely to have been Catholic and Gaelic-speaking. It is probably not coincidental that most were located in North Down, an area of intense Scottish settlement. Interestingly, some were implicated in the United Irish Rebellion of 1798, on the side of the insurgents.[16]

The McIldoons, again a small, heavily localised Gaelic sept in north Armagh, may be another case in point. In 1911, according to the census, there were only 56 McIldoons in Ireland, virtually all located in east Ulster (Antrim, Armagh, Down), and all Protestant with the exception of two Catholic households. Out of the total of 56 McIldoons, a majority or 32 were affiliated to the Church of Ireland, that is, 57 per cent of the total. Less than 10 per cent were Presbyterian. Again this might suggest wholesale conversion from Catholicism to the Church of Ireland in Anglican-dominated and denominated north Armagh. These two cases, those of the McIldoons and the McGimpseys, suggest that group conversions were possible, for a variety of motives perhaps, and the presumption might be that this was more likely in the seventeenth century, when political, economic and religious conditions were more fluid than in the later periods when the denominational boundaries were more strictly policed.

Such wholesale conversions are likely to have been the exception, and are probably confined to rather small groups of people in the thinly populated countryside of Ulster in the 1600s. It might be illuminating to take a more common Gaelic Ulster name such as Doherty, noting in passing Sir Cahir O'Doherty's quixotic uprising in 1608 which had the effect of precipitating a much more extensive plantation of Ulster than the one originally envisaged. There were more than 17,000 individuals bearing the Doherty name in 1911. If we focus on the Dohertys who lived in County Antrim in 1911, we have a more manageable sample of 847. Of these, as one might expect, most were Catholic. But the perhaps surprising point is that one in three was Protestant. One in five (21 per cent) gave their religious affiliation as Church of Ireland, one in ten (9 per cent) as Presbyterian, and one in thirty-three (3 per cent) as Methodist. Hardly any had been attracted to the small Protestant sects. None, for instance, adhered to the Plymouth Brethren, the Baptists or the Independents but thirty-seven-year-old Jessie Doherty, handkerchief folder, living in the Dock area of Belfast, a poor part of the city, was returned as 'Salvationist'. Her brother, William, a printer by trade, was one of the few in the city returned with 'no religion'. The religion of the remaining two members of the family, including the widowed household head, Ellen, was given as Church of Ireland.[17]

In the neighbouring county of Down there were 288 people by the name of Doherty in 1911, and 25 per cent of these were of a Protestant persuasion. Even in County Londonderry, where the greatest concentrations of Dohertys were originally located, some 12 per cent out of the total of 2,598 were Protestant. What all this suggests is that defections or conversions from the pre-Reformation religion of the O'Dohertys could be considerable, being especially pronounced in the majority Protestant counties of east Ulster. What is true of the Dohertys is likely to be true of other major Gaelic surname holders in Ulster as well.

Ethno-Religious Blocs

This might begin to suggest that the battery of state legislation, or Penal Laws, directed against Catholics and non-conformists from the end of the seventeenth century and in force, to varying degrees, for more than a century after, was taking its toll on the Catholic community in Ireland. Earlier persecutions on religious grounds, going back to the days of the Tudors, would have worked in the same direction. There is some truth in this. A broad spectrum of motives, from religious conviction to economic, sexual, status and security considerations, is likely to have motivated movement across the ethno-religious boundaries and the adoption of Protestantism. But, if anything, the net flow of defectors or converts would seem to have been from the Protestant to the Catholic ethno-religious bloc. This may seem counter-intuitive, at least by reference to certain European precedents. The persecution of Muslims and Jews by the Spanish state – the Inquisition of the later Middle Ages – resulted in forced conversions or exile. The profession of Muslim or Jewish beliefs was simply no longer possible. The repression of French Protestants by the state during the seventeenth century, which was intensified with the revocation of the Edict of Nantes in 1685, was largely successful in producing civic and religious uniformity within France, though at a terrible cost in human terms.

One test in the Irish case is to look at the outcomes, in terms of religious affiliation in 1911, of a sample of the descendants of those English and Scottish who were new to Ireland in the post-Reformation period. With some small exceptions these may be presumed to have been Protestant at the time of arrival in Ireland. But were they still Protestant some three hundred years later?

A systematic analysis, using a large sample of new British surnames, is not attempted here. But the findings from a small sample of such names is certainly suggestive. We focus on three such surnames, those of Anderson, Bell

Table 2.1

Protestant British surnames from the 1600s, and the proportion (%) who had been absorbed into the Catholic ethno-religious bloc by 1911

	ANDERSON	BELL	ROBINSON
	% Catholic	*% Catholic*	*% Catholic*
Leinster	74	46	60
Munster	58	51	46
Connacht	53	51	43
Ulster	8	6	10

Source: calculated from the National Archives of Ireland: http://www.census. nationalarchives.ie [accessed 5 February 2011].

and Robinson (see Table 2.1 above). The assumption is that all, or virtually all of the people bearing these surnames were newcomers from Britain in the post-Reformation period and that they were of a Protestant persuasion. Table 2.1 then displays the proportion of these who reported their religious affiliation as Catholic in 1911.

The table above indicates remarkably high levels of attrition sometime in the preceding three hundred or so years affecting all three surname groupings. Thus, to take the most extreme case, that of the Andersons: three out of every four (74 per cent) of those resident in Leinster had shifted across to the Catholic (and presumably nationalist) camp. Three out of every five Robinsons in that province made a similar itinerary across religious and, one suspects, ethnic and political boundaries as well. The Bells seem to have been more persistent in their attachment to their original faith. Nonetheless, outside of Ulster, one in every two Bells had switched allegiance by the eve of the First World War.

It is apparent also from Table 2.1 that the experience of change of religion in Ulster was very different from that of the other three provinces, and this requires more detailed and more intensive study. Suffice it to say at this stage that, within 'Protestant' Ulster, British newcomers were much more likely to retain a Protestant religious and ethnic identity. The attrition rate in our sample was 10 per cent or less.

Ethno-Religious Flows

Rather like miners prospecting for hidden minerals, we have taken test borings in the rich archives of the Irish census of 1911. The picture that is beginning to emerge is that there was considerable 'traffic' of Catholics across boundaries in east Ulster, where Protestants were in a clear majority. But where the demographic balance tilted the other way, as in the southern provinces of Ireland, the traffic ran the other way, with widespread 'defections' from Protestantism to Catholicism. That this had social class and social geographic dimensions is highly likely, and there may have been a gender dimension to these social processes as well. It would be interesting, and indeed feasible, to compare the socio-economic status of the stratum of Andersons, Bells and Robinsons who retained the Protestant faith with the socio-economic characteristics of those Bells who transferred to the Catholic ethno-religious bloc.

An illustration of how this might be done is presented in Table 2.2. There was a total of 7,359 Bells in Ireland in 1911, of whom 2,289 belonged to the Church of Ireland, 2,953 to the Presbyterian Church and 987 to the Roman Catholic Church. There was a strong regional pattern to the distribution of Bell households, as most were to be found in the northern counties of the island. In the sample reported in Table 2.2 the occupations of the Bells who were resident in County Dublin in 1911 have been classified by religion (Catholic or Church of Ireland). Needless to say, the sample is small and only selected occupations have been examined, so the findings should not be used to support generalisations beyond the experience of these holders of the Bell surname in County Dublin at the end of the Edwardian era. By contrast with the northern counties, Catholic holders of the Bell surname, at 283, were in a majority; Church of Ireland Bells in County Dublin were fewer in number at 176, indicating a high incidence of conversions of one kind or another.

Table 2.2
The Bells of County Dublin in 1911: a comparison of selected occupations by religion

	Catholic	Church of Ire.	Catholic	Church of Ire.
	Number	Number	%	%
Land owner	1	1	0.4	0.6
Merchant	0	1	0.0	1.1
Solicitor	0	2	0.0	1.1
Civil servant	0	2	0.0	1.1
Teacher	0	1	0.0	0.6
Clerk	6	8	2.1	4.5
Labourer	28	3	9.9	1.7
Servant	20	9	7.1	5.1

Source: calculated from the National Archives of Ireland: http://www.census. nationalarchives.ie [accessed 10 February 2011].

The results are fairly clear cut. In relation to the higher status professions, the Bells who adhered to the Church of Ireland were more likely to be in higher status occupations than Bells with a Catholic affiliation.[18] The numbers are, admittedly, small. But when we come to lower status occupations such as labourers and servants, where the numbers are larger, a strong contrast is evident. There were four times as many Catholic Bells in these lower socio-economic strata as compared to their Church of Ireland counterparts. The contrast is a bit less than this, however, once one takes into account the fact that the number of Catholic Bells exceeded that of the Anglican Bells in Dublin at this time (by 283 as against 176, as mentioned above). Columns three and four in the table allow for this difference in absolute numbers, showing the contrasts in proportional form. It is still clear that Anglican Bells enjoyed a higher socio-economic status and that they were underrepresented among the servant and labouring classes.[19] Whether lower socio-economic status preceded or coincided with absorption into the Catholic community, or gave rise to this outcome in the form of downward social mobility, opens a further intriguing set of possibilities. This rich research agenda might be further enlarged by pondering the role of emigration in shaping these patterns. Emigration may well have been selective as between Catholics and Protestants,[20] though how this worked out in practice in relation to the Bells and other originally Protestant families is not known. Finally, it is worth adding that some distinctive cultural markers tended to accumulate along the way: while none of the Anglican Bells living in Dublin had a knowledge of Irish, eight of the Catholic Bells, predominantly male and in their twenties, claimed a knowledge of 'Irish and English'.

The Language of Identity

In the Gaelic or Irish language a common word for Protestant is *Sasanach* (English person). This conveys the strong impression that Protestants, typically members of the Church of Ireland, were English, hence foreigners and outsiders. They were not, therefore, Éireannaigh, or members of the Irish nation, at least outside of the realm of more sophisticated nationalist discourse. Of course, attitudes to Irish Protestants within Irish society and within Irish nationalism varied considerably and have also evolved over time but, in demotic speech, and hence in popular consciousness, there was a sense of 'otherness' at the very least.[21]

There is a fascinating twist on this in areas of the Donegal *Gaeltacht* (Irish- or Gaelic-speaking areas). Traditionally a Protestant was referred to as an *Albanach* (Scottish person).[22] This applied and still applies whether the person in question is Anglican, Presbyterian or other Protestant. In view of the fact that many Donegal Protestants are, and have been, affiliated to the Church of Ireland, and hence were largely of English rather than Scottish origin,[23] it seems curious that the different strands of Protestantism have been conflated into this one ethnic entity. Presumably because many of the early settlers were Presbyterian, of Scottish origin, the title stuck and was applied indiscriminately to other outsiders as well. In any case, it is an interesting example of how religion and ethnicity can be used interchangeably, even though the ethnic labelling may be of a rough and ready kind. It also raises the question of how the social identities of these outsiders were initially perceived: in ethnic terms or in religious denominational terms, or as a fusion of the two? The use of the ethnic rather than the denominational label might suggest that non-religiously-based cultural differences, including place of origin, were seen as the predominant elements in the identity imputed to the other.[24]

None of this is to suggest that Protestants could not be native Irish speakers. The census enumerators' returns for Glencolumbkille, in south-west Donegal, for instance, show a number of Church of Ireland households in which Irish and English were spoken.[25] One might wonder, though, if Irish- or Gaelic-speaking Protestant households, or their offspring, might have been particularly vulnerable to absorption into the majority Catholic population in the isolated areas where Irish speaking still survived in the early twentieth century. One straw in the wind is the experience of the Connor family from the Great Blasket Island, off the coast of County Kerry (a copy of the completed census form for the Connors may be seen on the National Archives website, Census of Ireland 1901).[26] This was a Gaelic-speaking island, until the last inhabitants were evacuated in the early 1950s.[27] Eugene Connor, the fifty-five-year-old head of household, was returned in the 1901 census as a farmer and fisherman. Both he and his wife Kate belonged to the 'Irish Church', that is the Church of Ireland, and both had Irish as well as English.[28] But the eldest son, the twenty-nine-year-old Maurice, who actually signed the census form, was returned as Roman Catholic. So also was the daughter-in-law, his wife Mary, and *their* two sons. Presumably he had been born into the faith of his parents but at some stage he must have moved across to the Catholic religion. His marriage to a Catholic bride, Mary, might seem the most likely occasion for this conversion. But it is curious that his three younger brothers and a sister, all unmarried, were also returned as 'Roman Catholic'.

For whatever reason – social isolation, communal pressure, access to education and other opportunities are some of the possibilities – the parents had agreed to or had acquiesced in having their children incorporated into the Catholic Church. The result was that future generations of Connors became exclusively Catholic and the Church of Ireland line on the island simply died out. If one were to trace the family history backwards in time, it is quite possible, perhaps even likely, that the Anglican lineage did not go that deep in time. An earlier generation of the Connors may well have converted from

Catholicism to the Church of Ireland as a result of early to mid-nineteenth-century missionary activity in the Dingle peninsula.[29]

Conclusion

Ireland has long been a land of invasions and inward migrations, giving rise to complex genetic, ethnic and cultural inheritances. The pure Gael, once held as an ideal, was always little more than a piece of ideological make-belief. Notions of Anglo-Saxon racial homogeneity, not to say superiority, with distinctive traits and characteristics, were similarly the product of political imaginings. The evidence of this chapter suggests that mixing and intercourse between different ethnic groups, even in the post-Reformation period when religious difference served to harden ethnic boundaries, have been features of Irish society for centuries. John Hewitt may be reassured: there is no necessary conflict between a 'planter' origin and a twentieth-century Irish or Ulster identity, or indeed between a Gaelic or Old English ethnic origin and an Ulster or Irish unionist identity.

We have developed and deployed, in this chapter, one measure of traffic across denominational and ethnic boundaries. It is clear that the traffic was not one way,[30] and the net outcomes would seem to have depended primarily on social and demographic variables at the local level rather than on state policy or other supra-local influences. The extent of this traffic, it would seem from our sample findings, was considerably greater than many believed or were prepared to admit. The phenomenon has attracted relatively little overt recognition; why this might be so is itself an interesting question.

It has to be said that our method does not allow us to say in what time periods conversions or transfers from one ethno-religious bloc to another were most prevalent. Until the chronology is filled in, even if only in a rough fashion, the task of identifying the determinants of these movements will be little more than guesswork. What has been attempted here is a necessary first stage along the road towards a more complete analysis of the dynamic processes at play.

Having highlighted fluidity at a personal and a local level, it may seem paradoxical to conclude by emphasising the resilience of social divisions originating in the seventeenth century.[31] This is particularly true of Ulster, where the sense of the 'other' sometimes assumed virulent form. Thus, while the major ethno-religious groups gained and lost significant numbers during the course of time, thereby enlarging and complicating the genetic pool, it remains the case that each bloc assimilated entrants so thoroughly that the capacity to reproduce divisive social structures was not seriously impaired.

CHAPTER THREE

Nationalism and Unionism in Ireland

The first necessity for the obtaining of prosperity to Ireland is the banishment of English misrule from Ireland.

Charles Stewart Parnell[1]

Introduction

Political theorists, such as the late Ernest Gellner, suggest that nationalist ideology is a product of the modern industrialising world.[2] It is, therefore, a nineteenth- and twentieth-century phenomenon, not an ideology that can be found in pre-industrial or medieval times. Brian Boru was not a nationalist; neither was Oliver Cromwell. Nationalism, it is argued, is more likely to emerge in the context of rapid economic and democratic change, where there is a sense among some ethno-cultural groups that they are somehow losing out or being disadvantaged. The growth of national sentiment, therefore, forms part of a political and ideological backlash against the disruptive impact of economic and social change and the state structures that appear to house these forces. In response to the challenges and pressures of modernisation, nationalist intellectuals and ideologues strike out for political autonomy or even complete political independence. Over time, nationalist claims take on a more assertive tone, possibly culminating in political violence.

Within the emerging nationalist movement it is the middle classes – those involved in industry, commerce, commercialised agriculture and the professions – who tend to assume leadership roles. This is, in substantial part, because national demands serve the particular economic, social and prestige interests of these social groups, or so it is argued. Though it is not usually said, irrespective of social class women tend not to be to the fore in such movements, the occasional exception notwithstanding. You would not, therefore, expect the impoverished cottier-fishermen of the Aran Islands, or the women of the

Scottish Highlands and Islands for that matter, to be the early activists in campaigns for national independence.

Might Gellner's framework of ideas help to illuminate the emergence of nationalism and unionism in nineteenth-century Irish society?[3] Ireland was deeply affected by the forces of modernisation emanating from the epicentre of the industrial revolution, the neighbouring island of Britain. By the end of the nineteenth century, much of Ireland was seen as economically underdeveloped and nationalism had swept the board as far as most elective bodies in Ireland were concerned, be it in parliament, on the boards of poor law unions, or in the new county councils. Political autonomy for Ireland, of one kind or another, seemed inevitable. Contrariwise, one part of the island, the north east, had experienced modern industrialisation and a majority of the inhabitants were wedded to the union with Britain and a form or dialect of British nationalism.

The primary interest of this chapter is the role of economic *forces* and the *experience* of economic change – a rather more subjective notion – in the development of nationalist and unionist movements in nineteenth- and early twentieth-century Ireland. There is no suggestion, of course, that only economic forces mattered, nor that they operated in isolation. Monocausal explanations for complex political and ideological formations have long been out of fashion, and rightly so. But there is no sympathy here either for the more modish interpretations of historical change in which virtually everything is held to be related to everything else, and causal links are only weakly specified, if at all. By focusing attention on the economic dimensions, there is at least the possibility of probing the explanatory power of a major constellation of forces held to be relevant both by nineteenth-century Irish and British nationalists and by modern-day theorists of nationalism and Marxism.

Five Indicators of Economic Progress

A micro-historical perspective, attentive to temporal, regional and local variations, would no doubt identify an extensive range of economic issues with a bearing on nationalism and unionism in Ireland. The strategy pursued here is different, however. An attempt is made to locate a small number of overarching themes, as summarised in Table 3.1, which most people, it is suggested, would regard as basic to economic well-being. The emphasis is on change over time. To this end each of the chosen economic indicators has been assigned a score of one or zero – one indicating substantial gains or improvement, and zero indicating little or no advance, or even deterioration within a given time period. If, however, a satisfactory position in relation to a particular indicator had been reached by the start date and was being maintained, then a satisfaction rating of one is recorded. The scoring system is simplicity itself, and it is also held to be additive across the five indicators. It would not be difficult to develop a more complex schema, but the principle of Occam's razor has much to commend it in the present context.[4]

In a similar spirit of parsimony the geo-political entities are defined as nationalist Ireland, embracing most of the island and holding large or overwhelmingly Catholic populations, and unionist Ireland where Protestants were in a majority, that is, the four north-eastern counties of Antrim, Down, Londonderry and Armagh. Needless to say there were Protestant communities and enclaves elsewhere on the island, most notably in Dublin and its environs, but the rock of Protestant and unionist identity, on which the ship of Home Rule eventually foundered, was deeply embedded in the North.

Table 3.1
Five Indicators of Economic Progress or Non-Progress in Ireland, North and South, 1800–1914

Nationalist Ireland (South)

		1800–50	1850–80	1880–1914
1	Living Standards	0	1	1
2	Economic crises	0	0?	1
3	Industrialisation	0	0	0
4	Emigration	0	0	1
5	Economic Justice	0	1	1
		0	2	4

Unionist Ireland (North)

		1800–50	1850–80	1880–1914
1	Living Standards	0	1	1
2	Economic crises	0	1	1
3	Industrialisation	1	1	1
4	Emigration	0	0	1
5	Economic Justice	1	1	1
		2	4	5

Note on the scoring scheme: a score of 1 means a substantial gain over the period in an economic indicator (for example, achieving gains in living standards or reducing economic crises), or having already attained a satisfactory position in relation to that indicator, while a score of zero means there was either an actual loss or there was little improvement in what was an unsatisfactory position to begin with.

From the Union to the Famine

1. Trends in Living Standards, 1800–1840s

We may begin by looking at the first half of the nineteenth century, starting with what might loosely be termed Southern Ireland. The first indicator relates to the living standards of the mass of the population. There are various measures of living standards but income is one of the most widely used. Can we say, in terms of the wages of agricultural labourers, the incomes of farmers, or the earnings of artisans and industrial workers, that there were substantial gains between 1800 and the 1840s? It seems unlikely, if only because, in the neighbouring country of Britain – the world's first industrial nation – gains in living standards were meagre in this period. Feinstein, for instance, calculated that the standard of living of the average working-class family improved by less than 15 per cent between the 1780s and the 1850s.[5]

But there are more substantial grounds than argument-by-analogy to suggest that broadly-based improvement was not the order of the day, or the half century. As Louis Cullen has argued, the voracious demands of the United Kingdom's wartime economy helped maintain high levels of economic activity during the course of the French Wars (1793–1815), though some underlying economic weaknesses were apparent in retrospect.[6] After the war, demobilisation of the armed services, economic recession and deflation affected the whole of the United Kingdom.[7] The impact was particularly severe in Ireland where far more people, proportionately speaking, lived close to the margin of subsistence. As discussed later in the context of industrialisation and de-industrialisation, living standards in much of urban Ireland were also under pressure. Moreover, population growth was still remarkably exuberant, despite narrowing economic opportunities. Symptomatic of these economically troubled times, the tide of emigration was rising in the decades between 1815 and 1845.

Not that all was doom and gloom. The Catholic middle classes, in town and countryside, may well have improved their positions in the decades before the mid-century crisis. While wages and incomes fell in monetary terms, the cost of living probably fell more steeply, by one-third or so between 1813 and the mid-1830s.[8] The terms of trade moved in favour of the better-off tenant farmers,[9] who were the backbone of O'Connell's agitations for Catholic Emancipation and Repeal of the Union. Catholic clergymen enjoyed greater security and substantial incomes.[10] In addition, there were various innovations, some state-sponsored, in policing, education, communications and banking services which, on balance, favoured the commercial or market-oriented segments of society.[11] The picture is not, therefore, a monochromatic one when viewed through the prism of social class. Still, in terms of the welfare of the mass of the people, inequality appears to have widened and there was no significant amelioration of their wretched material conditions before 1845.[12]

Worse was to follow in the later 1840s, as living standards collapsed for large sections of the population and there was outright starvation. So a score of zero for changes in living standards is surely the appropriate one for proto-nationalist Ireland in the period 1800–1850.

In the more Protestant North the strains of economic and structural change were also apparent. The same economic forces affected the Protestant smallholders of outer Ulster, while in inner Ulster, where the combination of small-scale farming and handicraft weaving predominated, the earnings of weavers were being squeezed by the competitive pressures of the Lancashire cotton industry.[13] The objective reality was a decline in the position of farmer-weavers and cottier-weavers, as well as the hand spinners of linen yarns. This was also the subjective perception.[14] Asked in the mid-1830s how their position compared with that at the Peace of 1815, many Ulster parishes reported either no improvement or a decline in living standards.[15] So, a score of zero rather than one seems the better fit for the northern experience as well.

2. Economic Crises

Trends in living standards are important. More important, though, for most people are the year-to-year fluctuations. In pre-industrial societies the availability of food might change violently over time, being heavily dependent on unpredictable climatic and environmental factors. In the Irish case, severe shortages of the staple food crop, potatoes, affected the country in 1800–01, 1816–17, 1824–25, and again in 1836 and 1839, as indicated by the evidence of potato prices.[16] Hunger, at irregular intervals, visited the millions mired in the poverty and squalor of the potato economy, on top of the recurrent seasonal 'hungry gap' between the exhaustion of one potato crop and the arrival of the new potatoes.[17] It is clear that fluctuations in food supply, and the attendant food insecurity, were a common feature of the pre-Famine economy, and that significant improvements had not materialised in the four decades after the Union. By the same token, there is no evidence either of more frequent or increasingly severe food crises – warning shots as it were – as one approaches the Great Famine itself. Then out of the blue, and with the force of a tsunami wave, the potato blight *Phytophthora infestans* swept across the countryside, leaving devastation in its wake. It is true that the Union gave more secure access to the main market for Irish agricultural exports.[18] It is also the case that the United Kingdom offered a protective framework against European competitors to agricultural and linen producers in Ireland, but these may have been among the less tangible or less visible benefits of the economic union, going largely unremarked by contemporaries. In any case, it is difficult to chart major gains in food security or the cushioning of the poor against economic misfortune in this period. The Irish poor-law system, inaugurated in 1838, was, on balance, beneficial but was soon overwhelmed by the scale of the Famine tragedy.

The same was true, by and large, for Protestant households in the Ulster countryside. Industrialisation in the Lagan Valley, which is discussed further in the next section, conferred benefits on the emerging industrial proletariat, one in which women and children featured more prominently than adult male workers and in which Protestant workers were more firmly entrenched than Catholics. The likelihood is that this broadened the economic base of some households. But these households were also vulnerable to a new type of economic fluctuation, the business cycle. When these coincided with harvest failure, as in Belfast in 1846, the result was intense deprivation and vulnerability to famine-related disease.[19]

3. Industrialisation

The Industrial Revolution was gradually transforming modes of industrial production in the British and Irish Isles from the later eighteenth century onwards, with profound implications for industry in Ireland. Significantly, the earliest sectors to be mechanised were in textiles, first in cottons and later in linen and woollens. Ireland's major industries consisted of the *handicraft* production of linen and woollen goods. The Irish woollen industry went into severe decline after the business recession of 1824–25. Populist critics of the Union plausibly but misleadingly linked the decadence of the industry in the southern towns of Ireland to the Union rather than to the more fundamental forces of technological and organisational change associated with modern industrialisation. There is debate as to the extent of industrial decline in Ireland before the Famine,[20] but decline there undoubtedly was in the once extensive woollen and worsted industries. Cheaply manufactured British textiles displaced handicraft production. Though a small number of Irish firms made the transition to factory conditions,[21] the more visible result was unemployment and underemployment in the Munster towns, Carrick-on-Suir in County Tipperary and Bandon in County Cork being particularly good examples.

The picture in relation to the leading industrial export sector, that of linen textiles, is more complicated. The mechanisation of the spinning branch of linen textiles from the end of the 1820s onwards, as a result of technical breakthroughs in the handling of flax fibres, deprived tens of thousands of hand-spinners of a livelihood.[22] These were principally women and children, located not just in Ulster but in north Connacht and the north midlands as well. Again, it was easy for ideologues of the Home Rule cause to invoke the familiar fallacy of *post hoc ergo propter hoc* in relation to the Union and its alleged consequences.[23]

The other side of the story, which apologists for the Union liked to stress, was the mushrooming of textile mills in east Ulster, building on an earlier foundation of factory-based cotton spinning in the Belfast region.[24] Mill workers, mainly women and children, displaced the thousands of dispersed domestic spinners in the rural economy. The new mill-spun yarn complemented and also helped break down gender divisions of labour in the handloom weaving sector.[25] More generally, Belfast and its environs represented the local Irish expression of the Industrial Revolution.

Mr and Mrs Hall who visited Ireland in 1838 and again in 1840 were almost euphoric in their praise of the 'new town' of Belfast, its rise, and its favourable topography:

> It was something new to perceive, rising above the houses, numerous tall and thin chimneys, indicative of industry, occupation, commerce, and prosperity; the volumes of smoke that issued from them giving unquestionable tokens of full employment; while its vicinity to the ocean removed at once all idea that the labour was unwholesome, or the labourers unhealthy….the contrast between this town and the towns of the south startled us, making us for the moment believe we were in a clean Manchester, where hearty breezes swept into the neighbouring sea all the impurities usually inseparable from a concourse of factories.

The good health and environmental conditions might easily be challenged (though it is interesting to see these welfare issues being raised at this time) but the progressive image of the North and the relative industrial backwardness of the South certainly accorded with the self-image of proto-unionists.[26]

O'Connell's adversary, the redoubtable Reverend Henry Cooke, asked provocatively: 'Look at Belfast and be a Repealer if you can.'[27] (Cooke was the leader of the politically conservative wing of Presbyterianism and sought to effect an alliance between Presbyterians and Irish Anglicans, largely in opposition to burgeoning Catholic assertiveness in the public sphere.) But uneven economic development served to heighten the contrast between an industrialising North and a largely non-industrialising or de-industrialising South, thus sharpening perceptions of underdevelopment over much of southern and Catholic Ireland. The even larger contrast of course was with Britain itself. In terms of industrial progress, therefore, it seems appropriate to award the North a gain (arbitrarily set at one) and the South a score of zero.

4. Emigration

One and a half million people are said to have emigrated from Ireland, North and South, between 1815 and 1845. This migration affected Anglican,

Catholic and Presbyterian communities, and the middling elements in Irish society rather than the very poor.[28] Another million emigrated during the terrible Famine years of the late 1840s. Though the attitudes of Catholics and proto-nationalists towards emigration were ambivalent during the early decades of the nineteenth century, these hardened after the Famine into firm critiques of the Union.[29] As far as public discourse went, emigration was seen primarily as a problem rather than an opportunity. Protestants may or may not have possessed a more 'modern' or entrepreneurial set of attitudes towards life beyond the Irish shores,[30] but Protestants remaining in Ireland were unlikely to have viewed mass emigration as one of the fruits of the Union, not least as it drained Protestant numbers as well as those of Catholics. As the Reverend William Fry lamented from a part of Ireland where Protestants were thinly represented: 'I fear many more [Protestants] will shortly leave their old habitations, to seek for peace and quietness in every foreign land where they think such is to be obtained.'[31] Emigration was increasing rather than diminishing in intensity by the 1840s, so a score of zero seems merited for both the northern and the southern political constituencies.

5. Economic Justice

Members of an ethno-cultural group, such as the Catholics of Ireland in the early nineteenth century or Ulster Protestants for that matter, were concerned not only with their own economic and social situation but their position relative to other groups as well. A sense of relative deprivation was vitally important in informing political consciousness, particularly in an era of democratising reforms.

Irish society at the time of the Union was stratified, not only along the lines of social class but on the basis of religious affiliation as well. This was particularly noticeable at the level of the landed elite, which was overwhelmingly associated with the Church of Ireland, and in much of the public sector, at local and national level, in the professions and the higher echelons of the army and later police. There was, in effect, a hierarchy of occupational roles with a strong religious coloration at the top. The origins of this cultural division of labour, to use Michael Hechter's terms, went deep in time to the seventeenth-century confiscations, plantations and migrations, and proved remarkably enduring.[32] Presbyterians had largely gained acceptance for public office by the early nineteenth century, though there were still residues of hostile attitudes towards Presbyterians on the part of Church of Ireland ministers and landowners, but it was Catholics who found the greatest difficulty in penetrating the higher strata of society.

It is likely that cultural differences between Catholics and Protestants have been exaggerated in the past, as Donald Akenson argues in his aptly-titled book, *Small Differences*.[33] But economic and social differences certainly existed and were *perceived* to exist.[34] There is little to suggest that these inequalities were being seriously eroded for Catholics during the first half of the nineteenth century, with the exception of a brief period in the 1830s under the Drummond administration when attempts were made to reform local administration and remind landlords of their obligations to their tenants.[35] Notions of 'justice for Ireland' were certainly in the air but converting expressions of good-will into more concrete measures was far from easy.[36] The score for change in economic equity or justice, as this related to the Catholic population is, therefore, held to be zero. Up north the diversification of women's occupations in the first half of the century, perhaps particularly among Protestant women in east Ulster, might be held to signal an advance, however slight, in the long march towards gender equality. By the standards of the time, and notwithstanding cross-cutting tensions between Presbyterians and Anglicans on issues such as tithes, theology and tenurial relations, the position of the main Protestant groupings, male and female, is taken to be satisfactory on issues of economic justice.

Winners and Losers

We may sum up by saying there were no visible or perceptible gains in southern Ireland in relation to any of the five economic indicators for the mass of the people in the decades following the Union. This had little to do with the Union itself. Indeed it can be argued that the Union, in its economic implications, was beneficial for Ireland.[37] But so many forces – economic, political and demographic – were at play after 1801 that it is difficult to separate out the different causal strands. Paradoxically, this made it easier to ascribe the problems of making a living to a single cause: the union of Great Britain and Ireland had to be the fountainhead of the manifold ills of Ireland. Both at the level of personal experience and of political interpretation, there was apparently little to commend the Union to nationalist Ireland. The catastrophe of the Great Famine served to confirm the emptiness of the relationship.

Broadly speaking, the situation in the north of Ireland was not very different for most of the indicators, though there is no doubt that living standards were a bit higher to begin with and that the Famine had a less severe impact. In relation to the latter, some Protestants saw the Famine as mainly affecting Catholic communities, thereby serving to confirm their sense of economic superiority and the value of the Union.[38] More importantly though, the North scored positively in terms of the rise of modern industry and in terms of the representation of Protestants in the higher echelons of economic and status hierarchies.

Mid-Victorian Ireland

The next two periods may be reviewed in much the same fashion, but more quickly now that the basic approach has been established. In southern Ireland the long wave of economic expansion after mid-century resulted in expanding incomes for farmers and agricultural labourers. Improving standards of living were reflected in rising levels of literacy, housing conditions and religious piety. Urban Ireland also participated in these gains, though housing conditions in Dublin were shocking by any standards.[39]

The impact of the Great Famine was still being felt in the 1850s and arguably beyond. There was a severe downturn in the rural economy at the beginning of the 1860s. The onset of an international agricultural depression after 1876 revealed how economically vulnerable some rural households still were, especially in the west of Ireland. This helped ignite the Land War of 1879–82.[40] While the judgement is a bit harsh, in that differences of degree are being neglected, it seems preferable to return a negative verdict in relation to economic crises facing southern Ireland, even in the mid-Victorian period.

It would be hard to argue a case for industrialisation. Improved sea communications and, internally, an elaborate railway system, opened up small-scale industry in southern Ireland to more intense outside competition. Success stories such as Jacob's biscuit factory in Dublin or O'Mahony's woollen mills in County Cork did not an industrial revolution make. The withering away of artisanal occupations and small-scale provincial industry that catered for essentially local markets was far more characteristic of the period. The southern economy still balanced on an agrarian base. Over time, and despite a strain of rural fundamentalism within Irish nationalist thought, this came to be viewed as a further injury. It was assumed that industrialisation was the normal expectation; if it did not happen, then there was something deeply wrong with the political and constitutional arrangements of society. As Professor James Meenan once put it: 'There has been a natural feeling that this country was cheated out of an industrial revolution in the nineteenth century by the Union with Great Britain…'[41]

Emigration cut deeply into southern Irish society as a result of the Famine exodus. The expectation of leaving was built into the strategies of many an Irish household.[42] At the level of political discourse, emigration was increasingly viewed as a by-product of the Union itself. Alternative interpretations, such as that emigration was inevitable in the light of surplus labour in the countryside as well as easy access to two major and expanding labour markets, those of Britain and the United States, found little favour. The haemorrhaging of the Irish population was viewed as one further, and indeed powerful indictment of the Union.

Economic justice might take a variety of forms. Most salient is Catholic–Protestant differences, but one might also consider the dimensions of social class, region and gender. Social inequality was probably less pronounced in the decades after mid-century, as were regional inequalities but, to a large extent, these were an artificial creation, the product of death and emigration among the poorer classes in Ireland during the Famine. Public policy had little to do with it. Wage differentials between the western and eastern counties diminished, and there was some convergence in terms of quality of housing.[43] The Catholic middle classes expanded in relative importance, enjoying the fruits of economic expansion, while the disestablishment of the Church of Ireland must have been a source of symbolic satisfaction. Whether the status of women advanced is a more open question. A rising incidence of unmarried females in Irish society seems open to conflicting interpretations. Less ambiguously, the gap in literacy standards between males and females narrowed, with important implications both for women's social role and their life chances as emigrants overseas. Thus in the census of 1851 only a quarter of females were returned as being able to read and write, as compared to 41 per cent of males. Differences still persisted three decades later, but the gap was much smaller. While 62 per cent of males were recorded as readers and writers in 1881, some 56 per cent of females were similarly accomplished. Protestant–Catholic gaps in the literacy stakes also declined. In terms of objective measures, therefore, there are grounds for claiming some gains in economic justice, albeit of a modest kind, in southern Ireland in this period.

In the North, there were broadly-based gains in the mid-Victorian period. Living standards advanced, subsistence crises were less pronounced (in part because of the increasingly industrial character of the North, though this, of course, exposed the province to the cyclical downturns of the industrialising world). Vast engineering and shipbuilding enterprises complemented earlier developments in linen textiles. Belfast was emerging as one of the great industrial towns and ports of the United Kingdom.[44] Poverty and urban degradation were also part of the story. Emigration from rural Ulster continued, though movement to Britain and to 'loyal' Canada almost certainly had less politically charged connotations for Protestant migrants as compared to Catholic and self-styled exiles.[45] So, in terms of broad brush strokes, it is the consolidation of economic gains and further industrial advance, not the shortcomings, which command attention.

'... The last years of the Union were the best...'

What is most striking for the period 1880–1920 is how substantial were the gains made in southern Ireland by comparison with its own past and by comparison also with the North. Incomes, on average, undoubtedly rose, probably faster than in the United Kingdom generally.[46] There were massive schemes of land reform, special assistance for the west of Ireland (through the efforts of the Congested Districts Board), the formation of a Department of Agriculture and Technical Instruction to promote rural development, and the introduction of pensions for older people. Perhaps overly cynically, as this was a period of social reform within the United Kingdom more generally, these diverse measures (with the exception of the last) are sometimes bundled together as an attempt to kill Home Rule with kindness. Even emigration was on a steep downward incline after the exodus of the 1880s had subsided and movement out of Ireland, North and South, largely dried up during the years of the Great War itself. Rural housing schemes promoted by the British state benefited the most degraded elements of Irish society, the agricultural labourers. Looking at another marginalised category, there were modest gains for women also, both in home life and in the public sphere.[47] Despite these advances, this was also the period in which Irish nationalism made its most spectacular gains, culminating eventually in the creation of the Irish Free State in 1922 and the declaration of an Irish Republic a generation later. David Johnson has crisply summarised the economic experience: 'In economic terms, the last years of the Union were the best ones.'[48]

Is this not paradoxical? Does it not cast doubt on any significant role for economic factors in the rise of Irish nationalism? Ulster unionism fits better within an economic framework of interpretation: the North witnessed a spectacular transformation from a largely agrarian and proto-industrial society at the time of the Union to a technologically advanced industrial society by the end of that century. Adherence to the Union, relative to the alternatives (a Home Rule Ireland or an independent Irish Republic), made good economic sense, for the Ulster unionist middle classes *and* the Protestant working class. Political allegiance and economic interest were remarkably congruent. It is the relationship between economic forces and the rise of Irish nationalism which seems curious.

On reflection, perhaps the story is not quite so contradictory. As will be suggested shortly, a more complex model of relationships between the economic and the political is necessary. Moreover, the formative period for Irish nationalism was before the 1880s, with linkages deeper in time.[49] While it would be foolish to pursue a deterministic view of the making of the Irish nation, it would be equally wayward not to recognise the channels of mobilisation and agitation from the 1820s onwards that were conducive to the rise of an essentially Catholic constitutional nationalism. Economic failure in relation to industrialisation, employment and famine intensified the sense of alienation from the metropolitan centre and favoured the development of an oppositional, territorially-based ethnic politics. It is thus in the earlier two periods, rather than in the slow countdown to political independence, that

Gellner's insights appear to carry most weight. It is surely right also to allow for the role of time lags in the system of economic and political relationships, as well as allowing a role for contingency, when seeking to trace the causal sequences.

It is true that the demands for the devolution of power from Westminster to Dublin waxed and waned over time,[50] but by 1881 the nationalists of town and countryside had been mobilised behind the banner of land reform and Home Rule, in the course of a crisis that owed its origin and intensity to the severe economic downturn of the late 1870s. These feedback mechanisms, from the economic to the political spheres, suggest a type of path dependence in the evolution of Irish nationalist politics.[51] Once mobilised and locked into an inconclusive power struggle, no amount of economic improvement was likely to deflect Irish nationalists (in effect Irish Catholics) from the goal of self-government nor Ulster unionists (in effect Protestants) from support for the Union.[52]

Economic Forces and Nationalism

It may be helpful to attempt a summary of the links between economic forces and the evolution of nationalist politics, taking account both of the long and the short term. There are four elements to this understanding.

First, going deep in time, there were the structures of power, authority and property relationships laid down in the seventeenth century under conditions of conquest and confiscation, which had become normalised over time, some limited challenges notwithstanding. These formed part of the larger architecture of power relationships enveloping the two islands, and whose ultimate focus was located in London. The enduring economic as well as political significance of the seventeenth-century convulsions, including the inflows of settlers and economic migrants from Britain, was that the hierarchy of occupational and authority roles established then was reproduced, *mutatis mutandis*, into the nineteenth. These structures, imbued with latent economic power, conditioned social action, though in a far from deterministic fashion. While the social order had acquired a fair degree of stability during the eighteenth century, notwithstanding the stresses and strains of an evolving market economy and a variety of political challenges, there remained an ethno-religious fault line that ran through the society.[53] The upper reaches of the social hierarchy, be it in terms of land ownership, political power or status, were occupied by Protestants. Social class and religious demography intersected one another. Or, as Kerby Miller puts it: 'Irish society around 1800 seems analogous to a pattern in a kaleidoscope: turned one way the design forms along sectarian lines, but when turned again the socioeconomic and cultural divisions within each religious community seem most prominent.'[54]

The Protestant and unionist aspect of the class structure came to be viewed as a source of grievance by aspiring Catholics (see indicator five in Table 3.1) from at least the 1820s onwards and probably earlier.

There is, of course, the danger of assuming that the stratification of society in Ireland was somehow peculiar to Ireland. As Sean Connolly has advised, 'we must see the whole structure of confessionally based inequality as itself existing within a wider structure of hierarchy and privilege that Ireland shared with other [European] societies of the *ancien regime*'.[55] There is a danger also of succumbing to notions of historical inevitability, that the actual pathways traced out were, in fact, the only possible pathways. Modern Irish history (which of course cannot be divorced from its higher-level context of British-Irish relations), was more branched and pathway *independent* than is sometimes allowed. Yet it is only fair to recognise also the deep structures of modern Irish history, the intertwining of social class, religious demography, and external political authority that, at the very least, constrained the range of possible developments.[56]

Then, secondly, there were the *generalised* economic and technological changes of nineteenth-century western society, in which Ireland also participated, that facilitated, albeit indirectly, the mobilisation of nationalist groupings and the transmission of nationalist ideas. These included a more differentiated occupational structure (reflecting a more complex division of labour), improved communications by road and railway,[57] effective postal and telegraph services and increased access to learning in the English language. We see the rise, not only of national newspapers, but also of a provincial press that was often avowedly nationalist in tone. New or expanding occupational roles such as teachers in the state-funded national schools, along with journalists and lawyers, were frequently carriers of the idea of the nation.[58] These developments were part and parcel of a wider process of modernisation – economic, social and technological – in which the spread of the English language and of mass literacy was implicated. The market for ideas, particularly ethnic nationalist ideas, expanded exponentially during the course of the century, with positive feedback mechanisms lowering the unit cost of producing and diffusing these ideas. As the networks of people and institutions thickened, the benefits of adopting a nationalist stance in public affairs became all the more rewarding, leading to the further expansion of existing networks.[59] The cumulative effect was to scoop the ideological pool for ethnic nationalism, as shown by the breakthrough of the Home Rule party at the general election of 1885. An important aspect of this process was the spread of the English language which made the propagation of Irish nationalist ideas less costly, in turn encouraging the further use of the medium of English, and so on in a mutually reinforcing upward spiral.[60] Ironically, English was the language of Irish nationalism and British public finance the source of mass literacy and a reading public.

Third, at the level of populist discourse, there was a long litany of 'wrongs', including economic wrongs and frustrated expectations, which could be formulated into arguments decrying the Union. Some were undoubtedly valid, others were of antique origin and of doubtful relevance in the context of debates on the effects of the Union, and others again rested on misunderstanding.[61] The economic grievances, which formed a large subset of the total, ranged from restrictive legislation by the British parliament on Irish trade and commerce in the eighteenth century to claims of a capital drain of funds out of Ireland as a result of absentee landlords, excessive increases on whiskey duties and over-taxation of the Irish more generally.[62] It was William Gladstone, later a great Liberal prime minister, who took the unpopular step of raising taxes on Irish whiskey towards British levels, saying that 'he did not know that the rights of man demanded that an Irishman should get drunk more cheaply than an Englishman'.[63] He may even have had a point. Selective recitations of injustices and wrongs were, of course, the stuff of political discourse, shaping and reflecting a collective sensibility attuned to the politics of grievance. The library of past and present wrongs, including those of an economic nature, were articulated in a continuous present tense that seemed to give historical depth and legitimacy to newly-minted notions of nationalism.

Conveniently the counterfactual view of Ireland's potential implied by these criticisms was not only pleasing but located in future space. Imagined communities, to use Anderson's term for national groupings, also tend to have imagined destinies toward which history and nationality are apparently straining.[64] The sequel to Irish independence, in a mysterious but seemingly assured way, would be a prosperous, populous Ireland. Arthur Griffith, for one, saw no reason why the island could not provide a living for a population of 15 million people.[65] Nationalist priests dreamt of an Irish-Ireland in which small-scale industry complemented the endeavours of the field, with noble peasants and rural industrial workers fashioning a new civilisation in contradistinction to the ugliness and immorality of the modern, urban-industrial world.[66] The images were utopian, and even archaic; the realities of independence in the Irish Free State, epitomised by the cutting of state pension benefits in 1924 by 10 per cent (from 10 shillings to 9 shillings per week) soon punctured the make-believe world of the ideologues. But this observation is with the benefit of hindsight. Such expectations were all the more beguiling because imagined material benefits could not be sampled until *after* the threshold of independence had been crossed. In this respect, Ulster unionists were at a disadvantage in having to argue for an imperfect current reality as against the weakly-specified but alluring possibilities of liberation premised and promised in the nationalist vision.[67] Or as one economist has put the point in a more general context, 'it is always easy to contrast the observed deficiencies with the unknown advantages'.[68]

Annoyingly also for Ulster unionists, the industrial achievements of Belfast – 'Tis the bad, Orange, immoral hole of a place is the same Belfast'[69] – were belittled and pronounced alien by the new cultural nationalism associated with the Gaelic Athletic Association, the Gaelic League and the Irish-Ireland movement.[70] It is true some nationalist thinkers, such as Tom Kettle, recognised that there was likely to be an economic cost to Irish independence, but these tended to be minority voices. In the generic nationalist discourse the reassuring fact was that there was no necessity to sacrifice economic interests on the altar of nationalism.

This brings us to the final point: the actual experience of economic and social change in the century after the Union. In the final analysis, one might presume it was the *personal* and *social* experiences of material change in the century after the Union that most directly influenced Irish national sentiment and sensibility. This may well be so, but these experiences cannot be separated from the preceding discussion: the evaluation of all significant change is mediated by political entrepreneurs and public knowledge-makers (not to mention the filtering effect of individual and family ideologies), which in turn of course are likely to chime with wider political discourses locally and nationally. In other words, there is no such thing as direct, unmediated experience of change: normative and evaluative mechanisms are inevitably involved. But having conceded this, only the most incorrigibly anti-materialist thinker would dispute the importance of objective economic and social structures and forces external to the individual, family and community in shaping political attitudes and orientation.

This returns us to the simplified world condensed in Table 3.1. If this model is a roughly credible representation, then for the first seven or eight decades under the Union the grand conclusion must be that there were no great gains for the nationalist or proto-nationalist peoples of Ireland. Dominating all other experiences was the catastrophe of the Great Famine. That the problems at mid-century of a potato-dependent society – *the* greatest indictment of the Irish social system – had their roots well before the Union, in ecology as much as in economy, was something beyond the national gaze. With the promptings of political activists, in Ireland and Irish-America, much of the economic experience of life in Ireland was plausibly interpreted and re-worked to fit a paradigm that indicted the Union as the key source of Irish ills, economic and otherwise.

Two Case Studies and a Model

The model of interactions between the economic and the political spheres, as sketched above, has four strands: deep historic structures, processes of modernisation, political and cultural discourses, and contemporary experience of the social world. All four form an interactive system of relationships, shaping but not necessarily determining social outcomes. By way of illustrating and testing this explanatory sketch we may take two formative episodes in the development of Irish nationalism. These were the campaign for Catholic Emancipation of the 1820s and the Land War of 1879–82. Each owed much to the organisational and oratorical skills of O'Connell in the first case and to Parnell and Davitt in the second. But in both instances deep-seated inequalities of wealth, status and power, as well as the correlation with religious demography, served to structure the conflicts.

Catholic Emancipation: Daniel O'Connell's campaign for Catholic Emancipation unsurprisingly assumed a largely Catholic coloration, despite some backing from liberal Protestants, while much landed wealth, particularly in Ulster, was thrown into the scales against pro-Emancipation candidates. By and large, the longer-run forces of modernisation – a concept that is not without its problems – favoured the popularisation of the agitation. The years of prosperity for commercial farmers, traders and exporters during the French Wars improved both the fortunes and the numbers of a small but growing Catholic middle class, one that was later to form the basis of O'Connell's reform campaign. The progress of the English language in the eastern parts of the island, as well as rising literacy levels, opened up the localities to wider messages of identity and communal solidarity. The hierarchical arrangement of the Catholic Church, with its foundations in parish-based communities, was also evolving into a ready-made communication system. At the level of discourse, the appeal to a mass audience invoked past wrongs and an appeal to the wider material interests of the Catholic people, and not simply a narrow focus on Catholic representation in the House of Commons.[71] Mass demonstrations, marching men and flag be-decked platforms served to multiply the messages and the circulation of ideas.

Then there was the issue of contemporary economic experience. While the Catholic middle classes may have been motivated primarily by considerations of status and civil liberties in the 1820s, smallholders in the countryside and the poorer dwellers in the towns had little to gain from such recognition. Their participation, which was concentrated mainly in the anglicised or rapidly anglicising parts of eastern Ireland, can only have sprung from wider dreams of 'emancipation', particularly some amelioration of their impoverished state.[72] Thus, the violent fluctuations in living conditions after the French Wars must have found some reflection in the discontent that was channelled into O'Connell's mass movement.[73] The course of agricultural prices in the early 1820s suggests severe economic distress. The prices of wheat and oats for the years 1820, 1821 and 1822 were only a half of those prevailing in 1817, which admittedly was a high-price year. The same was true of pig meat and there were substantial falls in butter prices, beef prices and mutton prices.[74] The implication is clear. There was a major squeeze on farm incomes which, in turn, had adverse knock-on effects for other parts of this essentially rural economy.

The effects of these economic shocks were reflected in collective political action at the time, most notably in the form of the Rockite insurrection in the Munster counties of Limerick and Cork that preceded the Catholic Emancipation campaign.[75] Conversely, the improved prices and incomes of the commercially-oriented farmers and traders between 1823 and 1826 may have furnished the relatively better-off sections of Catholic society with the confidence and the resources to back a very different kind of agitation, that is, O'Connell's radical but largely peaceful constitutional campaign for Catholic Emancipation.

Seemingly inevitably there were ethno-religious reactions. An ill-conceived plan to hold a massive demonstration in the North set off an Orange counter reaction.[76] Taking the longer view, from the 1820s onwards there are signs that there was dual path-dependence in the making of Irish politics, as evangelical Protestants mobilised to challenge Catholic 'gains'. The conflictual dance of Orange and Green, so apparent in rural Ulster in the later eighteenth century in clashes between Peep O'Day Boys and Defenders, was emerging from the localities and edging on to the national stage.[77] As dual path-dependence took firmer shape, relations between the major ethno-religious blocs became less and less responsive to economic shocks. The drawing together of Presbyterians and Anglicans in a pan-Protestant political alliance from the 1830s onwards facilitated this duality.[78]

Land War. Switching to the second half of the century, despite the social convulsions associated with the Great Famine and the operations of the Incumbered Estates Court, the structure of property and power relationships underpinning the rural social order remained largely intact. Such steep social and economic inequalities, when caught in the headlights of a new political consciousness furnished the *opportunity* for land claims from below. Of more recent vintage, in terms of the structural features of Irish society, was the large-scale destruction, through famine and emigration, of the semi-proletariat of cottiers and labourers. This cleared the way for a confrontation between tenant farmers and landowners in a crisis uncomplicated by cross-cutting social conflicts between farmers and labourers.[79] The winds of modernisation helped the propagation of the new political consciousness. The continuing decline of the Gaelic language and the rise of a literate, newspaper-reading populace proceeded apace, even in the western regions of Ireland where the origins of the Land War were situated.[80] Post-Famine economic change, most notably the deeper penetration of market relationships in the countryside, strengthened the numbers of farmers, traders, priests and townspeople available to assume local leadership roles in the politico-agrarian movement.[81]

However, without the economic downturn of the late 1870s, it is unlikely that the dissident landlord, Charles Stewart Parnell, or the former Fenian prisoner, Michael Davitt, could have succeeded in mobilising the mass of the rural population behind the demand of 'land for the people' and Home Rule for Ireland. It was helpful also at the level of political discourse that the tenant farmers and their representatives could, as part of the critique of landlordism, re-vision Irish landlords as 'alien' by virtue of their historic origins and religious affiliation. Thus, in the space of a few years, economic stimuli (including economic critiques) and political reactions conjoined to produce a nationalist mobilisation on a mass scale.[82] Individual and collective economic interests helped fire an agitation that was structured by power and property relationships, and, increasingly, that used the language and practices of Catholic nationalism.

In the final analysis, it is not easy to see how one might attach primacy to one or the other, to politics or to economy in relation to the Land War. Each would seem to be a necessary condition for the undermining of the long-established social order in rural Ireland, that of landlordism. Thinking about these issues more generally, perhaps it makes sense to see the economic as inextricably bound up with the political and the cultural in the development of nationalism, with multiple actions and reactions unfolding in time. So, sometimes these short-run interactions might contribute mildly, perhaps additively, to the historical flux, as for example during the tenant right agitation of the early 1850s; at other times, depending on contingent forces and particular conjunctures as during the Land War, the mutually-reinforcing effects might be multiplicative, resulting in profound change. But always there were the economic and power structures, deeply embedded in time, modified by short-run processes of change (cumulatively or otherwise), serving not so much to determine as to channel and constrain political action. While omnipresent, only in times of crisis did these reveal themselves visibly.

Economic Forces and Ulster Unionism

One might wonder if the narrative on the unionist side of the street is pretty well the mirror image of that on the nationalist side. It is apparent that Ulster Protestants, unlike Irish Catholics, had made modest economic gains during the first half of the nineteenth century, downward pressure on the piece rates of handloom weavers notwithstanding,[83] and that substantial gains had accrued during the next quarter century with the growth of shipbuilding, engineering and factory weaving. These business achievements were extended further in subsequent decades. By 1914 the North of Ireland had two of the world's leading shipyards, Harland & Wolff and Workman Clark. It was a world leader in the manufacture of linens. A range of smaller industries including

Mackies and Sirocco in engineering, Dunville and Bushmills in distilling, Gallahers in tobacco manufacture, Cantrell & Cochrane in mineral waters, the Belfast Ropeworks and the shirt-making industry in Derry, helped fill out the picture of industrial progress.[84] So, looking across the nineteenth century, and viewing particularly the second half of that century, it seems clear that the favourable economic experience of Ulster Protestants under the Union gave ample reason to support the Union (Table 3.1).

Was that how Ulster businessmen saw the story? We may turn to one of the best-informed and articulate members of the business class, John Milne Barbour, for an answer. Milne Barbour was president of the Belfast Chamber of Commerce when he gave evidence on the Home Rule controversy before members of the Committee on Irish Finance on 20 July 1911.[85] Later on, he was to become Minister for Commerce in the Northern Ireland government. In a series of remarkable exchanges, principally with the Roman Catholic bishop of Ross, Dr Kelly, Barbour set out the business objections to devolution for Ireland. By implication, the benefits of Union membership were asserted.

> Chairman: 'Have you personally much apprehension of the effect on trade of the establishment of Home Rule?'
> Barbour: 'I should be very sorry indeed to see it introduced.' [86]

The first worry voiced by Barbour was that access to loan capital on the London financial markets, on which much of Ulster industry depended, might be adversely affected. Under close questioning by the committee he conceded that a solvent firm in Ireland would be able to raise loan capital just as cheaply in the wake of Home Rule as beforehand. However, he (and other investors) worried about the uncertainty the new constitutional arrangements might entail. While he did not anticipate a flight of capital from Ireland in the event of a devolved parliament in Dublin, in his view 'new capital certainly would not be attracted'. He was not, however, able to explain very satisfactorily why an Irish parliament, admittedly dominated by agricultural interests, should seek to damage the industrial sector.[87] A sharp reminder from the Bishop of Ross, Dr Kelly, that there was the beginning of an industrial awakening in the south of the country brought forth the rejoinder that the major manufacturing enterprises in Ulster, and Ireland more generally, were dependent on British, American and world markets. The implicit criticism here was that the Irish industrial revival – paralleling the literary, cultural and language revivals – was oriented, in the main, towards the very limited home market. Some of its more parochial advocates were overtly protectionist. Ulster industry, by contrast, competed profitably and proudly in Empire and world markets. Should an Irish state go down the road of economic protectionism (as in fact it did for several decades after 1931), this would be at the expense of the export-oriented industry of the North.[88]

Bishop Kelly returned to the attack: surely he, Mr Barbour, would agree that, just like an ordinary household, the public finances of the national household would be more effectively and more efficiently conducted by an Irish administration? The reply was discomfiting: 'I often think there has been very little legislation initiated by Irishmen; nearly all our greatest benefits have been initiated by Englishmen.' While agreeing that 'national extravagance', or high public spending should be curtailed, he added that he had never seen 'any really good proposal for the more economic administration of Ireland'.[89] The only major point of agreement between the Bishop and the captain of industry was that the recently-introduced National Insurance scheme – one of Lloyd George's great reform measures aimed at protecting workers' livelihoods in times of unemployment and denounced by the Irish bishops – bore heavily on Ireland. Even on this issue, there seems to have been some distance, as Barbour professed himself happy with the reform *in principle* while the Irish bishops were arrayed against reform.

Barbour was polite but unyielding on the key economic issues as they touched on the Union. Then the cross-examination took an unexpected and, as it turned out, a prophetic turn. In the world of politics Barbour opined that minorities sometimes controlled the state of play. 'So it is conceivable', he worried, 'that a minority interest in Ireland might be the more virulent minority, and that a separatist party might eventually be able to control things in an Irish parliament. It is a strange thing, but it does happen.' This was indeed prescient when one considers that these opinions pre-dated the arming of the Ulster and Irish Volunteers and the 1916 rising. But perhaps most surprising, having addressed the major economic problems at length, was Barbour's dramatic admission, if it was such, later in the session:

> Sir William Plender: 'Is the feeling against Home Rule more religious than economic?'
> J. Milne Barbour: 'I think it is very largely religious.'
> Plender: 'More so than economic?'
> Barbour: 'Yes, I really think it is.'[90]

The Unimportance of the Economic?

So, is the game up for the advocates of economic interpretations? It begins to look as if the real issues in Ulster were ethnic and cultural after all. (Religion, in the context of the exchanges quoted above, should be understood as an ethnic and cultural signifier – with religious affiliation, world view and denominationally-controlled socialising patterns at the heart of a nationalist or a unionist identity.) If true, this would also open up a striking asymmetry in the argument of this chapter: economic structures and forces seemed to be profoundly important in the evolution of nationalism but of secondary import, if even that, in the Ulster unionist case. In this topsy-turvy world the material motivations of the South begin to contrast with the less-material leanings of the Protestant North.

This will not do, even if there is much of substance in what Barbour had to say in relation to the nationalism and unionism *of his time*.[91] Unionists liked to parade apparently cool, largely rational arguments about free trade, fiscal responsibility, and the like, but the politics of the late period of the union were infused with hot, emotion-charged issues about identity, militarism, masculinity and culture, notions that had a particular attraction for the younger age cohorts.[92] By the beginning of the twentieth century, if not a decade or two earlier, economic experience as a determinant of political affiliation had been superseded by more holistic concerns (as was conceded earlier in the discussion of the five indicators for the sub-period 1880–1914). The ethno-political pathways were now well marked, and the passions of Orange and Green tended to trump material calculation, particularly among the rising generations.

But economic forces still mattered for the development of unionism, broadly in the manner expounded earlier for Irish nationalism. The outward-oriented, dynamic nature of the Ulster economy helped to secure Protestant allegiance to the unionist cause, from at least the 1840s onwards. This is simply to say that the Protestant and unionist position was grounded in positive economic experiences under the Union, one reflected in and reinforced by unionist discourses surrounding these experiences.[93] The generalised economic forces making for the propagation of a nationalist sense of identity, as discussed above, operated in parallel fashion to produce a mass Protestant and unionist populism. But the contemporary did not exist independently of the past. Again, as in the case of nationalism, the institutional legacy of the seventeenth century was present in the social structure of the nineteenth century. But in Ulster the social structure had been radically amended and supplemented by the emergence of a new class of industrial capitalists. With few exceptions its members were Protestant in religious outlook and unionist in terms of political identity, and these new elites – John Milne Barbour is a representative voice – shared with the older, landed ascendancy a fear of Dublin-based devolved government.[94] A potential cleavage in the social structure, in the form of divisions between industrial and agrarian capital, was resolved through a commonality of economic and class interests. (An intriguing counterfactual supposition might be to wonder what the attitudes to Irish nationalism might have been, had a substantial fraction of the capitalist class in Ulster been Catholic.)

Northern Catholic Workers

However, there was another division, wearing familiar ethnic and religious markings, that seems to confound this economic reasoning. What of northern Catholic workers, whose livelihoods were also bound up with the success of industrialisation in the Lagan Valley, but who remained resolutely attached to Irish nationalism during the various Home Rule crises? Had the economic issues really mattered, it might be argued, then the Catholic shirt-makers of Derry or the Catholic mill workers of Belfast should have been aligned politically with the Protestant textile, engineering and shipyard workers, whose various livelihoods depended on international markets and the emerging social reforms of the British state. It was not so: political allegiance cut across putative class alliances. In Belfast, Catholic workers supported the nationalist Joe Devlin while Protestant workers, in the main, supported unionist candidates, and, later on, the labour unionist association.[95]

One way out of this dilemma might be to adopt an orange Marxist position: that urban-based northern nationalists were the victims of 'false consciousness', in thrall to the hegemonic influences of an Irish Catholic bourgeoisie.[96] This, however, is no more convincing than putting the boot on the other foot: northern unionists were the dupes of an Ulster Protestant bourgeoisie who failed (and continue to fail) to see their 'real' class interests and their place in the Irish nation. Short of an appeal to congenital worker stupidity, it must be said that ideologies, political alliances and mobilisations, be they of the orange or green variety, that have endured for more than a hundred years and that show no sign of dissolving, can hardly be understood in terms of what is essentially wishful thinking. If anything, false consciousness resides in the mind of the analyst.

There are, in fact, reasons why northern Catholic workers should not necessarily identify their interests with unionism. Admittedly the arguments are weaker in relation to the economy but, even here, some qualifications are in order. Catholics were concentrated in lower-paid sectors, and they experienced job discrimination in the labour market as well as artificial ceilings to their career aspirations.[97] While the extent of these barriers is still a matter of controversy, a role for discrimination is not in doubt.[98] Moreover, northern Catholic workers had no difficulty in adopting trade unionism which served a subset of their interests, though not the rounded set of political, cultural and economic objectives to which they subscribed under the banner of nationalism. The most compelling economic argument of all resided in the calculus of the imagination, or rather the incalculable calculus of the imagination. Ireland free *would be* Ireland prosperous, as nationalist discourses from O'Connell to Parnell, and onwards to Arthur Griffith and Sinn Féin, had reassured generations of nationalists. Visons of an as yet unrealised future were worth the risk and could be far more compelling than prosaic policy prescriptions, as demonstrated down the ages in virtually all countries by social movements of a religious or secular hue. Moreover, nationalism, in Ireland as elsewhere, appealed to the whole person, and travelled well across gender and class boundaries, satisfying needs as diverse as the rational, the emotional, the symbolic, the aesthetic and the aspirational, as well as the irrational, the vindictive and the neurotic.

Returning to Ulster unionism, industrialisation had manifold implications for the practice as well as the making of unionist politics. Industrialisation generated wealth and resources which helped fund Ulster unionist political campaigns and later the arming of the Ulster Volunteer Force in 1913–14.[99] From the captains of industry there emerged some effective political leaders, the most prominent example being that of James Craig of the Ulster distilling family. Indeed the economic and political timing was fortuitous: the era of the home rule challenge was also the period when the business strength of Ulster unionism was reaching a triumphant crescendo. The implications at the level of ideological discourse and collective self-image have been mentioned above. But the most powerful contribution from the economic sphere to Ulster Unionism arose indirectly rather than directly. Business success bred, literally, demographic strength, a necessary condition for successful resistance to Home Rule and the later brands of Irish nationalism in an era characterised both by democratic reform and resort to political violence.[100]

Conclusion

By the late nineteenth century, the two ethnic groupings were 'locked-in' to either unionist or nationalist postures. The mutually hostile embrace ensured positive feedback mechanisms within each camp, thereby reinforcing the sense of group solidarity and commitment to Irish nationalism or Ulster unionism, as the case might be. In effect, this was, and it still is (in the twenty-first century), a type of dual path dependence. To borrow an image from econometrics, unionist and nationalist positions on a range of political and constitutional issues tracked each other through time in a closely-bound relationship in which the political stance of one was typically the inverse of the other.

The role of the economic, if comprehended more broadly to embrace the three dimensions of structure, process and economic discourse, interacted in complex ways with emerging political, cultural and even theological stances. Indeed, taking the longer view, what we have is something akin to cumulative causation, as outlined by Gunnar Myrdal in a very different historical context.[101] It probably does not make much sense to try to find a *primum mobile* or original mover in the system of historical relationships from the seventeenth century onwards. Rather, the emphasis might be on the economic as both cause and effect of the unfolding historical forces that helped form nationalism and unionism in the nineteenth century.

Having reinstated the case for the importance of the economic, as understood in the three-fold sense of structure, process and discourse, a word of caution is due, perhaps overdue. Whether these deeper structures and the experience of economic change in nineteenth-century Irish society were a *necessary* condition for the development of Irish nationalism and unionism, in the absence of which alternative historical pathways might have opened up, is difficult to say. An agnostic position, while emotionally unsatisfying, may be the better part of intellectual valour. The intuitive sense of this chapter is that the rise of regionally-based nationalisms is compatible with a wide range of economic circumstances, beyond those sketched by Gellner and his followers, particularly if there is a substantial inheritance from the past of cultural and ethno-demographic materials for nation-building.[102] Ulster unionism is anomalous in terms of such earlier frameworks, as there was no sense of missing out on the heart beats of economic modernisation and industrialisation. Sure enough there is a case for emphasising the relatively recent origins of nationalism in world history, but this too can be overdone. It is hard to make much sense of the two ethno-nationalisms on the island of Ireland without reference to the deeper historical foundations. A parting economic shot is in order in relation to the triumph, or partial triumph, of Ulster unionism, as distinct from the making of British nationalism in Ireland. The process of industrialisation in north-east Ireland was critical, though not in the sense usually understood. It was the demographic implications of industrialisation and urbanisation that really mattered. This is because, in the absence of industrialisation, there would not have been a sufficiently populous Protestant presence for effective opposition to Home Rule and the creation of the statelet of Northern Ireland. But unfolding that particular argument is work for another day.[103]

PART 2
FAMINE IN IRELAND

CHAPTER FOUR

Cry Holocaust: The Great Irish Famine and the Jewish Holocaust

Introduction

The most traumatic event of modern Irish history was undoubtedly the Great Famine of the mid-nineteenth century. Before it had run its awful course, at least one million people had perished of hunger and famine-related diseases. A million more had been dispersed, in a panic-stricken exodus, to Britain, the United States of America, Canada and other parts of the English-speaking world.[1] Viewed globally, it was one of the worst famines of modern times[2]

In some parts of the countryside, rather like a tragedy unfolding in slow motion, famine conditions dogged the local community for a full five years. Process servers, bailiffs and ultimately the 'crow-bar brigade', acting on behalf of evicting landlords, tumbled the cabins of small farmers and labourers, throwing their inhabitants at the mercy of the rain, the wind and the workhouse.[3] Presiding over these policies was the parliament at Westminster, itself representative of large property holders in England, Scotland, Wales and Ireland.

For many, both contemporaries and later commentators, the autumn of 1847 was a turning point. Under cover of the mantra that Irish property should pay for Irish poverty, thereby shifting responsibility for the crisis from British to Irish shoulders, the Whig government of Lord John Russell turned its back financially on a starving people in the most westerly province of the United Kingdom.[4] This was at the height of the catastrophe, the year known in popular memory as Black '47. The *Times* of London exulted: 'The attempt to make Ireland maintain its own poor is one of the greatest experiments of this day.'[5] The famine was to run for a further two or three years, making it the longest-running famine in modern Irish and European history. By way of comparison, the dismal inventory of European famines includes the great Finnish famine of 1867–68; the Russian famines of 1890–91 and 1921; the Ukrainian famine of 1932–33; and the Dutch winter famine of 1944.[6] Leaving to one side for a moment the varying severity of these crises, it is evident that, in terms of duration, Ireland's famine was a case apart.

For the Jewish peoples of Europe their darkest hour belongs to living memory. The mass destruction of some six million Jews in the mid-twentieth century at the hands of the German Nazis, and their enthusiastic collaborators in Poland, the Baltic countries, the Ukraine, Hungary and in parts of the former Yugoslavia, seemed to mark a turning point not only in Jewish but in world history.

The Holocaust and the Great Famine

Can we somehow associate these two searing episodes in the life histories of the two peoples? In a sense the question is redundant. It has already been considered. James Pius Sweeney of New York, writing in the Irish-American paper, the *Irish Echo*, while acknowledging that there were differences between the Famine and the Holocaust, went on to argue:

> The genocide of the Holocaust was remarkable because of the macabre efficiency of freight cars, camps and gas houses. The genocide of the Great Famine is distinct in the fact that the British created the conditions of dire hopelessness, and desperate dependence on the potato crop through a series of sadistic, debasing, premeditated and barbarous Penal Laws, which deliberately and systematically stripped the Irish of even the least semblance of basic human freedom.[7]

When blight struck the Irish were 'totally vulnerable'. This was a 'nuanced genocide', he continues, one that manipulated fate 'by pushing a people to the brink of annihilation and turning away so not to hear the wailing ....'[8] Putting it briefly, and more bluntly, professors Charles Rice and Francis Boyle asserted that Britain was guilty of genocide. They argued that this had been achieved by deliberately inflicting on the Irish conditions of life 'calculated to bring about the destruction in whole or part of the Irish people'. And this had been done 'with intent to destroy'.[9] Bob Scally, in his elegantly crafted work, *The End of Hidden Ireland*, when discussing the hunger-stricken exodus of people from the island, speaks of 'the odor of racial hatred surrounding the emigrant's treatment' and argues that Famine-era emigration should be seen as 'a movement in "coffin ships" that bears more resemblance to the slave trade or the boxcars of the Holocaust than to the routine crossings of a later age'.[10]

Turning to the internet for a moment, a Google search using the words 'Irish famine genocide' yields about 465,000 results. 'Irish famine holocaust' yields one-third of a million 'hits'.[11] These are truly astonishing figures, even if many of the results are only incidentally relevant. It also suggests, not only a huge interest in the Irish Famine but the likelihood that understandings of the past are formed primarily on the internet nowadays, with only limited reference to evidence-based research. My tiny sample of these internet interventions suggests strong support for the genocidal interpretation.

However, what is striking in all this is that while the Famine–Holocaust connection is being made (and this of course is a recent construction), the nature of the parallels is rarely spelled out in detail. Perhaps it is time to spell it out, possibly to the mutual illumination of these two major fields of study. There is, in principle, no end to the number of comparisons one might run in terms of the two catastrophes. It is necessary, therefore, to select a number of themes that many might regard as being of major importance, though there is no pretence to being comprehensive in these overviews of the two collective tragedies. The five themes chosen for comparative analysis are as follows: the approach to crisis; racism, racialism and group prejudice; the Irish workhouses compared to the Jewish ghettoes; mass mortality; and the challenge to Enlightenment thinking.

Approach to Crisis: Ireland and Germany

Given the centrality of the state during both historical episodes, as good a starting point as any is to look at the attitude of the British state to the Irish people, or peoples, in the lead up to the Famine, and then to go on to compare this with the attitude of the Nazi state to Germans who happened to be Jews, in the decade or so before the Final Solution. These sketches are, of necessity, greatly compressed.

Irish Catholics, and to a lesser extent Irish Presbyterians, had experienced discrimination from the early modern period onwards, but the most severe manifestations of this were well in the past.[12] Indeed the Drummond administration of 1835–40, marked a major drive to curb the powers of landlord and Orange influence in local administration, the judiciary and control of policing. Though the pace of reform slackened with the untimely death of Thomas Drummond in 1840 and the advent of a Tory administration under Sir Robert Peel in the following year, these gains were not reversed. The fundamental Irish question on the eve of the Famine, it hardly needs emphasising, was poverty, not the status of Irish Catholics within the British state, even if there were some minor disabilities still to be remedied. The same is true of Irish Presbyterians who, along with Anglicans and other Protestants, numbered close on two million in the 1840s, out of an island-wide population of perhaps eight and a half million.[13]

In the decade before the Holocaust, the German state, under Nazi control from 1933, moved beyond discriminating against Jews to active persecution, a process that, in only a decade, would result in their liquidation. The Nazi accession to power was followed by a nationwide boycott of Jewish businesses on 1 April 1933, and was followed a few days later by mass expulsions from the civil service on the grounds of race, in the name of 'purifying the state'.[14]

Unlike the British and Irish case, the state orchestrated a climate of fear and repression: verbal assaults, physical attacks, public humiliations, became an-all-too 'normal' occurrence. In effect, the new regime portrayed Jews as a leprous, parasitic element within German society: the enemy within, an evil, malignant and implacable force, which had to be eliminated at all costs. The Nuremberg Laws of September 1935 stripped Jews of their citizenship and made sexual relations with non-Jews illegal (the grotesquely titled Law for the Protection of German Blood and German Honour). The persecution of a helpless and passive minority was taken a stage further on 9 and 10 November 1938: Kristallnacht (Crystal Night, an image suggestive of the sound and sight of broken glass) was the occasion for terrifying attacks on Jewish homes, businesses and synagogues right across Germany. In less than a year, Europe was at war, and the skies darkened further for the 'inferior races' of central and eastern Europe.

Racism, Racialism and Group Prejudice

One can discern racist, or perhaps more accurately racialist attitudes towards the Irish, particularly the Catholic Irish, at all levels of British and American society in the mid-nineteenth century, not least the lampooning of Irish people in periodicals as brutish creatures who were overly given to drink and violence.[15] Images of Chartists and English trade-union agitators were certainly unflattering but even in caricature form they did not get quite such a bad press in early Victorian Britain. George Lewis's *State of the Irish Poor in Great Britain,* published in 1836, presents in its witness statements a compendium of anti-Irish prejudice,[16] while Frederick Engels helped immortalise the human-animal intimacy of Paddy and his pig.[17]

Perceptions of the Irish are important as these are likely to have coloured British attitudes towards Ireland when it came to making policy during the Famine. There is little doubt that Irish immigrants, whether they were Catholic or Protestant, were perceived as undesirable outsiders by the working classes in England and Scotland in the years before the crisis. But when malnourished, impoverished and diseased famine refugees poured into Liverpool, Glasgow and other British ports in huge numbers and competed for jobs in an already overstocked labour market, ethnic animosities were inflamed still further.[18] In MacRaild's words, 'it is no mere coincidence that levels of anti-Irishness mirrored large-scale immigration from Ireland' and these fears were exacerbated by perceptions of Irish people as bearers of contagious diseases, including a particularly virulent strain of typhus known as the 'Irish typhus' or 'Irish fever'.[19] With extreme poverty comes overcrowding, dirt and squalor, and inevitably greater vulnerability to infectious diseases. Thus the stereotypes had a basis in fact, but they took on a life of their own even as the Famine influx subsided. Conflict and contempt, sometimes of a mutual kind between natives and newcomers, was the outcome.

Irish immigrants to Britain brought their own cultural baggage, including a variety of social prejudices. Communal, sectarian and xenophobic images were also present within Irish society, finding their expression in taunt, riot or broadsheet ballad more so than the print medium. There were the Orange and Green clashes which had bubbled to the surface from the later eighteenth century and which contributed to the suspension of the Orange Order in the 1830s. Faction fighting, which drew on neighbourhood and kinship bonds but possibly also embodied conflict along social class lines, featured prominently in the Irish countryside in the 1820s and the 1830s.[20] A further and perhaps more pervasive form of prejudice found violent expression in traditions of local and regional xenophobia. The moral economy of rural society, in Ireland as elsewhere, was not always benign.[21] In the North Riding of Tipperary, which touches the provinces of Connacht and Leinster, labourers from across the Shannon were sometimes subjected to threats, intimidation and expulsion, should they dare to seek work or even try to buy potatoes locally.[22] Similarly, labourers from Kilkenny and Tipperary eyed each other with a sense of competitiveness and hostility that sometimes erupted into pitched battles.[23] Such small-scale xenophobia could be carried across the water to Britain. This is the testimony of a Liverpool builder, Samuel Holme, who employed large numbers of Irishmen: 'I am unable to hire a Connacht man; he is always spoken of in terms of contempt.' He added that 'the other three provinces consider the Connacht men as lower caste'.[24] Once a Connacht man was discovered, he was persecuted until forced to quit. Holme was speaking in the 1830s but the likelihood is that such prejudices persisted long afterwards.[25]

Still, emaciated famine refugees, washed up on the shorelines of Britain, might have hoped for a less hostile reception than was frequently their lot. Anti-Irish prejudice in America, as well as the Irish contribution to racism in the United States, is a whole other story, which is fleetingly touched on later. But in the nearest country of refuge, Britain, some of the traditions of collective violence Irish people brought with them probably had some survival value in a new and hostile environment.[26] Edward Lengel argues that 'racialism became in the decade after the Famine a dominant factor in English thought on Ireland'.[27] However, he is careful to note that English perceptions of the

Irish were far from constant through time, as some older histories tended to assume, adding that attitudes on the eve of the Famine were not so highly charged as later. The Famine and its many disruptions, affecting British as well as Irish society, hardened attitudes of hostility towards Irish immigrants.[28]

In time, the *descendants* of Irish famine refugees – one or two generations down – melted into the British working classes, with some coming to play prominent roles in the labour and trade union movements.[29] Completing the circle, and embodying the circulation of progressive ideas in the two islands – the Union of ideas and letters as it were – two British-born evangelists of the labour movement, Big Jim Larkin and the temperamental James Connolly, played seminal roles in the evolution of labour politics in Ireland. Both were of Irish migrant lineage.

High Politics

It is, of course, the attitudes towards Ireland and the Irish held by members of the political establishment that matter most and, in particular, those of the key decision-makers. These included: Sir Robert Peel, prime minister during the first year of famine; his successor Lord John Russell; Charles Wood, who was chancellor of the exchequer during the worst years of the famine; other members of the cabinet, and the administration at Dublin Castle; and, of course, Charles Edward Trevelyan, assistant secretary at the Treasury and the person chiefly responsible for the delivery of government relief during the whole course of the Famine. There were many others of course, of equal or lesser significance.

The high politics of the Famine years have been ignored or simplified by a number of writers bent on offering populist versions of responsibility for the Famine. *The Famine Plot: England's Role in Ireland's Greatest Tragedy* is but one, and one of the more curious contributions to this subgenre.[30] Fortunately, there is Peter Gray's authoritative study of high politics, and important contributions also by Bew, Delaney and others.[31] In broad terms, we may say that Peel had an active and constructive interest in Irish affairs, Russell had a long-standing desire to deliver 'justice for Ireland', Charles Wood was doctrinaire and parsimonious but could hardly be accused of racialism. Key figures in the administration in Dublin Castle, including Lord Clarendon (Lord Lieutenant of Ireland, 1847–52) and Edward Twisleton (Chief Poor-Law Commissioner, 1847–49), at various points, chafed at the limitations being placed on them by the Treasury. Twisleton was driven to resign in March 1849 because of the 'indifference of the House of Commons' to death and destitution in Ireland.[32] Differing degrees of intimacy and senses of urgency with the problems of hunger, as between Dublin and London, in fact formed part of the problem.[33]

The Westminster parliament, especially following the 1847 General Election, was increasingly opposed to further aid for Ireland. Middle-class public opinion had moved to the right, with the arrival of more economic ideologues in the parliament, which in turn circumscribed Russell's room for manoeuvre. Lord John Russell, a prime minister whose leadership weaknesses were all too apparent, presided over a divided cabinet and a fragile coalition of support at Westminster. Ethnic prejudice is likely to have played its part, particularly as the crisis dragged on and on and famine refugees crowded into the north of England and the west of Scotland. But most MPs were more critical of the Irish gentry than of Irish smallholders. The *Times*, the mouth-piece of middle-class opinion, argued vehemently that Irish property should discharge that 'which in this country has always been considered a primary obligation of nature'.[34] It also drew attention to the large rent rolls of landed proprietors in Ireland. Some in the parliament, and even in the cabinet, had estates in Ireland, and countered claims such as those of the *Times* with arguments that the disaster should be treated as a crisis of the United Kingdom and not just of Ireland.

Moderate liberals, such as Lord Lansdowne and Lord Monteagle pleaded the impossibility of Irish landlords shouldering the burden unaided. Others have acquired a less savoury reputation. An intervention by a west of Ireland landlord, Sir William Gregory, of Coole Park, Gort, led to the infamous Gregory Clause whereby landholders in possession of more than a quarter acre were excluded from public relief.[35] Others, such as the 'relatively humane' Marquess of Sligo, were responsible for clearances of paupers from their estates.[36] According to Donnelly, mass clearances gathered pace during the late 1840s; the official figures for those thrown out of their dwellings in 1849 and 1850 alone were in the region of 150,000 persons.[37] The numbers evicted or persuaded to give up their dwellings between 1846 and 1854 may have been as high as half a million.[38] In all of this, ruthless self-interest rather than racialism was the motivating force.

The villain of the piece is often taken to be Charles Trevelyan. Was the potato blight a punishment from Heaven on the Irish, as some providentialists argued? This seems not to have been Trevelyan's philosophical position,[39] though it was one held by a diverse range of individuals, from some of the Irish poor to Catholic priests and Protestant evangelicals.[40] But there is little doubt that he was high-minded, tunnel-visioned and recklessly self-confident regarding the efficacy of the policies he advocated.[41] Like many Whigs he felt the Irish landed ascendancy was heavily responsible for the evils that assailed the common people. As a doctrinaire free-marketeer he believed that the most beneficial outcomes for society issued from the free and unfettered operation of market forces. Any 'unnatural' interference, such as state intervention in the market for food, was likely to prove counterproductive. The doctrines of political economy taught that this was so. It must, therefore, be so.

As a moralist, he worried that deviations from strict adherence to the 'laws' of the market (which were taken to be a refraction of divine laws) would prove ruinous, not only economically but morally as well. A dependency culture, cultivated and propagated by state hand-outs, would result in indolence and worse in the long run. The common-sense realisation that a hungry people *had* no long run seems not to have penetrated his ideologically-insulated mind set.

Meanwhile, on the political and ideological front, the *Times* of London and the *Economist* blazed away at the dangers of state interference and the evils of Famine aid. The *Times* was prepared to acknowledge in early 1848 that 'during the great part of last year Ireland was suffering a terrible famine', but remained firmly of the view that Irish property should pay for Irish poverty.

> Nor is it our chief, although an important consideration that England may now hope to hear fewer calls on her purse in the name of Irish destitution. Indeed, as soon as Ireland can show that she is really self-supporting, so soon as the proprietor has got into the way of giving employment, and the peasant of submitting to labour, the wealthier part of the empire will be all the more ready to contribute to its aid.[42]

In the meantime, the Irish propertied classes should get on with paying their rates to support the local poor-law administration and its chief instrument, the workhouse. How this might have been possible under the weight of repeated famines between 1845 and 1850 in regions of the west of Ireland where much of the land was infertile, where population densities were high and farm sizes small, was not explained.

There is much to criticise in the handling of the Great Famine, and a more detailed critique of the policies pursued by the British (and Irish) government will be taken up later. But ethnic prejudice of an extreme kind, which readily translated into ethnically-discriminatory policies, is not what we find among the political elite of mid-nineteenth century Britain and Ireland.[43] True enough there were condescending references to the Celtic temperament which was associated with impulsiveness and backwardness but this bore little resemblance to the anti-Semitism coursing through German society a century later, and given steely expression through punitive legislation and the activities of paramilitary street gangs. The bible of racism, *Mein Kampf*, first published in two volumes in 1925 and 1926, raged against the Jews, 'under whose parasitism the whole of honest humanity is suffering today more than ever'.[44] Sexual imagery served to embellish the narrative. The 'Jewish problem' was at its most potent where it threatened the purity, quite literally, of the German womenfolk.

> With satanic joy in his face, the black-haired Jewish youth lurks in wait for the unsuspecting girl whom he defiles with his blood, thus stealing her from her people. With every means he tries to destroy the racial foundations of the people he has set out to subjugate.[45]

A chilling speech by Hitler to the Reichstag in January 1939 foreshadowed the 'final solution':

> Today I will once more be a prophet. If the international Jewish financiers in and outside Europe should succeed in plunging the nations once more into a world war, then the result will not be the Bolshevization of the earth, and thus the victory of the Jewry, but the annihilation of the Jewish race in Europe![46]

Within a few years the Fuhrer's words would be made flesh in villages, towns and cities across the Third Reich and beyond.

Workhouses and Ghettoes

Moving from the pre-crisis to the crisis period in the two societies, one might wonder if there are some parallel experiences that are identifiable. Perhaps the congregating of people into Union workhouses in Ireland during the Famine and the concentration of Jews in ghettoes during the early years of the Second World War bear some comparison?[47] Under the then recently introduced Irish poor law the country was divided into 130 unions, each with its associated workhouse. By the end of the Famine the number of unions had increased to 163, as some of the very large unions were subdivided. As an example, the Dingle union was partitioned off from the huge Tralee union in 1848, so as to cater for the remote and stricken communities on the Dingle peninsula. That was the administrative framework. What of the operations of the workhouse system? Some deeply disturbing accounts may be found. In the workhouse attached to the Cork union, more than two thousand people died in the first four months of 1847. A report in the *Cork Examiner* noted caustically: 'Had the workhouse, instead of being an asylum for distress, been a machine for depopulating the country, it scarcely could have answered its object with more terrible effect.'[48]

James Hack Tuke, the English philanthropist who did much to relieve poverty in the west of Ireland, made a point of visiting workhouses in his famous tour of Connacht in the autumn of 1847. He was happy to state, though there may perhaps be a touch of diplomacy here, that some ('a large number') of the Union workhouses were well-managed. However, he went on to say that:

> The worst which I visited was that of Carrick-upon-Shannon: it was in a miserable state, and the doors were closed against further admissions; and although built for seven hundred, had but two hundred and eighty inmates; the gates were besieged by seventy or eighty wretched beings who in vain implored for admission. Numbers of them were in various stages of fever,

which was terribly prevalent in the neighbourhood, and the fever sheds over-crowded. Two months before my visit, the doors of the poor-house were opened and the inmates expelled, entailing upon them most dire misery.[49]

Still worse, arguably, were the conditions of those beyond the reach of the workhouses. The Ireland correspondent of the *Times* relayed to British readers the grim fate of the inhabitants of the scattered coastal strips of Mayo and the islands in Clew Bay. This was in the winter of 1847.

> We have heard the most heart-rending accounts of the frightful destitution which prevails in several of the remote districts, threatening a more fearful catalogue of mortality than even last year, with all its horrors. We have been informed that in the neighbourhood of Belmullet, and within the Mullet, instantaneous death from starvation can only be expected – that the people are already sinking into premature graves from lack of food – and that disease is rapid in its ravages. ... In the populous islands in Clew Bay and along the sea coasts the peasantry are in a most dreadful condition ... And we have been assured, by an official who visited Clare Island and Inishturk, that he saw several emaciated wretches expiring in agonies from utter want.[50]

The account, which was taken from the *Mayo Constitution*, goes on to anticipate the reactions of some readers: they have the Poor Law to support them. But the workhouse at Westport was far distant, and had it been possible to transport the islanders to the mainland the workhouse was already overcrowded and refusing admission.

Some workhouses were better managed than others; some were better financed from local taxation; and some faced less severe challenges than others. But conditions in some of the workhouses, particularly but not only in the western half of Ireland were appalling, even by the standards of the time. Gross overcrowding, poor hygiene and sanitation, and the presence of famine diseases afflicted the inmates. Little wonder that many families only sent a hunger-weakened and diseased relative into the workhouse when close to death. The prospect of access to food and shelter had to be finely balanced against the grim reality of workhouse life and the danger of exposure to infectious diseases. Little wonder that death rates in these workhouses soared during the Famine years, peaking in 1847 and again in 1849. A quarter of a million deaths in public institutions were recorded during the Famine years.[51] For all the squalor, misery and death – sometimes amplified by inefficiency, penny-pinching and incompetence – the intention of the system was to save as many lives as possible. The pleas for more resources and the elevated death toll of doctors and workhouse staff during the catastrophe are testimony to this.[52]

Descriptions of life in the Polish ghettoes a century later contain accounts of material deprivation, of hunger and disease. Attitudes to the inmates, even before the Final Solution was conceived, were different. As one German official put it in November 1940, and this before the 'Final Solution' took firm shape: 'A rapid dying out of the Jews is for us a matter of total indifference, if not to say desirable, as long as the concomitant effects leave the public interest of the German people untouched.'[53] Once the ghettoes had been sealed off from surrounding society, the penalty for leaving was death.[54] The workhouses in Ireland were ghettoes in a very different sense, that is, if the term is applicable at all. The acid test is that, as the Famine deepened, the famished and the disease-ridden were clamouring to get *into* rather than out of the workhouses.

Mass Mortality

In the end, what matters most is death. This shifts the spotlight to the numbers of people who died or were put to death. It is surely not enough to say, in relation to the Irish Famine for instance, 'that many, very many people died'.[55] Death is a democracy, it is sometimes said: all victims are equal and hence comparisons are likely to be unrevealing. As against this, one might argue, the *manner* and the *circumstances* of death differentiate one type of tragic event from another in quite profound ways.

The circumstances of death for Jews were different. Many died of hunger, disease, ill-treatment and exhaustion: during the vast resettlement schemes, in the ghettoes, on death marches, and on the trains taking them to the extermination camps. But many, perhaps most in the case of Poland, were killed directly: by shooting or gassing. Christopher Browning, in *The Path to Genocide*, describes the work of one killing unit used in 'ghetto-cleaning'.[56]

The date was 12 July 1942; the place was a small Polish village, some distance from Lublin. The objective was to round up the 1,800 or so Jews in the area and bring them to the market square. The orders were that those too sick or too frail to walk, as well as infants and anyone offering resistance, were to be shot at once, in their homes, in their beds, wherever was convenient. The rest – over a thousand – were assembled in the village square. The young Jewish men were separated out for work as slave labourers in a camp at Lublin. The remaining women and children, and the elderly, were to be trucked, batch by batch, to the edge of a nearby forest, where other members of the police unit (Police Battalion 101) awaited them. As they disembarked:

> The individual squad members paired off *face-to-face* with the individual Jews they were to shoot, and marched their victims into the forest… The Jews were forced to lie face down in a row. The policemen stepped up behind them, and

on a signal from the first sergeant fired their carbines at point-blank range into
the necks of their victims …

When the first salvo was heard from the woods, a terrible cry swept the market
place, as the collected Jews now knew their fate. Thereafter, however, a quiet
– indeed 'unbelievable' – composure settled over the Jews, which the German
policemen found equally unnerving.[57]

That is but one detail from the destruction of the European Jews and the
lethal hatreds that shaped their fate.

Scale and Intensity

Can one also explore mass mortality in the two historical periods by reference
to the scale of mortality and its relative intensity? The Great Famine of the
1840s claimed in the region of one million women, men and children. These
are *excess* deaths, not *total* deaths. It is an inescapable fact of life that people go
on dying even in the best of times. 'Normal deaths' in normal times during
the quinquennium 1846–50 would have been about one million.[58] That the
figure is close to the toll exacted by the Famine itself is both surprising and
counterintuitive but is accounted for by the fact that the time period of the
Famine was a protracted one, extending over five years or so.

'Excess deaths' refer exclusively to those who died of hunger or hunger-
related diseases. This mountain of mortality, of more than a million dead,
is the equivalent of one in seven or one in eight of the population and,
in proportional terms, compares with the other Great Famine of modern
Irish history, the largely forgotten famine of 1740–41.[59] A death toll of
one in seven or one in eight marks out the Irish Famine of the 1840s
as one of the most severe in the history of famines internationally.[60]
Contemporary Third World famines, however terrible, would not remotely
approach this degree of death, though the key to this less unhappy state of
affairs is due primarily to advances in medical technology and, to a lesser
extent, improved communications, transport and storage facilities, as well as
international food aid. Had these been available in the 1840s, innumerable
lives would have been saved but that, of course, is merely wishful thinking.
The more interesting question is how many more lives could have been
saved, using alternative policies but working within the constraints imposed
by the existing technologies of the time, thereby avoiding ahistorical and
anachronistic judgements.

The death toll varied greatly by region, by social class and, to some degree,
by age and gender. As is well known, the greatest concentration of suffering
was in the far west of Ireland, where an impoverished peasantry scraped a

living from the beautiful but barren lands of west Connacht and west Munster. The impact of the Famine was also highly selective in terms of social class. Those most likely to die were the cottiers, rural labourers and town labourers. Or as the *Cork Examiner* put it at the outset of the crisis: 'What do we find in this mis-governed world? Peers know no poverty, while the poor perish.'[61] In gender terms, the chances of survival were slightly greater if you were female rather than male, an outcome found in many famines.[62] Whether this was due to biological or social factors, or indeed a combination of the two, is not altogether clear. There was also, as one might expect, an age profile to the victims, with the old and the young being particularly vulnerable to famine conditions. In the Nenagh workhouse in county Tipperary, for instance, over half of all deaths were of children (less than fifteen years of age), with children under two years being particularly vulnerable.[63]

How does all this compare with the Holocaust? Well, in absolute terms, the numbers dying unnaturally during the Nazi era were higher: in excess of five or six million. In proportional terms, relative to population that is, the story is incomparably bleak. The killing rate was of the order of 80 to 90 per cent in many European countries; in some villages it was 100 per cent.[64] In Belzec, an early extermination camp in the south-east of Poland, well over half a million Jews were exterminated in the interval between May 1942 and the spring of 1943. There was only one known survivor.[65] In Poland, of some three million Jews, fewer than one in ten survived.

This was industrialised sadism and murder, a bastard progeny of industrialisation and modernisation, and conducted with an efficiency the world had never known. But, lest there be some misunderstanding, it is as well to insert a qualification here. There is nothing in the logic of industrialism, nor more generally in the technological mastery of nature, that leads inevitably to the perverted outcomes witnessed under the Third Reich. Neither is industrialism a necessary condition for mass slaughter, as the low-technology killings of Hutus and Tutsis in Rwanda in more recent times remind us.[66] Within one hundred days or so some 800,000 are believed to have been slain, most of them Tutsis, and nearly two million were forced to flee their homes. Hand-held machetes were among the most lethal instruments of destruction.

Region, Class, Gender

As with other catastrophes, whether natural, people-made, or a combination of the two, we could look at the Holocaust by reference to region, class and gender. There are regional dimensions to the Holocaust and temporal variations in its incidence, but these perspectives do not take us very far. While it is true that death rates varied across Europe, in all German-occupied areas the end of policy was the 'Final Solution': the destruction of the European

Jewry. Consequently, death rates approached saturation point where there was German occupation.

Neither does it make much sense to speak of age, gender or occupational factors in shaping overall death rates. It is true that those chosen for slave labour were selected on the basis of age, gender and special skills – and these factors could prove vital to the survival of individuals and small groups of survivors. Helen Lewis, the Belfast survivor of Auschwitz, in addition to her indomitable spirit, was aided by her dancing and choreography skills.[67] But the remarkable fact about Nazism was how it subordinated major forms of social hierarchy – class, status and gender – to a hierarchy of race. In relation to gender, as Gisela Bock argues, 'the core of Nazi rule and its novelty (compared with other countries and other historical periods) was not patriarchy but racism'.[68]

Challenge to the Enlightenment (or the Progress of the Human)

In the search for parallels or similarities we might want to shift to a different level, more in the realm of ideas. The tyranny of ideology, one might say, is present in both episodes but this is hardly a point to be pushed very far, if at all. Dogmatic visions of society have the potential to distort and deform when it comes to public policy, be it of the free-market or the national socialist variety. While *laissez faire* economics was naïve in its assumptions, wrong-headed in its application to the Ireland of the 1840s, and brutal in its consequences, it was not *intended* as an instrument of destruction. In the Nazi case the vision was founded on race hatred and racial extermination. It was one of such perversion that it belongs to a different moral sphere and it was implemented with the iron fist of totalitarianism. Whether the Shoah was unique in human history is itself the subject of intense debate among scholars but this is certainly not a claim one would make, in any substantive sense, for the Irish Famine.[69]

Perhaps one can argue that the Irish Famine and the Shoah, each in their different time periods, posed similarly powerful challenges to enlightenment ideas and the European enlightenment project. There is no doubt that the Shoah or Holocaust served to undermine the optimistic assumptions coming out of the eighteenth century which stressed human rationality, perfectibility and progress. These values were clearly incompatible with the operation of slave labour camps and the gas chambers. Along with other examples of genocide from the blood-steeped twentieth century – the massacres of the Armenians, of Gypsies, of Cambodians, of different ethnic groups in Africa – the Holocaust has served to challenge some of our most deeply cherished notions of human behaviour and human progress.

The same cannot be said of the Irish Famine. In time it produced some modifications to ideas of political economy, though hardly of a profound kind, but the striking thing is how little influence the Irish Famine had on the existing constellations of intellectual ideas.[70] On the contrary, it served to corroborate enlightenment thinking, dramatising the dangers of reliance on outmoded economic practices and slovenly class relationships.

Intentionality

It is time to move to the heart of the matter, that is, the question of intentionality. No major historian, however critical they might be of particular Famine policies, believes that the British state intended the destruction of the Irish people. The Famine–Holocaust comparisons that have been invoked in this chapter provide no support either. Yet one million died. Does intentionality matter?

It does matter, for at least three reasons. Firstly, it directly determines the scale of the tragedy. It is easy to forget, had Germany not lost the war, that many more Jews would have been killed, such was the strength of commitment to the Final Solution. Even as the German empire was collapsing and as the victorious Soviet troops pushed westward towards Berlin, the orders from Hitler's headquarters were to prosecute ever more vigorously the extermination of European Jews. By contrast, when the Irish economy recovered some strength at the end of the 1840s the crisis was largely, though not wholly over. This was to the evident relief, not only of people in Ireland but of British policy makers as well.

Secondly, the cruelty, often wanton cruelty which attached to the treatment of Jews has virtually no parallels in the Irish case. The Irish Constabulary and detachments of the army which protected grain shipments, granaries and other forms of private property during the 1840s generally behaved with restraint.[71] Army officers played a key role in the organisation and distribution of relief rations, though as James Hack Tuke noted: as far as the poor people evicted were concerned, the 'law, police, military, magistracy and proprietary must have seemed alike confederated against them'.[72] Medical doctors, by and large, did their best, though hampered by ignorance of the means whereby infectious diseases were transmitted.[73] But no one has uncovered cases of deliberate medical ill-treatment of a systematic kind. The record of the German medical profession a century later is forever tainted by abominable medical experiments on hapless victims. True enough, evictions were heartless affairs and on a massive scale, affecting perhaps 6 per cent of the pre-Famine population if one includes also the 'voluntary' surrender of holdings. Even in these cases there was the assumption that alternatives, however bleak, existed.

Thirdly, intentionality is relevant to the question of responsibility, a question inextricably bound up with the politics of memory. John Mitchel, the fiery Young Irelander, was in no doubt. Do we accept John Mitchel's verdict, that whistles like a bullet through Irish popular memory: 'The Almighty, indeed, sent the potato blight, but the English created the Famine…'.[74] I have sometimes thought the Almighty got off rather lightly in this particular formulation but the preceding sentence reads: 'The British account of the matter, then, is first, a fraud – second a blasphemy.' I am not qualified to comment on the latter but the former derives from the mistaken assumption that this was an 'artificial famine'.

Mitchel makes a useful distinction, albeit implicitly, between causation and responsibility. The Famine was an ecological disaster but it wasn't *simply* that. I think it is important to distinguish between three distinct notions: causation, responsibility and blame. And at the bar of history we might want to call to account, not only Lord John Russell and his Whig administration, but a host of other historical actors as well, from landlords to Young Irelanders and the strong farmers and merchants of eastern Ireland. These are themes pursued in the next chapter.

To narrow the focus simply to the role of the British government for a moment: for all the massive irresponsibility and buck-passing that characterised the five years of crisis, the state succeeded in organising public relief schemes that employed three-quarters of a million workers and, at one point, was responsible for feeding three million people on a daily basis. These are not the actions of a government or a state bent on genocide.

British and Irish Famine Relief

A closer look at the workings of Irish famine relief brings out more fully the contrasts with the Nazi case. The Great Famine was a story of two halves, as it were, in terms of famine relief measures. The two phases, roughly speaking, were as follows.

Phase One (1845–47) or what might be termed the British and Irish phase. This was the period from the blight-afflicted harvest of autumn 1845 to the early autumn of 1847 when there was heavy reliance on the United Kingdom government and the UK Treasury. The principal relief measures included food imports, employment on public works' schemes, soup kitchens and food rations. In addition, there were the more Irish-based schemes to assist the destitute, essentially the work of local relief committees, charitable bodies and individuals (including some landlords), and the final if porous safety net, the poor-law system with its workhouses, dispensaries and fever hospitals.

Phase Two (1847–50): the Irish phase, from the autumn of 1847 onwards, when most of the burden of famine relief was thrown back on Irish property. There was now a single statutory mechanism, the Irish poor-law system as the means of delivering relief.[75] This was financed from local rates, of which the great barrack-like institution of the workhouse was the centrepiece. Thus, the poor-law amendment act of 1847, which brought this new phase into being, transferred the financing of Famine relief, and hence responsibility for the Famine, to the poorer partner within the union of Britain and Ireland.[76] This was a momentous change. Is this proof of the more 'nuanced genocide' that some have claimed?

Apologists for this fundamental shift, as they did at the time, would argue, firstly, that Irish landed property was largely responsible for the bloated population and the rural slums found in mid-nineteenth century Ireland and, secondly, that Irish property holders had the resources to cope with the crisis. Arguing about historical causation and attributing blame in the depths of a famine was hardly the most appropriate response to a crisis, though, of course, there was collective self-interest as well as ideology at play. On the face of it, the second argument has some substance. Irish rental incomes before the Famine were of the order of £12 million per annum.[77]

Of course, arrears of rent mounted during the Famine, landlords were responsible for the poor-rates on holdings valued at £4 or less, and this was especially onerous in the western counties where many land holdings had low valuations.[78] Though hardly known at the time, the real value of rental incomes due to Irish landlords was falling in the decade before the Famine, in striking contrast to the fortunes of English landowners in the same period.[79] These points are easily overstated, however. What evidence we have of arrears on rent suggests this was not a large problem generally, though it may have been so on particular estates.[80] The taxation burden can be exaggerated as well, bearing in mind that landlords in Ireland did not pay income tax, unlike their counterparts in Britain, and an estimate by Ó Gráda suggests that poor-rates, even in badly affected poor-law unions, can hardly have exceeded one-tenth of the rental income.[81]

More to the point, many estates were deeply indebted by 1845 because of the profligacy of owners and their predecessors and because family settlements meant that large portions of rental income were already spoken for.[82] Thus, a minority of landlords were so indebted before the Famine that the crisis itself pushed them over the financial edge and into the Incumbered Estates Court from 1849 onwards. The extent to which Irish landlords were encumbered with debt was hardly known at the time, so this may have misled the more doctrinaire critics of Irish landlordism. Still, if many in the Whig–Liberal administration believed that Irish landlords had failed in their social duty, then it seems curious to have entrusted that same class with the massive task of responsibility for famine relief from late 1847 onwards.

This points to the conclusion that the cabinet and the Westminster parliament failed to face up fully to the seriousness of the crisis, partly out of a mistaken faith in the doctrines of political economy, partly out of concern for the public finances of the United Kingdom following the financial crisis of autumn 1847, but also out of selfish economic interest in passing this particular 'hot potato' back to Ireland. Trevelyan encapsulated much of the logic of the establishment view in a remarkable letter to Edward Twisleton, chairman of the Irish Poor Law Commission, in the spring of 1848.

> The state of the case is simply this: The only hope, not only for saving the whole Empire from Bankruptcy, but also of arriving at a satisfactory permanent settlement of Ireland is by making the support of the Irish Poor a local charge, and this cannot be done without much painful discipline of this kind. You will strive against it [additional funds from the Treasury] as far as you can, but where it cannot be avoided, it must be submitted to as a smaller evil by which a greater good is to be attained for Ireland and the whole British Nation.[83]

There was genuine concern, particularly on the part of Charles Wood at the Treasury, of possibly severe damage to the public finances of the United Kingdom as a result of the Irish crisis. His responsibility was for the whole of the United Kingdom and not just for one populous region therein. Naturally, the Lord Lieutenant and Chief Secretary for Ireland begged to differ on the priorities. It is understandable also that there should have been concern about the poverty burden the Irish potato failure imposed on Britain, as well as apprehension that its effects might roll on indefinitely. Trevelyan was alarmist and possibly self-serving in his comment but he laid bare a dilemma that certainly existed. Reform of the ramshackle Irish agrarian economy and dealing with the problem of a large, economically-redundant population were desirable policy ambitions. On the whole, historians have taken the luxury of offering soft-option sentiment in place of assessments that recognised the gargantuan nature of the problem; this option was not available to contemporaries. It is simply the case that escape from grinding poverty, not least the monotony of a largely single-food diet, necessitated fundamental changes. It was also desirable that the government should seek to minimise the extent to which the structural problems of the Irish economy were reinforced when devising relief policies. But to risk implementing societal reforms in the midst of famine was reckless and inhumane. The British government failed in its responsibilities as, unfortunately, did many others in Britain and Ireland. How one expresses this failure is a difficult problem in terms of rhetoric, representation and judgement, but it has nothing to do with the kinds of policies enacted by the Nazis in the 1940s dealing with the livelihoods of their victims. Reaching melodramatically for terms such as *holocaust* and *genocide* does little to advance the historical enquiry, however subjectively satisfying that may be when confronted with harrowing accounts of eviction, starvation and death.

Useful Histories?

After having suffered so much, Irish people can immediately empathise with people who suffer all over the world. [84]

The burden of the story so far is that it is difficult to find any significant parallels between the Famine and the Holocaust, either in terms of their respective prehistories, the actual events themselves, or the intellectual shock waves unleashed. This will come as no surprise to professional historians, but it may give pause for thought to the ideologues who feast on Famine 'memories'. This prompts one further set of questions that seems worth pursuing: perhaps the *handling* of the two catastrophes in later time offers more fruitful grounds for comparison. In what follows, three areas of intersection are elaborated.

When Jewish and Irish people are placed in the same frame, one suspects *guilt* can't be far away. Almost inevitably, it would seem, the Holocaust and the Famine imposed burdens of guilt on those who survived. On the Jewish side, there were those who cooperated with the Nazis in the menial operations of the death camps and lived, perhaps not to tell the tale. Then there were those who survived the camps and bore an existential guilt simply because they had survived a world of terrifying and nihilistic violence in which most had perished. As one survivor, the Italian writer Primo Levi reflected: 'Are you ashamed because you are alive in place of another? And in particular, of a man more generous, more sensitive, more useful, wiser, worthier of living than you?' He continued in ironic vein: 'The worst survived, that is, the fittest; the best all died.' Some, haunted by a sense of guilt in not helping close friends at the extremity of existence, invented stories to cover up perceived acts of betrayal. Again, in Helen Lewis' memoir, *A Time to Speak*, there is a poignant account of human frailty and betrayal on the part of one of her friends. 'I can still hear her words, that night, on the final stretch of the icy road. "She has had it, she is finished, if we allow her to hold on to us, she will drag us along with her, to her and our end." And I can still remember Mitzi's arm slipping from mine as she let go of me.'[85]

The lineaments of guilt are more difficult to trace in relation to the Great Famine, and not only because the experiences are buried deeper in time. In a society haunted by hunger and the spectre of death, it is hardly surprising that some family members turned on each other, fighting over a morsel of food or abandoning a dying relative to his or her fate. There are cases of neighbour turning against neighbour; of ambitious or avaricious farmers and merchants swallowing up the land vacated by dispossessed smallholders; of farmers prosecuting cottiers and labourers for stealing food.[86]

Breandán Mac Suibhne relates a harrowing story from Arranmore, an island off the west coast of Donegal. This was during Black '47. Mary Gallagher was found stealing potatoes from a neighbour. Using a reaping hook, and assisted by his wife, the neighbour cut off one of Mary Gallagher's ears and nearly severed the other.[87] This was struggle for survival at its most elemental; similar scenes of violence must have happened where the Famine struck most severely. For the *survivors*, not to say the beneficiaries of the Famine, there were things to feel guilty about.

If guilt is a point of connection between the two catastrophes, perhaps there are other shared psychological after-effects. Irish communities and Jewish communities were traumatised by the terrible events of the 1840s and the 1940s respectively. One might wonder if individual and collective trauma, borne on the wings of popular memory, might have had the longer-term effect of sensitising people to the sufferings of other groups, leading to new or different patterns of social behaviour. The expectation might be that out of suffering come acts of empathy and redemption.

There seem to be some rough parallels between the handling of the Holocaust by some Jewish groups and the handling of the Famine experience by some sections of Irish nationalism, but it is the inverse in both cases of the empathy hypothesis. I neither wish to trespass on the politics of the Middle East, nor prejudge issues relating to the Arab–Israeli conflict but it would be hard to argue that the aggressiveness with which the Israeli state polices the occupied territories bears testament to a heightened sense of ethnic empathy and historical understanding. Susan Sontag is only one of those voices from within what might loosely be called the Jewish diaspora who has argued in sonorous prose for a more sensitive reading of Palestinian experience.[88] There is even less to suggest that Palestinian groups have read their history or histories with an eye to the emancipatory potential of shared suffering and tribulation. The forces of repression *within* Palestinian communities may help to explain the fewer instances of internal critics and revisionists as compared to Israeli society.

Race Riots

In the Irish case we have a remarkable test of the hypothesis linking suffering and subsequent behaviour. Some will have seen Martin Scorsese's extravagantly funded film, *Gangs of New York*.[89] Towards the end of the film, we witness scenes of the Irish and other ethnic groups rioting in New York. The film is evasive about *why* the poor, Catholic Irish are rioting and *who* the targets of their communal hatred really were. The historical backdrop is, in fact, the early stages of the American Civil War. The occasion represented was the introduction of legislative moves to draft men into the Union armies in the war against the secessionist and segregationist southern states of the USA. The New York riots of July 1863 were labelled the Draft Riots. Putting it more bluntly, these were race riots. Immigrant workers, particularly Irish immigrants, feared competition in the labour market from emancipated black slaves. There was also resentment against those of a wealthy background who could buy their way out of military service.

Racial antipathy, however, had preceded the draft. The previous year several thousand people from the mainly Irish South Brooklyn had demanded that the Watson and Lorillard tobacco companies get rid of several hundred Black women and children. When the employers refused, the crowd laid siege to the buildings and attempted to set them on fire. This was in an attempt to 'roast the niggers alive'.[90] Fortunately the police intervened.

'Kill all niggers' was the cry of one band of white workers, led by Irish longshoremen during the Draft Riots. In an explosion of communal hatred, thousands of Irish and other ethnic whites turned on Black neighbourhoods, lynching and burning before them. Irish Catholic rioters targeted Protestant charities such as the Five Points Mission. One infamous case of arson resulted in the destruction of the Coloured Orphan Asylum, though the children – more than 200 of them – managed to escape to safety. Many Black people were beaten, at least eleven were lynched or otherwise murdered, and hundreds were driven from their lodgings.[91] The following month *Harper's Weekly* featured a sketch of a gang of Irish or Irish-American rioters, armed with cudgels, attacking an elderly Black man who is depicted in a cowering posture, down on one knee and seeking to shield a Black girl from the fury of the mob.[92] The ethnic and racial colouration of the scene could hardly be clearer. The official death toll for the four days of rioting, in itself probably an underestimate, was 119.[93]

This was New York, 1863. Mark the time. This was little more than a decade after the Irish Famine. Most of these rioters were recent immigrants. Many would have experienced childhood or adolescence during the horrors of the Great Hunger. *These were the children of the Famine.*

Death Camps and Ireland

We may take a second historical episode to underline the point of a lack of a necessary relationship between historically-defined communal suffering and broadened human sympathies. This example links wartime Ireland, the Irish Famine and the Holocaust. From May 1945 onwards, following the end of wartime censorship, the Irish national newspapers began to reveal details of the Nazi death camps in central and eastern Europe. On 13 May 1945, the *Sunday Independent*, the largest-circulation Irish national newspaper, published photographs of hundreds of corpses from the death camps at Buchenwald, Nordhausen and Ohrdruf. 'If there was one year when the power of photographs to define, not merely record, the most abominable realities trumped all the complex narratives [of verbal accounts], surely it was 1945, with the pictures taken in April and early May at Bergen-Belsen, Buchenwald, and Dachau in the first days after the camps were liberated…'[94] Susan Sontag might think so; however, two weeks after the images appeared in Irish newspapers, *An Taoiseach*, Eamon de Valera, speaking at an election meeting in Galway, defended the wartime censorship of news, and then added rather sourly: 'You see more atrocity pictures, and so on, and are you any the better for seeing them?'[95] The *reception* into Irish society of the news of the extermination centres was of a more hostile kind in some quarters: it was either denied, and as such is an early example of Holocaust denial (before the term had established itself) or denounced as lending support to a 'small Ascendancy group'.[96] Ascendancy was a code word for Irish Protestants and unionists. There is more than a touch of what might be called *ethnic autism* in these reactions to the photographic images of the emaciated victims of Nazi persecution.[97]

Thirdly, and seemingly inevitably, there is the use of history in the service of present-day politics. James Donnelly speaks of the public memory of the Famine,[98] or what less reverently might be called the reprisals of selective memory-making. Famine images were honed into powerful ideological weapons by 'advanced nationalists' (to use that quaint phrase) in the decades after the 1840s. During the Land War of the later nineteenth century, as also during the revolutionary fighting of the early twentieth century, images of Famine suffering – Remember Skibbereen![99] – supplied motivational energies for political recruitment, mobilisation and confrontation. Famine themes and images of genocide underwent a further reincarnation during the sesquicentenary commemorations of the Great Famine in the 1990s. The context then was the Provisional IRA's 'war' against the British state in Northern Ireland. One can't help sensing similarities across time and space from the British–Irish conflicts of the nineteenth and twentieth centuries to the use of history and memory in the Israeli–Palestinian conflict of recent decades.

This is not to say the memory of the Holocaust does not need to flame brightly in the consciousness of the peoples of the world, both because of what it was in its own historical right, and what it reveals of human potentialities for evil as well as good. Not many would want to go down the road with Norman Finkelstein, a fierce critic of the uses to which the Holocaust has been put.[100] The phrase 'There's no business like Shoah business' – a wonderful piece of Jewish black humour and self-caricature – is not his creation but it could be.[101] There are, however, calmer Jewish and Israeli voices that have expressed concern about the uses to which memories of the Holocaust have been put. It seems clear that images of the Holocaust, and the vast representational infrastructure that constantly reconstitutes and memorialises that awful event, have also been exploited to serve the interests of Israeli foreign policy and the ambitions of ultra-nationalists and religious zealots. This is within the context, it is only fair to add, of the most open, democratic and secular society in the Middle East.

Concluding Comments

There was the Great Famine of the 1840s in the United Kingdom of Great Britain and Ireland. There was the Holocaust or Shoah of the 1940s on the European mainland. The Famine demonstrated that the Union, in political practice, was less complete than the constitution makers had imagined. It is true no other European state faced the test set by nature for the repeated destruction of its main food source.[102] The devastation spread across five consecutive years. As Peter Solar has demonstrated, in what is probably the single most important article on the Great Famine, a series of consecutive crop failures on this scale was beyond all reasonable statistical expectation.[103] The peoples of Ireland were unfortunate in so many ways. An ecological curse of this duration was unprecedented and virtually unimaginable. The timing of the catastrophe was also unfortunate, not least in that population levels were at an all-time high.[104] The population of Ireland in 1841 was one-half that of England and Wales, a ratio which highlights the size of the potential dependency. Britain had its own swathes of deep poverty, though not the absolute poverty present in Ireland. Many landed estates were deeply indebted due to the financial irresponsibility or ill fortune of their owners, or their owners' ancestors. The political and ideological constellations now in the ascendant favoured individual and local responsibility, the ideology of the free market, and minimal state intervention. Changing attitudes to poverty at elite levels had been apparent from the 1830s, with the introduction of the new and harsher English Poor Law and its extension to Ireland soon afterwards. This was the brave new world of political economy. One of the cruel ironies is that the most doctrinaire economists – wedded to notions of free trade and *laissez faire*, half-drunk on the conviction that they had uncovered the laws of nature that governed society – were not misanthropic monsters but well-intentioned individuals on the whole.[105]

Despite the scale of the problem, the fact that Britain could carry Ireland through two years of famine without disastrous consequences for the public finances would seem to indicate that existing levels of support, insufficient though they were, could have been maintained for another two to three years.[106] Outrage might be and indeed was expressed at the failure of United Kingdom solidarity in the face of the crisis in Ireland and, indeed, in the Highlands and Islands of Scotland as well. The failure in relation to Ireland led to a statement of regret by the prime-minister of the United Kingdom, Tony Blair, in June 1997. However, unlike the case of Nazi Germany and the Jewish Question there is no evidence of a 'plot' or campaign to wipe out the famine-stricken Irish.

Margaret Kelleher has warned: 'Dangers exist that analogies between the Holocaust and the 1840s Irish famine, for example, may become trite and simplistic and obscure the complexities of both catastrophes.'[107] The clear conclusion to this chapter is that direct comparisons of the Famine and Holocaust fail. So, it is something of a surprise then to find that in terms of the *legacies* of the two catastrophes, and their handling through time, some loose parallels may be drawn.[108] Feelings of guilt on the part of survivors, though better documented in the case of the Holocaust, suggest some commonality of experience. Secondly, there is the negative finding that traumatic collective experiences do not necessarily translate into inter-ethnic empathy in another time period or in another society. Finally, there is little doubt that a history of tragedy in the one case and a history of atrocity in the other makes for historical representations that have ideological uses in contemporary times in Ireland, Irish-America, Israel and Jewish-America.

Still, these are lesser considerations. It is more appropriate to draw to a close by recalling the cautionary note – one I recall vividly – struck by the American historian of Ireland, Don Akenson. Here he is, speaking at one of the early sesquicentenary Famine commemorations at the Ulster-American Folk Park, Omagh, Co. Tyrone in September 1995: 'One word, however, is not open to our usage… This is the term "holocaust". When you see it, you know that you are encountering famine-porn. It is inevitably part of a presentation that is historically unbalanced and, like other kinds of pornography, is distinguished by a covert (and sometimes overt) appeal to misanthropy and almost always an incitement to hatred.'[109]

CHAPTER FIVE

Ireland, Irish-America and the Man who 'Invented' Genocide

If the history of the western moral imagination is the story of an enduring and unending revolt against human cruelty, there are few more consequential figures than Raphael Lemkin – and few whose achievements have been more ignored by the general public.

Michael Ignatieff[1]

Introduction

The social and economic policies pursued by the British government during the five or so years after the first appearance of blight in the late summer and autumn of 1845 amounted to genocide. This is an interpretation that has gained renewed currency in the last two decades, stimulated in large part by the sesquicentenary commemorations of the Great Irish Famine. While not absent from discourses in Ireland, this view is especially prevalent among one section of the Irish diaspora, that of the United States of America. As the Irish-American activist James V. Mullin relates: 'In 1995, when I first learned that the New Jersey Holocaust Education Commission had been empowered by the legislature to consider course materials on "a wide range of genocides", I contacted Dr Paul Winkler, Executive Director of the Commission, and asked him if the Great Irish Famine could be included.'[2] Mullin's opinion, in view of the scale of the catastrophe in Ireland, was that 'serious consideration must be given to the concept of genocide'.[3]

Where Jewish America had led, Irish America would follow. After intense political lobbying, the study of the Irish Famine was made mandatory for children in public schools in New York and New Jersey. The 'Famine curriculum movement' also got hearings in Massachusetts, Connecticut, Oregon, Maryland, Missouri, New Hampshire, Nebraska, Illinois, California and Pennsylvania. Despite the passage of various resolutions and education bills, by 2002 only two states, New Jersey and New York, had implemented an Irish Famine Curriculum.[4]

This indicates unease and opposition at various levels. The British Embassy in Washington had a clear interest in downplaying criticism of British responsibility for the death toll during the Irish Famine because this reflected badly on Britain and its political system. More immediately, it was aware that the Northern Ireland peace process was at a delicate stage. It voiced a sharply-worded rebuttal when Governor Pataki of New York claimed: 'History teaches us the Great Irish Hunger was not the result of a massive failure of the Irish potato crop but rather was the result of a deliberate campaign by the British to deny the Irish people the food they needed to survive.' Ambassador John Kerr came up with a series of counter arguments, including the allegation that the Great Famine was being equated with the Holocaust. Strictly speaking this claim was not true, though the various subtexts pointed in that direction, and there was more than a degree of coyness on the matter on the part of some advocates of the new curriculum.[5] Political campaigners in New Jersey spoke of a tragedy akin to genocide.[6] The positioning of the Famine alongside the Holocaust in the New Jersey and the New York curriculum units also invited such an inference. John J. McEneny, an Assemblyman from Albany whose ancestors were said to be Famine refugees, conceded that the actions of the British government could not be compared to 'the methodical brutality of the Nazis'.[7] He went on, however, to charge that the British wanted to eradicate the Irish and their culture: 'we have less a case of the deliberateness of a Buchenwald and much more a case of the ethnic cleansing in Bosnia'. Moreover, the repeated use of the term 'mass starvation' in relation to the Famine was ambiguous at best (was the starvation only a condition or was it also an act?), though some had no difficulty in claiming that 'England's policies during the nineteenth century had been intended to spread the famine and starve the Irish people.'[8] No one picked up on the irony that the implicit (retroactive) demand for massive state intervention in food provision and health care emanated from a society in which large sections of the electorate esteemed free-market capitalism and denounced state interference as dangerously socialistic. Followers of James Connolly, the Irish revolutionary socialist and star of many a late-night ballad session, might have recognised a little cognitive dissonance.[9]

Other voices criticised the curriculum idea on other grounds. A scholar at New York University worried that it would allow politicians 'to decide what history to teach and how to teach it'.[10] Some spoke of pandering to ethnic interests and foresaw pressures from other ethnic groups to have their favoured historical experiences crammed into an already stretched school curriculum. Jewish representatives, perhaps surprisingly, were not unanimously opposed to making additions to Holocaust courses. Some, it is true, condemned attempts to include coverage of the Armenian genocide or American racism as undermining the unique character of the Holocaust.[11] Others were less resistant, possibly from mixed motives. A letter to the *New York Times* noted that the proposal to implement the Famine curriculum could not have passed without support from Jewish legislators.[12] In Israel some scholars were more relaxed and argued for the inclusion of other genocides alongside the Holocaust: otherwise, as one put it, 'how can we know why and how the Holocaust was unique, if we don't know what happened to other people?'[13] Whether he would have regarded the Irish Famine as a fit example to be included within the same frame as the extermination of gypsies, Armenians or Jews, we do not know.

In any case, the initiative was successful. Assemblyman Joseph Crowley, who represented a largely Irish section of Queens, sponsored the legislation that teaching the Irish Famine would become part of the school curriculum. A budget of $100,000 was allocated to this effect. This was reported by the conservative *New York Times* under the heading of 'Pork-Barrel Spending Alive and Well in Albany', and added rather mischievously that Crowley's constituents might well 'remember his effort on Election Day'.[14] The article, it is only fair to mention, gave many other instances of 'member' items in the State's budget plan.

The two states that adopted Famine curricula early on were New York and New Jersey, but there the similarity ends. The New York curriculum was carefully designed under the direction of a leading scholar in Irish Studies, Professor Maureen Murphy and colleagues at the University of Hofstra. A panel of eminent historians of the Famine, drawn from both sides of the Atlantic, guided the work of the project. The result was a multi-disciplinary, multi-faceted set of units that met the needs of schoolchildren, of varying abilities and ages, as well as experts on the Irish Famine.[15] Though criticised by some Irish-American activists as insufficiently accusatory of England, it represents an educational achievement that is even-handed and creative.[16]

The development and delivery of the New Jersey curriculum was very different. A librarian and Irish-American activist, James Mullin, led the early work in course design. A glance at the content, as described by him, would give historians of Ireland pause for thought.[17] Restrictive legislation by the British is said to have hindered the progress of the linen industry, which will come as a surprise to historians of the hugely successful Ulster linen industry; the Penal Laws against Catholics are mentioned, and properly so, but the fact that these were directed against Irish Presbyterians and other non-conformist groups as well is not mentioned in Mullin's summary; 'coffin ships' and Gross Isle feature but the larger context that these were not representative of emigrant experience during the exodus to the New World is glossed over.

There is a strong critique of British colonialism but on a matter of much interest to Americans, then and now, that is the slave trade, Britain's leading role in outlawing slave trading (having profited from it in earlier time periods), merits not a mention. The understanding of political decision-making during the crisis itself borders on the simple-minded.

In response to criticism from British and American sources, the New Jersey Holocaust Commission insisted that it needed letters from two prominent academics who would testify to the effect that the Famine was a case of genocide. No such testimonies were forthcoming from historians but two members of law faculties, professors Charles Rice and Francis Boyle, supplied legal opinions to this effect. Neither had been widely known for their expertise on the Irish Famine prior to this. In his supporting letter Boyle asserted that during the years 1845–50 the 'British government pursued a policy of mass starvation in Ireland with intent to destroy in substantial part the national, ethnical and racial group commonly known as the Irish People.'[18]

Irish-American interest groups, including the Irish Action Coalition, the American Irish Political Association and the Ancient Order of Hibernians, rowed in behind the initiative.[19] The upshot of this politicised process was that the Irish Famine was incorporated as a subset of the New Jersey Holocaust/Genocide curriculum, thereby providing students and teachers with a 'framework in which to consider the mass starvation as a form of genocide'.[20]

Raphael Lemkin

'New conceptions require new terms.'[21]

The path of the advocates of an Irish Famine curriculum in American schools would have run more smoothly had they realised that the originator of the term genocide had once entertained the idea that the Irish Famine might have constituted a historical example of genocide. The Polish lawyer, Raphael Lemkin, was born in 1900 on a small farm near the town of Wolkowysk, then part of imperial Russia.[22] His early interests centred on the need for the legal protection of ethnic, religious and social groups. His advocacy in the 1930s of such safeguards met with little success in international conferences. The German invasion of Poland caused him to flee for safety, first to Sweden and then to the United States. Forty-nine members of his family, including his Jewish parents, died in concentration camps, the Warsaw ghetto and on death marches.[23]

His early legal interest in the decimation of ethnic groups came not directly out of Jewish history, as one might have expected, but from the tragic history of Armenians during the First World War.[24] Some historians regard this as an instance of genocide perpetrated by Turkish forces, though spokespersons for the Turkish state hotly dispute this. Lemkin worked for the US War Department and, in 1944, published his monumental study, *Axis Rule in Occupied Europe*, which carefully documented Nazi policies of repression against various minorities and national groups. In this work he coined and defined the term 'genocide'.[25] 'Crimes of barbarity' had been an earlier phrase of his as he groped towards a way of encapsulating the enormity of certain kinds of mass destruction. After the war, Lemkin lobbied national delegations at the newly formed United Nations in New York. His objective was to have certain categories of murderous activity outlawed. Michael Ignatieff paints this picture of his frenetic behaviour: 'He took up residence in the corridors of the United Nations, camping out in the delegates' lounge, a lonely, balding refugee with an overstuffed briefcase and a fanatical mastery of every comma in the convention draft.'[26] Just before Christmas 1948 the United Nations approved the Convention on the Prevention and Punishment of the Crime of Genocide. The Convention did not mirror Lemkin's ideas in their entirety; they were rather more diffuse, but his efforts were hugely influential in the drafting of the document. As he acknowledged, 'wars of extermination' had marked and disfigured the historical record for millennia. The archetypal case of his time was of course the Shoah or Holocaust: the systematic destruction of five to six million European Jews during the Second World War at the hands of the German Nazis and their collaborators in Austria, Hungary, France, Croatia, the Baltic states (Latvia, Lithuania, Estonia) and farther east in the Ukraine.

United Nations Convention on Genocide

Different definitions of genocide abound in the literature, and one can find loose or self-serving formulations that can be mobilised to demonstrate almost anything. The most widely accepted definition is that of the United Nations, which, as mentioned above, was ratified at a general meeting of the assembly in December 1948. Whether it is meaningful to employ even widely accepted criteria such as these and project them back into other time periods is debatable. Some would see this as anachronistic. Moreover, there is no general agreement on the incidence of genocides, even for the twentieth century, which is both a well-documented century and a particularly blood-thirsty one. Still, as a heuristic exercise, it may have some limited utility, if only because some contemporary ideologues are wedded to the imagery of genocide and its application to the Irish Famine.

Article One of the Convention confirms that genocide is a crime under international law, whether committed in time of peace or in time of war. Members who have signed up to the Convention undertake to prevent and to punish this crime. Article Two states that 'genocide means any of the following acts committed with intent to destroy, in whole or in part, a national, ethnical, racial or religious group, as such:

- killing members of the group;
- causing serious bodily or mental harm to members of the group;
- deliberately inflicting on the group conditions of life calculated to bring about its physical destruction in whole or in part;
- imposing measures intended to prevent births within the group;
- forcibly transferring children of the group to another group.'[27]

Most would accept that the Rwandan massacre of the 1990s, in which at least three-quarters of a million, mainly Tutsis, were murdered in the space of a hundred days or so, fell readily within the frame of the UN Convention, though, incredibly, some denied that the ideological and ethnic purges of the Pol Pot regime which consigned millions to death did not.[28] Some would argue that the Armenian massacres, at the hands of the Turks during and after the First World War, constituted genocide.[29] Some twenty countries, and many historians, have accepted this view, but others have not. Similarly, the old Soviet Union dismissed claims that mass deaths from malnutrition, famine-related diseases, food seizures and deportations of people from the Ukraine in the early 1930s added up to genocide. An Irish–Ukrainian research collaboration compared the Irish Famine (*An Gorta Mór*) with Holodomor (the Ukrainian famine of 1932–33), though the focus was not on the tragedies themselves but on subsequent representations of these terrible events.[30] Several contributors to the volume treated the mass deaths in the Ukraine as genocide ('death by forced starvation'), though there was no attempt to present the Irish Famine in such terms. The brutal repression and banishment of certain tribes in South West Africa (present-day Namibia) under German colonial rule is sometimes referred to as the first genocide of the twentieth century. For years the German government resisted demands to acknowledge the atrocities; it later conceded there had been human rights' violations but not genocide; finally, in 2004, a German government minister travelled to Namibia and accepted that the massacre of some 65,000 Herero tribal people had amounted to genocide.[31] She ruled out, however, financial compensation for the victims' descendants. Discussions of the Armenian massacres, as already noted, generate sharp disagreements and disavowals of genocidal intent. The Irish-born, Pulitzer prize-winner, Samantha Power, has argued passionately that western powers, and in particular the United States of America, have been reluctant to acknowledge the existence of genocide during the course of the twentieth century.[32] What all this adds up to is the realisation that what constitutes genocide is not easily agreed, though there is no doubt that mass killings of civilians characterised all of the episodes mentioned above.

Ukrainian Famine

Switching the focus back to New York in the year 1953, we encounter Lemkin once again, this time in the context of the anniversary of the Great Famine in the Ukraine twenty years earlier. The newspaper of the Ukrainian exiles in New York announced to its readers that a parade and later a mass rally at the Manhattan Centre would take place on Sunday, 20 September, with Lemkin as one of the principal speakers. The paper referred to the suffering of millions of the Ukrainian people and charged that the famine was 'purposely arranged by the Kremlin in order to crush Ukrainian resistance to Russian enslavement and Communism'.[33] It claimed that the 'Soviet Russian-made famine in 1932 and 1933' resulted in the deaths of over six million people.[34] It further charged that, in addition to this 'genocidal act', further genocidal actions were taken against the Ukrainian people, including mass executions and deportations to prison camps in the course of which some ten million died.[35]

The following day, according to the *Ukrainian Weekly*, 15,000 Ukrainian Americans gathered at Washington Square and later a capacity crowd of 5,000 was addressed by Professor Raphael Lemkin, of Harvard University.[36] He spoke at length on the different genocidal actions or 'racial murder' inflicted by the Soviet regime on the Ukrainian nation. There is no reference to Ireland in this report. Intriguingly, in a much shorter account of the day's proceedings in the *New York Times* there is a fleeting reference to the Irish Famine of the 1840s. Under the heading 'Ukrainians March in Protest Parade', the *Times* reported: 'Prof. Rafael Lemkin, author of the United Nations Convention against genocide, said that [that?] high crime had been employed 100 years ago against the Irish.'[37] In view of the Soviet–Ukrainian context to the remark, the charge would seem to be that the British government had used famine as a means of destroying some or all of the Irish people. The question that immediately arises is this: was this a considered opinion? If so, then the pronouncement by someone of Lemkin's stature carries much more authority than politically-motivated claims to this effect, then and subsequently.

The likely text of Lemkin's address to the Ukrainian rally has only come to light relatively recently among his papers in the New York Public Library. It was published in the *Journal of International Criminal Justice* in 2009, with a foreword by Roman Serbyn, professor of history at the Université du Quebec, Montreal, and has appeared in other locations as well.[38] According to Serbyn, Lemkin's views on the Ukrainian tragedy are 'virtually unknown and hardly ever figure in scholarly exchanges on the Ukrainian famine of 1932–33, or on genocides in general'.[39] The paper is hugely interesting in its own right, and of great interest for those seeking to understand Soviet–Ukrainian relations. There is no reference to Ireland or the Irish Famine, and Serbyn makes no reference either to an Irish dimension in his introduction. The most likely explanation, assuming the reporter for the *New York Times* got it right in the first instance, is that the comment was a spontaneous aside. There is nothing to suggest that Lemkin had studied the Irish Famine or had any detailed knowledge of its history.[40]

So why might this reference have crept into his speech? We do not know if Lemkin delivered all of his set speech. In any case the likelihood is that he departed from his text at some point. Possibly he made a quick allusion to Irish history to illustrate his point that hunger might be used as a weapon in the service of genocide. Where this vague knowledge might have come from I do not know but the key may be the social milieu of New York itself. Highly politicised renderings of the Famine narrative were embedded in the popular memory of Irish-America and it is possible in a city like New York (or elsewhere on the east coast of the USA) that he picked up claims relating to the Irish Famine through contact with the Irish diaspora or through some writings on Ireland. Lemkin was something of a polymath but his wide reading did not always pick up on distinctions others might have found important. In his autobiography, published posthumously, he makes reference to Edmund Burke, 'the famous English historian of the seventeenth century'.[41] Whatever the reason for his comment at the Ukrainian rally, it seems not to have been followed up with any further reference to the Irish Famine.

In the Dock

The satiated never understood the emaciated.[42]

The opinions of certain Irish-American activists (and others) to the contrary, the Great Famine was a complex affair, as is its interpretation. It was not a tragedy waiting to happen. Once the potato blight struck, and struck repeatedly, a tragedy could not have been avoided.[43] However, its worst effects could have been mitigated. In other words, many more lives could have been saved. How many we may never know. In terms of culpability for the severity of the Famine there is no doubt that Lord John Russell, Charles Wood at the Treasury, other members of the cabinet, and the wider UK parliament failed to discharge their duty of care to a great number of the subjects of Her Majesty, Queen Victoria. Charles Trevelyan, as the principal architect of Famine relief, bears a special responsibility, one which he did not acknowledge in his own *apologia pro vita mea*.[44]

One might speak of a hierarchy of culpability. Others who bear major responsibility included the Irish landlord class whose ten thousand households monopolised land ownership in Ireland. Most reprehensible of all were those who engaged in mass clearances of their estates during the Famine itself. Some behaved honourably and benevolently, such as Elizabeth Smith in Wicklow or the Godreys in Kerry.[45] Many did not. How the representative landlord behaved awaits the accumulation of detailed local studies. In William Smyth's opinion perhaps a third of landlords tried to meet their obligations, perhaps a further third were incapable of doing much because of deep indebtedness, and a further one-third or more rode roughshod over their tenantry, using the Gregory clause to rid themselves of tenants.[46] This is as good a summary statement as any in our present state of knowledge but the author would probably agree that it has much the same status as Caesar's opening remark in his account of the Gallic Wars that 'All Gaul is divided into three parts…'[47] It may well be an understatement of the degree of landlord neglect but we just don't know.

Some of these landowners were members of parliament and the cabinet, so they held leadership roles at different levels of the propertied and political systems. Some were members of O'Connell's Repeal party which agitated for repeal of the Act of Union and the restoration of an Irish parliament. It cannot be said that the Repealers presented a united and coherent set of demands in parliament. Some were overly favourable towards the Whig administration, such was their dislike of the Peelite alternative. The overwhelmingly urgent issue for the rural poor was the Famine, not Repeal, and the priorities and the rhetoric of the Repealers failed to reflect this adequately. In the process, they succeeded in alienating large sections of British public opinion through their mistaken sense of priorities.

Members of the radical breakaway from the Repeal party, the Young Irelanders, hardly covered themselves in glory either, much as some of them might have coveted that mantle. Comfortably wrapped-up in their own idealistic rhetoric, they missed the main issue until it was too late. The hubris that animated some Young Irelanders, that alms from Britain should be spurned, is barely comprehensible to the modern mind. The fiasco of the 1848 'rising' was as much a manifestation of irrelevance and despair as of anything else. Yet the Young Irelanders contained within their tiny ranks some of the most brilliant minds of their generation. Along with other political groupings, they also failed the Irish poor, though least of all at the Widow McCormack's field.[48]

It was once conventional to speak of the pre-Famine Irish as if they were one homogeneous peasant mass. That simplified representation gave way to a realisation that there was a substantial rural and urban middle class, mainly Catholic, and composed of middling-sized and strong farmers, shopkeepers, merchants and members of the professions. The treatment of cottiers and labourers by these employers and rentiers is shrouded from historical view. In view of the deep divisions running along social class lines in the commercialised regions of the country, it is hard to believe that much empathy or largesse was involved. Of the many occupiers of dwarf holdings and conacre gardens, their effective landlords were commercial farmers whose withholding of access to land helped swell the ranks of the dispossessed. In County Cork, farmers employed guns and watchmen to stop labourers stealing turnips from their fields, in one documented case killing the intruder and in another causing severe wounding.[49] Such aggressive responses were not confined to the county.[50] Farmers also invoked the rigours of the law against labourers for stealing food. Some rejoiced in the fact that the poorer, more unruly elements were being driven out by Famine conditions.[51] In a more avaricious vein, there are instances of farmers assisting either openly or covertly in the ejection of neighbours, with a view to taking over the land of the evicted tenants.[52] Hugh Dorian, who lived through the Famine in north Donegal, resented the fact that 'the miserly, the narrow-living class of people, those who were little thought of before, creeped up [sic] in the world and became possessors of land such as never was in the tribe or family before'.[53] As the numbers dependent on the land declined by a quarter or so through death and emigration, surviving tenant farmers expanded their holdings. Silence surrounds such dark deeds, this not being the palatable stuff of popular memory within tightly-knit communities.[54]

There is a corollary. The more simplified narratives of the Irish Famine read the catastrophe in classless, essentially nationalistic terms, with Ireland as the victim of English malevolence, or worse. Writers with unionist sympathies, and the unionist community more generally, have largely obliterated the Famine from memory.[55] But the cataclysm can also be viewed through the prism of class conflict, in which property holders in Ireland, irrespective of religion or political affiliation, acted like property holders anywhere else in the capitalist world, with the added benefit of the ideology of the free market economy as their rationalisation. They protected their assets and continued to maximise their incomes. For them, attacking the basic precepts of capitalism such as charging the maximum price the market could bear, be it for corn or beef, would have been uncongenial, and they would have resisted any radical redistributive measures with grim determination. The writer Colm Tóibín makes the point in relation to Catholic Ireland – the only Ireland worth remembering during Famine times? – with characteristic eloquence: 'Catholic society in Ireland in the 1840s was graded and complex' and to suggest that 'it was merely England or Irish landlords who stood by while Ireland starved is to miss the point.' He continues: 'An entire class of Irish Catholics survived the Famine; many, indeed, improved their prospects as a result of it…'[56]

In the film adaptation of John B. Keane's play, *The Field*, there is the claim that no priest died during the Famine. This is, of course, untrue. Priests, ministers and nuns almost certainly did more for the Irish poor than did Irish politicians, for instance. As in the case of doctors, priests died disproportionately because of their close contact with the people they served.[57] The work of the liberal-minded but aged Archbishop of Dublin, Dr Murray, in channelling charitable funds to distressed areas surely borders on the heroic and maybe even the saintly. The close relationship between priests and people in post-Famine Ireland is also evidence of this service. Within this broad picture of concern there are, however, some more subsidiary stances that are questionable. It is curious that, in some dioceses, church building continued through the Famine years, as at Maynooth and at Enniscorthy for example, and such activity presumably took precedence over more immediate expenditure on the destitute.[58]

Pope Pius IX contributed somewhat less than a thousand pounds for Famine relief, though he did exhort the Catholic faithful world-wide to donate. But surprisingly Irish dioceses were still channelling funds to Rome during the Famine. Moreover, it hardly needs the benefit of hindsight to wonder about the distracting expenditure of time and energy that went into denouncing the non-denominational university colleges at Cork, Galway and Belfast ('the Godless Colleges') which were in the course of construction during the Famine.[59] Higher education can only have been of the remotest concern to the malnourished rural and urban poor. Two archbishops in particular, John MacHale in Tuam and Michael Slattery in Cashel and Emly, poured enormous energy into these controversies.[60] But perhaps the most ill-conceived clerical denunciations related to emigration schemes. Emigration was one of the possible escape routes from the Famine and was bitterly opposed by some clergymen, including MacHale.[61] As archbishop of some of the worst affected western dioceses, MacHale was an outspoken critic of government policy, and commendably so, but his own record in relation to education, emigration and the treatment of poor Catholics who converted to Protestantism during the 1840s was as doctrinaire as that of the most intemperate political economists.[62]

The well-endowed Church of Ireland merits a portion of criticism as well. True enough, some of its ministers hurled themselves into danger in helping their less-fortunate Catholic neighbours, through participation in relief committees and in directly dispensing charity.[63] Some of them paid the price with their lives. A small minority used the occasion of hunger during the Famine to proselytise and win souls on the basis of extreme need. This is an area fraught with controversy. However, the proselytising activity had commenced well before the Famine and it is possible that the competition for souls between denominations resulted in a greater availability of food in remote areas such as the Dingle peninsula and Achill island, than would otherwise have been the case. But it is interesting to look at a less ambiguous piece of evidence, that relating to 'the rebuilding, enlarging and repairing of churches' by the Church of Ireland during the years of dearth and disease. In the year 1844, on the threshold of the Famine, the expenditure was £26,697. It was marginally higher in 1847 and 1848, and it dipped to £25,726 in 1849.[64] To give a sense of proportion, a figure of £25,000 in 1845 would have a value of more than two million in today's money.[65] It is thus remarkable that there was little or no change in the level of capital expenditure on the part of the Church, despite the crisis engulfing sections of the wider society.

At times one might wonder if Irish society is best viewed as a dual or even multifarious society during the course of the Great Famine. Factor and product markets continued to function, albeit with greater reliance on the police and military. Extravagant ceremonies, dances and banquets co-existed with terrible deprivation. Newspapers carried accounts of hunger and death and, at the same time, advertisements for luxury goods such as beaver hats 'combining beauty with durability', or home furniture 'executed in the most superior style of workmanship, from the most modern London and Parisian designs'.[66] Even the mendicant Franciscan friars at Broad Lane, in the city of Cork, seem to have inhabited a world far removed from the famished poor. Their table was graced by expensive meats, fish, wine and whiskey.[67] The social life of many a Big House swirled to the rhythms of a pre-Famine lifestyle. For the later historian, innocent of the dilemmas posed by famine conditions, it is all very perplexing.[68]

Revival

A number of writers have commented on how little scholarly attention was focused on the Irish Famine before the 1990s, and the explanations have ranged from the plausible to the implausibly conspiratorial. It was the sesquicentenary commemoration of the Famine in the mid-1990s that unleashed a flood-tide of publications, locally, nationally and internationally. Television and radio programmes amplified the effect while there was also much popular commemorative activity in the Republic of Ireland, Northern Ireland,[69] and in Irish communities overseas. Creative writing, artwork, famine walks, a replica of a famine-period ship (the Jeanie Johnston), famine museums and drama re-presented *an droch shaol* or the bad times to contemporary audiences.[70]

The surprising point perhaps is that in the twenty-first century this interest shows little sign of abating. In 2012, four big books relating to the Famine appeared, a Famine tribunal at Fordham in the USA set out to ponder the issue of British culpability (postponed to the following year),[71] while a major conference at Nijmegen in the Netherlands, also in 2013, sought to explore the 'global legacies of the Great Irish Famine'.[72] At Quinnipiac, Connecticut in the United States the noted historian of the Famine, Christine Kinealy, was appointed head of a new Irish Famine museum in 2013. A conference to mark the thirtieth anniversary of the publication of Joel Mokyr's agenda-setting book, *Why Ireland Starved*, was organised by the Queen's University Centre for Economic History, Belfast at Eastertime 2014. Against this backdrop of busy academic activity may be found two works that take a radically different stance, in the sense that they argue explicitly for the genocidal interpretation. These are *The Famine Plot*, by Tim Pat Coogan and *A United Ireland* by Francis Boyle.[73]

The Famine Plot has received such a cool reception from scholars that there is little merit in pursuing it further.[74] Professor Boyle's work is more immediately relevant in that it connects with some of the developments in legal understanding outlined above, and we have already encountered him in our discussion of the New Jersey Famine curriculum. Boyle's study opens with the text of the Proclamation of the Irish Republic in 1916 and concludes with a suggested blueprint for a United Ireland from (what is termed) the perspective of international law and human rights.[75] The first chapter, the longest in the volume, is headed the 'Irish Hecatomb: The Legal Case for the Potato Famine as British Genocide'. It cites the UN Convention on the Prevention and Punishment of the Crime of Genocide and then proceeds to muster historical evidence to support the charge of the deliberate destruction of a substantial section of the Irish people by members of the British government. The twelve 'genocidaires' who are arraigned include Lord John Russell, Charles Trevelyan, Charles Wood, William Gregory and Lord Clarendon.[76] The evidence for genocidal intent, however, is merely a string of quotations from a small number of historians of Ireland, principally Christine Kinealy and the late Cecil Woodham-Smith. Most of the voluminous literature on the Famine is simply ignored. Neither is there any apparent attempt to engage with primary source materials or undertake original archival research. The style of writing is self-referential, and the quotations are not used in any systematic way to produce an argument for deliberate intent. It is a most curious enterprise.

Sites of Remembrance?

The main sites for the perpetuation of genocidal interpretations of the Great Famine are to be found in North America, and in the United States in particular. The Famine curriculum movement was a major manifestation of this tendency but some, and by no means all American memorialisations of the Famine come close to this. Thus the website for the Philadelphia Famine monument speaks in accusatory tone of the 'so-called Irish Potato Famine'. The monument itself is traditional in ideological as well as aesthetic senses. There was no Famine, it confidently declares, as 'food sufficient to feed the people several times over' was being forcibly exported by a foreign government.[77] So it goes, in commemorative talks, monuments, newspapers and websites within the North American diaspora.[78] In what is perhaps the most famous Famine memorial site in Canada, that at Grosse Isle, where a huge Celtic Cross commemorating Irish Famine victims dates back to 1909, the inscription *as Gaeilge* on one of the three panels speaks of the Gael (only), of foreign tyranny and of an artificial famine.[79] Significantly, despite its prominence in Irish emigration streams to Canada, the Protestant experience is ignored. This ethnic exclusiveness is replicated elsewhere in Irish Famine remembrance.

Misunderstandings Unlimited

More so than other media, and not excluding films on grand historical themes such as *Braveheart* (1995) or the *The Patriot* (2000), the internet has the capacity to propagate misunderstandings of Irish and other histories at a prodigious rate.[80] In relation to the Great Famine there is a recurring set of themes on the more polemical sites. The first is that of genocide, the principal subject of this chapter. Another is that of ships leaving the Irish ports laden with food, which understandably constituted a distressing image then and later. Food exports are indeed a complex issue, and many ideologues seem innocent of the realisation that there were massive food *imports* during the years of crisis. Grain imports dwarfed grain exports in Black '47 and also exceeded grain exports in the following year, 1848.[81] Livestock exports were at high and rising levels but these were far less calorie-intensive sources of food as compared to cereals or potatoes. More importantly, only an authoritarian, perhaps only a totalitarian regime could have effected huge transfers of livestock from commercial farmers to the rural and urban poor. The unintended consequences of such a policy of confiscation would have been ferocious class conflict and a collapse of rent, rates and hence the poor-law system. It is doubtful if the Irish poor would have been the beneficiaries. A third recurring theme is evictions and here the populist understandings are closer to the truth. There is no doubt that mass evictions greatly amplified Famine deaths. It may be added that, in addition to heartless or hard-pressed landlords, there were also commercial tenant farmers who effectively dispossessed the families of cottiers and labourers on their holdings. Finally, there are allegations of little or no spending by the British government during the Famine. There certainly could have been more effective intervention,[82] but the British government spent in the region of £9.5 million on relief efforts. This was not a large proportion of British public expenditure; still using money values for the year 2011, this comes to the not inconsiderable sum of £712 million.[83] A variant of this charge, that Queen Victoria only gave £5 to the starving Irish, is a tribute to ethnic myth-making.

Times Change

Contrary to what might be surmised, modern Irish society is not particularly receptive to the doctrine of genocide. The fact that virtually all historians of Ireland have reached a verdict that eschews that position, be they Irish-born or scholars from Britain, North America or Australasia, has weakened the traditional populist account. The historian, Liam De Paor, wrote many years ago that, in the early twentieth century, there was 'a widespread conviction among many Irish people at home and abroad that genocide had been attempted by Britain in Ireland, notably at the time of the Great Famine of the 1840s'.[84] That may be but times change, and in place of these accusations, more complex understandings of the Famine have gained a hearing. This in itself is a tribute to academic scholarship on the Irish Famine, though it probably also signifies deeper changes in Irish society that have to do with greater confidence and a stronger sense of national identity in the modern world.

There is an exception, though, and that is in Irish republican circles in Northern Ireland and among their minority supporters in the Republic of Ireland. Murals appeared in republican areas of Belfast in the 1990s which unambiguously proclaimed the Great Famine as genocide. One such mural, entitled *An Gorta Mór* (the Great Famine), on the Whiterock Road, in West Belfast, depicted Famine scenes, and also included as text 'Britain's Genocide by Starvation', 'Ireland's Holocaust 1845–1849', 'over 1,500,000 deaths'.[85] The organ of the republican movement, *An Phoblacht,* spoke of the 'Irish Holocaust' while Sinn Féin, the political wing of the Provisional IRA, seized the opportunity to present a case that meshed with its historical line of 800 years of oppression at the hands of the English and its more contemporary stance of 'Brits Out'.[86]

What was striking about the commemorations in Ireland was the extent to which individuals and local community groups took the initiative in creating memorials, art works, and other commemorative artefacts in relation to the Famine. The Irish government also took a hand in the proceedings. Its concerns seem to have been: firstly, that there should be knowledge of the enormity of the Famine amongst the Irish peoples and others and, secondly, that the subject should not be exploited for politically propagandist purposes. In the latter it was perhaps mindful of the fallout from the fiftieth anniversary commemoration of the 1916 Rising.[87] The political backdrop was the tentative steps towards peace, or at least the cessation of overt hostilities in Northern Ireland, following the Provisional IRA ceasefire of August 1994 and the ceasefire by loyalist paramilitaries two months later.[88] The Irish government funded various initiatives, including speaking tours involving not only hired academics but an Irish minister, Avril Doyle, who chaired the Irish government's Great Famine Commemoration Committee.[89] At the Catholic University, Washington, during the course of a coast-to-coast tour of the United States, the inevitable 'genocide' question came up. 'I don't call the Famine genocide,' Doyle responded, and then went on to elaborate: there was 'an appallingly inadequate response' by the British administration to the failure of the potato crop.[90] Her point, based on a more subtle reading of the Famine experience, was that the unsustainable charge of genocide let the British 'off the hook' of responsibility.

Much of this official activity, it is worth recalling, was catalysed by the actions of the President of Ireland, Mary Robinson, who highlighted the role of the Famine in the creation of an Irish diaspora and who linked the Great Famine to concerns about contemporary famines in developing countries.[91] This moved the debate out of the time-worn Anglophobic rut into a thoughtful dialogue between historical and present-day concerns.[92]

> Hunger and poverty need to become realities. They became a reality to me when in Somalia I sat beside women whose children were dying – children whose mothers were dying. As a mother I felt the sheer horror of that. But as the Head of State of a country which was once devastated by famine I also felt the terrible and helpless irony that this could actually be happening again. And quite frankly I felt then, and I have never lost, a profound sense of anger and outrage and, indeed, self-accusation that we are all participants in that re-enactment.[93]

The notion of *self-accusation* is revealing. Robinson acknowledged in her speech that Irish Famine victims had freedom to travel to wealthier parts of the world, but she and we also know that in the 1990s affluent western countries (including Ireland), had erected barriers against the free movement of the most impoverished of the earth. Primo Levi, a survivor of Auschwitz, used the self-same expression and perhaps in a sense that connects, however obliquely, with Robinson's striking admission. While reflecting on the phenomenon of survivors' guilt, Levi speaks of self-accusation, that is, the 'accusation of having failed in terms of human solidarity'.[94] Few survivors feel guilty, he says, about having damaged, robbed, or beaten a companion. But almost everybody 'feels guilty of having omitted to offer help'.[95]

Rather unexpectedly, we find that Raphael Lemkin, reflecting on his own demons, offers a further window on guilt, indeed one that is even closer to President Robinson's view. 'I was ashamed of my helplessness in dealing with the murderers of humanity, a shame that has not left me to this day.' Then in a resonant phrase he observes: 'Guilt without guilt is more destructive to us than justified guilt, because … catharsis is impossible.' Guilt without guilt seems to have haunted Lemkin all his days.[96]

Was a sense of guilt, in the Robinsonian sense, about world hunger felt widely in Ireland during the 1990s and subsequently? There is no direct evidence on this but there is an indirect test that is at least worth considering. Did Ireland meet the United Nations' modest target of donating less than 1 per cent (0.7 per cent) of its Gross National Income to Third World countries at any point in the last three decades? The target was set by the United Nations' General Assembly as far back as 1970. The answer is that Ireland, despite its Famine legacy and, in common with many other countries in the western world, failed year in and year out to do so. Even during the prosperous years of the Celtic Tiger economy this level of overseas development aid proved too onerous.[97] Ireland is also one of a number of well-off countries which prevaricates on setting a timetable for achieving this target anytime in the twenty-first century. Aid would have mattered. To take the example of Africa, which is the most poverty-stricken continent, millions died (and still die) each year due to preventable and treatable causes, including undernourishment, contaminated drinking water and various infectious diseases that could be controlled using modern public health measures.[98] Yet the dominant reaction in western countries falls far short of what is required. According to Leonardo Boff, drawing on UN statistics for the 1990s, 15 million children died of hunger or hunger-related diseases even before they were five days old.[99]

Aid contributions by the Irish state have been anything but generous. But two qualifications should be entered. In the first place, private and voluntary donations by individuals and families in Ireland historically have been high, and this seems to have been due to religious motives rather than the effect of a Famine legacy.[100] In part out of the same motivation, Irish doctors, nurses, teachers and others have devoted themselves to fighting disease and poverty in developing countries. These qualifications, unfortunately, are dwarfed by two further considerations: Ireland jealously supports agricultural protectionism as practised by the European Union, thereby imposing major financial losses on developing countries seeking to export to the protected European market; it also facilitates tax-avoidance schemes which means that multinational companies pay much lower taxes, sometimes zero taxes, for subsidiaries operating in developing countries.[101]

Viewed in comparative perspective, Ireland lagged behind the leading donor countries. In 2005 the Republic of Ireland earmarked 0.4 per cent of its Gross National Income as aid. Comparable ratios for some other European countries were as follows: Austria 0.52, Belgium 0.53, Denmark 0.81, France 0.47, Germany 0.35, Italy 0.29, Netherlands 0.82, Norway 0.93, Portugal 0.21, Spain 0.29, Sweden 0.92, United Kingdom 0.48. The relative contribution of the United States was one of the lowest in the western world at 0.22 per cent, though in absolute terms the amounts transferred were large. The peak Irish contribution almost touched 0.6 per cent of GDP (Gross Domestic Product) in 2008, when the Celtic Tiger was still roaring, but has fallen away since. In 2013 its contribution, relative to national income, was little more than half that of the United Kingdom.[102]

Raiding the coffers of the past is both an attractive and a costless task but these slices of contemporary history might suggest that historians, among others, might be a little more wary about moralising about historical behaviours in times of catastrophe. It might also suggest a degree of caution, as discussed in the previous chapter, in stressing the sensitising effect of earlier traumatic experiences on latter-day behaviour.

Irish America

In a remarkable, and some might say overdue pronouncement – President Mary Robinson had called for such an apology several years earlier – a British Prime Minister, Tony Blair, acknowledged that those who had been in government in London at the time of the Irish Famine had failed their people through standing by while repeated crop failures turned into a massive human tragedy.[103] This was soon after he took power in 1997 and was probably influenced less by concerns of historical justice than with political considerations and the contemporary Northern Ireland peace process. The commemorative dynamic was less conciliatory in the United States, as we have seen, though we need to bear in mind constantly that the Irish-American universe is a diverse one. It should not be assumed that nationalist organisations, still less ultra-nationalist groups such as Noraid (Irish Northern Aid), necessarily reflected the attitudes and aspirations of most Irish-Americans. Nor should it be forgotten that most Americans of Irish ancestry were of Protestant rather than Catholic origin and may well have entertained different visions of the Irish past.[104] Nonetheless, the contrasting responses to catastrophe in the homeland and in the USA, as well as the much stronger demand in the latter for a narrative of the Famine that supposed genocidal intent, cries out for comment, however speculative.

Peter Gray is almost certainly correct in arguing that shared memories of the Famine in America contributed to 'an emerging sense of collective ethnic solidarity, and provided the moral idea of strength through shared suffering'.[105] But should this still matter at the end of the twentieth century and beyond? One of the most public manifestations of Irish-American desire to memorialise the Famine was the drive to have the study of the Great Famine inscribed in school curricula in the USA. In a trenchant critique of this movement the American-born historian, Timothy Guinnane, put this down to the 'efforts of a small number of Irish-American leaders who have pushed this line for ideological reasons'.[106] This may well be true but still this kind of campaigning struck a responsive chord in wider sections of Irish-America. In defence of the initiative one might point out that the

Famine experience is crucial to understanding mid-nineteenth century and subsequent emigration to the United States and the formation of an Irish diaspora in the American republic.[107] This in itself would and should make the Famine of major interest to both historians of the Famine and members of the Irish diaspora. The case for its relevance to the education of American schoolchildren is more questionable, particularly when packaged in a form that lies towards the propagandist end of the pedagogical spectrum.

Another American historian, one possibly more sympathetic to the campaigners, Thomas Archdeacon, viewed the episode as an interesting case study in the making of popular memory.[108] One might readily agree with him that this particular episode underlined 'how important, in any given era, the popular memory of the past is to current political discourse'.[109] One might go a step further and suggest that manufacturing propaganda is an integral part of the political process, and, to the extent that political interests seek to buttress present-day positions by reference to a tragic or even a 'usable' past, the likelihood is that popular memory will be a mélange of partial truths, selective recollection and special pleading.

Archdeacon usefully situated the Famine controversy in the context of revived expressions of ethnic identity and ethnic distinctiveness within American society in the late twentieth century. *Some* Irish Americans sought to secure a place for the Catholic Irish within American history, just as Black Americans and other minority groups had succeeded in doing for their people.[110] A further line of interpretation argues that remembering the Famine gave Irish Americans from a Catholic background an opportunity to remind the nation that they too had suffered prejudice and discrimination when they first washed up on the shores of America.[111] One might be more convinced of the purity of this motive had there been a parallel acknowledgement of the role of Americans of Irish origin or descent in promoting racism within American society, be it the 'Indian Removal' policies of Andrew Jackson (a President of Ulster–Scot origin), the exclusion of Black Americans from certain workplaces by Irish workers, or the appalling vision of John Mitchel who dreamt of re-introducing the trans-Atlantic slave trade, with all its attendant cruelties and the mass destruction of helpless peoples.[112]

One might wonder if the urge to associate the Great Famine with notions of genocide sprang from a spirit of ethnic competitiveness on the part of some, perhaps a minority of Irish Americans. One of the great features of the United Sates is that it is a multi-cultural society that encompasses hundreds of different ethnic groups. The market-place for wider attention and distinctiveness is a crowded one and there seems, in certain senses, to be a cultural advantage in identifying oneself and ones 'people' as part of an oppressed group. Thus, the Jews had the Holocaust but, hold on, the (Catholic) Irish had the Great Famine as a veritable myth of origin and as an ethnic marker. Possibly, at the level of identity politics, a sharpened sense of ethnicity, honed on historical or pseudo-historical materials, was an unconscious reaction to secularist and assimilationist tendencies within American society. In the end, however, the primary motive may be a simpler notion, one that relates to the 'mindscape' of *some* Irish-Americans in which pleasurable feelings of righteous anger, historical pain and ethnic vengeance comingle with cognitive understandings of the great tragedy.[113] Irish-born visitors are sometimes struck by the gap in time between the political culture of the home country and a seemingly backward-looking and outdated nationalism that is deeply-ingrained in pockets of Irish America and which was re-energised by the 'Troubles' in Northern Ireland. It may be summed up in the text of the official political banner that is carried during the massive annual St Patrick's Day Parade in New York: 'England out of Ireland'.[114]

This is the nationalism of vocal sections of the diaspora in east-coast America. But it should be emphasised that this applies to some Irish only: the self-described Irish belong to a multi-generational ethnic group and its expressions of ethnicity have varied greatly across space and time. The stridently nationalistic manifestations of 'Irishness' in recent decades belong in the main to the Catholic Irish of America, rather than to Irish Americans generally, and even then to only a minority within that subset of the Irish diaspora. As mentioned earlier, a majority of the descendants of Irish immigrants to the USA were of Protestant origin and cannot be assumed to share the same sentiments and world view. Of those of Irish Catholic descent, most are not militant Irish nationalists and some had crossed over to other faiths or none. Thinking in gender terms, aggressive protestation of Irish diasporic identity appears to be more of a male affair. In the end, there may not be agreement on the reasons for the conspicuous consumption of the genocide myth in sections of Irish America and among a minority of ultra-nationalists in Ireland. However, there might be more agreement that there is neither benefit nor dignity in trading on another nation's wound, be it that of the Jews, the Armenians or other national groups whose awful tragedy was one of deliberately-inflicted mass destruction.[115]

PART 3
THE REVOLUTIONARY DECADE

CHAPTER SIX

Harbinger of Reaction: The Ulster Covenant

We have it on the best authority that orange bitters will mix with sherry, but I have never heard that orange bitters will mix with Irish whisky.

T. Agar-Robartes MP[1]

Introduction

The great constitutional question agitating British politics since the 1880s, albeit episodically, was Home Rule for Ireland.[2] The two general elections in the United Kingdom in 1910 paved the way for the abolition of the veto powers of the House of Lords the following year. But the ruling Liberal party did not achieve an overall majority in either election and hence found itself dependent on John Redmond and the Irish nationalist MPs at Westminster. The price of the alliance was the promise of Home Rule for Ireland. Irish nationalists, who were, in the main, constitutional nationalists, were jubilant. The reaction of Irish unionists was one of dismay. In Ulster the reaction was a call to arms, though not literally so at first.[3]

The hugely divisive Home Rule Bill was introduced to a tense House of Commons in April 1912. A few months later, and symptomatic of the anger apparent in unionist circles, the recently elected leader of the Conservative party, Bonar Law, went so far as to proclaim that he could imagine 'no length of resistance to which Ulster will go in which I shall not be prepared to support them'.[4] In similar extremist vein he warned that there were things stronger than parliamentary majorities.[5] Whether treason was one of them he did not care or dare to spell out.

Ireland itself was in a state of high political excitement, nowhere more so than in the north-east of the island. An Ulster Unionist Council had been formed back in 1905 and, five years later, as the spectre of Home

Rule threatened, a Dublin unionist and leading lawyer, Sir Edward Carson, was offered the leadership of the Irish unionists and the Ulster unionists. Significantly, Ulster unionists held their own counsel, while maintaining links with southern Irish unionists whom it was feared might be more open to compromise on the matter of legislative autonomy for Ireland. Rhetoric turned to action. The theatre of action or re-action was Ulster, not all-Ireland.

To signify the undying opposition of Protestant and unionist Ulster to Home Rule, the 28 September 1912 was proclaimed as 'Ulster Day'. Religious services were to be celebrated at 11 am on that Saturday in the localities across Ulster. Needless to say, this did not include the Catholic mass. At the close of the services the congregations would then 'proceed to places locally assigned to pledge themselves to a solemn covenant which will have been passed by delegates of the Ulster Unionist Council at their meeting in Belfast on Monday, September 23 and proclaimed throughout the Province on the following day'.[6]

These tactics were also a means of diverting crude Protestant proletarian anger and the dangers of spontaneous communal violence into more disciplined expressions of protest.[7] Earlier that summer an attack on Sunday school children at Castledawson by sectarian-minded Hibernians had prompted a wave of expulsions of Catholic workers from the Belfast shipyards. Communal passions had been simmering in the shipyards for some time. While there are different interpretations of the Castledawson affair, there is no doubt the response was wholly disproportionate and indicated deep reservoirs of violence within loyalist Ulster. However, this was not the kind of message unionist leaders wished to present to the wider world. A special covenant was drafted with the support of the major Protestant denominations, which was then to be signed by 'all loyal men of Ulster over sixteen years of age' and all loyal women of Ulster.[8] Venues where the Covenant might be signed were designated; many of these were Protestant churches or church halls, signifying the confessional character of the enterprise.[9] Unionist newspapers dutifully carried the news, typically giving the place of worship, the hour of services, the place for signing the Covenant and the name of the local secretary. Thus for example, we read off from a long list published in the *Belfast News-Letter* *(BNL)*: 'Comber, First Presbyterian church, 2.30pm, Orange Hall, Reading Room and Square, Geo. Spence'. Clearly there was little expectation that this was anything other than a petition by the Protestant people of Ulster. In what was a significant demurral, bishops of the Church of Ireland outside Ulster did not support Ulster Day. In the view of one historian of that church, the event was 'perceived in the south as a symbolic renunciation of all-Ireland unionism'.[10]

The signing itself was surrounded by great pageantry. Sir Edward Carson, using a silver pen, was the first to sign at Belfast City Hall, which was one of the many centres where signatures were registered.[11] That a Dubliner with no obvious Ulster connections was the first to sign was an irony that went largely unnoticed. The ritual and the spectacle were integral parts of what was, in effect, a massive exercise in ethnic mobilisation.

Subtext

One of the many subtexts to the occasion was paramilitarism. As early as September 1911 Carson had addressed a rally of 50,000 unionists at Craigavon in east Belfast and had advocated immediate resistance the moment Home Rule was enacted.[12] On Ulster Day itself one unionist paper featured a *Punch* cartoon of 'General Carson' as Wellington on a rearing charger, wielding a pen like a lance over his head with ink dribbling from its sharp nib. A sword in its scabbard hung from his waist. The heading: 'Ulster will write'. At the bottom of the drawing was the legend: 'The pen (for the moment) is mightier than the sword'.[13] Ink might yet turn to blood. Major Frederick Hugh Crawford, who was in charge of the bowler-hatted marshals who escorted Edward Carson, James Craig and other unionist leaders from the Ulster Hall to City Hall, was in no doubt that the sword would be needed. A mass write-in was simply not enough. Crawford had been involved in gun-running on a small scale as far back as 1893 during the course of the second Home Rule crisis.[14] In 1910, he was a key player in the establishment of a secret sub-committee of the Ulster Unionist Council to import guns.[15] In the spring of 1914 Crawford masterminded the import of 35,000 weapons and three million rounds of ammunition, which were unloaded at seaports along the north-eastern coastline, at Larne, Bangor and Donaghadee.[16] Crawford had long been clear as to how far he was prepared to go:

> From the very first I came to the conclusion that our resistance, to be successful, must eventually come to armed resistance. Judging from past history and the Government's treatment of political agitation in Ireland, I knew that mere words were useless. We knew our Ireland and that Home Rule would sooner or later mean complete severance from the British Empire, and I was determined to do all in my power to prevent this, even by force if need be.[17]

The signing of the Covenant was undertaken with quasi-military style precision in the major urban centres. The undertaking and the accompanying spectacle represented not only an impressive show of political, demographic and masculine strength but deep organisational and communal determination. The massive support of the Protestant womenfolk added strength in depth, taking the campaign into the workplace, the neighbourhood and the home. It is hard to be sure in retrospect, but possibly most of the participants had little or no sense that they might be on track for communal and civil war, that is, as distinct from the episodic riots, expulsions and acts of intimidation that accompanied moments of high political excitement. Even the nationalist *Irish News*, whose hostility to the whole venture knew no bounds, charged Carson and Craig, as well as the foot soldiers from the Ulster clubs and the Orange Order, with silliness rather than sinister intent. It could not have been more wrong when it ridiculed the whole proceedings under headings such as 'Carson's Covenant Comedy Concluded', 'Wearisome Reiteration of Previous Harangues', or 'A Silly Masquerade in Belfast'.[18]

More sensible and sensitive voices were ignored. The writer George Birmingham in *The Red Hand of Ulster*, published shortly before the Covenant campaign got underway, had already sent out clear warnings about the depth of unionist resolve and the likelihood of a descent into bloodshed.[19] In his imagined crisis the Ulster unionists did indeed fight; there were volunteers confronting troops on the streets of Belfast, and a British naval vessel sailed into Belfast Lough to bombard the city centre. Though the fictional story is executed with a comic touch, its deadly seriousness is indirectly vindicated by the unsettling parallels with what actually happened in another Irish city a few years later.[20] Rightly or wrongly, Ulster would fight as well as write.

Organisation and Scale

Before turning to the text itself it is worth dwelling on the sheer scale of the operation which, remarkably, had been executed in the space of a few weeks. Almost half a million people – 471,414 according to the website of the Public Record Office of Northern Ireland (PRONI) which has digitised the records – signed either the Covenant (for men) or the Declaration (for women). Most were resident in Ulster but some came from elsewhere in Ireland, England and Scotland, with small numbers from farther afield.[21] The total is likely to be an upper-bound estimate. In Ulster and Ireland there must always be the lingering suspicion of a variation on electoral impersonation playing its part, in this case signing at more than one centre.[22] This would have been relatively easy in some places where venues for signing were not far apart. In practice, it was also possible to sign on behalf of someone else.[23] Policing such activity would have been difficult. Moreover, there were no opposition impersonation agents present as would have been the case in electoral contests, though each male (but not female) signatory was obliged to promise on paper that they had not already signed. This gender exception was either an oversight or a presumption that women were more honest than men, at least in affairs of state. Occasionally, what looks suspiciously like identical handwriting appears in relation to two or more names.[24] Daniel Hugh Morrison of Killygullib, Kilrea, in the South Derry constituency seems to have signed twice. This may be a case of an uncle and a nephew, or perhaps two cousins, with one signing on behalf of the other, as, according to the census enumerator's return for 1911, two individuals of that name lived in the townland of Killygullib Glebe. However, they were residing in different households. In some instances, of course, identical signatures occur because of illiteracy. Sarah Jane Peoples of 15 Dark Lane, Londonderry and her neighbour Maggie Pims [or Sims] of 22 Dark Lane have the same handwriting, but the presence of an 'X' accompanying each name and the legend 'her mark' explains this.[25]

There was no age check that we know of and there is the issue of the retrospective signings by young men who wanted to join the Ulster Volunteer Force in 1913. It was a prerequisite to have signed the Covenant and some did so at that later stage. Using the age structure of the population of Ulster in 1911 and the size of the Protestant population in the same year, a measure of the extent of the turn-out for the Covenant may be calculated. This works out at 74 per cent of the Protestants eligible to sign, a truly remarkable figure when one considers that this embraces both genders and that some were ill, elderly and bed-ridden.[26] Some may even have been out of their mind. One newspaper charged that in the Newtownards workhouse forms were brought in specially to the institution where about thirty signed the Covenant, 'some of these being blind, lame, and armless, and two or three registered as lunatics'.[27] That three out of every four signed, not in one or two constituencies but on average across the province, might raise some doubts. It certainly suggests strong communal, neighbourhood and family pressure, as well as superb political organisation. The integration of religious services into the political choreography served to intensify communal consciousness and communal conformity. 'O God, Our Help in Ages Past' was sung lustily, and possibly with an edge of group hysteria, in churches and mission halls across the province.

There is also the elusive, largely invisible issue of intimidation on the 'compulsory holiday' that was Ulster Day, as naturally alleged by some nationalists but also by some liberal Protestants.[28] The *Ulster Guardian* complained that the workmen of Belfast Corporation were promised full wages, despite being absent from work on Ulster Day, though this seems more in the nature of a carrot rather than a stick. However, under the same heading of 'Intimidation' it also claimed that workers at a weaving factory outside Belfast had been ordered to sign the Covenant or face the sack.[29]

Coercion is unlikely to have been wholly absent, given the experience of communal politics in the North, but there is no gainsaying the tsunami of support, of varying degrees of intensity, within Ulster Protestant society for the anti-Home Rule cause. The unionist *Irish Times*, based in Dublin, was almost lyrical in its celebration of this 'holy day': 'Belfast displayed on Saturday such a civic harmony and passion as the world has hardly seen since Athenian or medieval times.'[30] Moreover, in parts of outer Ulster where unionists were in a minority, the hostility of nationalists and possible fear of sectarian retaliation by Hibernians must have deterred some. So, to sum up, even if the overall figures are exaggerated, as is suggested here, there is no doubting that the returns were anything other than a massive endorsement of the sentiments contained in the Covenant. By the same token, this show of strength was likely to have had an intimidatory effect on northern Catholics.

The collection of mass signatures, though more usually in the form of petitions, was not unprecedented in Irish or British politics. As recently as January 1912, the Ulster Women's Unionist Council had organised a petition that attracted 100,000 signatories protesting against the provisions of the *Ne Temere* papal decree on religiously-mixed marriages.[31] As far back as 1841 and before the Great Famine, the O'Connellite political machine had helped collect close to 160,000 signatures throughout Ireland as a testimonial to the reforming administration of Lord Morpeth, the Chief Secretary for Ireland during the years 1835–41.[32] (The actual figure may have been closer to a quarter of a million as some of the sheets have been lost.) Such an enterprise is astonishing in view of the unevenness back then in language, literacy and communication across the island. In British politics we can see parallels with the spectacle of the People's Petition of 1838 signed by tens of thousands of workingmen, artisans and others who were loosely grouped in what was called the Chartist movement. This pressed for reform of the British parliamentary system. In 1842, a new Chartist petition attracted more than three million signatures but failed to impress the House of Commons at Westminster.[33] There is nothing, however, to suggest that the Ulster Day committee had such precedents in mind. Covenanting came out of a deeper tradition that mingled religion and politics. In any case the Covenant was more in the nature of a warning to British politicians than a petition. Another difference is that it was not being presented to Parliament – it was a roll-call of Ulster men and women who supported the Union – though clearly it was intended to influence opinion at Westminster and among the general public.[34]

Ulster

So what were the Ulster unionist masses signing up to? We need to make a distinction between the signature sheets used on Ulster Day and thereafter, and the specially printed individual certificates that signatories were entitled to order. The sheets are plain and business-like. On the Women's form is printed 'Women' (in parentheses), and on the top right-hand corner the Sheet No., the Parliamentary Division, the District and the Place of Signing. In large lettering is the heading 'Declaration', followed by the text of the Declaration. Next come two columns labelled 'Name' and 'Address' respectively. Underneath are placed lined rows to receive signatures and addresses. The Men's version follows the same format, the differences being it is labelled 'Men' (in parentheses), the heading is 'Covenant', and this is followed by the text of the Covenant which differs from that of the Declaration.

The printed souvenir certificate is a more elaborate affair. Emblazoned on the top left-hand corner is the ancient symbol of Ulster, the Red Hand. This is an image that speaks to both unionists and nationalists but, in context, its meaning is unambiguous. The Covenant is for the Protestant and unionist people of Ulster whose collective identity was compressed into the bloody imagery of the severed hand. It is at once familiar and reassuring. A symbol might be worth a thousand words (to modify an adage about photographs), and perhaps this one was.

But words matter. The key one here is 'Ulster'. It is the first word in the title, set out on its own, and the one which enjoyed the largest typeface. This was not necessarily the idiosyncratically delineated nine counties traced out by colonial administrators several centuries earlier and subsequently fetishised and reified in much political discourse. Ulster in this context was an imaginative construct, though one with a geographical counterpart even if the boundaries were ill-defined and its inhabitants selectively envisioned. Roughly speaking, Ulster was the homeland of tens of thousands of individuals and families who professed loyalty to King, Country and Empire, who opposed Home Rule, who owned farms, factories and mills, and who worshipped in a variety of Protestant churches, chapels and mission halls. They traced their ancestral origins to Scotland and England, though not necessarily to the plantations of the seventeenth century. In reality the blood lines were more mixed than that (see chapter two), and there were, of course, small numbers of Catholic unionists. Whether any of these signed the Covenant or Declaration is an interesting if minor point of interest. The imagined homeland of Ulster unionists had little space for Roman Catholics or Irish nationalists, again despite the reality of their presence not only in rural Ulster but in the regional capital of Belfast itself, where they accounted for a quarter of the population in 1911.[35] The ethnic community that peopled and defined this ideological space tended to overlook Catholics and nationalists, while simultaneously fearing them in the political realm.

The full title of the Covenant is Ulster's Solemn League and Covenant. The font used on the individual souvenir certificates issued to signatories is in a version of Old English, which gives the impression of an age-encrusted, even sacred text.[36] Thus we are immediately conscious of a dialogue between modern and earlier texts, or what is sometimes called intertextuality. The notion of a covenant harks back to biblical times, as if the historic depth to the Protestants of Ulster had to be measured in terms of a Christian lineage and a continuity stretching back millennia. The ethnic group was not simply made up of planters and newcomers from the seventeenth century and subsequently. Here was a people self-consciously aware of their ancient origin.

The seventeenth century also mattered and had a more immediate historic resonance. The term Covenant recalled the Scottish Covenanters of the 1640s. In 1643, Scottish Covenanters had 'resolved and determined to enter into a mutual and solemn league and covenant' in defence of the reformed religion and liberties of Scotland.[37] This led them to join forces with the English Parliamentarians to throw off the oppressive rule of the Stuart king, Charles I, and the pretensions of his Established Church. Inevitably the Scots invoked the blessing of God on the enterprise or, as Joe Lee has mischievously put it, a Covenant was 'the traditional Presbyterian technique for reminding God whose side he was on'.[38] Additionally, it signalled group solidarity in times of danger, a challenge to established authority with a suggestion of the conditional nature of loyalty to the British or indeed any state.[39] The Scottish Covenanters had met steel with steel when they felt their religious and other liberties were threatened, sentimental notions of the Scottish origin of the Stuart monarchy notwithstanding.

It is also the case that covenanting in the more modern period, that is outside of its Biblical time frame, was associated with Presbyterianism rather than Anglicanism, these being the two great streams whose confluence was the pan-Protestant alliance that opposed Home Rule.[40] Presbyterians, with 421,000 adherents, formed the largest single denominational group within Ulster Protestantism, exceeding the Church of Ireland membership by 55,000 or so. Still, it was something of a coup by Presbyterians to have shaped the petition in terms of Presbyterian and Scottish precedents. A contemporary remarked a few weeks before Ulster Day that it was a 'compliment' to Presbyterians that this form of opposition to Home Rule had been adopted: the leaders of unionism had considered it wise 'to revive an ancient method of unifying strength – a pledge or oath binding the subscribers to it to mutual confidence and alliance in times of trial and danger'.[41] This was also a usable narrative involving victim status, endurance and survival against the odds.[42] The less than distinguished early history of Anglicanism in Ireland, with its persecution of Presbyterians and Catholics, was a much less helpful narrative for a political campaign against Home Rule.

The Covenant: Main Text

Being convinced in our consciences that Home Rule would be disastrous to the material well-being of Ulster as well as of the whole of Ireland, subversive of our civil and religious freedom, destructive of our citizenship and perilous to the unity of the Empire, we, whose names are underwritten, men of Ulster, loyal subjects of His Gracious Majesty King George V, humbly relying on the God whom our fathers in days of stress and trial confidently trusted, do hereby pledge ourselves in solemn Covenant throughout this our time of threatened calamity, to stand by one another in defending, for ourselves and our children, our cherished position of equal citizenship in the United Kingdom, and in using all means which may be found necessary to defeat the present conspiracy to set up a Home Rule Parliament in Ireland. And in the event of such a Parliament being forced upon us, we further solemnly and mutually pledge ourselves to refuse to recognize its authority. In sure confidence that God will defend the right, we hereto subscribe our names. And further, we individually declare that we have not already signed this Covenant.[43]

A long, elaborately constructed, opening statement dominates the text of the Ulster Covenant, occupying two-thirds of the whole. It is introduced with the weighty phrase 'Being convinced in our consciences....' At first glance, the word conscience seems out of place but on reflection one can see the deeper layers of meaning adhering to its surface presence in the text.[44] Where does truth for the Protestant reside, when all things are measured and weighed but in the inner sanctum of the individual conscience? The moral, the religious and the political find ultimate form there. But it is striking that the argument that is then given primary position in the opening sentence is of the material kind. Home Rule 'would be disastrous to the material well-being of Ulster as well as the whole of Ireland'. Home Rule would not only damage Ulster's economy and the livelihoods dependent on it but would also endanger the material interests of nationalists (if they could only realise it). The positioning of the economic argument is hardly accidental: it accords with the commonplace assumption that Ulster – really the north-eastern region of the island – was more economically and industrially advanced than the rest of the island.[45] This was, of course, true, to the chagrin of some nationalists. In polemical disputes, the economic superiority of the North could be belittled by suggesting that Protestant Ulster was more materialistic, less spiritual and less cultured than Catholic Ireland. Still, there was no gainsaying it, the economic argument was a strong one and its rational character was calculated to impress unionists of all social classes, as well as wider audiences in Britain and beyond.

Indeed, Carson himself reckoned that the exclusion of four, nine or six Ulster counties – the permutations varied from negotiation to negotiation – from a Home Rule Ireland would have made devolved rule for any part of Ireland economically unviable, that is, in the absence of the industrial heartland of the Lagan Valley. This, however, was a mistaken piece of political economy. Had there been a high degree of interdependence between the industrial North and the largely agrarian South, through the supply of raw materials or the provision of important consumer markets for instance, the proposition might have had some validity. Neither condition applied. The raw materials of coal, iron, timber and flax, which fed the giant factories of east Ulster came through the ports of Belfast, Derry and Newry. Moreover, the produce of industrial Ulster was destined in the main for British and overseas markets. Contrariwise, there is no reason to believe a largely rural economy in the South could not continue to plough its own furrow, economically speaking, in the manner of Denmark or New Zealand, as indeed it was doing in the 1910s while enjoying modestly rising incomes. Low incomes, little modern industry and a declining population meant that the South was a minor market for the staple industries of the North. The two regional economies on the island were simply not complementary,[46] either then or later, and so could disengage from each other without major economic repercussions. The thinking, though, illustrates a degree of economic illiteracy on the part of the leader of Ulster unionism, if not among his more able lieutenants. Craig, for instance, thought in largely Ulster terms – however defined – rather than of Ireland as an entity.

Unionists led with the economic objections to Home Rule and this fitted with the confident self-image of a prosperous region committed to the modern world, as compared to the more backward Catholic and agrarian South. West of Ireland *curraghs* contrasted unfavourably with Belfast-made transatlantic liners. Some saw a close association between Protestantism, industry, science and technological progress. Some would also argue that Catholic culture was less receptive to the opportunities proffered by modernity.[47] Having said this, economics was hardly the primary reason for unionist opposition to a devolved parliament in Dublin. Such arguments may well have counted heavily with the captains of industry – they certainly did – but for the citizen in the street, as the industrialist Milne Barbour had conceded, they were not the key.[48] Having led with the economic, the opening sentence piles on further arguments against Home Rule. It would be 'subversive of our civil and religious freedom, destructive of our citizenship and perilous to the unity of the Empire'. The Reverend Dr M'Kean hammered home the point at the religious service in the Ulster Hall on Ulster Day itself: 'Home Rule is a great religious issue which threatens the destruction of our most precious liberties … Home Rule is at bottom a war against Protestantism, an attempt to establish a Roman Catholic ascendancy in the country which would lead ultimately to the overthrow of the British Empire'.[49] Or to mix metaphors, Home Rule was the Trojan donkey calculated to upend the imperial apple cart, and much else besides.

Anti-Catholicism

The claims and counter claims are not so easily resolved. Anti-Catholicism was a strain in British political culture that was not confined to the Conservative party. Even the Liberal prime minister charged with introducing the Third Home Rule bill, H.H. Asquith, had been angered at the thought of Catholic ceremonial in public spaces a few years earlier.[50] (This related to the Eucharistic Congress of 1908 and the prospect of Catholic priests in vestments carrying the host through the streets round Westminster Cathedral.) At a less elevated level, the catchphrase 'Home Rule is Rome Rule' summed up popular unionist perceptions of the relationship between church and state in a Catholic-dominated society. Despite its exaggeration and simplification, the charge contained elements of truth. The Roman Catholic Church had embedded itself deeply in many areas of public life in Ireland, from education to healthcare, from the running of reformatories to the conduct of Magdalene asylums for 'fallen women'.[51] Most irksome of all, its seeming intolerance in the matter of 'mixed marriages' did not bode well for mutual accommodation and tolerance in a future in which Catholic Ireland was politically dominant. The infamous *Ne Temere* decree published a few years earlier, in 1908, could be cited to confirm Protestants' worst fears, though in fact this proclamation only codified what had been common practice already.[52] Moreover, from a liberal Protestant, women's rights or a labour perspective there was the problem of the Catholic Church's traditional identification with reactionary and authoritarian politics elsewhere in Europe, something French socialists, Italian liberals or Spanish anti-clericalists would have immediately understood. Even Dr M'Kean, quoted above, had prefaced his remarks with the observation that Ulster men would support political and social reforms but not Home Rule.

Still in the political arena priests were less active in the 1910s than they had been in the past, being primarily concerned with protecting their 'special interests' in education and welfare.[53] Traditionally unionists had been hugely critical of the idea of the 'priest in politics'; if anything, the minister in politics was more prominent in the period 1910–14. Moreover, as often as not, Catholic priests were moderating voices as was apparent from their role in local Land League committees a generation earlier.[54] Their reactionary stance during the Great Dublin Lock-Out of 1913, the year after the signing of the Covenant, should have offered some reassurance to unionist employers, if not their organised workers. The Irish Parliamentary Party under John Redmond could hardly be viewed as an adjunct of Maynooth College and the Conference of Catholic Bishops, however sensitive it might be to clerical interests in the education sphere. Nor is it obvious how a devolved parliament in Dublin, with limited powers and subject to the oversight of the Westminster parliament, could have seriously impaired the civil liberties of Ulster and Irish unionists, particularly as unionists would constitute a significant and voluble minority within the new parliament. The Home Rule legislation itself incorporated various safeguards to ensure an Irish devolved parliament would not interfere with religious freedom, while discrimination on sectarian grounds was also ruled out.

The point about Empire misses the fact that John Redmond and some leading nationalists were favourably disposed towards the British Empire. Even Arthur Griffith, the founder of Sinn Féin, seems not to have been averse to the idea of Ireland having its own colonies.[55] In any case, foreign affairs was the prerogative of Westminster, so imperial matters were hardly likely to have featured prominently in Irish debates. Nor is it obvious why a devolved parliament in one part of the United Kingdom, as distinct from a secessionist state (as indeed came to pass in due course, not least because of Ulster unionist intransigence), should hasten the disintegration of the Empire. There is an argument that it might well have strengthened the Empire, as had the creation of a Canadian confederation, for instance, nearly a half century earlier.[56]

It is difficult to strike a balance on these issues. The small numbers of secularists, liberals and socialists of Protestant or Catholic origin would certainly have reasons to be apprehensive about a parliament dominated numerically by orthodox Catholics. After all, in Catholic Europe, including in particular France, Italy and Spain, the Catholic Church was associated with religious supremacy, a denial of freedom of religious thought, and reactionary politics more generally. The anti-popery of the Protestant masses, on the other hand, was more visceral than intellectual, finding its source in preaching traditions laced with prejudice, hostility and hysteria. There seems little of substance in the civil liberties argument, other than its reverse, that the maintenance of the Union might have preserved greater civil liberties for all the peoples of the island in place of the erosion of Irish citizens' and women's rights that accompanied the formation of the Irish Free State, to the detriment of some Catholics and many southern Protestants. The idea of the Empire, and the connections of kith and kin, especially to the dominion of Canada, undoubtedly meant more emotionally and ideologically to Ulster unionists than to other Irish people, but there was no great anti-imperialist groundswell within parliamentary Irish nationalism and rather a fair degree of pride in Catholic Ireland's spiritual empire.[57]

These are 'Men of Ulster, loyal subjects of King George V', we are told. Indeed! That His Majesty should have been so lucky. He wouldn't have had to read much farther before coming to the uneasy realisation that the loyalty of his Ulster subjects was highly conditional. But that is to jump ahead. The Men of Ulster also trusted in the God who had delivered them safely in 'days of stress and trial' – biblical and more recent historical allusions commingling – and were resolved, by binding themselves together in solemn covenant, to defend themselves 'throughout this our time of threatened calamity'. The rhetoric, which so far had been relatively subdued, is beginning to heat up. It required an apocalyptic mind-set, and this was an easily accessed resource within evangelical Protestant thinking, to see Home Rule in such calamitous terms. Moses had to contend with much worse, as had the Scottish Covenanters when Cromwell sent in the Roundheads.

'All means... necessary'

Children are invoked in the next phrase, because these modern-day covenanters were nothing if not solicitous of the welfare of future generations. This raises the emotional temperature a bit further, as does the appeal to group solidarity. The most arresting phrase in the whole document follows soon after. It is the resolve to use 'all means which may be found necessary to defeat the present conspiracy to set up a Home Rule Parliament in Ireland'. This is the climax to the long opening sentence that is made up of no fewer than 137 words.

It is a culmination worth dwelling on. For some it meant purely peaceful means, but the formulation is certainly open to more sinister interpretation. Knowing as we now do that a conspiracy was already afoot to import weapons and to arm a paramilitary organisation, there is no doubt that some at any rate knew exactly what this might entail, and what did indeed come to pass with the formation of the Ulster Volunteer Force (UVF) a few months later. The UVF trooped onto the public stage in January 1913, though, of course, much planning preceded its emergence.

The reference to the 'present conspiracy' to set up a Home Rule parliament is risible as well as insulting. The great Irish parliamentarian, Daniel O'Connell, was a harbinger of future political demands when he introduced a bill for the repeal of the Union back in 1834. The matter had been debated seriously in the House of Commons and the House of Lords since the 1880s. The policy was voted for in election after election in Ireland during the quarter-century of elections since then, and one of the two great British political parties, the Liberals, had embraced the cause. Admittedly this was reluctantly so, and with an eye to other interests, as Ronan Fanning has demonstrated.[58] To think that the mass support evident across most of Ireland somehow constituted a conspiracy is to rob the word of all meaning. It is also significant that the reference is to the *present* conspiracy. The phrase, 'throughout this our time of threatened calamity' further de-limits the action, referring by implication to the Third Home Rule crisis only. This seems to have been a qualification insisted on by Presbyterian churchmen who feared giving a mandate for other or later political actions.[59]

That's Party Politics

One unionist and Tory justification for such terms was that the Liberal party had not made Home Rule an important issue in the two elections of 1910, and hence lacked a mandate for radical constitutional change (as they saw it). Some went so far as to say the constitution had been suspended and that the Liberal government was unlawful.[60] Less extreme voices claimed the Liberal party was being opportunistic in striking a bargain with Irish nationalists so as to stay in power. Some Liberals, it is true, had little or no time for the Home Rule cause and yet were involuntarily locked into it. However, the Conservative party also behaved opportunistically in using the Home Rule crisis to unify its ranks and intensify its attacks on the Liberals. That was party politics after all. But to threaten treason was a curious response to allegations that the Liberal government of the day was breaking somewhat vague understandings of constitutional conventions.

It is impossible to say to what extent the signatories dwelt on the open-ended commitment to resistance to Home Rule. It cannot be argued that the manifesto was sprung upon an unsuspecting public that had no time to register the content. The *News-Letter* had carried the text a week earlier. Still, in an emotion-charged atmosphere akin to a closely fought electoral campaign, the prospects for cool reflection and resistance to collective pressures were limited. According to one set of newspaper claims, some Protestant ministers worried on precisely this score.[61]

The *Irish News*, woefully deaf to the implications and wilfully blind to the depth of unionist opposition to an Irish parliament, shot and missed the proverbial barn door by a mile in its supercilious editorial on Ulster Day. The series of events were 'tame as a demonstration of enthusiasm and highly ludicrous as an indication of the "grim and determined spirit"'. It went on: 'The whole grotesque production has been a political failure, though a comic success…'.[62]

In this it showed the limitations of nationalist thinking on the North and the North's anomalous situation in relation to the emerging Irish polity. There is also, in the editorial, the characteristic tendency to seek refuge in make-believe when faced with uncomfortable realities. The dismissal of unionist opposition to Home Rule as the tactics of blusterers and bully boys – a view widely shared in nationalist Ireland – was tragically myopic, all the more so from a source that was better placed than most to hear and see. Perhaps the underlying thought pattern was that discerned by David Miller, that the disposition of nationalist Ireland towards Ulster unionists was 'unavoidably coloured by the attitudes of northern Catholics who were indeed prone to think in terms of the inevitable dominance of one side or the other by any means at its disposal'.[63] To which one might add, this was one of the many shared understandings between Ulster unionists and northern Irish nationalists.

Leaving 'all means necessary' echoing in the air, the mood of the Covenant then shifts, almost abruptly, from crescendo to diminuendo. The covenanters inform us that, in the event of a parliament being forced upon them, they will 'refuse to recognise its authority'. Thus the possibility of defeat, at least in round one, is conceded. God is invoked for the second time, lest he might have been caught napping earlier on, and the main text ends prosaically with the promise that the signatory had not already signed for the cause.

The footer to the document is 'God Save the King', set in large type. This mantra was the ritualistic end point to any loyal demonstration. Its sheer familiarity as well as the invocation of monarchy, must have warmed the hearts of the tens of thousands queuing to add their personal mark to the roll call for God, King, Empire and Ulster. The large question mark remains, however. Was this a document which paved the way to the mass mobilisation of an ethnic group that was determined to resist Home Rule with force if necessary? The liberal unionist, Thomas Sinclair, who drafted the text might well have said 'No' at this stage. Sinclair was a social progressive who had favoured the disestablishment of the Church of Ireland, had supported land reform, and had proposed passive resistance at the time of the passing of the second Home Rule bill in the House of Commons in 1893. Others, as we have noted, already thought differently. One of these was the unionist MP, William Moore, who had moved the following motion at a meeting of the County Grand Black Chapter of Belfast a few weeks before Ulster Day:

> … we hereby emphatically declare our determination never to submit to any such measure [Home Rule] in any shape or form, but to resist it to the uttermost by every means in our power, regardless of consequences, personal loss or inconvenience. We will, at any time, be ready and willing to adopt any plans of resistance that may be arranged by our Unionist leaders, and do assure them of our support in opposing all traitors who seek to dismember the United Kingdom.[64]

Though not claimed explicitly in the Covenant, one can almost sense in the text the fear that once a devolved parliament had been conceded there would be demands for further powers to be transferred to the Dublin parliament. This is not mere supposition. Opponents of Home Rule made this argument at the time. Milne Barbour, as we have seen in chapter three, articulated precisely this fear before the Commission on Financial Relations between Britain and Ireland in 1911. Later experiments with devolved assemblies as an antidote to secessionist nationalisms in Quebec, Scotland and Catalonia, point in that direction, though it is also important to note that these tendencies unfolded slowly in time and have so far failed to result in full independence.[65] Fear of radical change, not just in the short term but over a longer time period also helps explain the otherwise curious notion that Home Rule would lead to the disintegration of the British Empire. All of these apprehensions required and merited a creative response, not just from Irish nationalists but from the government of the day. They also required an intelligent Ulster unionist strategy, of which the Covenant campaign might have been one hymn in the repertoire.

What about the Women?

The text we have been considering is gender specific. It is for the Men of Ulster and they are presumed to be the prime movers in the political movement. The paramilitary-style trappings attending the lead-up to Ulster Day signalled the importance within Ulster unionist culture of the values of manliness, militarism, valour and self-discipline in the face of yet unrevealed danger. One woman rights' campaigner complained at the time that it was 'a man's show entirely'.[66] But hard men had been active off-stage as well: intimidatory Protestant gangs armed with hammers and cudgels had already driven huge numbers of Catholic workers from their places of work during the July disturbances a few months before Ulster Day. This did not form part of the stage-managed presentation of Ulster resistance to Home Rule. Only selected images, chief among them the towering figure of Edward Carson, were favoured in projecting the cause and the man (and the men).

Then there were the women. A variant of the Covenant labelled the Declaration was signed by women only.[67] This indicates the gendered nature of the unionist movement in its campaign against Home Rule. Remarkably almost as many women (234,046) as men (237,368) signed up, though perhaps the really impressive point is that almost a half million people signed in total, out of a Protestant population of all ages of 891,000.[68] This must make it one of the most remarkable and comprehensive ethnic mobilisations of its age.

It is usually assumed that the Declaration was simply the product of the same male hand that penned the Covenant. This is unlikely to be true as the tone of the two documents is different, thus suggesting that there was a significant female input. We know the text was submitted to and discussed by the Ulster Women's Unionist Council (UWUC). According to the minutes of the executive of the UWUC (17 September 1912), the executive adopted unanimously the wording supplied to it by its 'Advisory Committee' which had examined the text.[69] While the first draft probably originated with Thomas Sinclair – the Covenant after all was a male initiative – the likelihood is that the Advisory Committee made changes. Indeed it is difficult to believe that the imperious Theresa, Lady Londonderry, did not have some involvement and of course Sinclair's wife was also a member of the UWUC executive. That said, it is worth recalling the hierarchical power structure of the unionist community that conceived and delivered the Covenant. These were all-male councils, women were obliged to sign a separate document and not the Covenant *per se*, and they had to lobby initially to be granted this concession.

The fact that women did muscle in on the act tells us something about the growing confidence and assertiveness of women in Ulster, and particularly within the unionist community, in those days of crisis.

The Declaration: Main Text

> *We, whose names are underwritten, women of Ulster, and loyal subjects of our gracious King, being firmly persuaded that Home Rule would be disastrous to our country, desire to associate ourselves with the men of Ulster in their uncompromising opposition to the Home Rule Bill now before Parliament, whereby it is proposed to drive Ulster out of her cherished place in the Constitution of the United Kingdom, and to place her under the domination and control of a Parliament in Ireland. Praying that from this calamity God will save Ireland, we here to subscribe our names.* [70]

The thrust of the Declaration was similar to that of the Covenant, though its formulation is more concise, there being only two sentences in the whole text, with the first carrying the burden of the case. As it was for the men, it is presumed by these 'Women of Ulster' that Home Rule would be 'disastrous to our Country'.[71] The word 'country' in the opening sentence has an ambiguous flavour, the referent could be 'Ulster' or the United Kingdom (both terms are present in the text) or indeed Ireland. There is a predictable profession of loyalty to 'our gracious King', and an expression of concern that Ulster will be driven out of its place in the Constitution of the United Kingdom to be forced under the 'domination and control of a Parliament in Ireland'.

The most revealing passage, from a feminist perspective, refers to the 'desire to associate ourselves with the men of Ulster in their uncompromising opposition to the Home Rule bill now before Parliament'. The principal agents of resistance are to be the men, and, in line with traditional notions of propriety and gender roles, the women are accorded, indeed self-accorded the place of assistants and supporters. An alternative reading – this passage is not easily de-coded – is that a 'desire to associate' suggests a degree of female assertiveness that goes beyond a willingness to assist. That Belfast was the leading centre within Ireland for the agitation for female suffrage, as it was also for trade union organisation, might support this more active interpretation.

Too much might be made of the existence of two versions of the Covenant, each gender specific. It hardly needs saying, Edwardian times were different. Women did not, as yet, have the parliamentary franchise, though the issue was fiercely debated on the edges of the Liberal, Conservative and Irish Parliamentary parties. James Craig, second-in-command to Edward Carson, was in favour of women's suffrage, though Carson himself was not.[72] So, in terms of involving women of all social classes in the public sphere, the promotion of the Declaration marked a radically new phase in the mass participation of women in constitutional politics. There is nothing comparable in Irish or British politics, and perhaps not on the European mainland either.[73] Some of this new-found confidence and self-assertion found its way into women's contribution in the Great War shortly afterwards.[74]

The concluding sentence has a resonant tone and is a cross-over piece of political rhetoric: 'Praying that from this calamity God will save Ireland, we here to subscribe our names.' The anthem of nationalist Ireland, it may be recalled, was A.M. Sullivan's 'God save Ireland', composed back in the late 1860s in the aftermath of the hanging of the 'Manchester Martyrs' – a piece of unconscious *homage* perhaps. More importantly, it is an act of appropriation or re-appropriation. The welfare of Ireland is not the sole prerogative of Irish nationalists; the 'Women of Ulster' have their own conception of the many Irelands of the imagination, and it is one that sees all of Ireland located securely within the framework of the United Kingdom. That they were unionist to a man did not stand in the way of giving voice to Irish patriotic sentiments in the female register.

Venus or Mars?

There is less inflated rhetoric, less tendentious comment in the women's Declaration as compared to its twin, than for men, and it is more modest in length. Bellicose phrases are absent: on the surface at least, it is a document from Venus rather than Mars. The use of the verb 'praying' – to God rather than to man – suggests a less aggressive approach to the impending crisis than is to be found in the men's Covenant. Women are self-acknowledged as a force auxiliary to that of the men in the Declaration, but this conventional piece of rhetoric does not necessarily denote a passive or supplicant role in the great cause of Ulster and Britishness. The political and constitutional objective is the same and the womenfolk are in step with the martial tramp of the menfolk. Without the enthusiastic and organised support of the women, both in the private and the public spheres, it is well-nigh impossible to see how such a huge ethnic mobilisation could have been produced. In 1913 it was estimated, though probably with some exaggeration, that the UWUC had more than a hundred thousand members (104,301).[75] Much of the influence must have been exerted at family, street and townland level but that is where organisational and motivational forces were at their most potent. Through the UWUC and associated organisations, women were inspirational in turning out the masses of women, men, girls and boys right across the province on Ulster Day. Women were agents not passive participants in the whole enterprise.

But...

Returning to the high politics of the period, some argued passionately for simple-minded solutions, that is, either a devolved parliament for all-Ireland as advocated by John Redmond and the Irish nationalists or a continuation of the United Kingdom framework as it had stood for more than a hundred years (the first preference of most unionists). A tiny minority favoured an all-Ireland republic – an aspiration bound to be productive of ethnic and communal terror – but that is another story. A political settlement, composed of grand compromises on either side, was the most that could have been achieved in 1912–14 (though one suspects that Irish nationalism and Ulster unionism would have continued to evolve in not wholly-predictable ways). A pacific reading or re-writing of the Ulster Covenant on the part of Ulster unionists and its use as a barometer of mass democratic feeling might have helped take unionists to another place (including possibly a peaceful campaign of civil disobedience and continuing political persuasion). In 1913, however, Ulster unionists took the worst possible direction when alternatives were still available. The North began... as the nationalist scholar and Ulsterman, Eoin MacNeill, was quick to point out once the Ulster Volunteer Force was presented to the public.[76] He was right.

The Covenant spoke deeply to the hearts and minds of Ulster unionists. Unionists certainly had solid grounds for objecting to Home Rule. There was, however, an Ireland beyond Ulster, beyond the Ulster unionist community, which was giving voice to very different aspirations. The great silence or mute scream in the text is this: what of the nationalist Irish? What is not acknowledged, in either the Covenant or the Declaration, is the elephantine fact that three-quarters of the electorate thought Home Rule was good for Ireland and its peoples, and had been saying so for quite a long time. This was the crucial unacknowledged fact from Orange and Unionist platforms in the run-up to Ulster Day, and the dark days that lay ahead.

CHAPTER SEVEN

Bad Blood: the Proclamation of the Irish Republic

Unhappy the land that is in need of heroes.

Bertolt Brecht[1]

Introduction

Less than four years separate the publication of two of the iconic texts of modern Irish history, the Ulster Covenant and the Proclamation of the Irish Republic. Those were momentous years and by Easter 1916 the world had changed. A possible civil war between North and South, between the newly-formed Ulster Volunteer Force (UVF) and the copy-cat Irish Volunteers had been averted as martial energies were re-directed towards the European conflagration that was the First World War. But fissures within Irish nationalism were about to produce some unanticipated outcomes. On Easter Monday, groups of lightly-armed volunteers took over buildings in the centre of Dublin and the first serious uprising since the union of Britain and Ireland in 1801 was underway. In form it bore a resemblance to nineteenth-century risings in Europe, particularly those of the 1840s, in which street barricades and armed civilians were to the fore.

One of the set pieces of this theatre of the streets was the reading of the Proclamation of the Irish Republic in front of the General Post Office (GPO) by the schoolmaster, poet and conspirator, Patrick Pearse. The GPO was located on the main thoroughfare, Sackville Street (later re-named O'Connell Street), not far from the landmark Nelson's Pillar. Passers-by listened with varying degrees of bemusement and indifference. A short time earlier Mary Brigid, Pearse's sister, had arrived at the nearby Liberty Hall, as the headquarters' contingent of volunteers was about to set off. 'Come home, Pat, and leave all this foolishness', was her sisterly advice, no doubt to the considerable embarrassment of her brother.[2] These were the inauspicious beginnings to the enterprise.

Though Mary Brigid did not yet realise it, and may well have gone home for tea, the document Pearse unveiled was to assume greater significance as time went by, eventually achieving the status of a national heirloom as copies of the text found its way onto the walls of schools and homes all over Ireland and among the Irish diaspora.[3]

The Signatories

As good a starting point as any in breaking open the text is to start at the end, that is, with the signatories to the 1916 Proclamation. The numbers were small indeed, as befits a revolutionary conspiracy. Seven men and no women had their names on the document. The first signature belonged to Tom Clarke, and there is some dispute as to why this was so since Patrick Henry Pearse had been designated the president and commander-in-chief of the Republic. Clarke represented an older generation of Fenians, and more specifically the faction that believed in the benefits of a dynamite campaign to terrorise the English and Scottish public in the 1880s.[4] Perhaps these considerations entitled him to a place of honour. Two symmetrical columns of names appear beneath Clarke's, in no apparent order of precedence. Later on the matter of precedence was to assume some significance, with the widowed Mrs Tom Clarke clashing with Mrs Pearse on 'who owned 1916' (as some put it).[5] Included in the seven was the socialist and trade union organiser, James Connolly, who played a significant role as a military leader in the rising. The others, less well-known now and little known then, were Sean MacDiarmada, Thomas MacDonagh, Eamonn Ceannt and Joseph Plunkett.

The document is usually referred to as the *Proclamation of the Republic*, or more loosely as the *1916 Proclamation* or the *Easter Proclamation* or the *Proclamation of Easter Week*. There are other minor variants. The use of the definite article in the original text implies that this is not any old republic: this one has been in the making for some time. The Fenian oath drafted in the previous century spoke of 'the Irish Republic, now virtually established'.[6] So the virtual Republic, long whispered about by Fenians in backrooms and public houses, was now fully incarnated as the Republic.

Proclamations and Declarations

In a sense, the choice of the term 'proclamation' for the document is curious, being associated with established authority, particularly that of Britain and various royal proclamations down the centuries. Possibly it's an unwitting acknowledgement of the extent to which British and Irish political vocabularies had become intertwined. Taking a comparative historical view a 'declaration' might have seemed more appropriate in view of the precedents established by the American and French revolutions, both of which had strong reverberations in Ireland. The Americans opted for a 'Declaration of Independence', which was adopted by Congress in 1776. The French Assembly in 1789, at the outset of the revolution, promulgated its 'Declaration of the Rights of Man'.

Rhyming with history was not perhaps the most urgent need. A proclamation is usually the expression of a lawful authority – a monarch or parliament – and this term helped confer a sense of legitimacy on a gaggle of revolutionaries who were largely unknown to the Irish peoples and of whom only one among the leaders had subjected himself to the test of public opinion. This was James Connolly who was unsuccessful in various electoral contests.[7]

The principal architect of the Proclamation was Patrick Pearse, while James Connolly and Thomas MacDonagh added suggestions.[8] Almost certainly the main reason the term proclamation was chosen was because there are textual echoes here of the 'Proclamation of Independence' by Robert Emmet, prepared before the latter's abortive rising in 1803. The aim of Emmet and the remnants of the United Irishmen was 'a free and independent republic in Ireland'.[9] Emmet's manifesto was issued by a so-called Provisional Government and addressed to the People of Ireland, which is a form of words replicated in the headings of the 1916 Proclamation.

Then there is the question of the language in which the Proclamation was written. Some might find it surprising, if not actually ironic, that the Proclamation was penned in English, and not *as Gaeilge* to which Patrick Pearse and others were so deeply committed. Only two of the signatories attached their names in Irish and Pearse was simply P.H. Pearse. An Irish-speaking Ireland might be the vision but the reality was that the practice of republican and nationalist politics had always been through the medium of English.

In bold typeface across the top of the document, in what is a token nod towards language sensibilities, may be read 'Poblacht na H Eireann' (underlined in the original). In other words, the Republic of Ireland. This technique of the *cúpla focal* would find widespread usage in the independent Ireland of a few years later. There follows, also in capitals and across four lines, the legend: 'The Provisional Government of the Republic of Ireland to the People of Ireland'. The new source of authority after a successful war, we are led to believe, is the Provisional Government whose membership is not revealed.[10]

It is a formula borrowed from coup-makers from many places. The largest typeface is reserved for the words the 'Irish Republic'. Seemingly appropriately, the 'People of Ireland' is in smaller typeface, as befits their place within the melange of conspiracy, fantasy and make-believe that attached to the idea of a 'Provisional Government'.

The Proclamation of the Irish Republic: The Main Text

Irishmen and Irishwomen. In the name of God and of the dead generations from which she receives her old tradition of nationhood, Ireland, through us, summons her children to her flag and strikes for her freedom.

Having organized and trained her manhood through her secret revolutionary organization, the Irish Republican Brotherhood, and through her open military organizations, the Irish Volunteers and the Irish Citizen Army, having patiently perfected her discipline, having resolutely waited for the right moment to reveal itself, she now seizes that moment, and, supported by her exiled children in America and by gallant allies in Europe, but relying in the first on her own strength, she strikes in full confidence of victory.

We declare the right of the people of Ireland to the ownership of Ireland, and to the unfettered control of Irish destinies, to be sovereign and indefeasible. The long usurpation of that right by a foreign people and government has not extinguished the right, nor can it ever be extinguished except by the destruction of the Irish people. In every generation the Irish people have asserted their right to national freedom and sovereignty, six times in the past three hundred years they have asserted it in arms. Standing on that fundamental right and again asserting it in arms in the face of the world, we hereby proclaim the Irish Republic as a Sovereign Independent State, and we pledge our lives and the lives of our comrades-in-arms to the cause of its freedom, of its welfare, and of its exaltation among the nations.

The Irish Republic is entitled to, and hereby claims, the allegiance of every Irishman and Irishwoman. The Republic guarantees religious and civil liberty, equal rights and equal opportunities of all its citizens, and declares its resolve to pursue the happiness and prosperity of the whole nation and of all its parts, cherishing all the children of the nation equally, and oblivious of the differences carefully fostered by an alien government, which have divided a minority from the majority in the past.

Until our arms have brought the opportune moment for the establishment of a permanent National Government, representative of the whole people of Ireland and elected by the suffrages of all her men and women, the Provisional Government, hereby constituted, will administer the civil and military affairs of the Republic in trust for the people.

We place the cause of the Irish Republic under the protection of the Most High God, Whose blessing we invoke upon our arms, and we pray that no one who serves that cause will dishonour it by cowardice, inhumanity, or rapine. In this supreme hour the

Irish nation must, by its valour and discipline and by the readiness of its children to sacrifice themselves for the common good, prove itself worthy of the august destiny to which it is called.

Source: Marie Coleman, *The Irish Revolution, 1916–1923* (London, 2014), pp. 125–26.

In the Beginning

The Proclamation opens dramatically in vocative mode with the words 'Irishmen and Irishwomen'. The call of the Republic was directed not just at men, as was conventional but at the women of Ireland as well. This was a welcome departure, at least at the level of rhetoric, from phallocentric notions of Irish nationalism, but this form of address was used at some public meetings in the period, so it is perhaps not so exceptional.[11] The inclusion of women among those addressed may well be due to the influence of Connolly, a convinced suffragist but Pearse also favoured giving the vote to women. This was all the more commendable as Pearse was peculiarly uneasy in the company of women, an unease that must have been connected to his own conflicted sexuality.[12]

'In the name of God and the dead generations…' God gets pride of place, which is only fitting, and hopefully He remained unembarrassed by conflicting demands on divine time. Clergy of the Church of Ireland, the Presbyterian and the Methodist churches had already been in touch with the heavens, as we saw with the signing of the Ulster Covenant. The dead generations, renowned for their political sagacity, are invoked next and could always be counted on, though not necessarily in their lifetimes.[13] In a tight corner, such as that into which the insurrectionists had boxed themselves, sourcing authority from beyond the grave was no bad move.

When was the Nation?

The next piece of text is rich in meaning and connects with modern debates about nationalism: '… from which she receives her old tradition of nationhood'. This and later phrases in the document suggest a primordialist, one might say an ever-green view of nationalism: that the nation is of remote origin and naturally occurring, that it is bound up with lineage and descent groups ('children of the nation'), and that it is immutable (there is an essence, a kind of DNA, that remains unchanged down the generations while allowing circumstances and secondary manifestations of nationalism to change). Few scholars accept such an ahistorical conceptualisation of nationalism nowadays, though it has been a foundational assumption of ultra-nationalists, and not just in Ireland.[14] A school of thought that is the polar opposite in most respects – the *modernist* school of theorists, most notably Gellner and Kedourie – sees nationalism as of recent vintage and largely or exclusively associated with modernity.[15] Kedourie pronounces boldly: 'Nationalism is a doctrine invented in Europe at the beginning of the nineteenth century.'[16] In these Eurocentric accounts, nationalism typically emerges at the time of the French Revolution or later. In the case of Italy and Germany it does not flower until the later nineteenth century, and later still in many lands outside Europe and North America.[17] Thus nationalism is a modern creation, with its emphasis on self-determination (communal determination), and a notion of sovereignty which derives from the desires of the mass of the people rather than a monarch, dictator or oligarchy. Depending on circumstances, a drive for popular rule and independence, posited on a sense of belonging within a larger, imagined community, are the hallmarks of this historically new phenomenon. While the primordial and its close relation the perennialist perspective fail to capture the variation through time in flows of people into Ireland and the multiple divisions within and between lordships and other territorial units, it can also be shown that the modernist model hardly does justice to the Irish case where the consistency of demands for some form of 'Irish freedom' across several centuries stands out.[18]

The ethno-symbolic approach promoted by A.D. Smith, more realistically (many historians would argue), stresses the continuities between pre-modern and modern forms of collective identity and places emphasis on the storehouse of myths, memories, traditions and symbols that can be utilised in the formation of ethnic and national identities.[19] It is fair to say that Pearse and MacDonagh, abstracting for a moment from the essentialist core to their thinking on nationalism, would feel more at home with this perspective on the national past. After all, they proved remarkably adept at exploiting traditions and symbols, including the symbology of the Catholic religion, for revolutionary ends. Perhaps the most useful theoretical sketch of nationalism, and its many-sided attractions, comes from the work of Richard English.[20] English is sympathetic to the ethno-symbolic approach but would also underline material as well as symbolic aspects of the historical past (as would historians of a materialist bent) and he speaks of a proto-national sense of shared identity, tradition and territory. In the misty pre-history of nationalism a proto-nation may be discerned, though not possessed of all the properties of a modern nation. In relation to Ireland English argues:

> In the end, then, Irish nationalism has been a modern phenomenon. But it has possessed historically embedded, constricting and defining roots, which go back into the pre-modern period of an Irish proto-nation. As noted, there has now emerged a broad consensus among most scholars studying nationalism that the phenomenon represents something which is comparatively recent in

human history. But this need not rule out the importance of what we have here called the proto-nation, a pre-modern phenomenon which has influenced and helped to shape later Irish nationalism.[21]

Applying this perspective to the Proclamation, a generous reading might be that the history embedded in the text is anachronistic and wrong-headed in places, yet there are shadows, shapes and structures that are recognisable, including, of course, the vital political and power relationships binding the two islands. Thus the men of 1916 are right to speak of tradition and nationhood in the one breath. That there is a historic depth to Irish nationalism is undeniable. Many of the building materials for modern nationalism – from a distinctive language and religion to a sense of history and economic conflict – had accumulated down the centuries and were not capable of being set aside capriciously or fabricated in almost arbitrary fashion by an intellectual elite engaged in self-interested nation building. Of the regions of the United Kingdom and of the white populations of the British Empire, the majority denomination in Ireland was unusual and hence inevitably alienated by virtue of being Catholic and not being Protestant. Additionally, it bears restating that the expressions of nationalist sentiment in the nineteenth century were a different kettle of fish to earlier precedents and forms of political consciousness. Continuities with the past notwithstanding and measured from the temporal vantage point of Easter 1916, Irish nationalism was of relatively recent origin.

None of this is to say that a republican outcome was highly probable, still less inevitable – royalism, after all, was deeply-embedded in the Irish psyche – but it is to say that a collective identity emerged in the nineteenth century that sought political expression in the form of an Irish legislative assembly, that it held shared traditions and symbols in common, and that there was an evolving national consciousness. If anything, national longings at the popular level were taking on a more radical hue as the new century dawned. These were dreams and emotions which a devolved parliament would only partly have satisfied.[22] All this bore a family resemblance to burgeoning nationalisms elsewhere in Europe in that century of rising literacy, increased mobility and easier communication when the mass of people was finding some voice in the political arena.

Mother Ireland

In the name of the dead generations, 'Ireland, through us, summons her children to her flag and strikes for her freedom.' After a rambling introduction, this is cutting to the chase. It begs the question, though: who is she? Feminist historians and cultural critics have spilled much ink on that anthropomorphic invention, Mother Ireland.[23] Suffice it to say that the personification of the nation is simply a product of the romantic nationalist imagination (though not of the Irish unionist one), which rather like God, may be invoked to suit the circumstances.[24] Allusions to the mother reach deep into the psychology of the individual and have enormous potential in terms of manipulating the emotions. Those gathered round Mother Ireland's petticoats are mere 'children', presumably endowed with little intelligence or agency but possessed of the human instinct to defend the mother figure.[25] This is a Pearsian moment: in his writings Pearse tended to celebrate women as mothers and bearers of masculine heroes for Ireland rather than as comrades-in-arms.

It may be noticed, *en passant*, that the flag of the Rising seems to have been a green flag with a gold harp emblazoned on it.[26] A variety of flags flew from occupied public buildings during post-Easter Week, as it might be more accurately termed. The more pluralist green-white-orange tricolour was flown at some locations but was not recognised as the national flag (of nationalist Ireland) until after the Rising. The Starry Plough, the emblem of Irish Labour, flew from the Imperial Hotel in Sackville Street.[27] The presence of the different flags suggests the contradictions at the heart of the enterprise. In reality though, the revolutionaries had wrapped themselves in green in what was a largely Dublin-based Catholic and nationalist conspiracy, though not of course representative of the Catholics or nationalists of the capital city, still less of Ireland. Dublin still had some working-class Protestants but the conspiracy did not embrace this segment of the working class. The Dublin-born playwright, John Casey or Sean O'Casey (1880–1964), who was of Protestant working-class origins, had been a leading member of the Irish Citizen Army (ICA) but had fallen out through disagreement before the Rising. His nationalist and socialist sympathies, in any case, were untypical of his co-religionists, as were those of the handful of other Protestants who had joined the ICA.[28]

'Freedom's just another word …' Or is it?

One might wonder about the kind of 'freedom' being claimed as well as the question of freedom for whom. For the tens of thousands of Irish nationalists fighting in France and Belgium as part of the armies of the United Kingdom, in addition to their far more numerous supporters at home, their constitutional aspiration was freedom for Ireland in the form of Home Rule. Even among the small numbers of insurrectionists, some did not know they were going out to fight for an Irish republic.[29] For the hundreds of thousands of Irish unionists, North and South, Home Rule, never mind an Irish Republic, was deeply objectionable.

The second paragraph, which is also a single sentence composed of many sub clauses, introduces the principal organisations involved in the uprising, mentions the preparations and the timing involved, and concludes on a note of expected triumph. The three organisations identified were the Irish Republican Brotherhood (IRB) – rightly accorded the premier position because of its role in planning and organising the rising – the Irish Volunteers and the Irish Citizen Army (ICA). These were all-male organisations, with the partial exception of the tiny ICA.[30] Cumann na mBan or Iníona na hÉireann do not even merit a mention.[31] Lest there be any lingering belief that the Proclamation somehow bears a feminist imprint, the recourse to the term 'manhood' should dispel such illusions. Women volunteers constituted a small minority of the total turnout, and a minority of these were engaged in military action.[32] Some commanders such as Eamon de Valera actually refused to have women with his men in the fighting. The role of women during the Rising was largely confined to ferrying messages, nursing the wounded, and carrying the white flag of surrender. In other words, these were subordinate roles consistent with traditional notions of the role of women in warfare and peacetime.

The claim that Mother Ireland had 'perfected her discipline' is questionable, in view of the cold-blooded killing of an unarmed Dublin Metropolitan policeman, Constable Michael Lahiff, on duty at the gates of St Stephen's Green at the very outset of the rising. Lahiff was 28 years old, a Catholic from the west of Ireland, spoke Irish, and like most Catholics in the force was probably a nationalist in politics.[33] His execution was part of the less than 'casual comedy' of 1916, a phrase found in W.B. Yeats' poem of celebration and critique, 'Easter 1916'.[34] Constance Markievicz (neé Gore-Booth), who styled herself a countess as well as a republican, was the probable executioner, being one of a small number of women who used arms in the Rising.[35] De Paor seems to suggest as much in speaking of Constance Markievicz whom he sees as 'eager to bag her man early, like a novice proving himself on a grouse shoot'.[36] Other less than glorious episodes of Easter week include the shooting of Dublin workers who refused to hand over their carts and the firing upon rioters, including children, from the slums of Dublin who seized a rare opportunity in life to lighten their misery.

All in all, the combatants came off lightly. Some 2,600 people were wounded, and another 450 or so were killed in the Rising. Civilians suffered the most, accounting for more than half the fatalities. Losses by British forces made up under a third of the total and volunteer losses were on a still lower plane. Less than one-fifth of the total numbers killed were insurgents, and this includes those shot accidentally by other inexperienced comrades and also those executed after the Rising.[37] Roughly speaking, for every volunteer killed, three civilians were slain in the week-long fighting. McGarry identifies the key issue:

Whatever the circumstances, much of the moral responsibility for the civilian deaths must be attributed to the [IRB] military council's decision to base the insurrection in the densely populated inner city, a decision which conflicted with their perception of themselves as a conventional military force fighting by conventional means.[38]

Mother Ireland, or rather the phantasmagoric figure that was Mother Ireland (neé Eire, Banba, Cathleen Ni Houlihan, Dark Rosaleen, Shan Van Vocht, and so on) was also in the business of seizing the time ('having resolutely waited for the right moment to reveal itself, she now seizes that moment').[39] There is more to this than meets the eye. The minuscule IRB had long dreamed of a rising, subject to certain conditions, though it is worth emphasising the more numerous Irish Volunteers had no such ambition. After such a wait, for Pearse and his co-conspirators this had to be the right moment to strike. That England's difficulty was Ireland's opportunity was an article of faith among the brothers of the IRB. With Britain hard-pressed in an all-consuming European war, when would there be a more opportune time? Moreover, there were the pressures arising from a male sense of identity: if the opportunity was not seized, the brotherhood might well be accused of the weakness, even of the cowardice with which it dismissed the older generation of Irish nationalist politicians. In Tom Clarke's words, 'if they did not strike during the war, they were damned for posterity'.[40] In a sense, the IRB leaders were trapped in the rhetoric of their own militarism, which was reinforced by the spirit of militarism and male braggadocio that was sweeping Europe. The view of England's difficulty prevailed, and indeed made some military sense, while ignoring some awkward political realities.

For a start, it was not 'England' that was at war but the United Kingdom of Great Britain and Ireland. Even within Ireland a majority of nationalists favoured participation in the war, seeing it as the route to ensuring Home Rule for Ireland. Virtually all unionists in Ireland were in favour. In all, more than 200,000 Irishmen served in the British armed forces (fewer than 2,000 served in the Easter Week insurrection).[41] The tragedy of the peoples of Europe, of all social classes and varied ethnicities – Russians, Germans, French, Italians, Belgians, Serbians, Irish, British – caught up in a brutal, prolonged and fruitless conflict between their social elites may represent the perspective of later generations but was not that of most contemporaries. Pearse himself, even after sixteen months of appalling death and suffering in Europe, could still voice the sentiment that these were among the 'most glorious in the history of Europe'.[42] Moreover, when war came to Ireland, 'she must welcome it as she would welcome the Angel of God'.[43]

Secondly, there was the question of whether Irish and Ulster unionists, Irish born and bred, were among Ireland's 'children'. A similar question attaches to the small but unquantifiable numbers of Catholic unionists. Could more than a quarter of the population of the island be wished away, politically speaking? Would not a rising in time of war be seen as a stab in the back by this already disaffiliating section of the national household? Whatever chances there might have been of cobbling together a historic compromise between Irish nationalism and Ulster unionism before 1916 – and the Irish Parliamentary Party, the Liberal government and the Ulster unionists were already well down the partition pathway by the summer of 1914 – the rising put paid to any such prospects. In raising a green flag over the GPO, in shooting Irish policemen and British soldiers on the streets of Dublin, in aiding the German war effort, the men of 1916 struck a blow, as powerful as it was unintended, for partition. In that these deeds are consistent with the text of the Proclamation, we are, in effect, reading one of the foundational documents for the partition of Ireland.

Where were the People?

There is at least one other major problem. Clause 3 in the IRB's revised constitution of 1873 insisted that there had to be widespread support for any decision to go to war. 'The IRB shall await the decision of the Irish Nation as expressed by a majority of the Irish people as to the fit hour of inaugurating a war against England …'.[44] No such consensus existed in 1916, so it was necessary to dupe the supreme council of the IRB and also the leadership of the Irish Volunteers, a simultaneous coup which the leaders of the rising managed to pull off. Pearse, in particular, proved adept not only at dying for Ireland – *his* Ireland – but at lying for it as well.[45]

The leaders of the rising looked first and foremost to their own strength in securing victory, or so they said. Some volunteers during the Rising believed a landing of 50,000 German troops was imminent. In any case, there was a deep history of over-reliance on fickle foreign allies, be it the Spanish, the French, or Papal forces. These had proved disappointing, over and over again, a popular impression captured in the Cyclops episode of Joyce's *Ulysses*. The ranting 'patriot', named anonymously as the Citizen, dismissed the French as not having been worth a 'roasted fart' to Ireland in the past. Still, the rebels also drew support from their 'exiled children in America' and their 'gallant allies in Europe'. The exile motif is a time-honoured, self-pitying pretence as, in fact, most Irish people in the United States (and Canada, and England and Scotland and Wales) were economic migrants seeking a better life abroad and not exiles who had been banished from their native places.[46] The infantilising reference to these migrants as children is a further departure from reality.

Gallant Allies, No Less

But it is the glorification of Germany and its allies – a part of the text that is usually conveniently ignored – that sits like Yeats' stone in the romantic flow.[47] It is all the more curious from a socialist perspective in that Liberty Hall, the centre of organised labour in Dublin and the starting point for the Rising, had earlier proudly proclaimed that it served 'neither King nor Kaiser'.[48] Volte-face, right turn. That these 'gallant allies' had committed a series of atrocities in their occupation of Belgium or that the Balkans and Anatolia were theatres for civilian massacre seems not to have unduly disturbed the authors of the Proclamation. While highlighted for war propaganda purposes by the allies, there is no doubt about the savagery of German repression against civilians, right at the beginning of the war. To take but one of many examples from Belgium, on the 5 August 1914, German troops attacking Liege were forced into temporary retreat and fell back towards the village of Soumagne. They then vented their rage and humiliation on the unarmed villagers.

> They placed the inhabitants under armed guard in the church. Male victims were selected and shot in a field in front of women and children. The execution squad bayoneted the bodies to ensure that no one survived… Three hundred to 400 survivors were used as a 'human shield' by the Germans as they entered Liege on 7th August.[49]

Doubtless few dwelt then or later on the likelihood that if the armies of the German Empire had had to deal with the equivalent of the 1916 Rising in its own backyard, the post-Rising killings would have run into the hundreds or thousands rather than the sixteen actually executed. German soldiers and their officers seem to have had a pathological fear of armed civilian resistance and dealt savagely with real, anticipated or imagined examples of it.[50] By contrast, the inventory of state repression in Dublin belongs to another order, some scattered acts of unlawful killing notwithstanding. Many of the women and youths picked up after the Rising were treated as silly or misled by others and simply sent home. Alleged leaders had their death sentences reduced to lesser punishments. Most of those believed to have been involved in the hostilities were released the following year. The Prussian military elite would have been astonished and appalled at such leniency.

Still sixteen bodies were sufficient to divert the course of Irish nationalist history, while reinforcing at the same time the cause of Ulster unionist separatism. In a fatal policy error, the handling of the aftermath of the Rising was entrusted to the British military, as the civil administration headed by Augustine Birrell, the Chief Secretary, had been discredited by the outbreak of civil disorder on his watch.[51] Some leading politicians in Britain and Ireland felt the execution of less than a score of the combatants only compounded the Irish problem, even though the most popular nationalist newspaper, the *Irish Independent*, situated in the heart of Dublin, had stated unequivocally that the leaders of the Rising 'deserve little consideration or compassion'.[52]

The final clause of the paragraph is duplicitous. There was no expectation of military victory on the part of the two main draughtsmen of the manifesto, Pearse and Connolly, as it went to press. Some of the rank and file didn't even know the purpose of the mobilisation on Easter Monday. According to De Paor, the general terms of the Proclamation were agreed by January 1916 at the latest.[53] So, in part mitigation, one might say that the possibility of success was stronger at the time of the drafting of the document, that is, before the large arms shipment from Germany, on board the *Aud*, was intercepted by the British navy on Easter Saturday. The following day, Easter Sunday (23 April 1916), the final draft of the Proclamation was agreed. By then, hope of a successful rising had all but evaporated. Pearse, like two others of his fellow signatories, Joseph Mary Plunkett and Thomas MacDonagh, believed in the redemptive power of blood sacrifice, so on Easter Monday everything was on course for the fulfilment of their personal drama. Connolly, on the same morning, had told a fellow trade unionist that they were 'going out to be slaughtered'.[54] Full confidence of victory was 'both fantasy and propaganda', to use De Paor's words.[55] As with their khaki equivalents, Irish volunteers had become cannon fodder for the morbid ambition and vanity of their superior officers.

The third paragraph is, in large part, an assertion of historical rights and a statement about the sovereignty of the people. It begins on a socially progressive note, declaring the 'right of the people of Ireland to the ownership of Ireland'. This is very likely an insertion by Connolly or a joint product of Pearse and Connolly's thinking on social questions, which was converging in the months before the rising. What it means is more open to question. Workers could take solace in this claim, with its hint of nationalisation, but so also could all strong farmers in Ireland provided they were undisturbed in the possession of their property. The great majority of Irish farmers already owned their land, as a result of British government reforms of the late nineteenth and early twentieth centuries, and Irish farmers (no more than other property holders) had not the slightest intention of conceding any of their hard-won gains to landless labourers or to the state, British, Irish or whatever. The eventual reality in an independent Ireland confirms this. Another reading is that of Anglophobic concerns about foreign ownership of Irish resources, as later reflected in the Control of Manufactures Acts of the 1930s which made a distinction between Irish capitalists and foreign capitalists, without of course challenging the former or the system they inhabited.[56] Existing property rights, structured according to principles of private enterprise capitalism, remained firmly in place.[57] The writing of the Irish Constitution of 1937, as overseen by the Fianna Fáil leader, Eamon de Valera, also affirmed private property as the basis of the Irish social system, in accordance with the wishes of vested interests and, it has to be said, the great majority of the people of the Irish Free State.[58]

The word 'people' is also open to interrogation. It occurs six times in the text; only mentions of 'Irish' exceed this number of citations. Theorists of nationalism have written of the imagined community of the nation.[59] In ultra-nationalistic writing, as here, the people are doubly imagined. There is the aggregate of real persons who, in a demographic sense, add up to the population of the nation. But most are not known to each other, yet they share common values, identities and aspirations with which most members of the imagined national community can identify. But there is a more abstract or idealised notion of the people, approximating to a Platonic form, in which 'the people', rather like 'the working class' in some Marxist discourses, are invested with special or unique qualities by the propagandist. This imagined people has no counterpart in real life. What these honorifics or marks of approbation might consist of varies with the context: they might include proficiency in the preferred language (Gaelic, Serbian, Basque), love of 'native' sports, qualities of martial valour, heroic feats, attitudes of anti-Semitism or anti-materialism, xenophobia, religious orthodoxy, or any and other zealot-approved traits.

The Joyful Mysteries of Rebellion

The claim to sovereignty is rooted in history and asserted in arms, according to the Proclamation. The rosary beads of rebellion – 1641, 1798, 1803, 1848, 1867, 1916 – gives a simplified anatomy of Irish political history, with a teleological thrust that sees the Easter Rising as the inevitable outcome of centuries of resistance.[60] In none of these instances can it be truly said that the 'Irish people' were asserting national rights and the degree of participation and sympathy for these risings varied across space and time. The valorisation of taking up arms – almost as if it was an end in itself – is given emphasis through repetition. The sense of continuity is also questionable: the Fenian brotherhood bore little relationship to the United Irishmen of the 1790s, not least in the sense that only one ethnic category was now involved. The Fenians were almost exclusively Catholic and nationalist, whereas the United Irishmen had brought together, albeit sometimes in uneasy alliance, Presbyterians and Catholics, and even some Anglicans. The strangest inclusion, however, is the 1641 rising, given that it was ostensibly in support of the autocratic Stuart monarchy and that it inaugurated a sectarian bloodbath in Ulster.[61] This was a less than reassuring historical precedent for a movement that might seek a republic composed of northerners and southerners, of Catholics, Protestants and Dissenters.

The claim that, in every generation, the Irish people had asserted their right to freedom is baseless, though one might argue that in the modern period in each generation there was widespread sympathy, among nationalists only of course, for some notion of 'freedom', however inchoate at times.[62] Counterpointed to Irish nationalist aspirations were Irish unionist celebrations of 'liberty' (another elusive term). The nationalist hopes ranged from monarchist leanings to demands for the restoration of the old Irish parliament, and from republican separatism to forms of federal and devolved government. Whether the claim also meant that each generation in the previous three hundred years had risen in arms is unclear. It is best perhaps not to take that apparent implication literally. We do know from other writings, though, that Pearse was preoccupied with generational assertiveness and the reproduction of claims to sovereignty. 'There has been nothing more terrible in Irish history than the failure of the last generation.'[63] Not even the experience of the Great Famines of the 1740s or the 1840s, one is tempted to ask.

The 'Irish people', the Proclamation lays down, have a right to the 'unfettered control of Irish destinies'. This and other claims to sovereignty are axiomatic for a republican of any hue. But who has the right to decide on these matters? One might have thought it was not a clique that could have contested elections but met secretly in backrooms instead.[64] Equally troubling is an understanding of who constituted the Irish people. Most who cared to notice knew that Irish society was deeply divided. Whether one argues the divisions were primarily communal, ethno-religious or national is less important than the recognition that there were deep political and constitutional differences between the inhabitants of the island. The 'Irish people' of the Proclamation has as much a real-life existence as a ventriloquist's dummy. The real people who populated the country, from Tory Island and Malin Head in the north to Cape Clear and the Great Blasket in the extreme southwest – the MacSweeneys, the Armstrongs, the Connors, the Blennerhassets and the O'Sullivans, and the multitudes of other families – could not be harnessed through the alchemy of a few self-delusional words to a shared constitutional objective. Would that it could have been so simple. The differences and divisions within Ireland were too great and cried out for recognition both on the part of Irish nationalists and Ulster unionists.[65] Nor should one forget the weaker but still significant social movements of the day, those of labour in particular.

Aspiration is fused and indeed confused with reality. Not only is there now a Republic in being but it is also 'a Sovereign Independent State'. The nation and the state tend to be closely associated but conceptually and in practice they are quite different. The state is a set of institutions – legislative, legal, bureaucratic – that exercises power and has a monopoly of coercive resources (to adopt part of Max Weber's definition) within the territory of the state. Such an Irish state did not exist. The rebels crouched and waited for the inevitable in the small number of buildings they had commandeered in central Dublin. That was the extent of their rule.

The paragraph concludes with a pledge that the insurrectionists will give their lives, and this was certainly true of the signatories, for the cause of the freedom of Ireland and its 'exaltation among the nations'. It is noteworthy, though, that none of the signatories to the Proclamation were killed in action, though Connolly was wounded. Their execution, as some of the leaders acknowledged, became all the more necessary, to redeem honour and smear blood across the imagination of later generations.[66]

Conscription by Another Name?

The third paragraph opens with a claim that is breath-taking in its presumption. 'The Irish Republic is entitled to, and hereby claims, the allegiance of every Irishman and Irishwoman.' Without exception, every inhabitant has now been conscripted into a national household, as defined by the main conspirators, without so much as a by your leave. An implication is that those who refuse such allegiance could be seen as apostates and traitors to the Republic.[67] There is the making of assassination and civil war in these words. Later, and not many years later, republican ideologues would parse and execute the meanings attaching to allegiance, Republic and the legacy of Easter 1916. Henceforth, politically-motivated killing in Ireland would have God and Easter 1916 on its side.

In what is perhaps the most attractive and progressive section of the document, the Proclamation offers to guarantee a range of rights, as well as opening vistas of happiness and prosperity for the future. It is worth quoting in full:

> The Republic guarantees religious and civil liberty, equal rights and equal opportunities to all its citizens, and declares its resolve to pursue the happiness and prosperity of the whole nation and of all its parts, cherishing all the children of the nation equally, and oblivious of the differences carefully fostered by an alien government, which have divided a minority from the majority in the past.

Even Ulster unionists would have found it difficult to find fault with the emphasis on equal rights, and there are shades of the American Declaration of Independence here. Or to go back farther in time, some might say these were ideas of liberty inherited from the Glorious Revolution of 1688, though the notion of equal opportunities is more the product of socialist thinking emanating from Britain during this period (with Jim Larkin and James Connolly as the principal conduits between the labour movements of the two islands). The importance of British political ideas in the making of Irish nationalist and radical thought – one strand of the Union of letters and ideas – is often overlooked.

The phrase 'cherishing all the children of the nation equally' is often misunderstood and sometimes misused in contemporary debate.[68] The children are the peoples of Ireland, from age zero to more than a hundred years of age. Clearly this is a resumption of the infantilising language found in the opening sentence of the Proclamation, a rhetorical ruse deriving from Romanticism rather than the Enlightenment thinking that animated the American declaration of 1776 and the French declaration of 1789. The resort to child imagery is possibly also a sign of Pearse's unhealthy preoccupation with children as reflected variously in his roles as schoolmaster, poet and writer.

The elephant in the room, the reality of a divided society, is only given cursory recognition at the end of the passage quoted above. Disappointingly, the cause of division is simplified as being the result of the manipulative role of 'an alien government'. The government is not mentioned and the words Britain, British or the United Kingdom do not make it into the text. Still, the charge has some truth. During the 1798 risings use was made of Protestant loyalists, militarised in the form of the Yeomanry, in putting down the Presbyterian and Catholic rebels. However, the general thrust of government policy, both under the old, unreformed Irish parliament and the Union parliament from 1801, had been to contain communal violence. That this aim was sometimes subverted at a local level by Orange magistrates who indulged loyalist communal violence and applied the law partially, does not overturn the main argument. The suppression of the Orange Order for periods, the creation of a national police force in 1831, the reform of local police forces later in the century, as well as various public pronouncements and investigations into disturbances in Ireland are signposts for the direction of change.[69] Ironically, in 1911 the unionist heartland of Belfast was policed by a body of men, many of whom were Catholic and some of whom were native Irish speakers.[70]

Vanishing Unionists

The nationalist critique of unionism, as reflected in the *Irish News* editorial for Ulster Day, failed to recognise that there was another ethno-religious formation on the island, spread thinly across the countryside in the southern counties but heavily concentrated in Belfast and the Lagan Valley. This people had deep ancestral roots, a different view of Irish and British history, a sense of their own collective identity and worth, and varying degrees of commitment to the reformed faith of Protestantism. In every sense they constituted an ethnic group and now through a process of political *struggle*, centred on opposing

Home Rule, were assuming an ethno-national identity.[71] It hardly requires hindsight – a glance across the nineteenth century should suffice – to realise that a fundamental division in Irish life was being ignored.[72] Such deliberate myopia encouraged collective self-delusion on the part of republicans and the wider nationalist population. Surprisingly perhaps, some prominent upper-middle class Protestants in southern Ireland who came to identify with Irish national feeling, such as W.B. Yeats and Douglas Hyde (the founder of the Gaelic League), also shared this narrow and arguably proto-partitionist mind-set. By presuming not to see another, quite distinctive ethnic group on the island – one that was assuming ethno-national characteristics by the early twentieth century – the possibilities of negotiating some kind of political reconciliation were further reduced and partition was rendered more likely.

The resort to arms is recalled in the fifth paragraph, this being the fifth time arms is mentioned in the text. There is more than a suspicion that for some ideologues the use of arms constituted an end in itself. In bloodletting is national redemption. But this penultimate paragraph is primarily about the establishment of a national government, elected by the 'suffrages of all her men and women'. The reader is given a respite from the imagery of the children of the nation at this stage, and it is indeed noteworthy that women as well as men are being accorded full voting rights. Women's suffrage was a heavily contested position in European as well as Irish society at this juncture. It was granted in the United Kingdom, and hence Ireland, some two years later, though ironically French women who were heirs to the republican revolution of 1789 had to wait until the closing stages of the Second World War.[73] In the meantime, until 'our arms' have brought the opportune moment when elections could be called, a Provisional Government will administer 'the civil and military affairs of the Republic in trust for the people', that is, the same people who could not be entrusted with the task of deciding Ireland's constitutional future and hence unsurprisingly were not given sight of the membership of this government-in-waiting.

In the final paragraph the Republic is placed under the protection of the Most High God, 'whose blessing we invoke upon our arms'. It is as if we have entered the sanctuary of a great cathedral, where the sword is placed upon the cross, and all have bent low before the sacred script, *Pro Fide et Patria*. God's blessing is invoked, not on the volunteers in the rising (perhaps they were dispensable in the greater scheme of things), but on 'our arms' which is a curiously inanimate image, devoid of human sensibility. Alternatively this may be a metonymic use of language, for men standing erect with weapons and a cause, with God standing-by as a kind of army chaplain.

The sentence continues with the hope that no one will bring dishonour on the cause by 'cowardice, inhumanity, or rapine'. No doubt this aspiration was genuinely felt, though one may detect some insecure undertones about collective honour as well. The earlier Declaration by Emmet betrayed a similar uneasiness.[74] The slashing into small pieces of a portrait of Queen Victoria which once hung in the boardroom of the Royal College of Surgeons in Ireland by some volunteers lies at the mild end of inhumanity during Easter week.[75] The killing of the unarmed Constable Michael Lahiff or the summary execution of Michael Cavanagh as he attempted to retrieve his cart from a rebel barricade, suggests that the actuality fell well short of the ideal.[76] Some volunteers had to be restrained from firing on working-class Dublin women who taunted the rebels and expressed their disapproval in no uncertain terms. More atrocities, however, were committed by British troops, possibly because there were far more of them by the end of the week and because it was sometimes difficult to identify gunmen from other civilians. Let it be said, most of the 'men of 1916' behaved well. But almost inevitably because of limited training, some volunteers did dishonour the naïve sentiments published in the Proclamation. Of longer-term significance, the precedent of violence established in this 'supreme hour' opened the way to the far more numerous atrocities committed by Irish republicans against Irish civilians and others in the hours, days and decades that followed.[77]

Heroism and Shame

War alone brings up to its highest tension all human energy and puts the stamp of nobility upon the peoples who have courage to meet it.... Fascism, now and always, believes in holiness and in heroism; that is to say, in actions influenced by no economic motive, direct or indirect.

Benito Mussolini[78]

Words take flight in the final sentence: this is the 'supreme hour' of the Irish nation; valour and discipline must prevail; the 'children' (of the nation) must sacrifice themselves for the common good; the nation itself must prove itself worthy of the 'august destiny' to which it is called. It is tempting to dismiss this as high-flown rhetoric, and to leave it at that. The notion of the 'supreme hour', for example, was a hackneyed phrase from Great War propaganda, and illustrates how khaki and green jingoism could intermix. Nonetheless, in the furrows of the language there lie important clues as to ideological anxieties and elisions on the part of the leaders. The Irish peoples, however defined, had endured some searing moments, the Great Famine of the 1840s being the most traumatic. It was more than half a century later before Irish society, or at least parts of it, was again exposed to extensive mass mortality. As many as 40,000 Irish men may have died and many more were injured or wounded in the First World War which places the Easter Rising in the ha'penny place in terms of Irish suffering and death.[79] Easter 1916 in Dublin may have been the sacred moment, or hour, or week for the leaders. For the rank and file it was the adventure of a lifetime;[80] small numbers died in action; some were wounded and traumatised. For the Irish peoples as a whole, they had not even been consulted on the momentous decision to stage a rising in their name.

The children of the nation were being challenged to behave heroically and, if necessary, to sacrifice their lives. Characteristically, as in European nationalistic rhetoric, the emphasis is on dying rather than killing, on the masochistic rather than the sadistic impulse, though the latter is invariably the predominant reality as most, given the choice, show a preference for killing rather than dying. The exhortatory quality constitutes an appropriate climax to the manifesto, but there is also a hint of uncertainty, even admonishment in advance. The 'Irish nation *must...*' (emphasis added). A moment later and expressed more explicitly, we find the Irish nation must 'prove itself worthy of the august destiny to which it is called'. As with an All-Ireland final, for all the hopes invested, the team just might not turn up on the day. In this case, the people might fail the conspirators, as happened all through the preceding century, in 1803, 1848 and 1867.[81]

Not only were the stakes high; there was much to be redeemed in terms of notions of honour and masculinity, not least on the part of those members of the Irish Republican Brotherhood who constituted the leadership of the rising. With bodies in mortal combat on the killing fields of Europe, a phallic thrust at Brittania was overdue. Patrick Pearse carried additional, personal baggage that may have fed his weakness for overblown masculinity as evidenced by his glorification of the mythological heroes of the Fianna;[82] he had an eye deformity (hence the photographs in heroic profile), was latently homosexual, and was seemingly sexually attracted to children.[83] Another leading revolutionary, Sir Roger Casement, was an active homosexual and paedophile, though whether this 'outsider' status conditioned his ultra-nationalist leanings is hard to say. In Pearse's political writings there is also an obsessive interest in the obverse of his masculine ideal, with repeated references to a loss of manhood, a lack of virility, and male degradation. The worst of all, to his mind, were the 'men who have ceased to be men', men who were fearful of war. They 'deserved the most shameful of all penalties'.[84] This bears uncomfortable comparison to proto-fascist and later full-blown fascist writings.[85]

Irish nationalism is not, of course, unique in celebrating a love of country so surpassing that contempt for sections of its own peoples is a necessary correlative. The same sentiments surfaced in the great era of ultra-nationalisms – the interwar period – in countries as diverse as Spain, Germany, Austria, Hungary and Poland, to take some of the more extreme examples. The Irish nationalist writer, D.P. Moran, led the way in the early twentieth century with scurrilous attacks on the types of Irish people of whom he disapproved.[86] Some of the dismissive asides smack of racialism. Pearse also had doubts about his fellow countrymen.

Take his widely known but uncritically acclaimed poem, *Mise Éire*.[87] The poem was written in 1912 and opens dramatically with the announcement that 'I am Ireland', older than the old woman (or hag) of Béarra. This tunes in to primordialist notions of the nation. There is a swelling of pride in the second couplet:

Mór mo ghlóir,
Mé a rug Cú Chulainn Cróga.[88]

Cúchulainn (as mentioned earlier) was a mythical hero who has the doubtful distinction of appealing to latter-day republicans and loyalists.[89] Pearse, in the guise of Mother Ireland, has given birth to the hero. Following this boastful recollection which evokes images of ancient times of heroism and chivalry, there is a quick inversion of mood and a descent into shame and self-hatred:

Mór mo náir,
Mo chlann féin a dhíol a máthair.

The charge could hardly be more damning: great is my shame, my own children that sold their mother. The children of the nation could be whore masters as well as heroes. This implies that the Irish people might well sell out their self-anointed leaders in the supreme hour that the Rising represented for republicans: hence the anxious subtext to the closing sentence of the Proclamation.[90] In a few short years it would be found necessary to execute or exile fellow citizens and siblings in the name of the self-same Mother Ireland, with the less pure Irish categorised variously as base, Castle Catholics, West Britons, loyalists, informers, or worse. The jingoistic turn in Irish politics meant an emotion-charged lexicon was now in place to finger elements traitorous either to the 'Republic' or the soon-to-be created Free State. This was the subtext to the redemptive acts of terror in Sackville Street in April 1916.

Shadows

The phrase 'the august destiny to which it [the Irish nation] is called' concludes the text of the Proclamation. It is a superb choice of words, silver tongued and emotion-laden, as befits the end point of the manifesto. The adjective 'august' has connotations of the reverential, the magisterial, even of the sublime.

Notions such as the destiny of the nation might be dismissed as little more than a piece of mysticism. There is no denying the emotional charge and its motivational power, though. The vagueness of the wording is a strength rather than a weakness, while the teleological quality of the sentiment runs with the grain of the nationalist historical narrative. Even more psychologically satisfying, there is the prospect of good times ahead. As with most social movements, the vision of an entrancing future – the New Jerusalem or the Éire Nua – is held out, though predicated on the readiness of the insurgents and those who find themselves in the nation (whether they assent to their inclusion or not) to 'sacrifice themselves for the common good'. Less than a decade later the great Irish playwright, Sean O'Casey, would cast a cold eye on how the rhetoric turned to wreaths. In Act 11 of *Shadow of a Gunman*, Seumas Shields, one of the principal characters, observes bitterly: 'I hear the gunmen blowin' about dyin' for the people, when it's the people that are dyin' for the gunmen!'[91] And so it came to pass in early twentieth-century Ireland, and with renewed ferocity in later twentieth-century Northern Ireland.[92]

CHAPTER EIGHT

Texting Terror: 1912 and 1916

When we believe that the very foundations of our life as a community are in danger we cannot, we dare not, keep silence … We must face the fact that there are things worse than war – worse than torture and death …

Bishop Charles F. D'Arcy[1]

The last sixteen months have been the most glorious in the history of Europe. Heroism has come back to the earth …. The old heart of the earth needed to be warmed with the red wine of the battlefields. Such august homage was never before offered to God as this, the homage of millions of lives given gladly for love of country.

P. H. Pearse[2]

Introduction

The Ulster Covenant and the Proclamation of the Irish Republic are two concise, and in many respects revealing expressions of how Ulster unionists and Irish republicans wished to see themselves, and wished others to see them. It may be instructive to tease out points of comparison and contrast in the two documents. Hardly surprisingly, it is the contrasts that dominate, but there are some similarities that are worth bearing in mind. For one thing, in the minds of many these are iconic texts. They mark turning points in the evolution of unionist and nationalist politics, they each complicated Britain–Ireland and North–South relations, they each pointed directly towards the partition of the island, and, though neither is markedly triumphalist, each has its quotient of make-believe. They are each manipulative documents, as suggested in earlier chapters, replete with contradictions, evasions and silences. This is more apparent in the Proclamation of the Irish Republic, but it is, after all, a longer, more complete text.

Perhaps the similarity of most importance linking the Covenant and the Proclamation is the threat of political violence which seeps out from the mute hieroglyphics on the page. To take the Ulster Covenant first, the ceremonial preparations and the political pageantry, including the series of public meetings and demonstrations that preceded Ulster Day, served to amplify the message of militant resistance to Home Rule. In September 1912, eleven meetings, starting in the west of the province and building to a climax at the Ulster Hall in Belfast, prepared the way for the public signing of the Covenant. The first meeting in support of the Covenant was held on 18 September at Enniskillen. Edward Carson was met at the station by an escort of 200 mounted volunteers.[3] From there he was accompanied to Portora Hill, where 40,000 members of unionist clubs *marched* past him. There was talk of 'righteous resistance', though the nationalist *Irish News* dismissed the proceedings as the 'first act of Carson's Ulster comedy'.[4] In one of the final mass demonstrations before Ulster Day, that at Lisburn, Co. Antrim, men in paramilitary formation bearing dummy wooden rifles paraded past the reviewing stand. As dusk descended, torches illuminated the marching bands. Drum beats ramped up the emotions of the assembled masses. The communal voice was: 'We will not have Home Rule.'[5]

These were disciplined demonstrations of demographic power with coercive intent. Demographic power is usually latent, having both absolute and relative dimensions.[6] The concept might be applied to a wide range of societies and a range of public occasions from faction fighting to riot, and from communal and labour disputes to massed military demonstrations. The absolute size of the pro-Union population in Ulster was not too far off a million persons. (Protestants numbered 891,000 in 1911; Protestant nationalists were thin on the ground, as were Catholic unionists, thus their net influence would have affected the total of unionists only marginally.) Even if one takes the six counties of Ulster that came to form Northern Ireland, the protestant masses still accounted for well over three-quarters of a million people (820,000 to be more precise). As suggested earlier (chapter three), this was a critical mass of politically conscious persons, which was concentrated in the north-east of Ireland, and which had the absolute numbers and the geographical density necessary to mount a fierce opposition to its political opponents. In relative terms, and this is vitally important in relation to the territory under dispute, Protestants represented 56 per cent of the population of the province of Ulster but 66 per cent of the population of the partitioned Ulster that was later to constitute Northern Ireland.[7] A short sea journey away, their compatriots in England, Scotland and Wales were numbered in their tens of millions. Both absolute and relative numbers suggested that unionist Ulster, whatever boundaries it might occupy, would be difficult to digest within any variant of an Irish state. Set within the smaller context of the island of Ireland, Ulster Protestants were in a significant minority, accounting for only 20 per cent of the Irish population in 1911, hence many of the insecurities that gave Ulster unionism its defensive character.[8] Counting all Protestants in Ireland in 1911 moves the share upwards but only to 26 per cent of all the peoples of Ireland.

These are the demographic fundamentals but the traipsing of the unionists across Ulster in the run up to Ulster Day was a means of dramatising their demographic strength in their chosen territory. To transmogrify Marx, this was an ethnic group in itself and for itself. The demonstrations were designed to capture the public gaze and give expressive and indeed menacing representation to the passive numbers found in the census counts – a tactic that had been pioneered by Daniel O'Connell with his great rallies and 'monster meetings' in the preceding century.[9] Demographic power appeared at its most potent when presented in the form of massed masculine numbers, on public display, and arranged in disciplined formations in pursuit of a shared political objective. It was also intended to give re-assurance, opportunities for recreation (including the thrill of possible violence), and a sense of solidarity to the social group producing the display.

Bullet Points

The choreography of the 1916 Rising was different, going beyond threat to outright killing in the minutes leading up to the reading of the Proclamation at about 12.45 pm on Easter Monday. But Easter week, or post-Easter week as it was, also showcased Irish republican claims as embodied in the Proclamation. So in each episode – that of the unveiling of the Covenant or the Proclamation – the text was a bullet-point statement of the demands of the protagonists, with the threat of violence or the acting out of violence undergirding and magnifying the impact of the message.

In each case the message was directed not just at a home audience but at audiences overseas. The Covenant, as part of the campaign against Home Rule, was addressed to the peoples of Britain and then beyond the shores of the archipelago to the loyalists of the British Empire.[10] In Britain itself, support for the Home Rule cause was dwarfed by the contrary sentiment that extolled the inviolability of the union of Britain and Ireland. This was underlined the morning after Ulster Day. At the close of that momentous occasion Edward Carson left Belfast Lough on board a steamer bound for Liverpool. As morning broke and the ship docked on Merseyside, Carson was met by a crowd of cheering supporters. Later that evening he addressed a 100,000 strong meeting in Liverpool.[11] As was also becoming evident, there was support for the Ulster campaign beyond Britain in the far-flung fields of Empire.

The Proclamation of the Irish Republic was also projected to an international audience. In addition to signalling to the Kaiser and the German

High Command that nationalist Ireland (or sections thereof) was open to collaboration, the broader and not wholly unrealistic strategy was to place the case for Irish independence before the international peace conference that would inevitably follow the cessation of hostilities. If the Central Powers had gained the upper-hand in the war and German troops had occupied Ireland, then the problem of Ulster might have been disposed of at a stroke, presumably with mass executions and expulsions. The exploitation of Ulster and Irish civilians as forced labour can hardly be ruled out, which was a fate that befell tens of thousands of Belgians who were rounded up, transported to Germany and forced to work for the German war effort.[12] An 'independent Ireland', had it materialised, would, in all likelihood, have become a German dependency, but that particular future was never put to the test, and it is perhaps as well not to dwell too closely on the likely consequences for the Irish peoples. As elsewhere in Europe, the welfare of the people was not a priority as nationalist elites, acting in Moloch-like fashion, placed few limits on the human sacrifice they demanded of their citizens.

Other, perhaps more incidental similarities relating to the two documents may be noticed. Ulster Day and Easter Week represent points of origin for the two state formations on the island, those of Northern Ireland and the Irish Free State, later Republic of Ireland. This is especially true in terms of Irish republican thinking which venerates Easter 1916 and the Irish Republic it proclaimed.[13] To use Christian imagery, the Proclamation was the annunciation and the moment of birth of the modern Irish state rolled into one. Baptism by fire followed. More obviously, the timing at Easter suggested martyrdom and resurrection.

While the reading of the Proclamation outside the General Post Office (GPO) may be viewed as a moment of transition, indeed transfiguration between the old and the new order,[14] the origins of the Ulster unionist statelet, as inscribed in popular memory, are less clear cut. The subject might repay more detailed study, though the historian Alvin Jackson has argued (perhaps a little too strongly) that the events of 1912–14 have indeed 'served as a creation myth for Unionism in the twentieth century – as a kind of Orange Genesis'.[15] The Covenant and the banding together of the British-Irish of Ulster in solemn league and covenant can certainly be seen as a vital moment in the emergence of Northern Ireland. Those who orchestrated it saw it as a historic milestone and its fiftieth anniversary in 1962 was celebrated with enthusiasm by unionist politicians and people (see later), with the then prime minister of Northern Ireland, Lord Brookeborough exclaiming that 'the Covenant was the rock of Ulster's foundation'.[16] There is the complication, though, that Ulster unionists did not initially seek a devolved government. As well as that, so many dramatic events jostled for unionist attention. The establishment of the Ulster Volunteer Force in 1913, plans for a Provisional Government, the terrible experiences of the First World War, the 'betrayal' of the Irish war effort in Easter 1916, the conscription crisis and the emergence of the Irish Republican Army (IRA), were all interventions serving to snap the kinship, social and cultural bonds that, to varying degrees, linked North and South. The opening of the Northern Ireland parliament in accordance with the Government of Ireland Act on 22 June 1921 is perhaps the one fixed substantive and ceremonial point of origin.[17] Such ceremony, though, situated as it was in the midst of the national and communal conflict that ravaged parts of Ireland from January 1919 onwards, does not have the mythic power of the passions evoked by the sight of the burning shell of the GPO some five years earlier.

Having discussed various points of comparison between the two documents, and the occasions that surrounded each, we may now turn to some of the contrasts. These are substantial and they range from differences in popular support to imagery and mode of writing.

Demographic Dimensions

The Covenant represented the political views of almost half a million Ulster unionists and, by inference, the vast majority of the unionist population in the North. The text was available for inspection and consideration beforehand. It was, thus, an expression of the demotic will. The Proclamation, however, had no such breadth of support and was signed in secret by seven conspirators, some of them actively lying to close colleagues about their intentions, and all of them men; its content was only made public once the die had been cast.

The demographic dimension may be taken a stage further. Most of the participants in the 1916 Rising were adolescents or young men in their early twenties. Even the leaders, with the exception of Tom Clarke, were middle-aged or of a younger age group. Older generations were seen as a corrupting influence, unless of course they were dead.[18] Of the six other signatories to the Proclamation, the average age was thirty-six, the youngest being the twenty-eight-year-old and sickly Joseph Mary Plunkett and the oldest being the forty-seven-year-old James Connolly.[19] By contrast, the Ulster Covenant received the endorsement of vast numbers of all ages, excluding children. Revolution was a young man's business.

Women and Men

The women of Ulster were as well represented as men in showing their commitment to the political cause, possibly for the first time in the public sphere in Ireland. In fact, within Ulster itself, more women than men turned out, with 228,991 women signing compared to 218,206 men. True enough, in formal terms the women merely associated themselves with the men of Ulster and they signed a somewhat truncated version of the text. But the action of signing, which was the key outward expression of the political intent that lay behind the anti-Home Rule campaign, was undertaken by both sexes in great and more or less equal numbers.

The Proclamation was men's work for men, as was the Rising itself. Women auxiliaries such as Cumann na mBan were welcomed but their role tended to be a subservient one, drawn upon in time of crisis.[20] The gender contrast is more pronounced than that. The numbers of women mobilised at the time of the signing of the Covenant were on a huge scale compared to the minuscule body of women from the Irish nationalist population who participated in or supported the Easter Rising. Could it be that patriarchy was more deeply embedded in Irish Catholic as compared to Ulster Protestant culture?[21]

The social and religious composition of the two sets of protagonists also bears consideration. The rising in Dublin was manned by working-class Catholic men, in the main, thrown into the field by a petit bourgeois leadership. The mobilisation in Ulster was an all-class alliance of Protestants and unionists, which joined together the landed gentry, the captains of industry, the middle classes and the clergy, the farmers and the farm labourers, the shopkeepers and their shop boys and shop girls, the skilled workers and the unskilled workers in pursuit of the same political objective.[22] This was a united 'people', if ever there was such. It was very different in Dublin. The Rising had a much narrower social base, with the rank and file consisting mainly of labourers, tradesmen and clerks, quite apart from its tiny minority status within Irish nationalism. It was a Catholic uprising in all but name, with priests ministering to the rebels before, during and after the rising. More revealingly, the mantle of martyrdom quickly descended on the condemned leaders.

Then there is the differing penumbra of space associated with the two documents. The Covenant was signed, not just by people living in Ulster but by Ulster-born people elsewhere in Ireland – several thousand in Dublin alone – and across the sea in England and Scotland and even by at least one group of Ulster men out at sea.[23] These last were on the SS Lake Champlain and numbered thirty-nine signatories. Elsewhere in the British Empire, as far away as Canada and South Africa, there were supporters. Cape Town, for instance, contributed thirteen signatures for the Covenant though none for the Declaration.

Thus, Belfast City Hall, as befitted the municipal centre of a great export-orientated city, was the hub of a series of rays which extended outwards to different parts of the globe. The Rising in Dublin which launched the proclamation of the Irish Republic was just that, a rising in Dublin. There were a few skirmishes elsewhere in Ireland, the most serious being at Ashbourne in County Meath. Despite earlier plans for action in three of the four provinces in Ireland – volunteers from Ulster would head across to Connacht so as to avoid provoking communal conflict in the north east – this ended up being an essentially Dublin city affair.[24] It would be a mistake, however, to dismiss the episode as parochial. City-centre Dublin, with its monumental buildings and symbols of authority, was the cauldron in which the Rising bubbled and boiled. In the eyes of some, it was the second city of the Empire. It was the compression of action within a few square miles at the centre of modernity in Ireland that gave this 'propaganda by deed' much of its imaginative intensity and symbolic power. The imposing physicality of the GPO, with its great Ionic columns, portico and pediment, mirrored and reflected the scale of the ambition of those crouched in the cockpit of that desperate gesture that was the Easter Rising. (Almost a century later on the other side of the Atlantic, in another moment of ecstasy, this time fuelled by Islamist ideology, a group of militants crashed their bodies and their machines into the Twin Towers that dominated the lower Manhattan skyline and that symbolised America's global economic power. Wham. The very specificity of the action, the monumental architecture that was its target, and the visual imagery of the aftermath of the destruction passed into the global imagination.)

Turning back to the Covenant, it is noticeable that its stance is defensive when contrasted with the aspirational sentiments found in the Proclamation. On paper at least, the Covenant was simply a democratically-supported petition of protest; a referendum within the Ulster unionist population, it could be said. But, as noted earlier, there was more than a hint of an open-ended commitment to resist Home Rule by whatever means might prove necessary farther down the road.[25] Indeed in 1913, in the year following Ulster Day, an administrative organ of some seventy-seven persons was appointed by the Ulster Unionist Council.[26] This was a cabal in-waiting, in case Home Rule was imposed on 'Ulster'. This conceit of a Provisional Government prefigured the political architecture of Easter 1916 in Dublin.[27] While hidden from public view, some unionists were already contemplating armed resistance and localised drilling had already been underway since 1912 as Orange justices of the peace gave permission for such incendiary activity in their localities. The Proclamation, however, was a declaration of war, with no allowance for measuring popular support. It might be seen, in part, as a letter of explanation to a perplexed people (whose capital was being raked by gunfire and looted by rioters), but the justification was released only after hostilities had begun.

In style as well as content the two documents are very different, even if there are religious undertones to both. The fact that the Covenant is much shorter means that less is on show. But what is on show is in plain speak. There are flights of rhetorical fancy, especially in the male version, but on the whole the text attempts to present the case of the Ulster unionists in ostensibly rational terms, without too much by way of ornamentation. It is the penmanship of the plain-spoken, 'honest Ulsterman', drawing on a well of traditions that included the Scottish religious debates of the 1630s and 1640s and the Enlightenment thinking that found a regional home in Belfast in the later eighteenth century ('The Athens of the North'). Some of these traditions continued into the era of industrialisation,[28] though under pressure from more conservative and evangelical thinkers.

The Proclamation comes out of a very different tradition. The feminisation of Ireland may owe something to the *aisling* poetry of the Gaelic poets of the eighteenth century, with their monarchist nostalgia for the Stuart pretenders, but the mist of romantic longings has settled on the text. The high-flown rhetoric, the mystical assumptions, the call to sacrifice, the invocation of the spirit of the nation, and the appeal to Ireland's august destiny have the cumulative effect of short-circuiting the rational and bombarding the emotions. It is more poetry than argument. Metaphorically speaking, this is the equivalent of unfurling the battle flag and entering *an bearna baol*.[29] The hand of the dramaturge is there. Pearse had written and directed a series of 'patriotic' plays and pageants, which in effect formed the prologue to the greatest drama of all: the shedding of blood, including his own blood, in sacrificial ritual.[30] It might be primitive or pagan, messianic or mystical, but it is calculated to set the blood boiling.

It is worth reviewing briefly the architecture of the Proclamation which is structured in terms of six paragraphs. Firstly, there is the annunciation of the insurrection and a reveille-type call to arms. The second paragraph reveals both secret and open preparations for war and then the unsheathing of the sword. The third reaches back in history to legitimise the revolutionary struggle and goes on to proclaim the Irish Republic. The fourth makes claims on all Irish men and all Irish women, and in turn guarantees equal rights and equal opportunities for all. The fifth skirts round the little difficulty that a Provisional Government has to be created in view of the absence of a nationally-elected assembly of a kind the conspirators would claim to favour.[31] (By contrast, many of the leaders of Ulster Unionism, including Carson and Craig, had stood successfully for election.) All five paragraphs build toward the climacteric of the final section, in which the children of Erin pass through the vale of tears and surge forward to the greater destiny that most surely and deservedly awaits them. The tone and the subtext have a religious quality, like psalms invoking the heavens, but permeating the whole is the mood music of Romantic nationalism.

Not Small Differences[32]

These are, thus, two very different documents. Drawing on musical analogy again, the Proclamation has the tone of hot, martial music whereas the

Covenant is a cooler, less visceral composition. The Covenant leads prosaically with the economic argument whereas, in the Proclamation, there is the vaguest reference to happiness and prosperity. The Proclamation has a sonorous quality, which makes it suitable for reading aloud, as it has been on countless occasions from annual commemorations of the Easter Rising to demonstrations against the European Union. In 1966, in honour of the 50th anniversary of the Rising, national schools all over Ireland were asked to display copies of the Proclamation.[33] Yet there is a paradox here. The Proclamation doesn't have attentive readers or listeners; it has worshippers not analysts, as befits a national icon. The only phrase from the document that seems to have passed into popular parlance relates to cherishing the children of the nation and this is routinely misinterpreted, such are the pitfalls of romantic imagery. The reception of the Proclamation might be compared to the surge of emotion experienced by a crowd singing *Amhrán na bhFiann* in the Hogan Stand, Croke Park on All-Ireland day. Why should anyone bother (or dare) to deconstruct its passages as this is more holy scripture than political programme? The icon is the message, massaging the emotions in a way Marshall McLuhan would have recognised.[34]

Words

It may be illuminating to examine the relative frequency of key words within the two texts and to run a formal comparison of the two sets of outcomes in the manner employed by some literary critics.[35] This evidence should help confirm, qualify or reject the lines of interpretation developed above. Is it the case, for instance, that in form and style the Proclamation is a different text to that of the Covenant or that very different manifestations of ethnicity are present in each?[36]

One hardly needs quantification to notice that adjectives abound in the Proclamation. One in ten words in the rebels' manifesto is an adjective, suggesting a more ornamented text. In pleasing conformity with popular perceptions of cultural differences between nationalists and unionists, the texts of the Covenant and the Declaration are more austere. To put boundaries on this measure, the relative frequency of adjectives in the Proclamation is twice that of the Covenant or the Declaration.

It is the choice and deployment of verbs however that sets the competing documents apart. Words in the Proclamation such as 'seizes', 'strikes' (x2), 'perfected', 'asserted' (x3), 'proclaim', 'pledge', 'claims', 'guarantees', 'declares', 'administer', 'invoke', 'must' and 'prove' convey dynamism, muscularity and certitude. The elongated and somewhat convoluted opening sentence of the Covenant (male version), in contrast, takes some time to signal what kind of action or reaction is being prepared, while the women's Declaration is less definite again in its resolve: we 'desire to associate' (with the men of Ulster). Surprisingly enough, the Covenant gives explicit recognition to the possibility of defeat, at least in round one. There is a degree of self-doubt: the 'conspiracy' to introduce Home Rule may, in fact, succeed despite the best efforts of the Ulster unionists.

The Proclamation contains no fewer than fourteen references to the 'Irish' and a further four to 'Ireland' (seven if one includes the version *as Gaeilge* (Éire) and the two further mentions in the title of the document). There is no mention of 'Ulster' (the province that dare not speak its name in the Proclamation) or indeed of the 'United Kingdom'. Thus, although the Proclamation has the semblance of inclusiveness, at least on a quick reading, it is soon apparent that this is an ethnic document in the tradition of an exclusive Irish nationalism. Neither is there any concession to the idea that the island and the nation might not be coterminous.[37] Reinforcing this reading of the text, we find the nation, the people and the Republic are invoked at least six times apiece.[38] Freedom and sovereignty, understandably, also feature prominently (but not self-determination), as do references to men (including manhood). Right and rights are repeated insistently through the text, meriting seven mentions in all. 'Arms' is cited five times: this is, after all, a militaristic enterprise. Children, in the sense of members of the extended family who form the nation, get four mentions, twice as many as the Godhead.

The most frequently occurring key word both in the Covenant and the Declaration is 'Ulster'. There are five such mentions across the two. Bear in mind these are short documents: the Proclamation is two and a half-times the length of the Covenant and it is more than five times the length of the Declaration. This last consists of an especially concise, one-paragraph statement. So the frequency of the term Ulster is anything but accidental. Citizenship, empire and the United Kingdom are also recognised in the unionist texts. It is interesting to note that 'Ireland' receives two mentions in each of the documents. Still, there is no doubt these are a different 'Irish', with political aspirations that are fundamentally different from those of Irish nationalists. There are no counterparts to the more militaristic word images found in the Proclamation, with the important exception of the phrase 'all means … necessary'. The irony here of course is that when the Covenant was being drafted some unionists, unknown to most, were already turning their minds to the business of importing 'arms'. Strikingly, the Proclamation is infused with female imagery, arising from the gendered nature of Ireland as represented in nationalist discourse. The possessive pronoun 'her' appears no fewer than eleven times, including one touch of gender confusion as in 'her manhood'. Perhaps surprisingly, Ulster is presented in feminine form also (but only in the women's Declaration).

Table 8.1
Comparing the texts of the Ulster Solemn League and Covenant and
the Proclamation of the Irish Republic

	PROCLAMATION	COVENANT	DECLARATION
Number of words	472	189	96
Number of paragraphs	6	1	1
Number of sentences	11	4	2
Mean number of words	42.9	47.3	48.0
Proportion in Irish (%)	near zero	zero	zero
Number of signatories	7	237,368	234,046
Frequency of key words			
'Irish'	14	0	0
'her'	11	0	2
'nation'	7	0	0
'people'	6	0	0
'Republic'	6	0	0
'arms'	5	0	0
'rights'	5	1	0
'Ireland'	4	2	2
'children'	4	1	0
'man'	3	1	1
'freedom'	3	1	0
'sovereignty'	3	0	0
'equal'	3	1	0
'woman'	3	0	1
'God'	2	2	1
'strike'	2	0	0
'military'	2	0	0
'right'	2	1	0
'citizen'	2	2	0
'liberty'	1	0	0
'Ulster'	0	2	3
'Empire'	0	1	0
'United Kingdom'	0	1	1
'loyal'	0	1	1
'calamity'	0	1	1
'Parliament'	0	2	2

Afterlife

Deputy Gerry Adams: 'I remind all Teachtaí that all the main parties [in Dáil Éireann] came from that period of armed resistance that led to the armed proclamation of a Republic in 1916.'[39]

The Easter Proclamation has served a variety of political and ceremonial functions down the years. In the famous general election of 1918 in the United Kingdom, in which Sinn Féin had a resounding victory (in terms of seats) in Ireland outside of east Ulster, the Sinn Féin election manifesto offered homage to the original text.[40]

> Sinn Féin stands less for a political party than for the Nation; it represents the old tradition of nationhood handed on from dead generations; it stands by the Proclamation of the Provisional Government of Easter, 1916, reasserting the inalienable right of the Irish Nation to sovereign independence, reaffirming the determination of the Irish people to achieve it, and guaranteeing within the independent Nation equal rights and equal opportunities to all its citizens.

The manifesto continues by appealing to the doctrine of apostolic succession found in Pearsian revolutionary theology and also reminds readers of the martyrs of more recent times. Sinn Féin, it states, enters the election 'confident that the people of this ancient nation will be true to the old cause and will vote for the *men* who stand by the principles of Tone, Emmet, Mitchel, Pearse and Connolly' (emphasis added). The Democratic Programme of the first Dáil Éireann, convened in January 1919 following Sinn Féin's success in the general election of the preceding year, also paraphrases and echoes even more fully sentiments found in the Proclamation.

Annual Easter commemorations by the Irish state down the years, as well as by a variety of nationalist political factions, have highlighted the importance of the declaration of the Irish Republic. No such occasion is complete without a reading of the Proclamation, as often as not in a graveyard where past, present and future fuse in the reverie of the moment. It was also, of course, a central feature of the Irish state's commemoration of the fiftieth anniversary of the Easter Rising in 1966.[41] Less obviously, but seemingly not incongruously, public meetings to oppose Ireland's entry into the (then) European Economic Community featured a reading of the Proclamation.[42] If a threat to sovereignty arose, an appropriate text was to hand. Or so it seemed. The loss of economic sovereignty on the part of the Republic of Ireland in 2010, and the subjection of the nation's finances to the dictates of the European Union and the International Monetary Fund revealed, among many other things, the barrenness of high-flown rhetoric in the face of economic mismanagement.[43] Nonetheless, and almost ritualistically, the Proclamation was ransacked for inspiring, perhaps comforting phrases by journalists shocked at the national loss.

The market place has been good to owners of early copies of the Proclamation, with prices spiralling upwards in recent decades.[44] The Covenant was mass-produced and, while copies of individually signed souvenirs may be found in antique shops, their monetary value is trivial by comparison.[45] While relative scarcity must form the dominant part of the explanation – relics of the Rising are very limited in supply whereas hundreds of thousands signed the Covenant – demand may also be a factor. The Covenant, though treasured, never achieved the iconic status within Ulster unionist life that the Proclamation achieved in the world of Irish republicanism and beyond. Perhaps the magnetising force of violence is the missing ingredient. Ulster Day doesn't make good drama, if literary production is any guide. The subject of the Easter Rising has attracted a range of writers from Sean O'Casey – playwright, early member of the Irish Citizen Army, and author of *The Plough and the Stars* – to Roddy Doyle one of Ireland's leading contemporary novelists who wrote *The Dead Republic*. There is a slew of patriotic poetry, of variable quality, of which W.B. Yeats' 'Easter 1916' is the most celebrated. Foster's panoramic view of critically-neglected popular and minor novels published between 1890 and 1922 contains references to Easter 1916 on no fewer than two dozen pages, whereas the Solemn League and Covenant merits only a single fleeting mention: the writer Martin Ross (of Somerville and Ross fame) travelled to Belfast to sign the Declaration.[46] Ulster unionists have Rudyard Kipling as a possible poet laureate – a doubtful asset – whereas a sheaf of poets of some stature addressed the Easter Rising.[47] The Covenant just doesn't cut the mustard in literary terms.

It would be a mistake, though, to imply that the Covenant has dropped out of the memory of unionists and loyalists. Members of the unionist community to this day speak of the grandparents and great-grandparents who signed the Covenant and some have preserved colour-printed certificates testifying to the fact. With perhaps a note of exaggeration one respected historian of unionism feels that 'signatories and their descendants alike held it [the Solemn League and Covenant] with a reverence akin to that of Englishmen for Magna Carta and Americans for the Declaration of Independence'.[48] Fifty years after the historic event, in 1962, the Ulster Covenant Jubilee Committee organised a spectacular commemoration to mark the occasion.[49] In an editorial headed 'The Covenant Spirit', the *Belfast News-Letter* (BNL) expressed its joy (and its uncritical reading of earlier history): 'To-day tens of thousands of Ulster loyalists will celebrate the fiftieth anniversary of the signing of the Solemn League and Covenant, one of the most significant events in the history of the province.'[50] Interestingly, the commemoration gave rise to some anguished discussion as to whether or not the Covenant had been violated by agreeing to the exclusion of the 'three lost counties' of Cavan, Donegal and Monaghan.[51]

On the appointed Saturday the industrial sounds of Belfast fell silent and 40,000 unionists assembled at Carlisle Circus and marched eight abreast through streets packed by thousands of spectators to the show grounds at Balmoral. Newspapers of the time, the *Belfast News-Letter* and the *Belfast Telegraph*, show scenes of street parties, bunting, British flags, and cheering crowds (forms of celebration evident at the time of the coronation of Queen Elizabeth II a decade earlier). The Imperial Grand Master of the Orange Order, Sir George Clark, expressed the hope that the Jubilee celebrations would 're-kindle some of the fervour which our forefathers had and which gave us the Ulster we had today'. This was under the heading of 'Rekindling the spirit of 1912'. Could the spirit of 1916 be far away? On a more poignant note Mrs Nellie Cardwell, of Cluan Place, Mountpottinger Road, Belfast, although only a school girl at the time, had vivid remembrances of the day in 1912 when her seven uncles signed the Covenant. Within a few years all seven uncles had been wiped out in the carnage of the First World War.

One might speculate that the public memory of the First World War overshadowed Ulster Day, the signing of the Solemn League and Covenant, and all else. These pre-war years were marked by national and labour turbulence, so one can hardly speak of an age of Edwardian and post-Edwardian innocence,[52] but it might well seem so after years of mourning the deaths of brothers, sons, nephews and neighbours' sons. There was no such problem for the new nationalist Ireland. The massive nationalist involvement in the Great War was represented publicly as merely an aberration, a memory to be suppressed or derided. A new revisionism swept the writing of Irish popular history, with the scales tipped forcibly in favour of the 'men of 1916'. Thus the fate of fewer than 2,000 insurgents in 1916 – on the whole a light experience as military encounters go – outweighed the privations and sometimes heroism of the 200,000 Irishmen in the service of Britain and another Ireland.

There was a kind of reprise of Ulster Day in the early 1970s. These were the early years of the 'Troubles' in Northern Ireland and members of the Orange Order circulated a 'covenant' that bore a lineal resemblance to the original of 1912. Hundreds of thousands of signatures were allegedly collected but this claim has the ring of fantasy to it. In the following year, William Craig, the leader of the loyalist Vanguard movement, read out a covenant-style document at one of the Vanguard rallies.[53] Alas for the loyalist ultras, the broad consensus that marked Ulster unionism at the time of the Covenant was not there in the 1970s, not least because it now proved impossible to mobilise sections of the Protestant middle classes behind obscurantist political programmes. The passage of time had helped make the Covenant history in more senses than one.

In more recent times, the digitising of the books of signatures by the Public Record Office of Northern Ireland and the making of these available online has again boosted interest in the Ulster Covenant, making visible what was always true at the level of intimate family recollections. Family tradition preserved the memory of signing the Covenant but this did not, until recently, find major public or cultural expression. Still, in 2012, Belfast City Hall was the setting for a commemorative banquet marking the centenary of Ulster Day. The first minister, Peter Robinson, addressed the assembled guests in what was perceived as a conciliatory address, though it did sidestep the kinds of controversial questions raised here, in particular the association of Ulster unionism with paramilitarism during the second decade of the twentieth century.[54] A loyal order parade from Belfast City centre to Stormont also marked the centenary and attracted some 30,000 supporters, complete with marching bands, flags and sashes. Some participants were less than coy about displaying imitation weapons and Ulster Volunteer Force (UVF) insignia, albeit in the form of historical pageantry.[55] The commemorative message was mixed, to say the least, but then so was the original.

Legacies

The vicissitudes of the Covenant in popular memory might lead one to believe that the political repercussions of the production and staging of Ulster Day were slight. Any such impression could hardly be more wrong. The legacy of Ulster Day, the ceremonial frame to the mass signing of the Covenant, was profound. The text committed one of the two major ethnic formations on the island to a position characterised by intransigence and outright opposition to Home Rule for All-Ireland. The creation of a paramilitary organisation, to increase political bargaining power, was the corollary. The political and constitutional niceties can be debated. Lady Londonderry, a leading figure within the Ulster Women's Unionist Council, was far from being alone in her view that if the Liberal government made no provision for a general election so as to test British opinion on Home Rule, then 'Ulstermen will be fully justified in armed resistance.'[56] It is difficult to see such sentiment as other than an expression of conditional loyalty to the parliament of the United Kingdom, and one laced with treasonable intent in the event of unionists not getting their way.

Though it was not obvious at first, the dialectic that bound nationalism and unionism ensured there was a response to Ulster Day and its sequel, the paramilitary mobilisation of Ulster unionists within the ranks of the UVF. Pearse believed that it was good to see guns in the hands of Irishmen, of whatever political persuasion.[57] Might not the militant unionists and the militant nationalists one day turn their guns on the common enemy of 'England'?[58]

Wishful thinking apart, the Irish Volunteers were mobilised in response to the threat of the Ulster Volunteers and so conditions were rife for communal confrontation. Without this sequence of actions and reactions, it is difficult to see how the Easter Rising of 1916 could have been brought about. Even Sir John Maxwell, who was given control of the military and civil response to the Rising, was of the view that ministers had 'winked at Ulster breaking the law' and were now reaping the poisoned harvest of their weak response.[59] Thus the unintended consequence of covenanting was to give a tiny group like the Irish Republican Brotherhood (IRB) the leverage it required to catalyse a major revolt. Ulster Day had foreshadowed partition, just as Easter 1916 would bring it close to fruition.

Nothing should detract from the irresponsibility of the Ulster Unionist leadership but it is important to bring out a further dimension to the Ulster, the Irish and the British crisis. Irish nationalists under the leadership of John Redmond were also party to the increasing polarisation. By not taking the Ulster unionist movement seriously, by not acknowledging the genuine concerns of many Ulster Protestants, and by failing to engage in effective dialogue from the early 1900s, the Irish Parliamentary Party indirectly contributed to its own eventual demise at the hands of militant nationalists and republicans. Nor can it be said that there were no warning voices from within the world of Irish nationalism. William O'Brien MP and his small All-for-Ireland League were the most articulate advocates of constructive dialogue but their counsels on the North and avoiding Partition were drowned out by the voices of the politico-sectarian Ancient Order of Hibernians and the advice of northern nationalist politicians.[60] There were others also but the weight of tradition-bound, self-deluding nationalist rhetoric on Ulster unionism prevailed until it was all too late.

In any case, the union of Britain and Ireland was not safeguarded by the extravagant gestures and mobilisations of the Ulster unionists. One can go further. The militancy and the militarism of the Ulster unionists paved the way for a secessionist nationalism that brought into being something much more extreme than Home Rule. This was an independent, frequently hostile Irish state on the borderlands of a re-drawn Ulster. Moreover, this was one in which Catholic doctrine and culture, supplemented by Anglophobia, were the hegemonic influences. Ulster unionism had shot itself in the foot, as inflated fears of the implications of a Home-Rule parliament had given rise to political reactions that proved to be self-fulfilling. The covenanting imagination succeeded in creating ever-enlarging numbers of implacable foes which it mistakenly assumed had always existed. Following Ulster Day and the arming of the UVF, the law of unintended consequences kicked in with a virulence that upended almost everything that Carson, the alleged saviour of Ulster and Irish unionism, originally stood for. More so than most, it may be said that his career ended in political failure and at great cost to his uncritical supporters.[61]

The instigators of 1916 fared little better. The Proclamation and the actions that accompanied it copper-fastened the looming prospect of Partition, though a partitioned Ireland was one of the last things the authors purportedly wanted. While not apparent in the text of the Proclamation itself, the Gaelicised and Catholicised images projected by the condemned leaders from their death cells revealed the Catholic nationalist ethos that ran through the Rising. Comerford captures this perfectly: the cohort that seized leadership of Irish nationalism in 1916 'was probably the most devoutly and uniformly Catholic grouping in Irish political history'.[62]

A scene from the death-wait of one of the lesser known leaders illustrates the wider point. The detail relates to Eamonn Ceannt, a Dublin Corporation clerk and Irish language enthusiast. During his last hours he was attended by a priest, Father Augustine, and at the moment of execution he held the priest's crucifix in his hands. 'My Jesus, mercy' were his last words. His wife Aine stayed up all that night, reciting Rosaries, while his brother Michael who had a particular devotion to the Sacred Heart of Jesus said five rosaries, as many litanies, and many other prayers. Sometime after the execution Father Augustine told Aine that her husband had 'gone to heaven'.[63] Devotional images such as these, which were powerfully marketed by the survivors and their relatives, found easy entry into the imagination of Catholic Ireland.

The re-organised Sinn Féin, in which the survivors of the Easter Rising played a dominant role, boycotted the Irish Convention of July 1917 which was perhaps the last realistic opportunity for peaceful compromise between North and South.[64] The politics of exaltation,[65] spelled out in the Proclamation and enacted in blood on the streets of Dublin left little room for creative compromise, not that much was on offer from London or Belfast. In the short term, the enormous boost to zealotry and to political purism imparted by the Rising raised the likelihood of violent conflict on a number of fronts, in the first instance with the UK state but also with unionists and with other Irish nationalists. The political incompetence of the British government in acceding to Sir John Maxwell's policy of executions after the Rising and, two years later, threatening to extend military conscription to Ireland, increased such probabilities still further.

Viewed in the longer term, the fetishising of the 'Irish Republic' within republican and nationalist discourse – an almost mystical concept inscribed in the Proclamation and one little talked of before 1916 – sowed the seeds of rancour, dissension and murderous disputes within Irish nationalism. The killings continued sporadically into the twenty-first century as various factions styling themselves Óglaigh na hÉireann or the IRA attacked the Northern Ireland state or indulged themselves in the killings of fellow dissidents, alleged drug dealers, or simply 'anti-social elements'.[66] At Easter-time, year in and year out, in graveyards across Ireland, in obeisance to the notion of apostolic succession, the ceremony of reading the Proclamation sanctions and sanctifies the continued pursuit of the 'Irish Republic', pure and indivisible.

These readings, and indeed many other readings, do not address the fundamental problem that the conspiratorial group that engineered the Rising had no mandate whatsoever from the peoples of Ireland. The anti-democratic nature of the enterprise and its uncritical exaltation in nationalist mythology has meant that any group of gunmen, ostensibly 'fighting for Ireland', can and indeed have invoked the precedent of Easter 1916 to legitimise their actions.[67] Like volunteer Joe O'Shea on Easter Monday, many have felt the 'savage exultation' of taking up the gun for 'Ireland'.[68] The idea that the sweeping victory of Sinn Féin in the general election of 1918, any more than the sweeping victory of Ulster Unionists in east Ulster in the same election, somehow legitimised retrospectively either 1916 or 1913 is simply a resort to mysticism. The arrow of time travels in one direction only.

The Two Irish Questions

In summing up one might say that the two manifestos, the Ulster Covenant and the Easter Proclamation, have something very important in common: it is that each texted terror. Both failed to take seriously the reality that there was not one but two Irish questions. Irish nationalists wanted recognition as a distinctive Irish nation which would be endowed with its own state apparatus. Ulster unionists wanted no part of this constitutional re-arrangement. Both were separatists in their own way, and each had a good case to make. Unionists outside of Ulster – those footnotes to the story of twentieth-century Ireland – were increasingly bewildered and uncertain.[69] The prospect facing Ulster unionists initially was a modest one, but one for which they were prepared to go to extreme lengths. To its great credit, one of the Protestant denominations, the Methodist Church in Ireland, issued an apology in 2012 on the centenary of the signing of the Covenant on two grounds: one was the implication that God was on the side of the unionists; the other was that 'the language of using "any means necessary" implied approval of the use of violence, as was clearly understood by some at the time'.[70]

The framework for all of this was the British question: how Ireland was incorporated into the United Kingdom in 1801. While the Liberals and the emerging Labour party had conceded the right to limited Home Rule, the Conservative and Unionist Party seized on the problems of a divided Ireland with malign enthusiasm. This had nothing to do with a supposed colonial relationship between the two islands at this juncture and everything to do with the United Kingdom's party political system and, in particular, with the bitter competition that marked relations between the Tories and the Liberals. It is the intersection of British and Irish politics, and calculations of party political advantage that produced the constitutional impasse. Under more gifted leaderships the outcomes might have been different, more sensitive compromises might have been devised, though in the longer term this would have required the dismantling of some of the segregationist devices – in education, in work, in housing, in sport, in language and in inter-denominational relations – that the two major ethnic groups had been so assiduous in manufacturing.[71] Carson and Craig, Pearse and Connolly were simply not up to the task. Neither were Redmond and Asquith, while the leader of the Tories, Bonar Law, was like a rabid dog fighting for the bone of advantage. Constructive unionism and reforming liberalism had done much to help modernise Ireland and lay the basis for a more prosperous future. Paradoxically, some of the major social reforms such as the settlement of the land question, better housing for rural labourers and the extension of the franchise had narrowed the areas in the North of Ireland where the interests of the two major ethnic blocs overlapped, thereby limiting the possibilities for co-operative action.[72] In 1912, they faced each other across the barricades of the national question.

Both the Covenant and the Proclamation deserve close reading, not just the affective or emotional response that typifies the reception of iconic texts. Mediated through the minds of historical actors, these texts helped inspire deeds of little beauty to God or country. The mobilisations that framed each document, and the subsequent mythologising, produced radical swerves to the right in unionist and nationalist politics, setting in train a series of consequences that privileged the gun, the drum and the flag above social concerns and individual liberties. No amount of celebration and commemoration can escape the fact that the consequences have been almost wholly malignant, not just at the time but across the twentieth century. Britain could extricate itself relatively unscathed from the imbroglio of the 1910s. But in Ireland mythological orthodoxies hardened, North and South, thereby deepening the gulf between communities on the island.[73] The agents of reaction – ethnic scribes, 'troubles' entrepreneurs, politico-religious extremists – were to be found aplenty within the island of Ireland. Typically they projected their own failings onto others, be it the North, the South or the British. No doubt there was something in all of these contentions. But the mote was never in the ideologue's eye. The consequences have been communal bitterness that feeds on itself and is only now undergoing slow and uncertain deconstruction in the new and twenty-first century.

CHAPTER NINE

Was There an Irish War of Independence?[1]

One of my grandfather's brothers, James Savage, fought in the American Civil War, and lost an eye in battle, so the spirit of freedom was strong on my mother's side.

Mary Brigid Pearse (1934)[2]

Always Ireland, Ireland, Ireland: story, legend, song, poem, planning. Perhaps we, too, would get a chance to fight or die. That seemed to be the end of all, the beckoning fate.

Ernie O'Malley (1936)[3]

Beginnings

Less than ten miles from my father's home in the Tipperary hill country lies the village of Hollyford. In 1920, it was the scene of a determined effort by the Irish Republican Army (IRA) to burn out the barracks of the Royal Irish Constabulary (RIC). The night attack was on a large scale, involving scouts placed on the hills commanding the approach roads from Newport, Tipperary town and Thurles. These roads had been cut at various points to hinder the arrival of police and troop reinforcements. Other volunteers lay in ambush. The attack was led by experienced militants, including Sean Treacy, who had attended the national school in Hollyford, Seamus Robinson who worked on a farm near Donohill, farther down the road from the tiny village, and Ernie O'Malley, a member of the Volunteers' GHQ staff. This is one scene from O'Malley's evocative recreation of the action:

> We crawled on to the roof, smashed slates with hammers, poured in petrol from our tins. We lighted sods of turf and threw them through gaps. Flames came with a yellow roar. We crawled further along the roof banging with hammers. I lighted the fuses of two bursting charges. We lay flat on the roof.

> Then came two loud explosions, bits of slates flew; a piece hit me on the head. Police fired rifles and revolvers. We poured in more petrol.

> Flames flaunted out of the darkness. We got back to the edge of the roof. Below I saw flashes through the loopholes; police grenades burst […]. I used up both revolvers, re-loaded and emptied again. The police fired through the roof of the lean-to building. I lay flat on the chimney. We emptied our tins of petrol. There were great holes in the slate roof; smoke and flames were blown by the wind against, and away from us. Our hands were burnt […] I flung in grenades […].[4]

This account is the kind of image that has burned its way into the public memory of political violence in Ireland during the years 1919–21. More generally, for people of my generation, popular and populist representations of the period celebrated the re-awakened consciousness of the Irish people, the rise of a martial spirit in the nation and, above all, the heroism of young, lightly-armed volunteers throwing themselves into battle against the mighty forces of the Crown. This enemy used 'every device of civilised and uncivilised warfare, every cruelty, every cowardly meanness that could be conceived by the most depraved minds' to crush the Irish Volunteers.[5] By contrast, as represented in the dominant narrative, the campaign of guerrilla warfare by the IRA was conducted with chivalry and restraint, characterised by set-piece engagements such as attacks on well-defended RIC barracks, deadly battles as at Kilmichael and Crossbarry, and daring jail escapes.

The opening shots of the guerrilla campaign were fired at Soloheadbeg, not far from Tipperary town, on 21 January 1919. Two armed RIC men, guarding a horse and cart carrying commercial explosives to a nearby quarry, were confronted by nine members of the Irish Volunteers lying in ambush. The attackers were led by Seamus Robinson, Dan Breen and Sean Treacy.[6] Recalling his feelings towards the two Irish policemen, moments before their deaths, Breen felt: 'the men who were now approaching had deserted their country, and were the spies and hirelings of her enemy'.[7] The dead men were Patrick O'Connell of Coachford, Co. Cork, who was due to be married, and the older James McDonnell, father of five children and a native Irish-speaker from the peninsula of Belmullet in Co. Mayo.[8]

My father, who was nine years of age at the time, in later life always referred to this incident as murder: the cold-blooded killing of two fellow-Irishmen. This was puzzling to me. My father's family and relatives had supported the IRA during those fateful years, they knew some of the principal participants in Tipperary, and the 'home place', which was almost hidden down a boreen, off a remote country road, was used as a refuge by IRA units in West Tipperary. My father was a fierce admirer of the more distant exploits of Tom Barry and his flying column in West Cork. Michael Collins had an iconic status at home, as soldier and statesman. In virtually all respects, apart from reservations regarding two or three sets of killings that were within the purview of the local, he endorsed the orthodox account of the struggle. Here then was a smooth narrative, which I had absorbed at home, at national school and in local oral tradition in the 1950s and 1960s, which nonetheless contained a ripple of contradiction. It was the awkward intersection of the local and the national which yielded this apparent conflict of understandings, and which later caused me to wonder about the nature of the 'Irish war of independence'. What if the local, far from being aberrant, was broadly representative of the whole? After all, my father and most others had to rely on written or second-hand accounts for the national picture, as constructed in the 1920s and later.

Concepts Revisited

Irish society underwent a series of violent upheavals between 1919 and 1921. Historians have varied in their use of labels to represent, and thereby capture the drama of the last days of the Union in southern Ireland, itself suggestive of the need to look more closely at the terms of argument and the social realities that lay beyond these attempted conceptualisations. Inevitably there are issues of power involved. Ideologues, politicians and civil servants have all sought to impose certain definitions of the Irish past with a view to promoting a particular ideology or legitimising a political position. The politics of language and hegemony are inseparable, and find expression in the discourses of Irish nationalism and Ulster Unionism. To give one example, modern-day Sinn Féin tends to refer to the fighting during the period 1919–21 as the 'Tan War', presumably with a view to reminding its audience that Irish independence, in the form of a 32-county Irish republic, has yet to be achieved.[9]

Contemporary protagonists created meaning out of their experiences by talking of the 'struggle', the 'war for freedom', the 'Black and Tan' war, the 'troubled times', the 'fight for freedom', the 'war with England', and the 'defence of the Republic'. In a detached, almost dismissive sentence, the IRA intellectual and hell-raiser, Ernie O'Malley, wrote on the declaration of a Truce in June 1921: 'And so ended for us what we called the scrap, the people later on, the trouble; and others fond of labels, the Revolution.'[10] What the episode was not called, by friend or foe, was the 'Irish war of independence'.[11]

Perhaps there is justification in its retrospective application? After all, a people cannot be sure it has undergone a war of independence until hostilities have been terminated and the outcome is manifest. The American colonists who revolted against Britain could be confident in the late 1770s that they were engaged in a revolution of some kind but hardly that they were prosecuting a successful war of independence. Historians of the United States of America still vary in their usage: for some the warfare and associated political agitation between 1775 and 1783 was the American War of Independence; for others it was the Revolution or the American Revolution. Even here there are crosscurrents. There is no reason to believe native Americans – a term the various, often mutually antagonistic indigenous peoples would have failed to recognise – might have subscribed to such notions, no more than one supposes the peasantries of Russia, Byelorussia or the Ukraine recognised the Bolshevik *coup d'état* of 1917 as the Great October Proletarian Revolution.

In the Irish case, as in other contexts, there is merit in looking critically at the grand concepts, their scope and genesis, particularly where by dint of common usage these have come to assume the status of empirical entities. How adequately do the conceptual categories encompass and express the complexities of the past? In the light of reflection, is there a need for some re-conceptualisation, for new forms of representation and perhaps for the creation of new meanings?

The violence-torn decade of 1913–23 is the crucial chronological segment for exploration of the notion of a war of independence. The surges of killings, woundings and intimidation which broke out in Ireland during these years, and which connected in different and conflicting ways with the European conflagration of the Great War, can be framed in a number of different, partly overlapping ways. Moreover, the forms and motivations for violence varied regionally on the island, indicating the complex, changing and contested character of terms like 'Irish', 'Ireland', 'war', 'independence' and indeed 'freedom'. The following table contains an inventory, by no means complete, of various perspectives which have been brought to bear on these conflicts.

Table 9.1
Conceptualising the Conflicts in Ireland, 1919–23

- A series of local and regional conflicts
- A 'war' by assassins, pro-Germans, disloyal elements
- A sectarian war
- A social revolution, a) in towns; and b) in the countryside
- A war in defence of the 'Republic'
- A 'revolution-in-arms'
- An Anglo-Irish war
- A war of secession
- A civil war: a) of nationalist against unionist; and b) of nationalist against nationalist

A De-centred View

The Soloheadbeg ambush was a result of local initiative taken by an informal fraternal brotherhood within the Tipperary Volunteers. It was disapproved of by other volunteers in the county, and roundly condemned by local priests, politicians and the nationalist *Tipperary Star*.[12] Archbishop Harty delivered hard words from the altar of Thurles Cathedral, seeing it as 'an offence against the laws of God, and as an offence against the fair name of our county'.[13] The priest who had attended the scene of the killings, Fr Keogh, C.C., was still visibly shaken a week later. 'It was a crime that cried to heaven for vengeance, as they knew from the words of God when Cain slew his brother Abel.'[14] Even the volunteers' clandestine journal, *An tÓglach,* referred to the incident only obliquely, reproducing what it claimed was a letter from an imprisoned Tipperary volunteer. Resorting to what must be an early example of 'whataboutery', the anonymous correspondent attacked the *Star* for not condemning excesses by the Thurles 'peelers' during the previous year, and ended by commending the men at Soloheadbeg for having 'risked their lives for Ireland'.[15]

The Volunteers envisaged the gathering storm of violence as convulsing the whole island, but a striking feature of the struggle was how highly regionalised it was. The greatest concentration of activity was located in the southern counties of Cork, Tipperary, Kerry and Clare, and in the capital city of Dublin.[16] As late as the spring of 1921, *An tÓglach* was returning to what was a constant refrain: while in some counties the enemy had been driven back virtually to its barracks, the situation was still 'very unsatisfactory' in other parts of Ireland. 'It effects [sic] no credit on the Volunteers in these districts that they should leave the gallant men of the South to bear all the brunt of the enemy's activities.'[17] Commandant General Tom Barry was more scathing. Some IRA leaders, he believed, were useless; too timorous to attack in case of reprisals. 'At least a dozen counties had some such figureheads, who were surely greater traitors to Ireland in her hour of need than any spies or informers.'[18] An alternative interpretation might be that other parts of nationalist Ireland, never mind the unionist districts of Ulster, were less receptive to the militant separatist doctrine of killing and (possibly) being killed. Far fewer Irish males responded to the call-to-arms of the IRA as compared to that issued by the Irish Parliamentary Party (IPP) in regard to the British army a few years earlier.

The regionally uneven character of the IRA's activity, as well as the sometimes local and selfish motives which dictated particular acts of violence, have to be acknowledged, but the sum total of activity can hardly be dismissed as isolated, local struggles devoid of national significance. The guerrilla campaign of 1919–21 was no lineal descendant of the mock-heroic exchange of hostilities at the Widow McCormack's cottage in 1848.[19] There was a broad base of support for the Sinn Féin movement, as evidenced by the 1918 general election, and by the local elections of 1920 and the 'partition' elections of 1921. The objective of breaking the Union of Britain and Ireland had gained greatly in popularity in the aftermath of the bloody occupation of central Dublin in April 1916 and the conscription crisis of 1918. While the relationship between the General Headquarters staff in Dublin and local IRA units was at times tenuous, the military campaign of the IRA came to have a degree of central co-ordination, and was fought in devotion to the 'Irish Republic' proclaimed in April 1916.

More serious criticisms might be that, by 1919, the volunteers constituted only a small minority within the Sinn Féin movement; they were effectively independent of political control (though nominally owing allegiance to Dáil Éireann), and they had little respect for the views or wishes of fellow nationalists. They were militarists, with a fundamentalist political aim, the attainment of an ill-defined 'republic', come what may.

'Murder Gangs'

In the eyes of Ulster unionist politicians and commentators, the guerrilla war was simply a campaign of murder carried out by gangs of assassins, pro-German sympathisers, and Sinn Féin thugs. Many Southern unionists may well have held similar opinions but as the fighting intensified in 1920, and as state terror sought to outmatch terror by the IRA, it became increasingly dangerous to voice dissent. In West Cork, for example, the isolated and vulnerable unionist households might hold private opinions but any sign of support for the police, the army or the British administration could carry heavy consequences.[20] In an historical inversion, it was a case of 'croppies lie down' for Irish loyalists.[21]

Moreover, these depictions accorded with elements of the truth. The Irish Volunteers, a splinter group from the mainstream nationalist volunteer movement, had been engaged in German plots, even if the German plot of 1918 had been a hoax invented by British intelligence, coloured perhaps by paranoia.[22] The words 'our gallant allies in Europe', inscribed in the Proclamation of 1916, referred to the Kaiser's troops, and their allies: a soldiery which occupied Belgium and parts of France and which met civilian resistance with brutal reprisals.[23]

Sometimes plain robbery, the settling of local land disputes by resort to the gun, or the protection of an illegal racket was the motive for violence. It is difficult to understand, for example, what national purpose was served by the ordeal of Kitty Carroll, dragged from her home by armed and masked men on the 17 April 1921, forced to walk half a mile from her home, and then shot by the road side as an informer. She had given the police information on the existence of a still for the illicit distillation of whiskey.[24] Miss Carroll was a forty-year-old spinster who looked after an invalided brother and a feeble mother aged about eighty. Similarly, one might wonder about the attempted murder of a herdsman in north Clare, working on a farm 'over which there is agitation in the district'.[25] His wife, Mrs Kilmartin, died trying to protect him from the masked gunmen. In spite of such accounts, to read the disorder of the period *primarily* in terms of banditry, local vendettas and general mayhem was, and is, wilfully misguided.

Unionist rage and fear regarding so-called gangs of assassins, midnight murderers, robbers and cowardly assailants, pointed to a new reality. The nature of resistance to the state by militant nationalists had changed fundamentally. Face-to-face engagements, as in April 1916, in which armed bodies of men in uniform met the uniformed enemy, had been superseded by the new tactic of guerrilla warfare, or the 'reign of terror' as one writer put it.[26] Soloheadbeg was a beginning in more ways than one. Contrary to the deliberately-fashioned popular memory of the period, as epitomised by accounts of the attack on the Hollyford barracks or the derring-do exploits of IRA commanders as portrayed in their memoirs, the typical action was of a rather less heroic kind. Policemen were shot in their ones or twos, on or off duty, usually when armed but sometimes not. Some simply 'disappeared': abducted, interrogated, shot or beaten to death, with their bodies disposed of in unmarked graves.[27] Troops were sniped at from a distance. Irish civilians under suspicion of offering succour to the Crown forces were abducted by the IRA from their homes, from their places of work, from public places. Some were warned and told to leave the country. Others were assaulted or publicly shamed, like the young Miss Kinsella, whose crime was to socialise with the police. 'In the early hours of Friday morning [8 July 1921] armed and masked men forced an entrance into the house of Peter Kinsella, a Co. Wexford farmer, and, dragging his daughter out into the yard, cut off her hair.'[28] As state and anti-state terror deepened, those who aroused the displeasure of the IRA were more likely to be shot. The notice-of-convenience – Spies Beware – covered all eventualities. Whether the Black and Tans, and the police auxiliaries, were any more discerning in their choice of victim is a moot point but their bouts of terror were restricted more narrowly in space and subject to some disciplinary restraint.

This war of the assassin lay outside the boundaries of mainstream unionist conceptions of legitimate warfare and beyond the limits of romantic nationalism as well. Hence the obvious uneasiness within nationalist Ireland with many of the attacks on the state forces during 1919 and on into 1920. The appellation of the term 'assassins' by the nationalist and Sinn-Féin-leaning *Irish Independent* to the group which attempted to kill Lord French, the Lord Lieutenant, at Ashtown during Christmas week 1919, so outraged the IRA that it initially considered murdering the editor but later settled on smashing its printing presses.[29] Because the descent into terror violated conventional notions of a war, this may help explain why some are reluctant to accord the title 'war' to the hit-and-run tactics of the IRA.[30] The ambiguous relationship between the militarism of the IRA and the political agitation of Sinn Féin, and of course the interpenetration of the two, served to muddy the water still further. Moreover, a policy of reprisals, unacknowledged but officially understood, existed from 1920 under Lloyd George's government. Houses, shops and community institutions such as co-operative creameries were put to the torch. On occasion drunken soldiers shot unarmed civilians. There were a number of cases of prisoners being shot in cold blood on the transparent excuse of 'attempting to escape' while in custody. Perhaps the most notorious instance of state terror took place on 21 November 1920 ('Bloody Sunday') when British soldiers fired indiscriminately on a crowd attending a Gaelic football game at Croke Park, murdering fourteen spectators. This was to avenge the slayings earlier that Sunday by the IRA of thirteen alleged British agents in their places of residence around Dublin. It is clear from the pattern of casualties nonetheless that while the IRA did not have a monopoly of terror, it had the lion's share over the period 1919–21.

According to some definitions of war – 'a forcible contention between states with the purpose of overpowering each other by armed force, in order to secure certain demands or claims' – this was not a war.[31] The term is surely sufficiently elastic, though, in current usage to be stretched to embrace this particular campaign of political violence. Moreover, as time wore on, the excesses of the state forces had the effect of legitimising the IRA's offensive in some sections of Irish society.

An Irish Jihad?

The guerrilla war unleashed, in virulent form, some of the elemental forces of communal sectarianism long present in Irish society. In Munster, particularly in Cork and Clare, Protestant farmers and businessmen had their homes burned; some were assassinated; others fled.[32] On the edge of my home village, Borrisoleigh, the one Protestant farmhouse was regularly fired on, while in the neighbouring parish of Templederry Protestant farm yards were looted for machinery and implements.[33] In one case, as my father related, this took the form of dismantling and hauling away an imposing set of cut-stone piers from a farm entrance. He retold the story with amusement, as the stones were commandeered by one of his neighbours – a small farmer whose horse-and-cart was barely able to draw its load of contraband into the hill country. In general, he was reluctant to talk about the treatment of local Protestants, though they may have fared better than in some other parts of the county.[34]

Not far from the tiny village of Templederry lay the great ancestral home of the Dunalley family; today it is a ruin, its shattered structures enclosing emptiness. In those troubled times the mansion was raided many times, cattle and sheep were stolen from the demesne, and finally it was burned down by the anti-Treaty IRA during the civil war.[35] Some miles away, at Dualla, a Protestant chauffeur, David Cumming, in the employment of a gentleman farmer, was shot dead, as were a number of other Protestants in the county.[36] Farther north, in Mayo, Monaghan and Roscommon, Protestant farmers were the victims of possibly sectarian killings.[37]

But the real cauldron of sectarian hatred was in east Ulster. In January 1919, in the same month as the summoning of the first Dáil Éireann and the killings at Soloheadbeg, Catholic and Protestant workers in Belfast united in massive strike demonstrations to advance their demands for a forty-four-hour working week.[38] However, under the strain of the IRA mobilisation and subsequent offensive, passions boiled over. At the end of the holiday fortnight, July 1920, there were mass expulsions of Catholic workers from the shipyards, the engineering works of Sirocco and Mackies, and other places of work in Belfast, Banbridge and Dromore. Casualties were heavy on both sides. In the first few days of violence six Protestants and seven Catholics were killed, and this was only the prologue to a long summer of deadly sectarian rioting.[39] The trigger to the disturbances was the killing of an RIC divisional commissioner, Colonel G.F. Smyth, who had connections with Banbridge in the North. He was gunned down by the IRA in Co. Cork. Emotional scenes surrounded the homecoming and the funeral. Worryingly, the incident, and its sequel, demonstrated the lethal interconnectedness of violence in the North and in the South.

Outrage was heaped on outrage, with little respite over the following two years. Some of the shootings were three-way affairs, involving Catholic gunmen (usually but not invariably members of the IRA), Protestant gunmen and the RIC. Unlike the conflict in the South, street mobs played a significant part in the escalating violence, resorting to stoning, burning and looting. The sheer weight of Protestant numbers gave them an advantage, which had terrifying implications for isolated Catholic enclaves like the Short Strand in east Belfast.[40] In one of the worst months of violence, March 1922, sixty-one people died. This included the Catholic McMahon family, five of whom were murdered in their home by men believed to be members of the RIC.[41] John McMahon, aged twenty-five, who was badly wounded but survived the attack, described how the attackers smashed their way into the house and then set about their grim work.

> My mother and sister were hustled into a room, and the murderers, revolvers in hand, forced my father, brothers, and the manager into the sitting room.

The leader then remarked: 'Well, boys, do you say any prayers?' The words had scarcely been uttered when a fusillade of shots rang out, each member of the gang firing, and my father fell. They then fired at each of us in turn, and eventually I was shot.[42]

Sectarian killings were not confined to Belfast of course. Most towns with mixed populations reverberated to the drumbeats of communal hatred. Near Newry in south Armagh, the IRA, possibly led by Frank Aiken, a future Fianna Fáil minister, carried out a series of killings of Protestant farmers during the early hours of Saturday, 17 June 1922.[43] This was followed, in quick succession, by reprisals which left seven Catholics dead.[44] It was as if the ethnic warriors of loyalist paramilitarism and the nationalist IRA were trading body counts. And so it continued until the newly-created Northern Ireland state finally succeeded in suppressing the violence.

It is difficult not to see the period 1919–23 in Ulster, and to a lesser degree elsewhere on the island, as the working out of communal sectarian tensions long present in Irish society but stoked by the arming of the Ulster Volunteer Force (UVF) in 1914 and brought to a murderous climax by the IRA offensive after the First World War. While politics intertwined with religion, religious affiliation was more than simply a marker of unionism or nationalism.[45] The street-level antipathies and name calling, the self-segregation, the riots and expulsions, the Catholic trappings of Irish republicanism and the Protestant character of Ulster loyalism, all suggest that religious conflict was a potent force in its own right. While the patterns of violence of 1919–23 are not reducible to a sectarian war, one plane of the conflict is best represented as religious or sectarian. As with other dimensions of political violence, there was a marked but markedly different regional character to the outbursts of sectarian hatred.

Social Revolution

Perhaps at base the tumultuous events in Ireland during the revolutionary decade constituted a social revolution? Certainly there were agrarian agitations involving cattle drives, seizures of grazing farms, and demands for the redistribution of land in favour of local, land-hungry farmers. The radical land reformer, Lawrence Ginnell MP, who later defected to Sinn Féin, had long called for the breaking up of demesne farms and untenanted grazing farms.[46] A number of Sinn Féin activists took up the call in 1917, an auspicious year for social revolution in world history.[47] In this and the following year there were spontaneous outbursts of small-farmer militancy in several districts in Ireland, especially in the West of Ireland. In some places the Irish volunteers intervened on the side of the smallholders but by 1919 the official policy of restraining land hunger was being more vigorously enforced, much to the chagrin of republican socialists like Peadar O'Donnell.[48] 'All the leadership wanted was a change from British to Irish government: they wanted no change in the basis of society. It was a political not a social revolution', he asserted.[49] Expressions of rural class interest were perceived by Sinn Féin and the IRA as selfish distractions from the national struggle. Moreover, they raised the spectre of Bolshevism, a less than popular cause in a conservative, Catholic society. From a Sinn Féin point of view discouraging land seizures was almost certainly a sensible strategy, some of O'Donnell's fanciful rhetoric on small-farmer radicalism notwithstanding.

The truth was these localised land agitations were largely sideshows, confined in the main to parts of the west of Ireland and patches of the midland counties. The problem for agrarian radicals was that the social revolution in land ownership had already taken place. The landed ascendancy had been deprived of its ownership of the farm land of Ireland by virtue of a series of reforms stretching back into the later nineteenth century, and culminating in the Wyndham Land Act of 1903 and the Birrell amendment to this act in 1909. In Marxian terms, major contradictions within the foundations of the social order had already been smoothed: a largely peaceful social transformation in the countryside had been concluded, and farmers were happy to take the full benefit of the boom in agricultural prices and farm incomes between 1914 and 1920.[50]

There was more scope for conflict farther down the social hierarchy, between farmers and labourers, as had been common in pre-Famine Irish society. By the early twentieth century rural labourers were less numerous than farmers in the countryside, but there were still significant numbers in the tillage counties of the south east and in the rich dairying lands of Cork and Limerick. Some had joined the militant Irish Transport and General Workers Union during the Great War and had fought bitter strikes during 1918–20, involving violence and sabotage, to push up wages in the face of rampant price inflation. The local elections in urban Ireland in January 1920 witnessed remarkable gains, both by nationalist labour candidates and unionist labour.[51] The labour organ, *Watchword*, headlined its coverage with the claim of 'Red Flag Over All in Bantry, Lurgan, Mullingar, Athlone, Newbridge, etc', adding somewhat optimistically, 'surely Mullingar's next step is the Soviet'.[52] Some strikes seemed to threaten a revolutionary take-over of society: workers seized thirteen creameries, to form the 'Knocklong Soviet' in 1920, and two years later the red flag was hoisted once more in the Suir valley as workers took over creameries, mills and bakeries owned by the Cleeves manufacturing company.[53] To the worried owners of capital the apparent similarity at local level between Sinn Féin and labour activism, and the alacrity with which trade unions initiated political strikes – in April 1919 the Limerick Trades

Council organised a nine-day general strike against 'British militarism'[54] – seemed to threaten the existing social order.

Urban Ireland, particularly the cities of Belfast and Dublin, was a more obvious theatre for class warfare. Jim Larkin had remarkable success in organising the unskilled workers in factories, transport and docklands, and then in leading them to industrial defeat. In the later years of the First World War and its aftermath, labour militancy reached new heights. But the owners of capital need not have worried. Limited forms of class struggle and limited, if realistic, forms of worker consciousness ensured there was no fundamental challenge to the existing relations of production. Moreover, Sinn Féin, by and large, was not sympathetic to Labour.[55] The national question crowded out the labour question, most ruinously of all in the case of Ulster.

It is true that class tensions were never very far beneath the social surface, adding to the complexity of the period. But whatever way one seeks to conceptualise what happened in Ireland in the decade before 1923, it certainly did not eventuate in a social revolution. Ironically, the social reforms which redistributed income and wealth most effectively had been initiated by the Westminster parliament some time earlier: the land acts, the measures to improve the housing of labourers, the introduction of state pensions to combat poverty in old age, and forms of social insurance for selected categories of workers from 1911.

The Gun and the 'Republic'

'*Go dtugaidh Dia cogadh le n'ár linn*' [may God grant us war in our time] was the ardent wish of the young Sean Treacy.[56] If anyone may be said to have been dying to kill for Ireland, it was Treacy, and he, in fact, achieved both objectives. In April 1916, soon after the insurrection in Dublin, he had to be restrained by his uncle from pulling a gun on an elderly sergeant in the RIC and shooting him on the spot. The sergeant had asked him for his name and his business.[57] A committed gunman and veteran of innumerable ambushes with a limited interest in politics, Treacy was finally gunned down himself in a shoot-out in Talbot Street, Dublin. Another of the fatherless sons of the revolution, Terence MacSwiney, later to win international attention through his death on hunger strike, exulted in the prospect of war: 'glorious fruitful action. Oh God speed the day, God speed the day'.[58] A Cork volunteer, Florence O'Donoghue saw himself and his comrades working for the 'achievement of national independence in arms'.[59] Michael Collins, conspiring energetically in Dublin to produce an armed conflagration, would have embraced such sentiments and possibly the persons.[60] The father of Austin Stack, a leading IRA figure in Co. Kerry, instilled in his children the 'honour it would be to strike a blow in defence of our native land'.[61]

This opens a serious line of questioning. Were these militant separatists seeking an Irish Republic, through political means if possible, through violent action if necessary? The subtext of many of the memoirs and other biographical materials seems to be that a revolution-in-arms had become an end in itself, just as it was for some of the participants in the 1916 insurrection. The achievement of political independence without going through the purging experience of war and bloodshed was so inglorious, so lacking in heroic possibilities, so out of tune with an imagined past, as to be soulless and unfulfilling. Self-dramatisation and the destiny of the nation demanded more. Flag-waving, speech-making, resolution-passing and parading, and other such harmless pursuits, were all right for the faint-hearted, but a warrior race would redeem its honour in blood and sacrifice.[62]

There was also the consideration that the 'Irish Republic' had been proclaimed in 1916, admittedly by men who had considered it unnecessary to consult the Irish electorate on the imminent destruction of parts of its capital. Perhaps the most chilling sentence in the Proclamation reads: 'The Irish Republic is entitled to, and hereby claims, the allegiance of every Irishman and Irishwoman.'[63] This presumptuousness consigned scores of Dubliners, unconnected with the insurrection, to an untimely death, and later served to legitimise, albeit by a mystical sleight of hand, the operations of the IRA. In effect, the peoples of Ireland had been conscripted into a non-existent state. For a small number of extreme nationalists the rhetorical trick of a self-subsisting 'Republic', transcending democratic politics, was a matter of immediate and deadly seriousness. Liam Lynch, who later served and died as the commander of the Anti-Treaty forces, saw an inescapable obligation to fight for the 'Republic'.[64] So did others. The impressive Sinn Féin victories at the general election in 1918, and the decision of the first Dáil to opt for a republican form of government, were further sources of moral reassurance. However, these in themselves were not necessary to legitimise, in the minds of some, the drive towards a war: a war in defence of the 'Republic', as proclaimed on Easter Monday from the front of the General Post Office.

It may have been a world of ideological make-believe, but from the viewpoint of republican zealots, there is a real sense in which the warfare of 1919–21 was a war in defence of the 'Republic'. The argument (but not the closed logic) is a bit more strained when it comes to dealing with the conventionally-labelled civil war of 1922–23. This becomes simply the second war in defence of the 'Republic'. I stood in a country graveyard in the late 1950s, just after serving Sunday mass, as a republican speaker denounced those who used the term 'civil war', urging instead the more cumbersome 'second war in defence of the Republic'.[65] The great majority of Irish nationalists, and of course unionists, were not carried away by these rhetorical devices, but then their options were narrowing rapidly from early 1920 onwards. Depending on the voices one chooses to listen to, there *was* a war in defence of the 'Republic', just as the revolution-in-arms was a blessed experience for some.

Anglo, Irish, and War

The Anglo-Irish War is one of the most widely-used formulations by historians, and is sometimes used interchangeably with the image of a war of independence.[66] It was a term used, though not very often, during the period itself. But it begs some awkward questions. Even if we skip over the issue of how it deals with the Scottish and the Welsh – national groupings which formed an integral part of the British polity – there remains the most immediate question of who were the Irish. Many southern unionists saw themselves as Irish, while entertaining further political identities as well. They would not have perceived themselves in the one-dimensional form of loyalists and imperialists to which, for instance, Tom Barry reduced so many of them.[67] Lady Arnott, who presided over a meeting of unionist women voters in the Mansion House in December 1918 believed their ideal was 'service not for Ireland alone but for Ireland, the Empire and humanity'.[68] Petitioners to the coalition government of Lloyd George and Bonar Law, protesting against the partition of Ireland on behalf of 400,000 southern unionists, described themselves simply as Irishmen seeking to promote 'the true interests of Ireland'.[69] The social republican, Peadar O'Donnell, who was born into a poor, Gaelic-speaking family in west Donegal, had a different take on his fellow Donegal Protestants, people who were in the main unionist: 'I considered them to be as Irish as I was, but bad Irishmen.'[70] The West Britons and shoneens against whom the *Leader* newspaper and other Irish-Ireland organs railed so consistently must have had some numerical significance; otherwise so much propagandist energy was a waste of breath.[71] Northern unionists might have been more equivocal in their sense of identity – as with their nationalist compatriots this was defined most powerfully in relation to the 'other', that which they vehemently were not – but many would have seen themselves as Irish and also loyal to King and Empire.

It may be straining definitions of Irishness too much – though no more so than in the case of Eamon de Valera, Mary MacSwiney or Erskine Childers – to view the incumbent of the vice-regal lodge, Sir John French, as Irish. Born in England, of Anglo-Irish parentage, he had a deep affection for Ireland – his Ireland, that is – and his sister, Mrs Despard, was an outspoken republican and advocate of women's rights. Some months after the Ashtown ambush, Mrs Despard, walking down O'Connell Street in Dublin in the company of Maud Gonne MacBride, met one of his would-be killers, Dan Breen. Mrs Despard upbraided him for the attack on her brother. This is how Breen recalled that strange encounter:

'My only regret', I ventured to say, 'is that we did not get him.'

'You naughty boy! John is a good Irishman.'

'Your notion and mine differ about the meaning of the word "good"!'

'Imagine poor John killed by his compatriots', she exclaimed with tears in her eyes.[72]

In the circumstances of such cultural and ethnic complexity, and its accompanying diversity of ideologies and identities, the apparently neutral image of an Anglo-Irish war seems singularly ill-fitting. Even within nationalist circles, never mind the electorate of Ireland as a whole, there is no evidence of a widespread desire for violent struggle, still less of the kind which eventually emerged. It is true that the first Dáil Éireann, composed exclusively of Sinn Féin deputies, moved in 1919 to adopt the idea of the Irish 'Republic' as advocated in April 1916. It is also true that the IPP had warned during the general election of 1918 that a vote for Sinn Féin could be a vote for another insurrection. 'There is only one way in which an Irish republic can be got', argued Joe Devlin MP, 'and that is by an appeal to physical force'.[73] That was tried in 1916, and despite the fact that Britain was then at war, it failed. Predicting a rude awakening when these young fellows eventually woke up, Devlin dismissed the idea as foolish and impossible. While the impossibilists would have their day, it is not clear that the Irish party, or the electorate, had a clear view of what this might entail. There were many different motives for voting for Sinn Féin, only some of which were consistent with support for the policy of a republic, achieved by force of arms if necessary.[74] Certainly Sinn Féin, still less the secret Irish Republican Brotherhood (IRB), were in no hurry to enlighten the electorate regarding the direction of their militancy in advance of the polls in December 1918.

Moreover, the new assembly in Dublin was slow to take responsibility for the actions of the Irish Volunteers. There was no formal link until August 1919 when an oath of allegiance to the 'Republic' and to Dáil Éireann began to be administered to each volunteer, and, of course, no responsibility was taken for Soloheadbeg, Fermoy, Ashtown and other engagements during this early phase of armed hostilities.[75] While the more theologically-minded republicans would have regarded Ireland as being in a state of war with Britain since 1916, the coalition of political forces which was Sinn Féin did not feel itself in a position to declare war on behalf of the 'Irish people'. It was only during the final phase of the years of disturbances and violence that Dáil Éireann assumed a degree of public responsibility for the actions of the IRA. Nonetheless, the relationship was always loose. IRA activists were often suspicious or dismissive of the politicians in Sinn Féin: Ernie O'Malley laughed heartily at the idea of being mistaken for a 'Sinn Féiner'.[76] In the final resort, many in the IRA perceived themselves to be above politics; they represented an élite force which interpreted the true interests of the Irish people. Be it war or peace, the people might have a right to be consulted. But they had no right to do wrong.

After two years of terror and counter-terror many in nationalist Ireland had come to acquiesce in the idea of a war against the British state. By then, to have voiced criticism would have been distinctly dangerous. The degree of enthusiasm for political violence is difficult to gauge but it varied greatly, by age, by social class, by locality and possibly by gender. The unionist Irish, who alone constituted a quarter of the population, remained unsupportive: cowed into submission, as in much of the South, or violently hostile as in the North.[77] Viewed from a position of doctrinaire certainty on the course of action the peoples of Ireland should be pursuing, there was an Anglo-Irish war. For the majority, however, this was a terror-laden strategy which had been imposed on them.

Leaders of the IRA were quite open about this in later years. In fact it was a matter of pride to recall what little support they had initially enjoyed.[78] In recognition of the reluctance of the nationalist population to support an IRA offensive, Richard Mulcahy, the chief of staff of the Irish Volunteers believed that the people had to be educated and 'led gently into open war'.[79] Sean Treacy, the Tipperary commandant, was of a different mind. Alarmed at the melting away of the volunteers and the poor state of organisation of the remainder once the conscription crisis of 1918 had passed, he foresaw a more desperate remedy: 'If this is the state of affairs, we'll have to kill someone, and make the bloody enemy organise us!'[80] This, in fact, was how the spiral of confrontation and polarisation was accomplished. By deliberately provoking and inducing state oppression, elements within the IRA achieved their objective of engineering a confrontation with the British state, in the process pulverising their opponents within nationalist Ireland.[81]

This was not, however, easily achieved. One late and imperfect barometer of public opinion is the local elections in urban Ireland in January 1920.[82] Fought under a system of proportional representation, Sinn Féin decisively out-polled the Irish Party by a factor of more than two to one. Interestingly, the ratio between the two parties' share of the vote was much the same as in the general election of 1918. Moderate nationalism, outside of Sinn Féin, had not gone away. Equally significantly, Labour candidates did remarkably well, North and South, suggesting that the withdrawal of Labour from the electoral contest in 1918 was an important element in the scale of the Sinn Féin victory at the time. The shocking point for Sinn Féin in 1920, however, was that it took less than one in three of the seats.[83] As always, many motives went into the making of voting shares and Sinn Féin support would probably have been higher in rural as compared to urban districts. However, on the crucial issue of support for the IRA campaign, there was only one party to support, and that was Sinn Féin. Even discounting the likelihood that some voters supported Sinn Féin for other reasons, there was no mandate here for a 'war', however labelled.

The conclusion seems inescapable: nationalist Ireland was catapulted into a violent confrontation not of its choosing. It follows from this that the notion of an Anglo-Irish war is inappropriate and misleading. Whether a conscious strategy or not, the effect of the IRA offensive was to limit and eventually restrict choice to the twin polarities of Sinn Féin and the unionists, as in the 'partition' elections of 1921. When people in southern Ireland were again allowed to register their views, as during the general election of June 1922, they voted resoundingly for the Treaty and the peace it promised. True to character, IRA militants and the anti-Treaty Sinn Féiners were reluctant to allow free elections, and the contest was rigged to shield them from the full force of the electorate's rejection of further military adventures.

A War of Secession

The Union of Britain and Ireland had given rise to major devolutionist agitations, though none were sustained before the late nineteenth century. Contrary to the impression sometimes conveyed in writings driven by retrospective knowledge, the question of the union was not a leading political issue during most years of the nineteenth century. The union occasioned virtually no bloodshed before 1916, which contrasts remarkably with the bloody internal politics of France, Spain and Italy during the same extended time period.[84] This internal security and stability places Ireland closer to the political experience of the Scandinavian countries and the Netherlands rather than some of the polities of western Europe. The sheer density of interconnections between the societies of Britain and Ireland by the eve of the First World War, most powerfully expressed in the volunteering of at least 200,000 Irishmen (a majority of whom were Catholic) to fight against the armies of the Kaiser, makes it easier to understand why the great political question of the day was not a call for the end of the union but for devolution of power to a subordinate assembly in Dublin.[85]

The political agitation of Sinn Féin, and the accompanying violence of the IRA, strained and severed many of the connections. An Irish Free State was created which, in most significant respects, was an independent state. In addition, it had the potential to evolve further, so that by 1949 an Irish 'Republic' could be declared. It is an irony of history that the architect of many of these changes, Eamon de Valera, had originally been a fierce opponent of the notion that the Treaty of 1921 gave freedom, 'not the ultimate freedom that all nations aspire and develop to, but the freedom to achieve it'.[86] More significantly, the treaty between the representatives of Dáil Éireann and the United Kingdom government, agreed in London in December 1921, led to double acts of partition and secession: from a nationalist viewpoint the partition of the island of Ireland and the secession of the six northern counties; from a unionist viewpoint the partition of the United Kingdom and the secession of southern Ireland. These were classic acts of secession on a European pattern: as in the violent withdrawal of Belgium from the Netherlands in the early nineteenth century or the more pacific break up of Czechoslovakia into two distinct states in the late twentieth, but not very different in character from either of these. But then there is not much poetry in the idea of a war of secession, so whatever its partial congruence with the facts of the situation, it is unlikely to commend itself to those who demand glory from history.[87]

These acts of secession were derivatives or by-products of the civil conflicts that gripped Ireland in the decade after the formation in 1913 of the UVF and its nationalist mirror image, the Irish Volunteers. An undue preoccupation with the high politics of the period – the machinations of Asquith, Carson, Lloyd George, de Valera, Griffith and Collins – tends to obscure the deeper and contradictory social forces that drove, obstructed and re-synthesised politics in Ireland during the course of that terrible decade.

Civil War One: Orange and Green

If one considers the series of interrelated conflicts between 1913 and 1923 as a whole, then it is possible to discern a pattern of civil war within Ireland, albeit one powerfully influenced by external forces and circumstances. This is in two senses: one, that of a civil war between Orange and Green, between Irish nationalism and Irish (including Ulster) unionism; and two, as a war within Irish nationalism.

At the beginning of the year 1914 Ireland seemed poised on the edge of a civil war of North and South. This was both extraordinary and yet seemingly inevitable. Still, we need to remind ourselves that Irish politics for the preceding three decades had revolved on an east-west axis, with the problems of communal division within Ulster perceived rather like sounds off-stage, worrying in a provincial context but not really part of the grand plot. Now the private armies of North and South, the UVF and the Irish Volunteers, seemed destined to re-enact a modern-day drama of Planter against Gael. What we have, therefore, are the classic ingredients of a civil war: a deep ideological gulf, with masses of ordinary folk standing ready to join combat with similar others, for the sake of differing political aspirations within the polity of the United Kingdom. Even if one recognises the existence of two distinctive ethnic identities on the island of Ireland, the unfolding tragedy has the sticky intimacy of impending civil war.

In this moment of truth, British politicians and Irish nationalist politicians were forced to acknowledge the deeply antagonistic political formations on the island of Ireland. Though a direct confrontation was suspended until after the Great War, thus serving to conceal both the malign influence of the Tory party at Westminster and the bankruptcy of the Liberal's Irish policy,[88] the struggle of nationalist Ireland against unionist Ireland was now couched in the threatening language and practices of militarism. Moreover, the lurch into armed rhetoric set constraints on political compromise over the next decade and proved to be a principal tributary to communal conflict in the years after the Great War.

Fighting between nationalist and unionist in the northern counties of the island was no figure of speech. The pogrom directed against Catholics and nationalists in Belfast in the summer of 1920 has been mentioned earlier, as well as the counter-terror of armed nationalists. Even the Truce of Monday 11 July 1921 failed to cut across the communal savagery that ravaged Belfast and other parts of Ulster. Some, fearing an end to the sport of terror, intensified their activity in the weekend before the Truce. The newspaper headlines of the time chart the progress: 'Belfast's Bloody Week-End'; 'Sinn Féin Attack on Police Lorry'; '12 Killed and 100 Wounded in Night and Day Battles'; '42 Catholic Houses Burned'.[89] A day later: 'Belfast's Death-Roll 16'; '1,000 Homeless'; 'Snipers Again Active'.[90] Among the many civilian casualties was that of a young girl from a nationalist area:

> Between five and six o'clock a little girl named Margaret Walsh, aged 14, of No. 2 Ellis Court, received a fatal bullet wound, being shot in the head by a sniper when standing at the corner of York Street and Nile Street. She was taken in the ambulance to the Royal Victoria Hospital, and only survived for about an hour after admission.[91]

While Catholics and nationalists suffered most in the northern 'troubles', Protestants and unionists were the more likely victims in southern Ireland. Unlike northern Catholics, a minority of whom either supported or participated in the killing of policemen, soldiers and sometimes Protestant civilians, southern Protestants tended to abstain from paramilitary activity, though small numbers were involved in the RIC and some were to be found in the British army. Ideologically out of tune with the demands of Sinn Féin, their position was a vulnerable one: they were open to boycotting, intimidation, raids on their homes, abduction, wounding or, in extreme cases, murder.

This has been discussed briefly in relation to the religious dimension to the conflict, but it is worth emphasising that, while religion was bound up with theological beliefs and practices, it was also a critical force in the formation and makeup of ethnic identity. The predicament of isolated unionists or loyalists in regions like West Cork was especially pitiful, as republican paranoia, politico-religious hatred and personal greed combined to produce a reign of terror.

Among the worst atrocities was the killing in the early hours of 27 April 1922 of James Buttimer, an eighty-two-year-old Protestant. The old man was shot in the face at the doorway to his home on the main street of Dunmanway, Co. Cork.[92] His wife, Clarina, who had been awakened by the battering on the door, was with him in his last moments.[93] This was not an isolated incident. Along the Bandon valley, an orgy of killings was in progress. In the space of a few nights, as Peter Hart relates:

> Ten men had been shot dead, and another wounded. All were Protestant. Scores of Cork Protestants had been killed as 'spies' or 'informers' in the previous two years, but never so many at once or so (apparently) randomly. The spectre of mass murder had long haunted the unionist political imagination; when it arrived, the reality struck with the force of a nightmare. Hundreds went into hiding or fled their homes as a wave of panic, fanned by threats and rumours, raced through West Cork. Farms and shops were abandoned and in many households only women and children, or those too sick or old to travel, remained.[94]

Kathleen Keyes McDonnell, who, unusually, combined support for the IRA with membership of a wealthy Catholic business family in Bandon, even fifty years later had little sympathy for 'this alien stock in the Bandon Settlement', these descendants of Elizabethan and Cromwellian settlers, as she contemptuously put it. 'Blood would flow to cleanse the record,' she exulted, 'much blood and no regrets'.[95] Cork was an extreme example, where de-civilising processes had proceeded farther than in many parts of the country. Still, most counties in the midlands, the south and west of Ireland witnessed shootings of civilians who favoured the union, more particularly if they had participated in the Great War.[96] The penchant for murdering ex-servicemen had many motives and, by the Truce of July 1921, at least eighty-two of these, Catholic and Protestant, nationalist and unionist, had been struck down. The assassinations continued into the years of the Civil War. To take a single example, chosen more or less at random: some hours after midnight on the 3 August 1922, armed and disguised men entered a house at Irishtown, Mountmellick, and led away one of the occupants, an ex-soldier and married man by the name of John Fitzpatrick. Fitzpatrick's body was discovered later not far from Mountmellick. He had been shot through the heart, and in his coat pocket was a label bearing the words 'Robbers and Spies beware'.[97] Thus ended the life of this Irishman from Irishtown.

In the border county of Monaghan the balance of communal terror was potentially more evenly struck, as the county contained a substantial if minority Protestant and unionist population.[98] In the late summer of 1920, armed unionist volunteers turned out at Clones and Drum to guard bread vans from Belfast.[99] Belfast goods were the subject of a widespread nationalist boycott, set up in response to attacks on Catholics and nationalists in that city.[100] A unionist farmer was shot dead in Carrickmacross, and the sub-region seemed to balance on the edge of political and sectarian conflict. In fact, moderate opinion and traditions of mutual accommodation held sway, despite the further provocations of the Black and Tans and the local IRA. The killing of several 'loyalists' by the IRA in the spring of 1921 did not induce a unionist volunteer response,[101] and the county managed to slip past the worst excesses of the sharpening unionist and nationalist conflict in the northern counties.

In Belfast, as we have seen, it was otherwise, with the weight of numbers favouring unionists. There were fewer cultural resources to limit violence once it had been invoked. Indeed the traditions of communal fighting dated back to the early nineteenth century. Riots, street battles, looting and killings had long scarred life in the northern capital, but never previously on such a scale or for such a prolonged period as in the early 1920s. This was also true to varying degrees in other towns and villages in Ulster. Neighbourhood turned on neighbourhood, sometimes neighbour on neighbour. During the course of the massacre at Altnaveigh, Mrs Crozier addressed one of the killers: 'I would not have expected that of you, Willie', before she herself was put to death.[102] Assassins came out of the night, sometimes masked, sometimes not. Discipline in the police and the military at times snapped, and there were numerous claims of collusion between the security forces and loyalist volunteers.[103] The fight centred on territory, economic and symbolic space, and, ultimately, the constitutional status of Ulster and Ireland. These 'uncivil wars' took several years to burn themselves out. The figures for deaths underlined the communal nature of the strife: in the two years between July 1920 and July 1922 the security forces lost 82 men, while 303 Catholics and 172 Protestants were slain.[104] The great majority of Protestant and Catholic deaths was of civilians rather than loyalist or republican gunmen.

We have already seen how severely the IRA might deal with those fellow Irish or British ('loyalists', 'imperialists') who professed support for the union in a manner which seemed delusional to their nationalist neighbours. How did IRA commanders see the collective future of this minority in the new Ireland? Opinions naturally varied – members of the new government of the Irish Free State were genuinely shocked when a delegation of Protestant church leaders waited on them in 1922, wondering if their congregations were to have any place in the new Ireland.[105] Some of the field commanders, however, had seen little role for unionists in the idealised future. Ernie O'Malley discussed the question with the die-hard republican leader, Liam Lynch. They foresaw 'what hardening had to come'.[106] More specifically, they resolved that the peoples of Ireland, be they of Celtic, Viking, Norman or English extraction, would have to give their allegiance to an Irish republic. If, on the other hand, they wanted to support the Empire, they would have to 'clear out and support the Empire elsewhere'.[107] The bellicose Dan Breen had no hesitation in embracing the costs that might be incurred: 'to me a united Ireland of two million people would be preferable to an Ireland of four and a half million divided into three or four different factions'.[108] The totalitarian impulse revealed here anticipates the kind of sentiment soon to find radical expression in Nazi Germany and Stalin's Soviet Union. Images of ethnic cleansing – seemingly a cultural fantasy in some corners of republicanism and in loyalism also – and purges within nationalist Ireland rush to mind. It is to divisions within nationalist Ireland that I now turn.

Civil War Two: Green on Green

Communal conflict along nationalist–unionist lines was highly visible, being an almost palpable reality of Irish society in the early twentieth century. Less readily apprehended, but more pervasive, was the extent to which the decade 1913–23 harboured a civil war within Irish nationalism. In part, but only in part, is the use of the term metaphorical. By 1920 no such qualification is necessary, and in June 1922 a full-blown war of comrade against comrade broke out within nationalist Ireland. The new imperative was to 'wade through Irish blood' to achieve 'Irish freedom'.[109]

Taking a slightly longer time perspective, it is possible to see, from the later nineteenth century onwards, the making of a new kind of politics, a kind of 'long revolution' in Irish society.[110] George Boyce dates this from 1879, with the formation of the Land League which brings the rural masses onto the historical stage for the first time. Another, largely complementary perspective is also possible: that of a sharpening of divisions within nationalist Ireland in the two or three decades before the First World War. In their most influential forms, though with the operation of a time lag, these were cultural wars: dissecting notions of Irishness, investing particular formulations of Irish identity with superior value and subjecting others to obloquy. Thus the Gaelic Athletic Association (GAA) was formed in Hayes Hotel, Thurles, Co. Tipperary in 1884 under the eye and guidance of the conspiratorial IRB. At one level the GAA was a sporting organisation, but it pursued simultaneously a political and cultural programme which discriminated against those who did not subscribe to its nativist attitudes on athletics and the nation. Within a decade a more vibrant language revival body was born, the Gaelic League, which added Gaelic speaking as an essential attribute of being truly Irish.[111] The Irish-Ireland movement, most notably associated with D.P. Moran's paper, the *Leader*, developed a vigorous propaganda which helped popularise new hierarchies of Irish nationality. At the top were situated the *fíor* Gaels, the true and truly Irish, imbued with a heightened racialist consciousness; at the base there lurked the shoneens, the West Britons, the Castle Catholics, and the 'Catholic sourfaces'.[112] Protestants belonged to a separate layer entirely, being no more than 'resident aliens' who might one day be absorbed into the Irish nation.[113]

Many nationalists may not have subscribed to these categorisations but these were the images which were gaining imaginative ground in the decades before 1914, particularly among the younger cohorts of nationalists. In many respects these were the stirrings of a wider European racialist consciousness which animated young people from the peasant villages of Poland in the east to the streets of urban Catalonia in the west. It may have been a big step from culture to killing, but a nucleus of militants, steeped in romantic nationalism, was willing to take killing in its stride. This might mean shooting down an unarmed member of the Dublin Metropolitan Police as on Easter Monday 1916,[114] the death and wounding of several hundred Dublin civilians during the same week, or, in time, the assassination of fellow nationalists within the RIC. As time went by, the intimidation or murder of those who dared disagree with Sinn Féin or the IRA became an acceptable form of politics. The nationalist writer, Stephen Gwynn put it nicely: it was 'dangerous for a man to speak his mind unless that mind agreed with the Republican policy'.[115]

While the cultural purges within Irish nationalism, along ultra-nationalist and pietistic Catholic lines, laid the basis for the devaluation of certain kinds of Irish life, the more immediate catalyst was the split within the Irish Volunteers in 1914. The overwhelming majority of the Irish Volunteers followed John Redmond's lead, with tens of thousands going off to fight for the King, the empire and the 'rights of small nations', including, of course, the variously-interpreted Irish nation.[116] There were premonitions of violent conflict within nationalist Ireland. Abuse and ridicule were heaped on the dissident Irish Volunteers who marched in Limerick in 1915 and also on the insurrectionists of 1916 as they were led away as prisoners.[117] By 1918 the boot was on the other foot, and used freely against moderate nationalists. Those who were unworthy of the 'nation' and of the 'Republic' deserved no better. Such murderous bitterness flowed freely, especially freely during the weekend between the announcement of a Truce and its coming into effect on Monday, 11 July 1921. Of the many poignant losses one might recall that of Bridget Dillon. At 11.30 am on the Saturday, almost exactly forty-eight hours before the Truce was due to take effect, five armed men called at a house near Kilcash, outside Clonmel in Co. Tipperary. They asked Michael Dillon, an ex-soldier, to come out. As he did not, the raiders fired into the house, killing his sister Bridget, who was standing just inside the door. She was aged fifteen.[118]

The consummation of this conflict was the Irish Civil War. Cain closed on Abel.[119] It was bloodier than the troubles which preceded it. While estimates of the numbers killed vary, the total was probably in the region of 1,500 to 2,000.[120] More so than in the previous fighting, there were some large-scale engagements, at least in the early months of the civil war. The anti-Treaty IRA had occupied the Four Courts in Dublin and was eventually driven out by the new national army, under the leadership of Michael Collins. Other major attacks centred on Cork, Limerick and Waterford but there was also the steady drip of blood from assassinations. The ordeal of John Cole, aged nineteen, and of Alfred Colley, aged twenty-one, both Dubliners, was not unique for men of their generation. Abducted by armed men wearing trench coats, with hats pulled down over their eyes, they were taken by car to Yellow Lane on the edge of Dublin city. They were given a few moments to prepare for their deaths, even as people came out of their houses to view the commotion. They sat on the roadside moaning and, according to eyewitness accounts, had already been beaten and were in obvious distress. One was heard to ask: 'What have we done?' Each was then placed against the piers of a gate and the men in trench coats 'emptied their revolvers into them'. It is not clear who was responsible for the murders, though there is some evidence that the death squad consisted of Free State soldiers out of uniform.[121]

As the civil war progressed, atrocity succeeded atrocity, with savage impact on the lives of the people. In the later stages of the civil war, political banditry, house burning and assassination became the staples of the anti-Treaty IRA. The new state met terror with terror in a sustained policy of repression which would have been difficult to execute or excuse under British rule. By 1923 the 'glorious fight' initiated in 1916 had degenerated sufficiently to allow official executions of anti-Treaty IRA prisoners by their former comrades in arms. The dark harvest of ultra-nationalism was consuming the very people whose 'freedom' it was meant to sustain.

A War of Independence?

It should be apparent by now that the grand, even grandiose term of a 'war of independence' is a misnomer. It is, in truth, an ideological construct, popularised in later times, that distorts and conceals the realities of Irish life during the fateful years of 1919–21. The point may be brought out most clearly by reviewing briefly the other options, by no means mutually exclusive, set out in the earlier table.

The IRA offensive had a strong local and regional dimension, being heavily concentrated in Dublin and a small number of southern counties. Many counties, and not just those in Ulster, were relatively unaffected. The conflict had its share of social banditry, though this was much more apparent during the periods of the Truce and the later civil war. The fighting had its heroic moments, and it is easy to be moved by, for instance, Ernie O'Malley's dramatic account of raids on police and military barracks. There is no doubting his generosity of thought – 'it's easy to sleep on another man's wound', as he himself remarked – and his personal chivalry found expression during the conflict itself.[122] The typical male victim, however, was neither a soldier nor a policeman. He was a civilian, taken out by armed and masked men, and 'plugged'.[123] Men of the RIC were themselves often killed in the most unheroic of circumstances, on the way out of mass, at public entertainments, when visiting family, or after they had retired from the force.[124] The bodies of some were never recovered, secreted away in bog or mountain grave. The case of Tom Hannon, murdered in June 1921, cuts across several boundaries. He had resigned from the RIC in 1913 to take over the family farm. His body was found in a bog near Tullamore in the midlands. He had been shot in the right temple and his hands were tied together with a rope.[125] Members of the military, and the militarised police, fared better in this respect, being separate from the civil population, though a number were unarmed when captured and executed. This was primarily a war of sporadic assassination, in which undisciplined state forces played an increasing role from the spring of 1920. Two of Michael Collins' closest aides, Dick McKee and Peadar Clancy, were shot 'while attempting to escape'. Both had been tortured in Dublin Castle; their corpses showed the marks of bayonet wounds and their fingernails had been pulled out.[126]

It was a communal sectarian conflict, most notably in the northern counties. People were boycotted, burned out of their homes, or killed simply because they were 'other', Protestant or Catholic. It is a frightening revelation how, under conditions of political excitement, the embers of sectarianism might also burn brightly in some southern localities. In the North it was the mainly Catholic and nationalist RIC which damped the potential for ever more lethal sectarianism, while the Protestant B Specials, recruited in the main from former members of the UVF, were widely accused of anti-Catholic bigotry.[127] In the South the IRA could drive out Protestants at will, and sometimes did.

There were the sparks of social revolution, in the seizure and occupation of work places and land holdings, in the hoisting of red flags, and in the fiery rhetoric of militant trade unionists. Even the disinherited of Irish rural society, the farm labourers, succeeded in organising and securing some material gains from their employers. But there was no social revolution. Sinn Féin was deeply conservative and suspicious, when not actually dismissive, of the role of labour in the politics of the period. Labour was left waiting.

There was, though, a 'revolution in arms'. It was vitally important to kill, though the rhetoric was framed in the masochistic terms of dying for Ireland. 'Ireland', of course, was an anthropomorphic abstraction which, like other emotive fictions, could be manipulated to many ends, including the end of violence. Revolutionary violence was itself liberating. In a variation on the overarching imperial or khaki jingoism of the period, green jingoism lamented the shame of not having confronted Britannia in arms. In the social psychology of ultra-nationalism, collective shame and self-hatred, as well as Anglophobia, provided powerful motives for action. The redemption of Ireland had to be achieved through violence. For some, independence on a plate would not have sufficed. For these a calculus of the necessity, including the costs and benefits of the revolution, was beside the point.

Similarly, as lived in the minds of some of the activists, there was a war in defence of the 'Republic'. This republic of the imagination, and its phantasms, came to haunt subsequent negotiations between Dáil Éireann and the British government, but for those hypnotised by the spectre it was a sacred and compelling presence – to be defended, irrespective of the evanescent wishes of the people. The fantastical and the fanatical achieved both their zenith and their nemesis in the nationalist civil war of 1922–23, also known in some circles as the 'second war in defence of the Republic'.

One of the least satisfactory formulations is that of the Anglo-Irish war. As in the *putsch* of Easter 1916, the Irish peoples, north or south, nationalist, unionist or labour, were not consulted in relation to the struggle prosecuted on their behalf. Paul Bew has made the important distinction between a substantial vote for an Irish republic within nationalist Ireland (not all Ireland) in the general election of December 1918 and that of a mandate for violent struggle.[128] The latter was not sought and, therefore, was not handed to Sinn Féin, still less to the Irish Volunteers. Later attempts to read such an interpretation into the election results are, at best, contrived.[129] At least as revealing are the urban local elections of 1920, perhaps the last open elections in Ireland under the Union. In view of the relatively poor performance of Sinn Féin, it is difficult to see majority support for an armed offensive. Far from there being an Anglo-Irish war, the Irish nationalist people were presented with a series of *faits accomplis* by the storm-troopers of the 'Republic' and manipulated into military confrontation. Irish unionists, of course, were little more than awkward pieces of stage scenery in the playing out of the national drama, and certainly not deserving of speaking parts.

In the end there was, of course, a secessionist outcome. Far from being a colony, Ireland was an integral part of the British polity and was over-represented relative to its size of population at the Westminster parliament. It was this status and its fractious but intimate relationships with British society which facilitated the outcome. The impressive organisational achievements of Sinn Féin in creating the structures of an alternative state in Ireland and the force of the IRA's argument must be acknowledged. In the end, though, it was liberal opinion in Britain, disdaining to use the massive coercive force available to it, which was the key element in securing political independence for (most) Irish nationalists. Had Ireland been a colonial possession, the nature of the fighting would have been very different, the ratio between guerrilla deaths and security force deaths would have been much higher, and the overall casualties immeasurably more numerous. Thus, paradoxically, the decisive element in the drive for secession and the realisation of an Irish free state was not the flying column but British public opinion. Equally paradoxically, the achievement of the collective right of political independence was accompanied by a diminution of individual rights for people in the new Irish Free State. There was more than a grain of truth in the Reverend P. O'Doherty's fear that the 'worst of English social legislation', including divorce (whose very mention had 'stunk in the nostrils of every decent Irishman and Irishwoman'), would ensue unless the union was terminated.[130] As legislative change in the new state on divorce, contraception, censorship of books and films, and jury service for women was soon to reveal, the seemingly straightforward notion of 'independence' itself concealed more than a few contradictions.

'The North Began [...]'

To encompass the argument in its entirety it is important to widen the lens and consider the period 1913–23 as a whole. What the North began, it did not understand.[131] Ulster Unionists pointed down the revolutionary path in 1913, and were later surprised to find it had helped precipitate a political revolution in southern Ireland. Beneath the surface nationalist Ireland was already beginning to ferment. The polarisation of North and South brought the prospect of civil war between nationalist and unionist closer, and this found muted expression in the early 1920s. The split in the Irish Volunteers in 1914, the events of Easter week, 1916, and of January 1919 accelerated the process of purgation within Irish nationalism, reducing further the likelihood of an accommodation with either Ulster or Irish unionism. These civil wars within Ireland perplexed Liberal politicians and made it more difficult to devise political and constitutional structures that might accommodate such divergent tendencies. It is these variegated and interlocking civil wars which are at the heart of Irish politics during the revolutionary decade, and which supply the dynamic of change.

It may be objected, however, that there were three armies in Ireland in 1914 and again in 1920, that of the British state, that of the Irish Volunteers (now re-named the IRA), and that of the Ulster Volunteers (many now enlisting in the B Specials). The primary targets of the IRA, before it turned its guns on itself and its fellow nationalists, were the forces of the crown and those it suspected of supporting the state. Surely, then, there was an Irish war of independence, at least of sorts? The major problems with this formulation have already been noted: in a religiously and ethnically divided society, the notion of Irish or Irishness is itself a contested one; there was no popular or democratic mandate for widespread hostilities; nationalists were driven into a war not of their making; and political independence meant different things to different people. Even within Sinn Féin some aspired to a republic peacefully gained; some others would have settled for dominion status. Irish Labour, whose members were denied a choice of Labour candidates in 1918, harboured a range of aspirations, social as well as political and constitutional. The supporters of the IPP, who accounted for one in every three nationalist voters in December 1918, would have preferred an outcome that was closer to devolved government within the United Kingdom.

There is a further sense in which the latent role of the IRA was primarily to radicalise and brutalise nationalists, its civil war mission as it were. This is because its military campaign probably did little to affect the political outcome. We may consider this in two respects: firstly in relation to the position of the Ulster Unionists and partitionist tendencies within Ireland, and secondly in relation to the shape of the eventual Treaty in 1921. Partition in some form or other was firmly on the agenda by 1914. The Irish Volunteers and the diminutive Irish Citizens Army, by their actions in 1916, and their subsequent violence, virtually confirmed the inevitability of partition. When it came to the showdown, Sinn Féin and the IRA had neither a strategy of persuasion – having rejected negotiation within the Irish Convention convened by Lloyd George in 1917 – nor of coercion to prevent partition. While Sinn Féin and extreme nationalists might have ridiculed the failure of the IPP on the question of partition – the Party of Futility, as it was dubbed[132] – its own policy position was threadbare. Indeed the situation was worse than that. Not only had it failed to protect northern nationalists effectively against loyalist attack, its southern offensive imperilled their very existence. Collins's adventurism, in channelling arms and encouragement to the northern IRA, merely exacerbated the dangers of all-out communal warfare in the North.[133] Sinn Féin and the IRA not only failed on the question of partition, they added further poison to the wells of communal hatred in the North. This in turn conditioned the psychology and structures of the new Northern Ireland state.[134]

More fundamentally, it is not even clear that the IRA made more than a marginal difference to the eventual settlement. The Sinn Féin alliance that was constituted in the wake of Easter 1916, and which, in a short time, produced the triumph of Dáil Éireann, succeeded in developing a powerful set of civil organisations that gradually but cumulatively hollowed out the institutions of the British state in Ireland.[135] Not unlike the Land League of an earlier generation, this mass mobilisation demonstrated the need for a radical response to southern nationalist opinion. No doubt Lloyd George and the Tory die-hards in his cabinet needed to be jolted, if they were to contemplate outcomes that went far beyond the original Home Rule agenda. Still the former had indicated as early as 1918 that any settlement short of a republic and the 'coercion of Ulster' might be discussed, and by the spring of 1920, as the steep descent into terror and counter-terror was getting underway, British officials in Dublin Castle were ready to entertain radical proposals, this side of a republic, for southern Ireland.[136] The Sinn Féin movement possessed the resources, in the form of people, organisation, abstentionist tactics and stratagems to effect political movement. Moreover, had it conceded earlier on partition and on the republic, concessions it would make anyhow at the end of 1921, it would have disarmed much, although by no means all of the Ulster Unionist and the British Tory opposition to political independence in southern Ireland.

In essence, therefore, there was an alternative both to the pacific approach of the IPP, which might have yielded dominion status for southern Ireland over a longer time frame, and to the pathway of terror mapped out by the IRA. However, the dialectic of attack and reprisal was incompatible with the politics of a peaceful, mass nationalist mobilisation from January 1919 onwards, following the inauguration of the first Dáil. Even in Sinn Féin terms, the work of the loosely-controlled volunteers, banging away in their localities, was counterproductive. Richard Mulcahy, who was the head of the Irish Volunteers, remarked caustically of the Soloheadbeg killings: 'it pushed turbulent spirits like Treacy and Breen into the Dublin area from time to time, where their services were not required and their presence was often awkward'.[137] This understated comment could perhaps be generalised to the IRA as a whole, in terms of its contribution to winning an Irish state, with partition and short of a republic (it may be repeated). The IRA campaign of violence was neither a necessary nor a sufficient condition for political independence in southern Ireland. It is difficult, therefore, to see much validity in the notion of an 'Irish war of independence', though this is not to deny that, for the veterans of guerrilla warfare and their ideological followers, the idea of a war of independence came to assume a comfortable and dignifying appeal, and was indeed real in their own terms. It was a political and psychological necessity.

The 'Troubles'; 'The Troubled Times'

Some will find too radical the interpretation of the period 1913–23 as one of interconnected civil wars within an island society, albeit heavily conditioned by the politics of the British government and His Majesty's opposition. In any case, historians need to place in some kind of conceptual box the three-cornered violence of Irish and Ulster volunteers, and the security forces, for the sub-period from January 1919 onwards. What label or heading can be applied, without doing violence to the preceding analysis?

There is much to be said for that unpretentious summary phrase, the 'Troubles', or 'The Troubled Times' which was the term used by my older neighbours, including one former volunteer, in Tipperary in the 1950s. True enough the 'Troubles' has an amorphous quality and, to the ears of an uninformed audience, may seem euphemistic. It might also be objected that it does not capture the cruelty and the squalid character of much of the violence of the period. Yet it has the merit of being a relatively neutral, many-sided term. It serves to relate rather than artificially separate the waves of terror, North and South, which formed part of the same sea of troubles. It hints at the unorthodox quality of much of what passed for a 'war'. Unlike the value-laden phrases that have been pressed into service by ideologues and (sometimes) unreflecting historians, it opens up possibilities of analysis, without prejudging outcomes. The fact that it came to be used by people in Ireland during or soon after the period of conflict may suggest a demotic sense of the complexity of these episodes in near-contemporary history – a sense, derived from direct personal experience that should not be easily dismissed.

Endings

> Union conference, tomorrow Monaco. Aldergrove, Heathrow, London, Tooting Common tube station. 'Come in. Come in and see the revolution'. The welcoming words of historian Ruth Dudley Edwards at her Pope's Lane home in London. There it was, in full colour, live, on television: the storming of the federal parliament in Belgrade; streets crowded with masses of flag-wielding protesters; Slobodan Milosovitch's ultra-nationalist regime being torn down before our eyes.[138]

Much of the conflict of modern Ireland was born of ultra-nationalisms that overreached themselves. The leading antagonists were Ulster loyalism and Irish republicanism, neither endowed with any intelligent understanding of the other. The IRA campaign of violence wrote a fiery epitaph to the original Union, though perhaps little else in terms of constructive political achievement. Taking the long view, what is surprising is the lack of a serious separatist challenge to the Union until the second decade of the twentieth century. Mainstream nationalist critiques had centred on reforming the Union along devolutionary lines, not on breaking the connection with England, as F.S.L. Lyons so misleadingly put it.[139] Not only was the Union long-lived in the time perspective of other international treaties, the union in its material as distinct from its political and symbolic manifestations continued long into the twentieth century. The trading union between the two islands, and between North and South, continued largely uninterrupted until 1931; for a half century after independence Britain remained the major destination for Irish exports and also the major source of its imports; the currency union prevailed until 1979; and over the twentieth century as a whole Britain was the preferred destination for Irish people who could not find work at home. The new state bore the imprint of British institutional forms, from representative democracy to the practices of its civil service. The linguistic union, with its multiplicity of advantages in the world of the arts, entertainment and multinational business, has deepened through time. In Northern Ireland, the Union in its political, constitutional and economic forms, albeit with modifications as a result of the Anglo-Irish Agreement of 1985 (itself superseded by the Good Friday Agreement of 1998), is entering its third century.

Even the cultural estrangement of Irish nationalists from 'England', which constituted the bedrock of militant nationalism, was one of the continuities. But this is to play with one of the historical ironies. The relationship between economic, social and cultural forces in the making and unmaking of the original Union needs further unravelling. It looks increasingly as if the narrow socio-economic interpretations of nationalism and separatism, as discussed in chapter three, are inadequate. The cultural sphere, in Ireland as elsewhere, seems to have had far more autonomy than many structuralist writers and even the most revisionist Marxists would allow, but the elasticity of culture, including its potential for image making, political rhetoric, and divisive fabrications, is the stuff of another exploration, for another day, or, more likely, another writer.

It follows from these various reflections, I think, that such a disarmingly simple question as when did the Union end, is not easily answered. This is so, even in the case of the Irish Free State, later Irish Republic, once one steps beyond the important but partial sphere of political and constitutional relations. In practice, the Union involved much more and was itself an evolving set of arrangements, capable of adaptation and reform.[140] If it is not easy to give a simple answer to the question of when the Union ended, then perhaps it is impossible to declare when its formal demise, at least in southern Ireland, became inevitable. From the 1880s onwards, such was the momentum of Irish nationalism and the degree of deliberate cultural distancing, that a form of devolved political independence seemed inevitable, even to many contemporaries. The expectation must be that a devolved parliament in Dublin would have evolved into dominion status and, eventually, full-blown political independence. Be that as it may, a drive towards a republic only entered the realm of the possible a few minutes before midnight. Or viewed in real time, the original Union was only fatally undermined in the last quinquennium of its existence.

Endnotes

Introduction

1   The quotation is attributed to Sir Boyle Roche, an eighteenth-century MP noted for his 'Irish bulls'. See the Irishman's Diary, *Irish Times*, 14 February 2000.

2   Liam Kennedy, *Colonialism, Religion and Nationalism in Ireland* (Belfast, 1996).

3   My one major reservation is that I didn't give the terrors of famine sufficient emphasis, in part because I was working with colleagues on a major study of the Great Irish Famine at the time (*Mapping the Great Irish Famine*, Dublin, 1999). As my friend David Wilson has pointed out, experiences of hunger and famine need to be incorporated more fully into the comparative frame.

4   Brian Porter-Szucs, *Poland in the Modern World: Beyond Martyrdom* (Oxford, 2014).

5   Susan Sontag, *Regarding the Pain of Others* (London, 2003).

6   On emigration from early eighteenth-century Ulster and subsequently see D.H. Akenson, *Ireland, Sweden and the Great European Migration, 1815–1914* (Liverpool, 2011) and Kerby A. Miller *et al.*, *Irish Immigrants in the Land of Canaan: Letters and Memoirs from Colonial and Revolutionary America, 1675–1815* (Oxford, 2003).

7   The argument has led a life of conference papers, but I may get round to publishing it sometime. An early version was presented as 'Industrialisation and Ethnic Conflict in Ulster and Ireland', at a conference on Irish Studies, University of Ulster, June 2006, while variants were featured at the University of Toronto and the London School of Economics.

8   To strike a personal note, during the 1980s and 1990s I was invited to give talks at half a dozen local history societies in largely Protestant and unionist areas within Northern Ireland. Other academic colleagues could report similar engagements. My most memorable meeting was with a loyalist women's organisation on the Lower Newtownards Road in Belfast. I was repeatedly interrupted and asked if Protestants had died during the Famine. In exasperation I threw the question back: how could they believe otherwise? One woman, pointing in the direction of the nationalist Short Strand, told me that in cross-community encounters with a residents association from the Short Strand they had been assured that only Catholics died during the Great Famine.

9   Mary Daly, 'Revisionism and Irish History: The Great Famine', in George Boyce and Alan O'Day (eds), *The Making of Modern Irish History: Revisionism and the Revisionist Controversy* (London, 1996), p. 86.

10 I have touched on issues of reflexivity in an unpublished paper, 'Writing Irish history in the Shadow of the Troubles in Northern Ireland' (Queen's University, Belfast, 2015).

11 A conversation with Professor John Cronin, formerly of University College Cork and Queen's University, Belfast, circa 1995, when the sesquicentenary of the Great Famine was creating renewed interest in the catastrophe. Curiously, in terms of the trauma thesis, it is not claimed that the First World War was responsible for transmitting pain to the

present generation of Irish people, even though it was a horrendous experience for many of the 200,000 Irish volunteers, as well as close relatives. It is also much closer in time (but the pain of the Edwardian generation of Irish youths did not fit the dominant narrative of Irish suffering).

12 Liam Kennedy, 'Was there an Irish War of Independence?', in Bruce Stewart (ed.), *Hearts and Minds: Irish Culture and Society under the Act of Union* (Gerrard's Cross, Buckinghamshire, 2002) and chapter nine in this volume.

13 The terms 'war of independence' or the 'Irish war of Independence' had found a place by the mid-1930s in the columns of the *Irish Press*, the newspaper of the Fianna Fáil party but were less frequently referenced in other Irish newspapers of the time it would seem. See for example the *Irish Press*, 21 January 1935, 9 February 1935, 20 January 1936, 5 May 1936, 1 July 1936 but there are occasional references in the early 1930s as well. One might wonder also if the notion of an Irish revolution needs unpacking. A revolution for whom, by whom, against whom, and fired by what ideology or ideologies? Indeed, who are 'the Irish' in this context?

14 This is in Parker's play on the 1798 rebellions, *Northern Star* (1984). See Stewart Parker, *Northern Star, Heavenly Bodies, Pentecost: Three Plays for Ireland* (Birmingham, 1989), p. 36.

15 This provisional judgement is based on conversations with descendants of Church of Ireland farmers from the county and also some preliminary work on compensation claims filed by victims of the revolutionary period. In Templederry, a few miles from my home in County Tipperary, the Church of Ireland rectory (unoccupied) and the Church of Ireland school were burned down during the civil war in what seem to have been little more than acts of communal intimidation. See the *Nenagh News*, 9 September 1922.

16 Joe Lee, *The Modernisation of Irish Society, 1848–1918* (Dublin, 1973).

17 Ernie O'Malley, *On Another Man's Wound* (Dublin, 1979), p. 332.

Chapter One: A Most Oppressed People?

1 This chapter was first published as 'Out of History: Ireland, that "Most Distressful Country"', in Liam Kennedy, *Colonialism, Religion and Nationalism in Ireland* (Belfast, 1996), pp. 182–223.

2 K.T. Hoppen, *Ireland since 1800: Conflict and Conformity* (Dublin, 1989), p. 1.

3 Publisher's preface (Cameron and Ferguson) to Thomas D'Arcy McGee, *A Popular History of Ireland from the Earliest Period to the Emancipation of the Catholics* (Glasgow, 1860). Moreover, 'The fiercest whirlwind of oppression that ever in the wrath of God was poured upon the children of disobedience had swept over her [Ireland].'

4 Horace Plunkett, *Ireland in the New Century* (London, 1904), p. 26. As part of his mission (p. 26 also) Plunkett saw the need 'to fasten the mind of my countrymen upon the practical things of to-day, and to wean their sad souls from idle regrets over the sorrows of the past'.

5 *Freeman's Journal,* 23 November 1879.

6 *Hansard,* 19 May, 1881, col. 888, third series.

7 *Hansard,* 11 February 1878, cols.1439–40, third series. National revolts against Turkish rule broke out in the Balkan Peninsula in 1875. The revolt of the Bulgarians followed soon after. In a series of brutal repressions, the Sultan's forces exterminated whole communities in Bulgaria, while prisoners were tortured as a matter of course before execution brought a kind of release. See H.L. Peacock, *A History of Modern Europe, 1789–1939* (London, 1961), pp. 194–7.

8 Isaac Butt, *Land Tenure in Ireland, A Plea for the Celtic Race* (Dublin, 1866).

9   John Wiggins, *The 'Monster' Misery of Ireland: A Practical Treatise on the Relation of Landlord and Tenant* (London, 1844), pp. 146–8.

10 John Mitchel, *The Last Conquest of Ireland (Perhaps)* (London, n.d.), pp. 61, 67–8.

11 Ibid, pp. 192–3. In fairness, the passage is in part a satire on the British government's handling of the Great Famine.

12 From M.F. Cusack, *Speeches and Public Letters of the Liberator* (Dublin, 1875), p. 501.

13 Daniel O'Connell, quoted in R.M. Martin, *Ireland Before and After the Union* (London, 1843), p. iii.

14 *Shamrock,* 2 March, 1812.

15 A.D. Godley (ed.), *The Poetical Works of Thomas Moore* (London, 1910), pp, 180–234 (Irish Melodies).

16 Quoted in Barbara Solow, *The Land Question and the Irish Economy, 1870–1903* (Cambridge, Mass. 1971), p. 51.

17 K.H. Connell, *The Population History of Ireland, 1750–1845* (Oxford, 1950); idem, *Irish Peasant Society: Four Historical Essays* (Oxford, 1968); K.A. Miller, *Emigrants and Exiles: Ireland and the Irish Exodus to North America* (Oxford, 1985). There is a livelier mood and tone to a later work by Miller: K.A. Miller and Paul Wagner, *Out of Ireland: The Story of Irish Emigration* (New York, 1994).

18 Robert Kee, *The Most Distressful Country* (London, 1989), p. 8.

19 Personal observation.

20 Kenneth Griffith and Timothy O'Grady, *Curious Journeys: An Oral History of Ireland's Unfinished Revolution* (London, 1982), p. 313.

21 Thomas Gallagher, *Paddy's Lament: Ireland 1846–1847: Prelude to Hatred* (Dublin, 1985), p. xvi.

22 T.H. Jackson, *The Whole Matter; The Poetic Evolution of Thomas Kinsella* (Dublin, 1995).

23 Brendan Bradshaw, 'Nationalism and Historical Scholarship in Modern Ireland', *Irish Historical Studies,* 26 (1989), pp. 329–51.

24 Trevor Aston (ed.), *Crisis in Europe, 1560–1600* (London, 1965); Geoffrey Parker and Lesley Smith, *The General Crisis of the Seventeenth Century* (London, 1978).

25 J.I. Israel, *The Dutch Republic: Its Rise, Greatness, and Fall, 1477–1806* (Oxford, 1995).

26 Giraldus Cambrensis, *The History and Topography of Ireland* (translated by J.J. O'Meara, Mountrath, Ireland, 1982), pp. 50, 53.

27 A fine synthesis of Irish historical geography is to be found in B.J. Graham and L.J. Proudfoot (eds), *An Historical Geography of Ireland* (London, 1993).

28 Even in the late twentieth century there were 250 million cases annually of malaria in the world, giving rise to two million deaths annually. See *New Encyclopaedia Britannica, Micropaedia* (Chicago, 1992), 7, p. 725. For some historical insights into the terror of malaria and other diseases see A.W. Crosby, *Ecological Imperialism* (Cambridge, 1994).

29 Carlo Levi, *Christ Stopped at Eboli* (London, 1984); J.M. Synge, *Four Plays and the Aran Islands* (edited with an introduction by Robin Skelton, Oxford, 1962). Synge visited the Aran Islands for five summers between 1898 and 1902. Levi's account relates to fascist Italy in the mid-1930s.

30 Cusack, *Speeches,* ii, p. 336.

31 Ibid, p. 336.

32 Ibid, p. 337.

33 G.A. Hayes McCoy (ed.), *The Irish at War* (Cork, 1969) and Thomas Bartlett and Keith Jeffery (eds), *A Military History of Ireland* (Cambridge, 1996).

34 They may, nonetheless, have been underrepresented in the Union army relative to their share of the population, in part because of an antipathy to the cause of black emancipation. See James McPherson, *Battle Cry of Freedom: The American Civil War* (London, 1990), p. 606.

35   R.F. Foster, *Modern Ireland, 1600–1972* (London, 1989), p. 280.

36   H. L. Smith (ed.), *War and Social Change: British Society in the Second World War* (Manchester, 1986), p. 163. People in Northern Ireland had some experience of death from the skies: see Chris McGimpsey, *Bombs on Belfast* (Belfast, 1983).

37   Most of the data in Table 1.1 are from Marc Ferro, *The Great War, 1914–18* (New York, 1973), p. 227. The calculation of death rates is based on population figures in B.R. Mitchell, *European Historical Statistics, 1750–1970* (London, 1988), pp. 19–24. Ferro's estimate of UK war dead seems on the high side. Both Taylor and Smith indicate a total in the region of three-quarters of a million for Britain: see A.J.P. Taylor, *The First World War* (London, 1972), p. 279 and H.L. Smith (ed.), *War and Social Change: British Society in the Second World War* (Manchester, 1986), p. 163. For Irish casualties see David Fitzpatrick, 'Militarism in Ireland, 1900–1922', in Thomas Bartlett and Keith Jeffery (eds), *A Military History of Ireland* (Cambridge, 1996), pp. 392, 501 and Saorstát Éireann, *Census of Population 1926: General Report, 10* (Dublin, 1934), p. 12. [Irish deaths are probably undercounted in this table; more recent estimates tend to revise upwards, suggesting 35,000–40,000 Irish war dead.]

38   But see T.P. Dooley, *Irishmen or English Soldiers?* (Liverpool, 1995); also *Report on Recruiting in Ireland* (BPP, 39, 1914–16).

39   Fitzpatrick, 'Militarism in Ireland', p. 405.

40   Introduction to Hans-Adolf Jacobsen and A.L. Smith (eds), *World War II: Policy and Strategy* (Santa Barbara, 1979), p. 12.

41   Ibid, p. 12.

42   The risk of a soldier getting killed in the Second World War while fighting for the British was well under half that for the First World War. See Smith, *War and Social Change,* p. 163.

43   K.B. Nolan and T.D. Williams (eds), *Ireland in the War Years and After, 1939–51* (Dublin, 1969).

44   Fitzpatrick, 'Militarism in Ireland', p. 405. The 1916 Rising is usually held to have resulted in four to five hundred deaths. Fewer than 100 insurgents were killed.

45   Frank McGuinness's play, *Observe the Sons of Ulster Marching towards the Somme* (London, 1986) is a unique act of homage from within nationalist Ireland towards Ulster Protestant involvement in the Great War.

46   Bob Rowthorn and Naomi Wayne, *Northern Ireland: the Political Economy of Conflict* (London, 1988), pp. 19, 24.

47   Jonathan Bardon, *A History of Ulster* (Belfast, 1992), p. 554.

48   Michael Anderson, *Population Change in North-Western Europe, 1750–1850* (London, 1988), p. 24.

49   Agatha Ramm, *Europe in the Twentieth Century, 1905–1970* (London, 1984), pp. 286–7.

50   It is impossible to know how many died with any degree of precision, nor is it easy to disentangle war-related deaths from other causes. See Evan Mawdsley, *The Russian Civil War* (London, 1987), pp. 285–7, and Harold Shukman, *The Blackwell Encyclopaedia of the Russian Revolution* (London, 1988), p. 146.

51   Mawdsley, *Russian Civil War,* p. 287.

52   F.S.L. Lyons, *Ireland Since the Famine* (London, 1973), pp. 531–3.

53   Hugh Thomas, *The Spanish Civil War* (New York, 1961), pp. 631–2. A later edition (1990 p. 926) estimates 500,000.

54   Jan Read, *The Catalans* (London, 1978), p. 197.

55   Some Irish historians have adopted the practice of appropriating the term 'holocaust' for the Great Famine. This is both offensive and historically misleading. (I must admit myself to a slipshod use of the term in an article on the Famine many years ago.)

56 Estimates taken from D.M. Lang, *The Armenians: A People in Exile* (London, 1981), pp. 10–12, 25–38.

57 Patrick Buckland, *Ulster Unionism and the Origins of Northern Ireland, 1886–1922* (Dublin, 1973), pp. 153–75.

58 Ibid., p. 176.

59 In the words of Hopkinson, 'the conflict was of short duration and saw no major battles'. Estimates of military deaths through violence vary but seem to have been under, perhaps well under the 4 to 5,000 sometimes claimed. See Michael Hopkinson, *Green Against Green: The Irish Civil War* (Dublin, 1988), pp. 272–3.

60 The death rate per thousand of the population for the Irish Free State was 14.7 in 1922 and 14.0 in 1923. In the two subsequent years, 1924 and 1925, it was 15.0 and 14.6 respectively. See *Detailed Annual Report of the Registrar General for Saorstát Éireann* (Dublin, relevant years).

61 Well over 100,000, perhaps 150,000 Irish fought in the American civil war. I am indebted to John Lynch for information on this point. A typical death rate for this war would suggest, therefore, 30,000 Irish deaths as a direct or indirect result of the fighting, excluding any civilian casualties. This would make the battlefields of the South the largest site of mass mortality for the Irish since the Famine and roughly comparable to Irish war deaths in the First World War.

62 McPherson, *Battle Cry,* p. 854.

63 D.C North and P.R. Thomas, 'The Rise and Fall of the Manorial System: A Theoretical Model', *Journal of Economic History,* 31, 4 (1971), pp. 777–803.

64 For an overview see F.E. Huggett, *The Land Question and European Society* (London, 1975).

65 The best assessment of the landlord and tenant system in Ireland for the later nineteenth century, even if a shade indulgent of landlords, is W.E. Vaughan, *Landlords and Tenants in Mid-Victorian Ireland* (Oxford, 1994). Michael Davitt's *The Fall of Feudalism in Ireland: Or the Story of the Land League Revolution* (London, 1904) is still a good read.

66 Huggett, *Land Question,* pp. 97–8.

67 The economic dimension to the tragedy of the Russian peoples is explored in many works, including Alec Nove, *An Economic History of the USSR* (London, 1978).

68 Huggett, *Land Question,* chapter four; A.S. Milward and S.B. Saul, *The Development of the Economies of Continental Europe, 1850–1914* (London, 1977), *passim.*

69 Jordi Nadal, 'Spain 1830–1914', in Carlo Cipolla (ed.), *The Fontana Economic History of Europe* (London, 1973), pp. 553–68.

70 The degree of owner occupancy in Ireland today is one of the highest in the European Union. For sharecropping and rental arrangements in Europe before 1914 see Milward and Saul, *Continental Europe, passim.*

71 Eugen Weber, *Peasants into Frenchmen: The Modernisation of Rural France, 1870–1914* (London, 1979), p. 4.

72 Donald Winch, *Malthus* (Oxford, 1987), p. 1. Malthus, of course, opposed this traditional view (though it was voiced by Daniel O'Connell as late as 1843).

73 L.M. Cullen and T.C. Smout, 'Economic Growth in Scotland and Ireland', in L.M. Cullen and T.C. Smout (eds), *Comparative Aspects of Scottish and Irish Economic and Social History, 1600–1900* (Edinburgh, 1977), pp. 3–18.

74 L.M. Cullen, T.C. Smout and Alex Gibson, 'Wages and Comparative Development in Ireland and Scotland, 1565–1780', in Rosalind Mitchison and Peter Roebuck (eds), *Economy and Society in Scotland and Ireland, 1500–1939* (Edinburgh, 1988), p. 113.

75 The best contemporary window on pre-Famine Ireland is the *Poor Inquiry (Ireland)* (BPP, 1836, 30–35). For a modern assessment see Cormac Ó Gráda, *Ireland: A New Economic History 1780–1939* (Oxford, 1994).

76 Joel Mokyr, *Why Ireland Starved: A Quantitative and Analytical History of the Irish Economy, 1800–1850* (London, 1983), pp. 6–10.

77 For a glimpse of the gaiety, the humour and the pathos of Irish social life see William Carleton, *Traits and Stories of the Irish Peasantry* (two volumes, New York, 1862); Miller, *Emigrants and Exiles,* chapter six.

78 Peter Solar, 'The Singularity of the Great Irish Famine', in E.M. Crawford (ed.), *Famine: The Irish Experience, 900–1900: Subsistence Crises and Famine in Ireland* (Edinburgh, 1989), pp. 112–31.

79 D.S. Johnson and Liam Kennedy, 'National Income in Ireland on the Eve of the Great Famine', paper read to the Historical National Accounts Group for Ireland, Dublin, January 1995.

80 K.A. Kennedy, Thomas Giblin and Deirdre McHugh, *The Economic Development of Ireland in the Twentieth Century* (London, 1988), p. 14.

81 D.S. Johnson and Liam Kennedy, 'The Two Economies in Ireland in the Twentieth Century', in J.R. Hill (ed.), *A New History of Ireland, VII, Ireland 1921–1984* (Oxford, 2003), pp. 452–86.

82 Recorded by Paul Brady on *Matt Molloy, Paul Brady, Tommy Peoples* (CD, Green Linnet, Danbury, USA, 1985). Brady believes the song dates from soon after the Famine, though it may be later in time.

83 Liam Kennedy and Philip Ollerenshaw (eds), *An Economic History of Ulster, 1820–1939* (Manchester, 1985).

84 There are some exceptions to this summary statement. Episodically, during the eighteenth century especially, poor law administrators in England sought to limit the inflow of Irish paupers. There were controls on Irish immigrants during the Second World War, in part because of IRA collaboration with the Nazis. The USA sought to restrict immigration in this century, though the Irish received preferential treatment on occasions. More curiously, the Irish government considered bans on younger female emigrants on two occasions, in 1947 and again, after a change of government, in 1948. (I am indebted to Enda Delaney for information on this point.)

85 K.A. Miller, *Emigrants and Exiles.*

86 John Hicks, *A Theory of Economic History* (Oxford, 1969), p. 113.

87 Raymond Hutchings, *Soviet Economic Development* (Oxford, 1971), pp. 99–119.

88 Ibid, p. 111. The forced labour camps, through which hundreds of thousands passed, of course approximated this.

89 The benefit to workers and others remaining at home in Ireland is explored in Kevin O'Rourke, 'Emigration and Living Standards in Ireland since the Famine', *Journal of Population Economics,* 8 (1995), pp. 407–21.

90 See end note 84.

91 R.E. Kennedy, *The Irish: Emigration, Marriage and Fertility* (Berkeley, 1973), p. 84.

92 The Irish ill-treatment of Black Americans in the United States, sometimes taking the form of mob violence and killings, is among the less publicised aspects of the emigrant experience. Economic xenophobia based on local geographical distinctions was also deeply rooted within Irish as well as other agrarian regions of Europe during the early nineteenth century. See J.S. Donnelly Jr., 'Irish Agrarian Rebellion: the Whiteboys of 1769–76', *Proceedings of the Royal Irish Academy,* 83, C (1983), pp. 302–4.

93 D.H. Akenson, *The Irish Diaspora: A Primer* (Toronto, 1993).

94 The Irish record on anti-Semitism is difficult to compare with other European societies as so few Jews settled in Ireland. The attacks on Jews in Limerick early in the last century and the anti-Semitism displayed by Irish civil servants at the height of the Nazi persecution hardly give cause for complacency. See Gerry Moore, 'Socio-economic aspects of anti-Semitism in Ireland, 1880–1905', *Economic and Social Review,* 12 (1981); also Micheál Mac Gréil, *Prejudice and Tolerance in Ireland* (Dublin, 1977).

95   Cormac Ó Gráda, 'The Great Famine and Today's Famines', in Cathal Póirtéir (ed.), *The Great Irish Famine* (Cork, 1995), p. 254.

96   On the Vietnamese 'boat people' see *The Economist,* 12 November 1977 and 17 June 1978.

97   At the peak of the exodus, 20,000 Albanian refugees reached Italy in one week. See *The Economist,* 16 March 1991.

98   On the fortunes of the Irish language through time, see Brian Ó Cuiv, 'Irish Language and Literature', in T.W. Moody and W.E. Vaughan (eds), *A New History of Ireland, IV, Eighteenth-Century Ireland, 1691–1800* (Oxford, 1986), pp. 374–423; Garret FitzGerald, 'Estimates for Baronies of Minimum Level of Irish-speaking among Successive Decennial Cohorts: 1771–1781 to 1861–1871', *Proceedings of the Royal Irish Academy,* 84, C, 3, pp. 117–55; Reg Hindley, *The Death of the Irish Language: A Qualified Obituary* (London, 1990); Brian Ó Cuiv (ed.), *A View of the Irish Language* (Dublin, 1969).

99   Hindley, *Death,* p. 15. But the first census after the Famine shows both the marked decline in Gaelic speaking and the huge regional variations: in Ulster and Leinster less than one in ten of the population admitted to being Gaelic speakers in 1851, while in Munster and Connacht one in two (48 per cent and 52 per cent respectively) did so.

100 Table 1.2 illustrates a pattern of association – no more, no less – which is suggestive. It does not establish lines of causation. The picture would become more blurred if the coverage was extended to include Eastern Europe. For an overview see Meic Stephens, *Linguistic Minorities in Western Europe* (Llandysul, Wales, 1976).

101 It is also unique in the sense of being the only Celtic area of Europe which has achieved modern statehood, albeit rather late in European historical time.

102 See end note 98.

103 Einar Haugen, J.D. McClure, Derick Thomson (eds), *Minority Languages Today* (Edinburgh, 1990), p. 43; see Hindley, *Death,* p. 19.

104 Stephens, *Linguistic Minorities, passim.*

105 Read, *Catalans,* p. 152.

106 The survival of ethnic minority languages in regions which later achieved statehood after 1918 is more a feature of the shambling empires of Austria-Hungary and Czarist Russia than of the more centralised nation-states of western Europe.

107 Read, *Catalans,* p. 198.

108 Eugen Weber, *Peasants into Frenchmen,* p. 70.

109 Tokens of shame used elsewhere in France bear comparison with stories of the Irish tally-stick: being forced to wear a cardboard notice, a peg, a paper ribbon, or, the more physical punishment of holding out a brick at arm's length. Weber, *Peasants,* p. 313.

110 Stephens, *Minorities,* p. 369.

111 Ibid, p. 390.

112 Arthur Griffith, *The Resurrection of Hungary* (Dublin, 1918).

113 Stephens, *Minorities,* p. xix.

114 Quoted in Clare Murphy, 'The Social Basis of Irish Nationalism, 1867–1879' (unpublished Ph.D thesis, Queen's University, Belfast, 1993), p. 137.

115 Henry Kamen, *The Rise of Toleration* (London, 1967); O.P. Grell, J.I. Israel and Nicholas Tyacke (eds), *From Persecution to Toleration: The Glorious Revolution and Religion in England* (Oxford, 1991).

116 *Novena Prayer Book* (Down and Connor, 1975), p. 33.

117 An excellent modern treatment of the Catholic question in the eighteenth century can be found in Thomas Bartlett, *The Fall and Rise of the Irish Nation: The Catholic Question, 1690–1830* (Dublin, 1992).

118   Murphy, 'Nationalism', p. 137.

119   R.J. Dickson, *Ulster Emigration to Colonial America, 1718–1775* (London, 1966).

120   Bartlett, *Fall*, pp. 157–68; S.J. Connolly, *Priests and People in Pre-Famine Ireland, 1780–1845* (Dublin, 1982), pp. 31–53.

121   John Bossy, 'English Catholics after 1688', in Grell, Israel and Tyacke (eds), *Persecution*, pp. 369–387.

122   Kamen, *Toleration* (1967).

123   For an overview, from a Catholic viewpoint, of the tribulations of the Catholic Church in France, Germany, Austria and Italy, see E.E. Hales, *The Catholic Church in the Modern World: A Survey from the French Revolution to the Present* (London, 1958).

124   Hales, *Catholic Church,* pp. 234–5. The great English poet and Jesuit, Gerard Manley Hopkins, in melancholy exile in Dublin, dedicated his poem 'The Wreck of the Deutschland' to the memory of 'five Franciscan Nuns, exiles by the Falk Laws, drowned between midnight and the morning of Dec. 7th, 1875'.

125   Ibid, pp. 242–5.

126   The agrarian critiques of the likes of the 'patriot priest', Fr Lavelle, for instance, would never have seen the light of day: Patrick Lavelle, *The Irish Landlord since the Revolution* (Dublin, 1870).

127   Thomas, *Civil War,* p. 270.

128   J.S. Donnelly, 'Agrarian Rebellion', p. 308.

129   The Francoist state in Spain, for example, introduced limited freedom of worship for Protestants in 1964, against the advice of sections of the Spanish Catholic hierarchy.

130   Kamen, *Toleration,* pp. 240–42.

131   Emmet Larkin, *The Historical Dimensions of Irish Catholicism* (New York, 1976).

132   J.L. McCracken, 'The Ecclesiastical Structure, 1714–60', in Moody and Vaughan (eds), *New History, IV,* pp. 91–95.

133   Exceptions to this generalisation may be found during the 1798 rising in Leinster and on occasion during agrarian rebellions. An incident of group rape is noted in J.S. Donnelly Jr., 'Pastorini and Captain Rock: Millenarianism and Sectarianism in the Rockite Movement of 1821–4', in Samuel Clark and J.S. Donnelly Jr., (eds), *Irish Peasants: Violence and Political Unrest, 1780–1914* (Madison, 1983), pp. 134–5.

134   Peter Flora *et al., State, Economy, and Society in Western Europe, 1815–1975* (London, I, 1983), p. 81.

135   D.H. Akenson, *Small Differences: Irish Catholics and Irish Protestants, 1815–1922: An International Perspective* (Montreal, 1988).

136   R.E. Kennedy, *The Irish: Emigration, Marriage, and Fertility* (London, 1973), pp. 48–57.

137   Eurostat, *Statistiques Demographiques* (Luxembourg, 1994), pp. 76–7.

138   Kennedy, *Irish,* pp. 51–65.

139   On unhealthy working conditions in the linen industry see the *Report Upon the Conditions of Work in Flax Mills and Linen Factories* (BPP, 18, 1893–94).

140   David Fitzpatrick, *Irish Emigration 1801–1921* (Dublin, 1990), p. 7.

141   More precisely, 'the worker is the slave of the capitalist society, the female worker is the slave of that slave'. This is in Connolly, *The Re-Conquest of Ireland* (Dublin, 1917), p. 41.

142   Ailbhe Smyth, 'Ireland', in Claire Buck (ed.), *Bloomsbury Guide to Women's Literature* (London, 1992), pp. 36–41; also Edna Longley, *From Cathleen to Anorexia: The Breakdown of Irelands* (Dublin, 1990).

143   One might speculate that geography, and spatial shapes more generally, feature less in unionist as compared to nationalist ideology and imagination.

144   See, for example, Gerardine Meaney's 'Sex and Nation: Women in Irish Culture and Politics', in Ailbhe Smyth (ed.), *Irish Women's Studies Reader* (Dublin, 1993), pp. 230–44.

145 Flann O'Brien, *The Poor Mouth (An Béal Bocht), A Bad Story About the Hard Life* (London, 1993), pp. 99, 125. Published in 1942, the author parodies the self-pity and sense of victimhood – the peasant MOPE mentality? – he finds, or affects to find in autobiographical writings about life in *Gaeltacht* areas of Ireland.

146 Of course the extent of the gap between images of Ireland and the life experiences of the common people varied over time, being at its narrowest during the first half of the nineteenth century, which is surely significant as one of the formative stages in the making of Irish political culture. It may be added, while this study is primarily concerned with images relating to Catholic and nationalist Ireland, there are strands of maudlin self-pity in loyalist writings, particularly in the late twentieth century. See Anne Fleischmann, "The Blood our Fathers Spilt": Rhetoric and Poetry', in T.A. Westendorp and Jane Mallinson (eds), *Politics and the Rhetoric of Poetry* (Amsterdam, 1995), pp. 65–75.

147 On the learned classes see Kenneth Nicholls, *Gaelic and Gaelicised Ireland in the Middle Ages* (Dublin, 1972), pp. 79–84. Bliss quotes Fynes Morrison to the effect that before 1600 'the meere Irish disdayned to learne or speake the English tounge', and the 'English Irish' similarly. See Alan Bliss, 'The English Language in Early Modern Ireland', in T.W. Moody, F.X. Martin and F.J. Byrne (eds), *A New History of Ireland, III, Early Modern Ireland, 1534–1691* (Oxford, 1978), p. 546.

148 See the poems collected by Seán Ó Tuama and Thomas Kinsella in *An Duanaire, 1600–1900: Poems of the Dispossessed* (Dublin, 1990), though it must be added that the book title relates uneasily to a number of these poetic works. An important review article by Donnchadh Ó Corráin may be found in the *Cork Examiner,* 19 and 26 November 1981.

149 This refers in particular to Catholicism, even more particularly to the transformed Catholicism of the nineteenth century with its sado-masochistic images of wounds, scourging, crown of thorns, bleeding heart and climaxing in scenes of the crucifixion of Christ. The attractions of self-sacrifice and Messiah impersonation, to take the most extreme manifestations, are well known in the case of Patrick Pearse, perhaps less so in the case of the labour leaders, James Connolly and Jim Larkin. Pearse and Connolly consummated their lives through the passion, death and resurrection of Easter 1916.

150 Compare in the British context Eric Hobsbawm and Terence Ranger (eds), *The Invention of Tradition* (Cambridge, 1983) and Patrick Wright, *On Living in an Old Country: The National Past in Contemporary Britain* (London, 1985).

151 Slovenia and Poland also were all too frequently the playing fields for the rivalries of neighbouring great powers.

152 Theobald Wolfe Tone's famous dictum, that England was 'the never-failing source of all our political evils', could have been set to music for later generations of Irish radicals, and perhaps it was. On Tone's life and politics, see Marianne Elliott, *Wolfe Tone* (Liverpool, 2012).

153 This is not the place to develop the point but the fact that some 90 per cent of the killings were due to Irish nationalist and Ulster loyalist paramilitary organisations, rather than the security forces, suggests the communal rather than the colonial dimension to the 'Troubles', though the latter has some residual relevance. It also suggests that the conflict has been handled by the two states on the island of Ireland with a degree of restraint that must have few parallels elsewhere. For statistics on killings during the 'Troubles' see John McGarry and Brendan O'Leary, *The Future of Northern Ireland* (Oxford, 1990), pp. 318–330.

154 L.M. Cullen, 'The Irish Economy in the Eighteenth Century', in L.M. Cullen (ed.), *The Formation of the Irish Economy* (Cork, 1972), pp. 9–21.

155 See, for example, de Valera's conduct of the 'economic war' and, in particular, the discourses of justification surrounding the Anglo-Irish agreement of 1938, as told in Ronan Fanning, *The Irish Department of Finance, 1922–58* (Dublin, 1978), chapter seven.

156   The historian Joseph Lee has commented critically, over-critically perhaps, on what he terms the Irish 'begging-bowl mentality' in relation to the European Union. For a scorching critique of Irish performance relative to opportunities, see Lee's, *Ireland: 1912–1985* (Cambridge, 1989). A different view may be found in David Johnson and Liam Kennedy, 'The Two Economies in Ireland in the Twentieth Century', in J.R. Hill, (ed.), *A New History of Ireland, V11, Ireland 1921–1984* (Oxford, 2003), pp. 452–86.

157   Liam Kennedy, 'Modern Ireland: Post-Colonial Society or Post-Colonial Pretensions?' *Irish Review*, 13 (1993), pp. 107–21.

158   Relevant here is the rather jaded debate on revisionism in Irish history. See Ciaran Brady (ed.), *Interpreting Irish History: The Debate on Historical Revisionism, 1938–1994* (Dublin, 1994).

159   This was not always so. Before the 1820s colonialist models of Irish history, with the massacres of 1641 writ large, enjoyed widespread currency. See M.J. Burke, 'The Politics and Poetics of Nationalist Historiography: Matthew Carey and the *Vindiciae Hibernicae*', in Joep Leerssen *et al.* (eds), *Forging in the Smithy* (Amsterdam, 1995), pp. 190–94.

Chapter Two: The Planter and the Gael

1   Liam Kennedy, Kerby A. Miller, Brian Gurrin and Gareth Davies, 'The Planter and the Gael: Explorations in Irish Ethnic History', in Karin White and Julie Costello (eds), *The Imaginary of the Stranger: Encountering the Other* (Letterkenny, 2012), pp. 13–26.

2   There are variants of this statement attributed to John Hewitt. A more elaborate version is contained in an interview he gave to the *Irish Times*, 4 July, 1974. 'I'm speaking very personally here. I'm an Ulsterman, of Planter stock. I was born in the island of Ireland, so secondarily I'm an Irishman. I was born in the British archipelago and English is my native tongue, so I am British. The British archipelago are [sic] offshore islands to the continent of Europe, so I'm European. This is my hierarchy of values and as far as I'm concerned, anyone who omits one step in that sequence of values is falsifying the situation.'

3   Ian Adamson, *Cruithin: The Ancient Kindred* (Newtownards, 1974). See also Adamson *et al.*, *Cúchulainn, The Lost Legend* (Belfast, 1995). Both Irish nationalists and Ulster loyalists lay claim to the mythical hero, Cúchulainn.

4   For an account and critique of the notion that descendants of the lost tribes of Israel turned up in Britain and Ireland see Joseph Jacobs, 'Anglo-Israelism', *Jewish Encyclopedia.com*.

5   A.T.Q. Stewart, *The Narrow Ground: The Roots of Conflict in Ulster* (London, 1977).

6   Marianne Elliott, *The Catholics of Ulster: A History* (London, 2000), pp. 29, 36–7.

7   Art Cosgrove (ed.), *A New History of Ireland. II, Medieval Ireland 1169–1534* (Oxford, 1987).

8   T.W. Moody, F.X. Martin, F.J. Byrne (eds), *A New History of Ireland, III, Early Modern Ireland 1534–1691* (Oxford, 1978), p. 113.

9   Philip Robinson, *The Plantation of Ulster: British Settlement in an Irish Landscape, 1600–1670* (Dublin, 1984).

10   Robinson, *Plantation*, Map 10, p. 110.

11   Liam Kennedy, K.A. Miller and Brian Gurrin, 'The Protestant Population of Ireland since the Seventeenth Century: Numbers, Proportions and Conjectures', in Joseph Ruane and Patrick Cabanel (eds), *Religion et Violence: Protestants et Catholiques en France et en Irelande, 16ᵉ–21ᵉ siècle* (Université de Rennes, Rennes, forthcoming).

12   The revocation in 1685 of the Edict of Nantes, which had extended tolerance to French Protestants, prompted an outflow of Protestant exiles.

13 Liam Kennedy and Philip Ollerenshaw (eds), *An Economic History of Ulster, 1820–1939* (Manchester, 1985).

14 John Lynch, *An Unlikely Success Story: The Belfast Shipbuilding Industry 1880–1935* (Belfast, 2001); J.M. Goldstrom, 'The Industrialisation of the North East', in L.M. Cullen, (ed.), *The Formation of the Irish Economy* (1972), pp. 101–112.

15 National Archives of Ireland at http://www.census.nationalarchives.ie [accessed 5 February 2011].

16 Information supplied by the historian and unionist politician, Dr Chris McGimpsey.

17 Census enumerator's return for the Doherty household, 244 Hillman Street, Dock ward, Belfast, 1911.

18 Protestants were numerically in a minority in the Irish capital but, on average, enjoyed a higher socio-economic status than their Catholic counterparts in the Victorian and Edwardian periods. The same was true of the industrial capital of the island, Belfast. Unlike Dublin, though, it is also true that a majority of the Belfast working-class was Protestant. On Dublin see Mary E. Daly, *Dublin: The Deposed Capital: A Social and Economic History, 1860–1914* (Cork, 1984); and on Belfast see A.C. Hepburn, *A Past Apart: Studies in the History of Catholic Belfast, 1850–1950* (Belfast, 1996) and Sybil Gribbon, *Edwardian Belfast: A Social Profile* (Belfast, 1982).

19 This is further confirmed by a comparison of the extent of illiteracy as between the two kinds of Bells, illiteracy being an indirect indicator of status and potential earning power. There were three times as many illiterate Bells, aged ten years or above, from the Catholic section of the population as compared to the Church of Ireland section of the population in 1911.

20 For a general discussion see Kerby A. Miller *et al.*, *Irish Immigrants in the Land of Canaan: Letters and Memoirs from Colonial America, 1675–1815* (Oxford, 2003).

21 A good literary illustration of this binary worldview may be found in the 'The Connor Girls', a short story by Edna O'Brien, in her collection *A Fanatic Heart: Selected Stories* (New York, 1984). For a critical discussion see Irene Boada Montagut, *Women Write Back: Contemporary Irish and Catalan Short Stories in Colonial Context* (Dublin, 2002). O'Brien is by no means exceptional. One finds the same binary presentation of Protestant–Catholic otherness in much Irish writing, most notably perhaps in the short stories of William Trevor. Interestingly, O'Brien comes from a southern Catholic background while Trevor was born into a Church of Ireland family in County Cork.

22 We are indebted to Dónall Ó Baoill, Professor of Irish at Queen's University, Belfast, for this insight. The point has been corroborated by Aodán Mac Póilin of the Ultach Trust, Belfast.

23 This generalisation does not rule out the fact that some members of the Church of Ireland in County Donegal, as elsewhere, were converts from Presbyterianism.

24 For a theoretical discussion of different approaches to ethnicity see Joseph Ruane and Jennifer Todd, 'The Roots of Intense Ethnic Conflict May Not In Fact Be Ethnic: Categories, Communities and Path Dependence', *European Journal of Sociology*, 45 (2004), pp. 209–232.

25 In County Donegal as a whole there were 111 members of the Church of Ireland, though only 22 Presbyterians, who claimed a knowledge of 'Irish and English' at the time of the census.

26 http://www.census.nationalarchives.ie/reels/nai000861965.

27 Some of the finest autobiographical writing in the Gaelic language came out of this small community, including the recollections of Peig Sawyers (*Peig, A Scéal Féin*), Tomás Ó Crohan (*The Islandman*) and Maurice O' Sullivan (*Twenty Years A-Growing*).

28 Muiris MacConghail mentions one Protestant family on the island about 1900: see his *The Blaskets: People and Literature* (Dublin, 1994).

29 On Protestant missionary activity in pre-Famine Ireland, including the Dingle peninsula, see Irene Whelan, *The Bible War in Ireland: The 'Second Reformation' and the Polarization of Protestant–Catholic Relations, 1800–40* (Madison, 2005).

30 The traffic was in multiple directions, even if one confines the analysis to the three major ethnic and religious groupings on the island at the end of the seventeenth century. There is, furthermore, the issue of how one handles the distinctions within the Catholic population between the Old English and Gaelic, where some historians see differences of an ethnic kind surviving into at least the late seventeenth century.

31 This by no means assumes a deterministic view of modern Irish and Ulster history. For some further discussion of historical patterns, contingency and path dependence see Joseph Ruane and Jennifer Todd, *The Dynamics of Conflict in Northern Ireland: Power, Conflict and Emancipation* (Cambridge, 1996) and Liam Kennedy, 'Did Industrialisation Matter?: Nationalist and Unionist Conflict in Ireland', international conference on Politics and Demography, London School of Economics, September 2006.

Chapter Three: Nationalism and Unionism in Ireland

1 A speech reported in *United Ireland*, 15 October 1881.

2 Ernest Gellner, *Nations and Nationalism* (Oxford, 1983).

3 The life of this chapter goes back to a series of conferences in 2005 and 2006 (and perhaps earlier). I had not then had the benefit of reading Richard English's incomparable *Irish Freedom: The History of Nationalism in Ireland* (London, 2006).

4 Each time I presented this work at a conference I almost invariably received the comment that a more complex scale would work better. That may well be true, and it would be easy to experiment with alternative schemes.

5 Charles H. Feinstein, 'Pessimism Perpetuated: Real Wages and the Standard of Living in Britain during and after the Industrial Revolution', *Journal of Economic History*, 58 (1998), pp. 625–58. This debate still rolls on and, indeed, has gone global. See in particular Robert C. Allen and the references cited therein: 'The High Wage Economy and the Industrial Revolution: A Restatement'. *Economic History Review*, 68 (2015), pp. 1–22.

6 L.M. Cullen, *An Economic History of Ireland since 1660*, (London, 1972), pp. 103–4.

7 Roderick Floud and D.N. McCloskey (eds), *The Economic History of Britain since 1700, vol.1, 1700–1860* (London, 1994).

8 Liam Kennedy, 'The Cost of Living in Ireland, 1698–1998', in David Dickson and Cormac Ó Gráda (eds), *Refiguring Ireland* (Dublin, 2003), pp. 249–76; Liam Kennedy and Martin Dowling, 'Prices and Wages in Ireland, 1700–1850', *Irish Economic and Social History*, 24 (1997), pp. 62–104.

9 That is, the non-agricultural goods which farmers purchased declined in price more steeply than did the products they sold in the market place.

10 Emmet Larkin, *The Historical Dimensions of Irish Catholicism* (New York, 1976).

11 Cormac Ó Gráda, *A New Economic History of Ireland, 1780–1939* (Oxford, 1997), pp. 80–85, 131–46.

12 The Poor Law Report of 1836 paints a dismal picture of a narrow diet, widespread underemployment, as well as poor housing and clothing. Nonetheless, the supply of calories from a potato-dominated diet was more than adequate for much of the year, while turf or peat supplied a cheap source of fuel. See *Poor Inquiry (Ireland)*, British Parliamentary Papers, 30–35 (1836), Appendix D and Appendix E; Joel Mokyr, *Why*

Ireland Starved: A Quantitative and Analytical History of the Irish Economy, 1800–1850 (London, 1985), pp. 6–29.

13 Philip Ollerenshaw, 'Industry', in Liam Kennedy and Philip Ollerenshaw (eds), *An Economic History of Ulster, 1820–1938* (Manchester, 1985); Brenda Collins, 'Proto-Industrialisation and Pre-Famine Migration', *Social History*, 7 (1982), pp. 127–46.

14 Frank Geary, 'The Act of Union, British-Irish Trade, and Pre-Famine Deindustrialisation', *Economic History Review,* 48 (1995), pp. 68–88.

15 *Poor Inquiry (Ireland), Appendix* D (1836); *Reports from the Assistant Handloom Weavers' Commissioners on the West Riding and Ireland* (BPP, 23, 1840).

16 A year of dearth is signalled by a spike or surge in the price of potatoes. For a more detailed view see Liam Kennedy and Peter Solar, *Irish Agriculture: A Price History, from the mid-eighteenth century to the eve of the First World War* (Dublin, 2007).

17 James S. Donnelly, Jr., *The Great Irish Potato Famine* (London, 2001).

18 David S. Johnson and Liam Kennedy, 'The Union of Ireland and Britain, 1800–1921', in George Boyce and Alan O' Day (eds), *The Making of Modern Irish History: Revisionism and the Revisionist Controversy* (Routledge, London, 1996), pp. 34–70.

19 Jonathan Bardon, *A History of Ulster* (Belfast, 1992), pp. 292–3.

20 Geary, 'Act of Union', pp. 68–88; Mokyr, *Why Ireland Starved*, pp. 13–15.

21 Andy Bielenberg, *Cork's Industrial Revolution, 1780–1880* (Cork, 1991), pp. 31–8.

22 For the wider European perspective see Brenda Collins and Philip Ollerenshaw (eds), *The European Linen Industry in Historical Perspective* (Oxford, 2003).

23 Johnson and Kennedy, 'Union of Britain and Ireland', p. 37.

24 E.R.R. Green, *The Lagan Valley: A Local History of the Industrial Revolution* (London, 1949).

25 Collins, 'Proto-Industrialisation', pp. 127–46.

26 W.M. O'Hanlon, *Walks among the Poor of Belfast, and Suggestions for their Improvement* (Dublin, 1853). To take just one scene from O' Hanlon's account (page 15): 'Plunging into the alleys and entries of this neighbourhood [Barrack Lane, North Queen Street], what indescribable scenes of poverty, filth, and wretchedness everywhere meet the eye.'

27 Quoted in Bardon, *History of Ulster*, p. 257.

28 D. H. Akenson, *Ireland, Sweden and the Great European Migration, 1815–1914* (Liverpool, 2011), pp. 93–6; *Poor Inquiry (Ireland), Appendix F* (BPP, 1836, 33), p. 135.

29 Sarah Roddy, *Population, Providence, and Empire: The Churches and Emigration from Nineteenth-Century Ireland* (Manchester, 2014).

30 Contrasting viewpoints may be found in K.A. Miller, *Emigrants and Exiles: Ireland and the Irish Exodus to North America* (Oxford, 1985) and D.H. Akenson, *Small Differences: Irish Catholics and Protestants, 1815–1922: An International Perspective* (Kingston, 1988).

31 *Poor Inquiry (Ireland), Appendix F*, p. 506. Fry was minister for Ikerrin, Rathnavogue, and Finglass on the Offaly–Tipperary border.

32 Michael Hechter, *Internal Colonialism: The Celtic Fringe in British National Development, 1536–1966* (London, 1975).

33 Akenson, *Small Differences* (1988), pp. 142–9.

34 No normative judgement is being made here. Some of the differences may have had to do with heavier investment in the acquisition of skills, literacy and education more generally on the part of Protestant groups, though a more favourable endowment of land to begin with must have mattered.

35 R.F. Foster, *Modern Ireland, 1600–1972* (London, 1989), p. 310.

36 Peter Gray, *Famine, Land and Politics: British Government and Irish Society, 1843–1850* (Dublin, 1998), pp. 26–36.

37 Johnson and Kennedy, 'Union of Britain and Ireland', pp. 63–5.

38 Christine Kinealy and Gerard MacAtasney, *The Hidden Famine: Poverty, Hunger, and Sectarianism in Belfast 1840–50* (London, 2000). However, this is more true of later times as 'political memory' filtered out ill-fitting elements within the Ulster unionist historical narrative. During the Famine itself philanthropic Protestant organisations were active in seeking to alleviate suffering.

39 Mary E. Daly, *Dublin: The Deposed Capital: A Social and Economic History, 1860–1914* (Cork, 1984).

40 Joseph Lee, *The Modernisation of Irish Society, 1848–1918* (Dublin, 1972). This dazzling work of scholarship stimulated much of the best later work on the Irish Land War.

41 James Meenan in *Commission on Emigration and Other Population Problems* (Dublin, 1954), p. 402.

42 David Fitzpatrick, *Irish Emigration, 1801–1921* (Dundalk, 1984).

43 See regional maps in Liam Kennedy *et al.*, *Mapping the Great Irish Famine: A Survey of the Famine Decades* (Dublin, 1999). But note also that gains in regional equality could actually have the effect of increasing rather than diminishing disenchantment with the political status quo. Thus the gains in literacy in the English language and the rise of trading and other non-farming occupations in the West were conducive to the diffusion of Irish nationalist sentiment and more efficient organisation among the disaffected.

44 Olwen Purdue (ed.), *Belfast: The Emerging City, 1850–1914* (Dublin, 2013); S.J. Connolly (ed.), *Belfast 400: People, Place and History* (Liverpool, 2012).

45 The circulation of individuals and families within the Empire fitted naturally enough with an imperial consciousness, a link that has not perhaps received the attention it deserves.

46 Tom Stark and Frank Geary, 'Examining Ireland's Post-Famine Economic Growth Performance', *Economic Journal*, 112 (2002), pp. 919–35.

47 On rural women, see Joanna Bourke, *Husbandry to Housewifery: Women, Economic Change, and Housework in Ireland, 1890–1914* (Oxford, 1993) and Mary E. Daly, *Women and Work in Ireland* (Dundalk, 1997).

48 David Johnson, *The Interwar Economy in Ireland* (Dundalk, 1985), p. 5.

49 George Boyce, *Nationalism in Ireland* (London, 1982).

50 K.T. Hoppen, *Ireland since 1800: Conflict and Conformity* (Dublin, 1989).

51 Paul A. David, *Technical Choice, Innovation and Economic Growth: Essays on American and British Experience in the Nineteenth Century* (London, 1975).

52 I would add, despite this 'lock-in' to set political positions, the expression of Irish constitutional nationalism may nonetheless have been moderated by the extent of economic and social reform in the quarter century before the Great War. Nor should one neglect the role of radicals and nationalists from a Protestant background in the development of Irish nationalism. These do not admit of a ready economic interpretation but in a sense the exceptional character of their participation reinforces the case for deeper structural explanations including ethnic cleavages.

53 S.J. Connolly, *Religion, Law, and Power: The Making of Protestant Ireland, 1660–1760* (Oxford, 2002).

54 Miller, *Emigrants and Exiles*, pp. 84–5.

55 Connolly, *Religion, Law and Power*, p. 313.

56 Joe Ruane and Jennifer Todd, *The Dynamics of Conflict in Northern Ireland: Power, Conflict and Emancipation* (Cambridge, 1996).

57 Take, for example, the use made of Ireland's extensive rail network by Charles Stewart Parnell and his Home Rule colleagues when organising political meetings and demonstrations. The humble bicycle became an important carrier of people and ideas a little later.

58   Miroslav Hroch, *Social Preconditions of National Revival in Europe: A Comparative Analysis of the Social Composition of Patriotic Groups among the Smaller European Nations* (translated by Ben Fowkes, Cambridge, 1985).

59   There is a nice illustration of these processes at work (and being frustrated) in Brinsley McNamara's nationalistic novel, *The Clanking of Chains* (Dublin, 1920).

60   There is now a voluminous literature on 'feedback' processes and cumulative causation. For brief treatments see 'Circular and Cumulative Causation' by Allan A. Schmidt and 'Path Dependency' by Mark Setterfield in Phillip A. O'Hara (ed.), *Encyclopaedia of Political Economy* (London, 1999), pp. 87–90 and 841–3 respectively. A seminal work is Gunnar Myrdal, *Asian Drama: An Inquiry into the Poverty of Nations* (New York, 1968), though my colleague Graham Brownlow points out that notions of cumulative causation can be traced back to the writings of Thorsten Veblen, in particular *The Place of Science in Modern Civilization and Other Essays* (New York, 1919).

61   Johnson and Kennedy, 'The Union of Ireland and Britain', pp. 34–70.

62   *Report by the Committee on Irish Finance* (BPP, 34, 1912–13).

63   Quoted in L. Paul-Dubois, *Contemporary Ireland* (Dublin, 1911), p. 340.

64   Benedict Anderson, *Imagined Communities: Reflections on the Origin and Spread of Nationalism* (London, 2006). See also John Wilson Foster's discussion of teleology and historical foreclosure as found in Irish republicanism in his essay 'Guests of the Nation'. This is in Foster, *Between Shadows: Modern Irish Writing and Culture* (Dublin, 2009), pp. 151–73.

65   Arthur Griffith, *The Resurrection of Hungary* (Dublin, 1918), p. 166.

66   Liam Kennedy, 'The Roman Catholic Church and Economic Growth in Nineteenth-Century Ireland', *Economic and Social Review*, 10 (1978), pp. 45–59.

67   A point made to me by my colleague Graham Brownlow.

68   Aaron Director, 'The Parity of the Economic Market Place', *Journal of Law and Economics*, 7 (1964), p. 8.

69   Brinsley MacNamara, *The Valley of the Squinting Windows* (New York, 1919), p. 20.

70   On Irish Ireland see D.P. Moran, *The Philosophy of Irish Ireland* (edited by Patrick Maume, Dublin, 2006).

71   Fergus O'Ferrall, *Daniel O'Connell* (Dublin, 1998), pp. 44–6.

72   The term 'Catholic Emancipation' is something of a misnomer: the main Catholic grievances had been redressed before the formation of O'Connell's Catholic Association in 1823, and parliamentary representation was hardly of direct relevance to the mass of the people.

73   Liam Kennedy, 'The Cost of Living in Ireland, 1698–1998', in David Dickson and Cormac Ó Gráda (eds), *Refiguring Ireland*, Dublin, 2003), pp. 249–76.

74   These price changes may be traced in some detail in Kennedy and Solar, *Irish Agriculture* (2007), pp. 132–73.

75   James S. Donnelly Jr., *Captain Rock: The Irish Agrarian Rebellion of 1821–1824* (Madison, 2009).

76   Jonathan Bardon, *A History of Ulster* (Belfast, 1992), pp. 245–6.

77   Ibid, pp. 223–7, 253–4.

78   Still, for many purposes, it makes sense to speak of three ethno-religious groupings on the island during the nineteenth century, even though, on the major constitutional issue, Presbyterians and Anglicans were increasingly as one.

79   Samuel Clark, *Social Origins of the Land War* (Princeton, 1979) offers a close sociological analysis of social relations in the countryside.

80   According to the Census of Ireland, just over one-in-three persons in Connacht in 1911 were Gaelic speakers and most of these had English as well. The proportion of speakers in the other provinces was smaller still.

81 Clark, *Social Origins* (1979); Liam Kennedy, 'Farmers, Traders and Agricultural Politics in Pre-Independence Ireland', in S. Clark and J.S. Donnelly Jr. (eds), *Irish Peasants: Violence and Political Unrest, 1780–1914* (Madison, Wisconsin, 1983).

82 Liam Kennedy, 'The Economic Thought of the Nation's Lost Leader: Charles Stewart Parnell', in George Boyce and Alan O' Day (eds), *Parnell in Perspective* (Routledge, London, 1991), pp. 171–200.

83 *Reports from the Assistant Handloom Weavers' Commissioners on the West Riding and Ireland*, (1840).

84 Philip Ollerenshaw, 'Business and Finance, 1780–1945' and John Lynch, 'Labour and Society, 1780–1945', in Kennedy and Ollerenshaw (eds), *Ulster Since 1600* (2013).

85 *Minutes of Evidence taken before the Committee on Irish Finance* (BPP, 30, 1913), pp. 174–85.

86 Ibid., Q. 4395.

87 Industrial protectionism, for instance, was against the economic interests of farmers. The farming sector benefited from internationally competitive prices for its farm inputs and for consumer goods. Protection would have had the effect of raising costs and prices, something which both export-oriented industrialists and farmers in Ireland would have wished to avoid.

88 David Johnson, *The Interwar Economy in Ireland* (Dundalk, 1985); Cormac Ó Gráda, *A Rocky Road: The Irish Economy since the 1920s* (Manchester, 1997).

89 *Minutes of Evidence*, QQ 4476–4478.

90 Ibid., QQ 4565–4566.

91 Graham Brownlow, 'The Political Economy of the Ulster Crisis: Historiography, Social Capability and Globalisation', in D. George Boyce and Alan O' Day (eds), *The Ulster Crisis, 1885–1922* (London, 2005), pp. 27–46.

92 David Fitzpatrick, 'Militarism in Ireland, 1900–1922', in Thomas Bartlett and Keith Jeffery (eds), *A Military History of Ireland* (Cambridge, 1997), pp. 379–406.

93 As with Irish nationalist narratives, Ulster unionist interpretations of the past were characterised by silences and selective recall. To fix on an egregious illustration, the Great Famine of the 1840s found little or no place in the folk memory and populist writings of Ulster unionists. Kinealy and MacAtasney, *Hidden Famine* (2000), pp. 1–9.

94 Stephen A. Royle, 'Workshop of the Empire, 1820–1914', in S.J. Connolly (ed.), *Belfast 400*, pp. 199–235. The interesting major exception is Lord Pirrie, chairman of the famous Harland & Wolff shipbuilding firm. Pirrie was initially supportive of Home Rule but later retreated from that position, thereby reproducing the more conventional association between religion, social class, politics and business. These issues are well-discussed in Glenn Simpson, 'William Pirrie, the Titanic and Home Rule', *History Ireland*, 20 (2012), pp. 30–34.

95 Henry Patterson, 'The Decline of the Collaborators: The Ulster Unionist Labour Association and Post-War Unionist Politics', in Francis Devine, Fintan Lane and Niamh Puirséil (eds), *Essays in Irish Labour History: A Festschrift for Elizabeth and John W. Boyle* (Dublin, 2008), pp. 238–56.

96 This seems to be implicit if not actually explicit in the influential publication, *The Economics of Partition*, produced by the Irish Communist Organisation, later the British and Irish Communist Organisation (Belfast, 1969).

97 A.C. Hepburn, *A Past Apart: Studies in the History of Catholic Belfast, 1850–1950* (Belfast, 1996).

98 John Whyte, 'How much Discrimination was there under the Unionist Regime, 1921–1968', in Tom Gallagher and James O'Connell, *Contemporary Irish Studies* (Manchester, 1983), pp. 1–35.

99 Timothy Bowman, *Carson's Army: The Ulster Volunteer Force, 1910–22* (Manchester, 2007).

100 Liam Kennedy, 'Did Industrialisation Matter? Nationalist and Unionist Conflict in Ireland' (unpublished paper, Institute of Irish Studies, Queen's University, Belfast, 2005).

101 Gunnar Myrdal, 'Institutional Economics', *Journal of Economic Issues*, 12 (December 1978), pp. 771–83.

102 The comparison with economically-developed Catalonia and the emergence of Catalan nationalism, for instance, is instructive, and the contrasts – a separate language but also a separate and powerful Catalan capitalist class – suggest there were different pathways into the world of nationalisms.

103 Kennedy, 'Did Industrialisation Matter?' (2005).

Chapter Four: Cry Holocaust: The Great Irish Famine and the Jewish Holocaust

1 It is not easy to calculate *excess* mortality, that is, the numbers who died because of the Famine but excluding those who would normally be expected to die during the same period. Joel Mokyr calculates a massive toll of one million to 1.2 million excess deaths. See Joel Mokyr, *Why Ireland Starved: A Quantitative and Analytical History of the Irish Economy, 1800–1850* (London, 1983). Cormac Ó Gráda suggests a death toll of around one million in *Ireland Before and After the Great Famine: Explorations in Economic History 1800–1925* (Manchester, 1993).

2 Cormac Ó Gráda, *Ireland's Great Famine: Interdisciplinary Perspectives* (Dublin, 2006), p. 198, and by the same author *Famine: A Short History* (Princeton, 2009).

3 J.S. Donnelly Jr., 'Mass Evictions and the Great Famine', in Cathal Póirtéir, (ed.), *The Great Irish Famine* (Cork, 1985), pp. 155–73; Christine Kinealy, *The Great Irish Famine: Impact, Ideology and Rebellion* (London, 2002), pp. 141–2.

4 Peter Gray, *Famine, Land and Politics: British Government and Irish Society, 1843–50* (Dublin, 1998), pp. 284–304.

5 *Times*, 9 February 1848.

6 An interesting recent work draws attention to parallels in the public memory of the Ukrainian famine and the Irish famine of the 1840s. See Christian Noack, Lindsay Janssen and Vincent Comerford (eds), *Holodomor and Gorta Mór* (London, 2012).

7 James Pius Sweeney, in a letter to the *Irish Echo* headed 'Famine study does not diminish Holocaust suffering', 29 May – 4 June 1996.

8 Ibid.

9 Quoted in James V. Mullin, 'The New Jersey Famine Curriculum: A Report', *Éire-Ireland* (2002), pp. 127–8. See also Francis A. Boyle, *United Ireland, Human Rights and International Law* (Atlanta, 2012), pp. 20–23.

10 Robert J. Scally, *The End of Hidden Ireland: Rebellion, Famine, and Emigration* (Oxford, 1995), p. 230. Despite the borrowed imagery, Scally did not subscribe to the genocidal interpretation of the Famine.

11 Accessed 22 April 2014.

12 S.J. Connolly, *Religion and Society in Nineteenth-Century Ireland* (Dundalk, 1985).

13 Liam Kennedy, Kerby A. Miller and Brian Gurrin, 'The Protestant Population of Ireland since the Seventeenth Century: Numbers, Proportions and Conjectures', in Joseph Ruane and Patrick Cabanel (eds), *Religion et Violence: Protestants et Catholiques en France et en Irelande, 16ᵉ–21ᵉ siècle* (Université de Rennes, Rennes, forthcoming).

14 The literature on the fate of European Jews is now vast. Choosing almost arbitrarily, the following provide overviews of different dimensions to the Holocaust: Raul Hilberg, *The Destruction of the European Jews* (Chicago, 1961); Martin Gilbert, *The Holocaust: The*

Jewish Tragedy (London, 1987); Robert Browning, *The Origins of the Final Solution: The Evolution of Nazi Jewish Policy, September 1939–March 1942* (Lincoln, Nebraska, 2004); Dalia Ofer and Lenore Weizman (eds), *Women in the Holocaust* (New Haven, 1998); Paul Valent, *Child Survivors of the Holocaust* (New York, 2002); Tom Lawson, *Debates on the Holocaust* (Manchester, 2010); Alvin Rosenfeld, *The End of the Holocaust* (Bloomington, 2011); Alan S. Rosenbaum (ed.), *Is the Holocaust Unique? Perspectives on Comparative Genocide* (Colorado,1996); and for the experiences of a survivor who found a new life in Northern Ireland there is Helen Lewis, *A Time to Speak* (Belfast, 1992).

15   Strictly speaking, racist images are inflected with pseudo-scientific assumptions. Following the Darwinian revolution of the second half of the nineteenth century, and hence outside the time frame of this chapter, corrupted and corrupting versions of evolutionary ideas swept Europe and America. One manifestation was simian-featured representations of Irish people in magazines and newspapers. A pioneering and still controversial study is Lionel P. Curtis, *Apes and Angels: The Irishman in Victorian Caricature* (London, 1997).

16   This was despite Lewis's temperate introduction to the body of oral evidence collected by the Commission. G.C. Lewis, *State of the Irish Poor in Great Britain* (BPP, 34, 1836). Donald MacRaild, 'Irish Immigration and the "Condition of England" Question: The Roots of an Historiographical Tradition', *Immigrants and Minorities*, 14 (1995), p. 72.

17   Frederick Engels, *The Condition of the Working Class in England in 1844* (London, 1950), p. 92. Some of Engels' comments on the Irish, though generally sympathetic, on occasion border on the racialist, that is, by modern-day standards but presumably not by those of the time.

18   Donald MacRaild, 'Irish Immigration' (1995), pp. 67–85; idem, *The Irish Diaspora in Britain, 1750–1939* (London, 2010).

19   MacRaild, 'Irish Immigration', p. 70 and also MacRaild, '"No Irish Need Apply": The Origins and Persistence of a Prejudice', *Labour History Review*, 78, 3 (2013), pp. 287–8.

20   Paul E. Roberts, 'Caravats and Shanavests: Whiteboyism and Faction Fighting in East Munster, 1802–11', in Samuel Clark and James S. Donnelly, Jr. (eds), *Irish Peasants: Violence and Political Unrest, 1780–1914* (Madison, 1983).

21   E.P. Thompson's valuable concept is interpreted by Thompson and others in unduly mellow terms and might be usefully expanded to take in some less pleasant dimensions to popular economic morality. See E.P. Thompson, 'The Moral Economy of the English Crowd in the Eighteenth Century', *Past and Present*, 50, 1 (1971), pp. 76–136.

22   Daniel Grace, *The Great Famine in Nenagh Poor Law Union, Co. Tipperary* (Nenagh, Co. Tipperary, 2000), pp. 16, 40.

23   James S. Donnelly, Jr., 'Irish Agrarian Rebellion: The Whiteboys of 1769–76', in *Proceedings of the Royal Irish Academy*, C, 83 (1983).

24   *Poor Inquiry (Ireland)* (BPP, 34, 1836), p. 503.

25   I have no idea how representative the following personal experience might be. I worked with a group of Irish navvies from County Kerry 'on the buildings' in London in the summer of 1966. 'Never trust a Connemara man' and 'watch out for his *scian* [knife]', were repeated pieces of advice.

26   The young Michael Davitt, himself a Famine refugee, was an active defender when his Irish neighbourhood in Haslingden ('Little Ireland'), in Lancashire, was regularly attacked by English workmen. These scenes must have been replicated in many parts of northern England and western Scotland. See T.W. Moody, *Davitt and the Irish Revolution, 1846–82* (Oxford, 1981), p. 12.

27   Edward Lengel, *The Irish Through British Eyes: Perceptions of Ireland in the Famine Era* (Westport, CT, USA, 2002), p. 14. Contrary to what might be expected, biological science and its scientific practitioners were not driving forces behind the simianised

representations of Irish people found in British popular culture in the second half of the nineteenth century. See Peter Bowler, 'Race Theory and the Irish', in Seán Ó Síocháin (ed.), *Social Thought on Ireland in the Nineteenth Century* (Dublin, 2009), pp. 135–46.

28 Lengel, *The Irish*, p. 152.

29 MacRaild counsels that it is important to see Irish settlement in Britain, and the reactions this provoked, in long-range perspective rather than in static terms largely dominated by the experiences of the Famine period. MacRaild, 'Irish Immigration', p. 81.

30 Tim Pat Coogan, *The Famine Plot: England's Role in Ireland's Greatest Tragedy* (New York, 2012).

31 Peter Gray, *Famine, Land and Politics* (1998); Paul Bew, *Ireland: The Politics of Enmity, 1789–2006* (Oxford, 2007); Enda Delaney, *The Curse of Reason: The Great Irish Famine* (Dublin, 2012).

32 Gray, *Famine, Land and Politics*, p. 314.

33 Delaney, *Curse of Reason*, p. 161.

34 *Times*, 12 February 1846.

35 James S. Donnelly Jr., *The Great Irish Potato Famine* (Sutton, 2010), p. 96. For a very different, largely favourable assessment of Gregory see B.M. Walker, 'Villain, Victim or Prophet? William Gregory and the Great Famine', *Irish Historical Studies*, 38 (2013), pp. 579–99.

36 Gray, *Famine, Land and Politics*, p. 180.

37 Donnelly, 'Mass Evictions', p. 155.

38 Ibid., p. 156.

39 Bew, *Politics of Enmity*, p. 97; Robin Haines, *Charles Trevelyan and the Great Irish Famine* (Dublin, 2003), pp. 2–5.

40 Cathal Póirtéir, 'Folk memory and the Famine', in Cathal Póirtéir (ed.), *The Great Irish Famine* (Cork, 1985), p. 219.

41 Delaney, *Curse of Reason*, pp. 158–160, 230–1

42 *Times*, 9 February 1848. It is conventional to give the *Times* a bad press. While at an editorial level it may be said to have had a bad Famine, it is also the case that through its Ireland correspondent it gave publicity to harrowing accounts of famine, disease and death in Ireland. Of many such accounts, there is the report (extracted from the *Mayo Constitution*) of the death by starvation of Pat M'Donnell whose body was found in a field in Mayo and the death also of Bridget Joyce, a widow with four children, who died of hunger in a sheep-hut (*Times*, 1 January 1848).

43 Bew, *Politics of Enmity*, pp. 202–205.

44 Adolf Hitler, *Mein Kampf* (translated by Ralph Manheim, London, 1969, reprint 2009), p. 138. This part-memoir is laced with self-pity, which reads rather curiously in the light of his later merciless persecution of socialists, gypsies, Jews and other impure or degenerate elements (as seen by national socialists) within German society.

45 Ibid, p. 295.

46 *Documents on Nazism, 1919–1945* (introduced and edited by Jeremy Noakes and Geoffrey Pridham, London, 1974), pp. 485–6.

47 Some of the more ideological Irish Famine websites have invoked this comparison.

48 *Cork Examiner*, 30 April 1847.

49 James Hack Tuke, *A Visit to Connaught in the Autumn of 1847: A Letter Addressed to the Central Relief Committee of the Society of Friends, Dublin*. Second Edition: *With Notes of a Subsequent Visit to Erris* (York, 1848), p. 16.

50 *Mayo Constitution*, quoted in the *Times*, 19 November 1847.

51 Liam Kennedy *et al.*, *Mapping the Great Irish Famine: A Survey of the Famine Decades* (Dublin, 1999), p. 128.

52   Peter Froggatt, 'The Response of the Medical Profession to the Famine', in E.M. Crawford (ed.), *Famine: the Irish Experience* (Edinburgh, 1989), pp. 134–56. See also T.W. Guinnane and Cormac Ó Gráda, 'Mortality in the North Dublin Union during the Great Famine', *Economic History Review*, 55, 3 (2002), pp. 487–506.

53   Christopher R. Browning, *The Origins of the Final Solution: The Evolution of Nazi Jewish Policy, September 1939–March 1942* (Lincoln, Nebraska, 2004). A year earlier, Hans Frank, the chief of military operations for occupied Poland, had exulted (page 45): 'What a pleasure, finally for once to be able to tackle the Jewish race physically. The more that die, the better.'

54   Raphael Lemkin, *Axis Rule in Occupied Europe* (Washington, 1944), p. 75.

55   R. Dudley Edwards and T. Desmond Williams (eds), *The Great Famine: Studies in Irish History 1845–52* (Dublin, 1956), p. vii.

56   Christopher R. Browning, *The Path to Genocide: Essays on Launching the Final Solution* (Cambridge, 1992), p. 176.

57   In a more emotionally-charged account of the same incident Daniel Goldhagen describes the close-range killing: 'the Germans often became spattered with human gore. In the words of one man, "the supplementary shot struck the skull with such force that the entire back of the head was torn off and blood, bone splinters, and brain matter soiled the marksmen"'. From *Hitler's Willing Executioners: Ordinary Germans and the Holocaust* (London, 1996), p. 218.

58   Using Mokyr's estimate of a normal death rate for Ireland in the 1840s of just under 24 per thousand per annum. However, in badly affected areas of the west of Ireland the ratio between Famine funerals and 'normal' funerals would have been much higher. A very rough estimate would suggest 160,000 normal funerals during the Famine years in Connacht, and thus well below Famine-related causes of death.

59   David Dickson, *Arctic Ireland* (Belfast, 1997).

60   Cormac Ó Gráda, *Ireland's Great Famine*, p. 198; Ó Gráda, *Black '47 and Beyond: The Great Irish Famine in History, Economy, and Memory* (Princeton, 1999), pp. 4–5, 84–5.

61   'Food or Famine', *Cork Examiner*, 24 November 1845.

62   Cormac Ó Gráda, *Ireland's Great Famine* (London, 1989), p. 101; Liam Kennedy *et al.*, *Mapping the Irish Famine*, p. 44.

63   Daniel Grace, *The Great Famine in Nenagh Poor Law Union, Co. Tipperary* (Nenagh, 2000), p. 131, table 11.3.

64   A more detailed table, country by country, of the numbers of Jews killed may be found at the website of the Jewish Virtual Library: https://www.jewishvirtuallibrary.org/jsource/Holocaust/killedtable.html [accessed 10 April 2014].

65   Doris Bergen, *War and Genocide: A Concise History of the Holocaust* (Plymouth, UK, 2009), p. 185. Other sources suggest perhaps a few more survivors after the war. Some idea of the scale of killing concentrated at this one small site may be gained by visualising a major football stadium, filled to capacity and multiplied some seven times over.

66   Gérard Prunier, *The Rwanda Crisis: History of a Genocide* (London, 1997).

67   Lewis, *Time to Speak, passim.*

68   Gisela Bock, 'Ordinary Women in Nazi Germany: Perpetrators, Victims, Followers and Bystanders', in Dalia Ofer and Lenore Weitzman (eds), *Women in the Holocaust* (New Haven, 1998), p. 94.

69   Alan S. Rosenbaum (ed.), *Is the Holocaust Unique? Perspectives on Comparative Genocide* (Colorado, 1996).

70   For example, whether potato consumption by the Irish poor conformed to the notion of a Giffen good, as suggested by some political economists and as disputed by others, is little more than a plaything for the amusement of social scientists.

71 J.S. Donnelly Jr., *The Land and the People of Nineteenth-Century Cork: The Rural Economy and the Land Question* (London, 1975), p. 91; Christine Kinealy, *The Great Irish Famine: Impact, Ideology and Rebellion* (New York, 2002), pp. 147–8. Some detachments of the army made charitable collections for the relief of Famine victims, actions hardly conducive to a desire to exterminate, but, as Kinealy also points out, the use of police and army to guard the shipment of foods and to assist in evictions evinced much anger among the populace. See also Hugh Dorian, *Outer Edge of Ulster: A Memoir of Social Life in Nineteenth-Century Donegal* (edited by Breandán Mac Suibhne and David Dickson, Dublin, 2000), pp. 225–7 where the author comments favourably on the sympathy shown by the Redcoats of the British Army towards the famished people.

72 James Hack Tuke, *Visit to Connaught*, p. 24.

73 Peter Froggatt, 'Medical Profession', pp. 134–56.

74 John Mitchel, *The Last Conquest of Ireland (Perhaps)* (Patrick Maume (ed.), Dublin, 2005), p. 219. This collection of writings was first published in book form in 1861.

75 This is to simplify a bit. During the 'Irish Phase' the Treasury did provide loans to financially-distressed poor-law unions and Trevelyan helped direct some remaining funds from the British Assocation into famine relief.

76 Gray, *Famine, Land and Politics*, pp. 291–8.

77 Joel Mokyr, *Why Ireland Starved: A Quantitative and Analytical History of the Irish Economy, 1800–1850* (London, 1985), p. 28. Mokyr's estimate is £13 million, which is perhaps a shade on the high side.

78 Donnelly, *Nineteenth-Century Cork*, pp. 104–6. For a detailed estate study see Joseph Knightly, 'The Godfrey Estate during the Great Famine', *Kerry Archaeological and Historical Society*, 3 (2nd series, 2003), pp. 125–33. The Godfreys were benevolent but deeply indebted long before the Famine.

79 Peter Solar, Liam Kennedy, Luc Hens, David Dickson, 'Rents in Ireland, 1730–1844', paper read to the annual conference of the Irish Quantitative History Network, January 2014.

80 Ibid., pp. 15–16.

81 Cormac Ó Gráda, *Ireland's Great Famine: Interdisciplinary Perspectives* (Dublin, 2006) p. 57. An awkward corollary of this might be that the British government and the (London) *Times* did have a point in claiming that the Irish landed gentry could have shouldered much more of the financial burden, not in each and every case of course, but as a class.

82 Ibid., pp. 57–9; Knightly, 'Godfrey Estate', pp. 135–6.

83 Quoted in Delaney, *Curse of Reason*, pp. 205–6.

84 Francis A. Boyle, *United Ireland, Human Rights and International Law* (Atlanta, 2012), p. 31.

85 Lewis, *A Time to Speak*, pp. 103–4.

86 J.S. Donnelly Jr., *The Land and the People of Nineteenth-Century Cork: The Rural Economy and the Land Question* (London, 1975), p. 87. John Crowley, William J. Smyth and Mike Murphy (eds), *Atlas of the Great Irish Famine:1845–52* (Cork, 2012); Breandán Mac Suibhne, 'A Jig in the Poorhouse', *Dublin Review of Books*, 31 April 2013.

87 Mac Suibhne, 'Jig in the Poorhouse' (2013).

88 This is in her more journalistic writing but there are echoes also in Susan Sontag, *Regarding the Pain of Others* (London, 2004).

89 The production budget was reported as 100 million US dollars at the end of 2002; see http://www.boxofficemojo.com/movies/?page=main&id=gangsofnewyork.htm [accessed 15 June 2015].

90 Edwin Burrows and Mike Wallace, *Gotham: A History of New York City to 1898* (Oxford, 1999), p. 884.

91 Ibid., pp. 888–895. However Iver Bernstein, in *The New York City Draft Riots: Their Significance for American Society and Politics in the Age of the Civil War* (New York, 1990), is at pains to argue that the street violence had complex origins and cannot be reduced simply to an expression of ethnic and racial hatred, though of course it was that as well.

92 The cartoon may be viewed at https://www.nytimes.com/learning/general/onthisday/harp/0801_big.html [accessed 14 March 2014].

93 Burrows and Wallace, *Gotham*, p. 895.

94 Susan Sontag, *Pain of Others*, p. 21–2.

95 *Sunday Independent*, 3 June 1945. See also the *Sunday Independent* of 13 May 1945, when wartime censorship had just ended, which featured shocking photographs of the inmates of the Nazi camps at Nordhausen, Buchenwald and Ohrdruff. I am grateful to Patrick Maume for pointing me towards the controversy surrounding these photographs.

96 See the correspondence in the *Irish Independent* following the publication of the photographs and also the feature 'Irish Doctor sees Belsen Horrors', *Sunday Independent*, 10 June 1945. The nationality of the eye-witness was emphasised, to deflect hostile critics and dispel any remaining doubts about the authenticity of the pictures. There is interesting work to be done on the reception of the Holocaust into Irish society, North and South, which might usefully be compared with similar-type studies for other societies.

97 Ethnic autism is a term I have made use of elsewhere to characterise relations between Irish nationalists and Ulster unionists in twentieth-century Ireland but it seems appropriate in this context also.

98 J.S. Donnelly, Jr., 'The Construction of the Memory of the Famine in Ireland and the Irish Diaspora, 1850–1900', *Éire-Ireland*, 31 (1996), pp. 26–61.

99 Miller, *Emigrants and Exiles*, pp. 280–81.

100 Norman G. Finkelstein, *The Holocaust Industry: Reflections on the Exploitation of Jewish Suffering* (London, 2003). From the Introduction: 'This book is both an anatomy and an indictment of the Holocaust industry.'

101 This quip has been attributed to a former Israeli foreign minister, the late Abba Eban. See Jonathan Freedland, 'An Enemy of the People', *Guardian*, 14 July 2000.

102 For example, the Finnish famine of 1867–68 carried away 8 or 9 per cent of the population. One can only dread what might have been the consequences of repeated ecological shocks on an Irish scale to its population.

103 Peter Solar, 'The Great Famine was No Ordinary Subsistence Crisis', in E.M. Crawford (ed.), *Famine: The Irish Experience* (Edinburgh, 1989), pp. 112–31.

104 The balance of population between the two islands mattered. The population of Ireland in 1841, astonishingly, was one half that of England and Wales. Scotland, it might be added, was thinly populated by comparison with Ireland.

105 For example, the founder-editor of the *Economist*, a brash new publication that excoriated relief offerings to Ireland, was of Quaker origin, deeply principled but exceedingly doctrinaire. A distant echo of the kind of misplaced confidence, born of ideological conviction that guided key actors and ideologues might be that of the neo-conservatives who instigated disastrous interventions in Afghanistan and Iraq during the US presidency (2001–2009) of George Bush junior. For the history of *The Economist* see Ruth Dudley Edwards, *The Pursuit of Reason: the Economist, 1843–1993* (London, 1993).

106 However, at least one scholar has cast serious doubt on this presumption, and the matter would benefit from further research. Charles Read (University of Cambridge), '"Laissez-faire", The Irish Famine and British Financial Crisis', paper read to the annual conference of the Irish Economic and Social History Society, Galway, November 2013.

107 Margaret Kelleher, *The Feminisation of Famine: Expressions of the Inexpressible* (Cork, 1997), p. 3.

108 But Kelleher also argues, quite reasonably and on the same page, that issues raised by Holocaust writers concerning 'the ethics and potential of representation have significant implications for famine literature'.

109 D.H. Akenson, 'A Midrash on "Galut", "Exile" and "Diaspora" Rhetoric', in E.M. Crawford (ed.), *The Hungry Stream: Essays on Emigration and Famine* (Belfast, 1997), p. 13.

Chapter Five: Ireland, Irish-America and the Man who Invented 'Genocide'

1 Michael Ignatieff, 'The Unsung Hero who Coined the Term "Genocide"', *New Republic*, 21 Sept. 2013. I should say, without implicating them in any way, that I am especially grateful for conversations with Maureen Murphy, David Wilson and Patrick Maume in thinking about this chapter.

2 James V. Mullin, 'The New Jersey Famine Curriculum: A Report', *Éire-Ireland* (2002), p. 119.

3 Ibid., p 126.

4 Ibid., p. 129.

5 There is a well-informed and informative review of the controversy in Thomas J. Archdeacon, 'The Irish Famine in American School Curricula', *Éire-Ireland* (2002), pp. 139–44, though it is perhaps a little opaque on political motivations.

6 'Schools to Teach about Irish Potato Famine', *New York Times*, 10 October 1996.

7 Raymond Hernandez, 'New Curriculum from Albany: The Irish Potato Famine, or one View of It', *New York Times*, 1 December 1996.

8 Ibid.

9 'No man who accepts capitalist society and the laws thereof can logically find fault with the statesmen of England for their acts in that awful period. They stood for the rights of property and free competition, and philosophically accepted their consequences upon Ireland; the leaders of the Irish people also stood for the rights of property, and refused to abandon them even when they saw their consequences in the slaughter by famine of over a million of the toilers.' James Connolly, *Labour in Irish History* (Dublin, 1973), p. 102.

10 *New York Times*, 1 December 1996.

11 Archdeacon, 'American School Curricula', p. 134.

12 Letter from James Mullin to the *New York Times*, 7 December 1996.

13 Quoted in Archdeacon, p. 134.

14 *New York Times*, 17 April, 1998. The article commented caustically that public spending that appears to have only honourable intentions, such as the Famine curriculum project, often has 'purely political roots'.

15 Maureen Murphy and Alan Singer, 'New York State's Great Irish Famine Curriculum: A Report', *Éire-Ireland*, (2002), pp. 108–118.

16 For an appreciative feature article on teaching the New York Famine curriculum, see 'Using the Irish Famine to Explore Current Events', *New York Times*, 21 March, 2001.

17 Mullin, 'The New Jersey Famine Curriculum' (2002). The more detailed curriculum is available on the internet and is 'dedicated to the millions of Irish who suffered and perished in the Great Starvation'. See: http://www.eirefirst.com/archive/intro.html [accessed 5 June 2014].

18 Francis A. Boyle, *United Ireland, Human Rights and International Law* (Atlanta, 2012), p. 21. A further initiative by Boyle and others (see pages 24–5) resulted in a 'Statement', signed

by 'approximately 125 distinguished personalities', re-stating the case for genocide. This was published in the *Irish Echo*, 26 February – 4 March 1997.

19   Archdeacon, 'American School Curricula', p. 136.

20   Mullin, 'New Jersey Curriculum', p. 122.

21   Raphael Lemkin, *Axis Rule in Occupied Europe* (Washington, 1944), p. 79.

22   'Coining a Word and Championing a Cause: The Story of Raphael Lemkin' in the *Holocaust Encyclopedia*, United States Holocaust Memorial Museum: http://www.ushmm. org/wlc/en/article.php?ModuleId=10007050 [accessed 20 March 2014]. Wolkowysk was re-allocated to Poland in 1920.

23   Ibid.

24   Raphael Lemkin, *Totally Unofficial: The Autobiography of Raphael Lemkin* (Yale, New Haven, 2013), p. 19.

25   Raphael Lemkin, *Axis Rule*. Chapter nine introduces the term 'genocide' and traces its implementation by the Germans in Europe during the Second World War. The more general point (page 79) is that 'Genocide is directed against the national group as an entity, and the actions involved are directed against individuals, not in their individual capacity, but as members of the national group.'

26   Ignatieff, 'The Unsung Hero', *New Republic*, 21 September 2013.

27   There are nineteen articles in all. The full text of the Convention may be found at the website of the United Nations. See http://www.un.org/en/ga/search/view_doc. asp?symbol=A/RES/260%28III%29 [accessed 19 February 2014].

28   Samantha Power, *'A Problem from Hell': America and the Age of Genocide* (London, 2003), pp. 149–54; Deborah Mayersen, *On the Path to Genocide: Armenia and Rwanda Reexamined* (New York, 2014).

29   Christopher J. Walker, *Armenia: The Survival of a Nation* (London, 1990).

30   Christian Noack, Lindsay Janssen and Vincent Comerford (eds), *Holodomor and Gorta Mór* (London, 2012).

31   *Guardian*, 16 August 2004. See also the BBC website: http://news.bbc.co.uk/1/hi/world/ africa/3565938.stm [accessed 28 March 2014] in which the German Development Aid Minister is quoted as saying, on 14 August 2004, that 'we Germans accept our historic and moral responsibility'.

32   Power, *'A Problem from Hell'*, pp. 503–06.

33   *The Ukrainian Weekly Section*, 19 September 1953.

34   Modern studies suggest lower excess mortality. For a range of estimates see Barbara B. Green, 'Stalinist Terror and the Question of Genocide', in Alan S. Rosenbaum (ed.), *Is the Holocaust Unique? Perspectives on Comparative Genocide* (1996, Colorado).

35   It is in no sense to minimise the extent of Soviet terror to suggest that these estimates are much too high.

36   *Ukrainian Weekly Section*, 26 Sept. 1953. One speaker recalled that when a Ukrainian demonstration against the Soviet handling of the famine had been held in New York twenty years earlier, it had been physically attacked by American communist sympathisers (or 'organised gangs of Communist hoodlums' as the paper put it).

37   *New York Times*, 21 September 1953.

38   Roman Serbyn, 'Lemkin on Genocide of Nations', *Journal of International Criminal Justice*, 7 (2009), pp. 123–130. See also the 16th Annual J.B. Rudnyckyj Distinguished Lecture, 'The Holodomor: Reflections on the Ukrainian Genocide', by Roman Serbyn at the University of Manitoba on the 7 November 2008. The text is at http://umanitoba.ca/ libraries/units/archives/media/Lecture_XVI_Serbyn.pdf [accessed 21 March 2014] and contains a passing reference to the mention of Ireland in the *New York Times* report.

39 Serbyn, 'Lemkin on Genocide', pp. 123–4.

40 I am grateful to Maurice Klapwald, librarian at New York Public Library, who arranged a selective search of the Lemkin papers. There is a folder labelled 'Soviet Genocide in the Ukraine' but a digital copy of its contents, kindly forwarded by Mr Klapwald, yields no reference to Ireland.

41 Raphael Lemkin, *Totally Unofficial: The Autobiography of Raphael Lemkin* (Yale, New Haven, 2013), p. 184. There is also a somewhat obscure reference (page 239) to 'the problem of ratification [of the Genocide Convention] by Ireland' (among other countries mentioned).

42 An old saying found in Hugh Dorian, *Outer Edge of Ulster: A Memoir of Social Life in Nineteenth-Century Donegal* (edited by Breandán Mac Suibhne and David Dickson, Dublin, 2000), p. 223.

43 On the huge dearth in food supplies see Peter Solar, 'The Great Famine was No Ordinary Subsistence Crisis', in E.M. Crawford (ed.), *Famine: the Irish Experience* (Edinburgh, 1989), pp. 112–31.

44 Charles E. Trevelyan, *The Irish Crisis* (London, 1848).

45 Elizabeth Smith, *The Irish Journals of Elizabeth Smith, 1840–1850* (edited by David Thompson and Moyra McGusty, Oxford, 1980).

46 W.J. Smyth, 'The Story of the Great Irish Famine, 1845–52: A Geographical Perspective', in John Crowley, William J. Smyth and Mike Murphy (eds), *Atlas of the Great Irish Famine* (Cork, 2012), pp. 10–11.

47 A thought suggested in conversation with Cormac Ó Gráda.

48 Some Young Irelanders, in part inspired by revolution in Europe, confronted a detachment of police at the farmhouse of a Mrs McCormack of Ballingarry, County Tipperary in the summer of 1848. This attempt at an insurrection soon fizzled out. Meanwhile famine still raged in many parts of Ireland.

49 J.S. Donnelly Jr., *The Land and the People of Nineteenth-Century Cork: The Rural Economy and the Land Question* (London, 1975), p. 87.

50 Smyth, 'Great Famine', p. 10.

51 Dorian, *Ulster*, p. 223.

52 Ciarán Reilly, 'Culpability and the Great Famine', paper read to the annual conference of the Irish Economic and Social History Society, Galway, November 2013.

53 Dorian, *Ulster*, p. 228. This reeks of social and personal resentment but Dorian speaks also of how some people undermined and injured their poorer neighbours, so as to get at their property, which has an authentic ring to it.

54 There are exceptions of course, as may be found in the archives of the Department of Irish Folklore, University College, Dublin.

55 A 'silence' pointed out by D.H. Akenson a generation ago in *Small Differences: Irish Catholics and Irish Protestants, 1815–1922: An International Perspective* (Montreal, 1991), pp. 144–5. For a later and fuller exploration see Christine Kinealy and Gerard MacAtasney, *The Hidden Famine: Hunger, Poverty and Sectarianism in Belfast* (London, 2000).

56 Colm Tóibín, *The Irish Famine* (London, 1999), p. 15. (The 'many' in the quotation above may be an overstatement, however. We really don't know for sure.)

57 Dónal Kerr, *The Catholic Church and the Famine* (Dublin, 1996).

58 Reilly, 'Culpability and the Great Famine' (2013); Colm Tóibín, *The Irish Famine* (London, 1999), pp. 13–15.

59 Don O'Leary, *Irish Catholicism and Science: From 'Godless Colleges' to the 'Celtic Tiger'* (Cork, 2012).

60 Slattery Papers, National Library of Ireland, P 6004.

61   Sarah Roddy, 'Spiritual Imperialism and the Mission of the Irish Race: the Catholic Church and Emigration from Nineteenth-Century Ireland', *Irish Historical Studies*, 38 (2013), pp. 600–619.

62   For a more sympathetic assessment of MacHale, see Delaney, *Curse of Reason, passim*. On reactions to proselytism (so-called 'souperism') in the west of Ireland see Irene Whelan, *The Bible War in Ireland: The 'Second Reformation' and the Polarization of Protestant–Catholic Relations, 1800–1840* (Madison, 2005). There is a choice of terms available to the student of religious conversion – missionary activity, evangelisation, proselytism, 'souperism' – depending on theological or ideological taste. On 'holy war' in Dingle, for instance, see the letter of the Reverend Thomas Moriarty to the *Cork Constitution*, 29 January 1846 and William O'Brien, *Dingle: Its Pauperism and Proselytism. The Operation of Proselytism Exposed, and its Results Exhibited. In a Series of Letters* (Dublin, 1852).

63   F.T. Blackwood (Marquess of Dufferin and Ava), *Narrative of a Journey from Oxford to Skibbereen during the Year of the Irish Famine* (Oxford, 1847).

64   William Shee, *The Irish Church, its History and Statistics* (London, 1863), p. 259, Table 8.

65   http://www.measuringworth.com/ukcompare/relativevalue.php [accessed 5 May 2014].

66   *Cork Examiner*, 8 February 1847 and 15 March 1847.

67   Liam Kennedy and Clare Murphy (eds), *The Franciscan Community at Cork, and its Account Books* (Dublin, 2012).

68   How innocent is of course debatable, in view of the reality of world hunger which is beamed into most households through the medium of television, newspapers and the internet.

69   Local history societies in Ulster were especially active, while Belfast City Council unveiled a commemorative stained-glass window at City Hall depicting Famine scenes. Nationalist and unionist councillors supported this initiative, though Mr Sammy Wilson of the Democratic Unionist Party opined that there was no evidence that the Famine played a major role in Belfast. In his view the initiative gave credibility to 'anti-British Sinn Féin propaganda'. See the *Irish Times*, 4 February 1997. My modest contribution was to give a public lecture on the Famine experience in Belfast as part of the unveiling ceremony. The content did not accord well with Mr Wilson's views.

70   The Jeanie Johnston is sometimes labelled a Famine 'coffin ship'. In fact its mortality record on crossings between Blennerville, Tralee Bay and Quebec was impeccable, with no loss of life (Blennerville Windmill and Famine exhibit, Tralee, Co. Kerry, visited in August 2013).

71   I agreed to participate in the Fordham event in 2012, and again in 2013 after the date of the Tribunal was re-scheduled at very short notice. In the end the arrangements for the event proved so chaotic that I withdrew, reassured in the knowledge that the organisation was unlikely ever to find itself in charge of a famine relief programme.

72   Enda Delaney, *The Curse of Reason: the Great Irish Famine* (Dublin, 2012); John Kelly, *The Graves are Walking: The Great Famine and the Saga of the Irish People* (Picador, 2012); John Crowley, William J. Smyth and Mike Murphy (eds), *Atlas of the Famine* (2012); Christian Noack, Lindsay Janssen and Vincent Comerford (eds), *Holodomor and Gorta Mór* (London, 2012). On the Nijmegen conference see http://www.ru.nl/faminelegacies/ [accessed 28 March 2014].

73   Tim Pat Coogan, *The Famine Plot: England's Role in Ireland's Greatest Tragedy* (London, 2012); Francis A. Boyle, *United Ireland, Human Rights, and International Law* (Atlanta, 2013).

74   See Cormac Ó Gráda's review in the *BBC History Magazine*, June 2013 and also the debate between Liam Kennedy and Tim Pat Coogan: 'Was the Irish Famine a Genocide?' reproduced in the *Dublin Review of Books*, No. 30, March, 2013. For critical comments on

Kennedy and an exploration of other aspects of the Famine see Breandán Mac Suibhne, 'A Jig in the Poorhouse', *Dublin Review of Books*, 32, April 2013.

75 Boyle, *United Ireland* (2012).

76 Ibid., pp. 34–35.

77 http://www.irishmemorial.org/ [accessed 14 April 2014]. For a detailed analysis of Famine memorialisation see Emily Mark-Fitzgerald, *Commemorating the Irish Famine: Memory and the Monument* (Liverpool, 2013).

78 Some American historians of Ireland have told me ruefully of the kinds of hostile emotions stirred up by their Famine talks in the USA. Many of the entries on the Irish Famine on the internet, particularly those urging genocidal interpretations, seem to emanate from Irish America.

79 Personal observation and my translation from a visit to Grosse Isle in the mid-1990s. The highly politicised campaign to make Grosse Isle a site of Irish-Canadian Famine memory is discussed in Mark-Fitzgerald (above), pp. 176–85.

80 *Braveheart* (1995) purported to tell the story of Scotland in medieval times while that other travesty of the historical past, *The Patriot* (2000), dealt with revolutionary America. Mel Gibson was the star in each.

81 The classic article on this is P.M.A. Bourke's 'The Irish Grain Trade, 1839–48', *Irish Historical Studies*, 20 (1976), pp. 156–67. My own view, following Bourke, is that a *temporary* ban on cereal exports at the outbreak of the crisis would have been helpful.

82 I am currently researching alternative and feasible policies that could have been implemented by the British government, with a view to forming some rough estimates as to how many lives could have been saved using other policies.

83 There are different ways, none of them perfect, to measure the relative value of the pound sterling through time. One widely used approach is to use the retail price index, as I have done here. See http://www.measuringworth.com/ukcompare/ [accessed 5 May, 2014].

84 Liam De Paor, *On the Easter Proclamation and Other Declarations* (Dublin, 1997), p. 52. These views derived from the hugely popular writings of John Mitchel and the then contemporary writings of Arthur Griffith, the founder of Sinn Féin. Griffith subscribed to the view that policies of extermination (driving the Irish out of Ireland) still existed in his time.

85 http://www.flickr.com/photos/gerryward/919237617/ [accessed 21 March 2014].

86 *An Phoblacht*, 11 Sept. 1997.

87 Mary E. Daly and Margaret O'Callaghan (eds), *1916 in 1966: Commemorating the Easter Rising* (Dublin, 2007).

88 Richard English, *Irish Freedom: The History of Nationalism in Ireland* (London, 2006), pp. 403–4.

89 *Irish Times*, 14 December 1996. Peter Gray, 'Memory and the Commemoration of the Great Irish Famine', in Peter Gray and Kendrick Oliver (eds), *The Memory of Catastrophe* (Manchester, 2004), pp. 54–5.

90 Report in the *Irish Times*, 14 December 1996.

91 Address to the International Conference on Hunger, Glucksman Ireland House, New York, May 1995 on the occasion of the sesquicentenary of the Great Famine.

92 The roots of anti-British feeling among the Irish in the United States go back well before the Famine. David A. Wilson argues that emigré United Irishmen were especially important in amplifying and propagating these sentiments, though, of course, their antecedents go deeper in time, back at least as far as the revolutionary period and the drive for an American republic. See Wilson, *United Irishmen, United States: Immigrant Radicals in the Early Republic* (New York, 1998), pp. 175–79.

93 *Irish Times*, 20 May 1995. The full address is at http://gos.sbc.edu/r/robinson.html [accessed 28 March 2014].

94 Primo Levi, *The Drowned and the Saved* (New York, 1989), p. 78.

95 Ibid., p. 78.

96 Lemkin, *Totally Unofficial*, p. 111.

97 For time series data on Ireland's official development assistance, for the years 1974–2013, expressed as a proportion of GDP and mapped against the contributions of other developed countries, see the dataset of the OECD (Organisation for Economic Co-operation and Development) [accessed 18 April 2014]: http://www.compareyourcountry. org/chart.php?cr=21andlg=enandproject=odaandpage=1.

98 The noted economist Jeffrey Sachs writing in the *New York Times*, 25 June 2005 ('Four Easy Pieces').

99 Leonardo Boff, *Cry of the Earth, Cry of the Poor* (New York, 1997), pp. 111–12.

100 As Cormac Ó Gráda has argued persuasively in the 'The Great Famine and Other Famines', in Ó Gráda (ed.), *Famine 150* (Dublin, 1997), pp. 129–31.

101 On protectionism and Ireland see Alan Matthews, *EC Trade Policy and the Third World: An Irish Perspective* (Dublin, 1991). Matthews identifies a range of trade polices practiced by the European Community that adversely affected developing countries. During the 1980s, the Republic of Ireland actively supported measures to restrict access to European markets (pp. 179–82) for manufactured and other goods. For a later study that charts the distorting effects of European Union agricultural protectionism, using import tariffs and export subsidies, see Nicola Cantore, Jane Kennan, Sheila Page, *CAP Reform and Development* (London, 2011), pp. 25–8. The use of transfer pricing as a means of tax avoidance is commonplace among multinational companies and is said to cost developing countries billions of dollars annually in terms of lost state revenue. Ireland's alleged role as an enabler of tax avoidance has drawn the ire of the European Union and the OECD. See the *Economist*, 18 October 2014.

102 OECD dataset, cited above.

103 *Irish Times*, 2 June 1997.

104 For a global overview see D.H. Akenson, *The Irish Diaspora: A Primer* (Belfast, 1996).

105 Gray, 'Memory and Commemoration', p. 49.

106 Timothy Guinnane, 'Historians reject Irish potato famine as genocide', *Washington Post*, 17 September 1997. In his concluding sentence Guinnane writes: 'To call the famine genocide cheapens the memories of both the famine's victims and the victims of real genocides.' Among a number of publications on Irish history, Guinnane is author of the award-winning *The Vanishing Irish: Households, Migration, and the Rural Economy in Ireland, 1850–1914* (Princeton, 1997).

107 Murphy, 'New York State's Famine Curriculum', p. 111.

108 The classic account of how popular memories of the Famine were forged is J.S. Donnelly, Jr., 'The Construction of the Memory of the Famine in Ireland and the Irish Diaspora, 1850–1900', *Éire-Ireland*, 31(1996), pp. 26–61.

109 Archdeacon, 'American School Curricula', p. 130. Archdeacon gave advice (see page 132) to Governor Pataki's office on the Irish Famine.

110 Archdeacon, 'American School Curricula', p. 131.

111 Ibid. p.131.

112 Mitchel was unambiguous in his attachment to the cause of human slavery: 'We deny that it is a crime, or a wrong, or even a peccadillo, to hold slaves, to buy slaves, to sell slaves, to keep slaves to their work, by flogging or other needful coercion.' He continued in slightly less sadistic tone: 'We, for our part, wish we had a good plantation well-stocked

with healthy negroes in Alabama.' Quoted in David A. Wilson, *Thomas D'Arcy McGee Vol. 1, Passion, Reason and Politics, 1825–1857*, (Montreal and Kingston, 2008), p. 320. For Mitchel's case for the re-introduction of the transatlantic slave trade in which multitudes perished, see James Quinn, 'John Mitchel and the Rejection of the Nineteenth Century', *Éire-Ireland*, (Fall/Winter 2003), p. 99.

113 The term mindscape is borrowed from my colleague Dr Rodney Cowie, School of Psychology, Queen's University, Belfast. It emphasises the partly-hidden emotional depths, in addition to the more apparent cognitive processes, that underlie human action. It might be argued that we historians, who are recruited on the basis of our cognitive abilities, characteristically understate the importance of emotion in our reconstructions of historical processes.

114 *Belfast Telegraph*, 17 March 2014.

115 The imagery is from Ernie O'Malley, *On Another Man's Wound* (Dublin, 2002).

Chapter Six: The Ulster Covenant

1 T. Agar-Robartes, a Liberal backbencher, in a speech in the House of Commons as early as June 1912. Fearing the possibility of civil war, he proposed that four Ulster counties (Antrim, Down, Londonderry and Armagh) be excluded from the provisions of any Home Rule legislation. House of Commons Debates, 11 June 1912, vol. 39, col. 773.

2 Conversations and communications with a number of people have deeply coloured my interpretation of the dramatic events of September 1912 and the crisis within the state of the United Kingdom. First and foremost I must mention Douglas McIldoon, Erina McIldoon and Christopher Loughlin. Eamonn Hughes, Ian Montgomery, David Fitzpatrick, Paul Bew, Kerby Miller, Cormac Ó Gráda and John Wilson Foster also offered important, sometimes contradictory observations. I am grateful to them all.

3 For a long-range view of Home Rule for Ireland – there were also contemporaneous demands for Home Rule in Scotland and Wales – see Alvin Jackson, *Home Rule: An Irish History, 1800–2000* (London, 2003).

4 *Times*, 29 July 1912. The only saving qualification, and it is not much, might be his reference to 'under present conditions'. See also Ronan Fanning, *Fatal Path: British Government and Irish Revolution, 1910–1922* (London, 2013), p. 71.

5 *Times*, 29 July 1912.

6 *Times*, 17 August 1912.

7 This helps explain also why many liberal-minded ministers of religion embraced the Covenant cause, as much (or more so) out of dread of the terrors of civil war as of anything else. Later on some Church of Ireland clergymen, and notably Bishop D'Arcy, saw the UVF as agents of social order and a means to restrain the rank and file. See Andrew Scholes, *The Church of Ireland and the Third Home Rule Bill* (Dublin, 2010), pp. 75–8, 81–4.

8 *Belfast News-Letter* (hereafter *BNL*) 20 September 1912. This issue of the paper, some eight days before Ulster Day, contains the text of the women's and the men's version of the Solemn League and Covenant.

9 *BNL*, 19 September 1912. It would be interesting to see if the sociological notion of a 'moral panic', fomented in part by radical clergymen, might prove useful in analysing aspects of the Covenanting campaign.

10 Andrew Scholes, *Church of Ireland*, p. 61.

11 *Irish News*, 30 September 1912.

12 Ronan Fanning, *Fatal Path*, p. 51.

13 *Belfast Evening Telegraph*, 28 September 1912. See also Gordon Lucy, *The Ulster Covenant: An Illustrated History of the 1912 Home Rule Crisis* (Newtownards, 1989), p. 35.

14 Ulster Scots Community Network, *Understanding the Ulster Covenant* (Belfast, no date, probably 2011 or 2012), p. 28.

15 F.H. Crawford, *Guns for Ulster* (Belfast, 1947), p. 17.

16 Ibid., pp. 56–7.

17 Ibid., p. 9.

18 *Irish News*, 28 September, 30 September 1912.

19 The author's real name was James Owen Hannay, a Church of Ireland clergyman. I am grateful to David Fitzpatrick for drawing my attention to this work.

20 The suppression of the Easter Rising in Dublin in 1916 involved thousands of soldiers on the streets of the capital and bombardment of rebel positions by a British gunboat which sailed up the Liffey. The key point, though, is that the Reverend Hannay had identified the potential for large-scale political violence within the Ulster unionist population.

21 On arrangements for signing the Covenant and the Declaration in Dublin at the headquarters of the Irish Unionist Alliance see the *Irish Times*, 5 October 1912.

22 One Belfast woman has assured me that her great-grandfather signed twice, using his then current address and another address from which he had moved not long before.

23 The *Irish News* alleged chicanery of this sort (30 September 1912).

24 http://applications.proni.gov.uk/UlsterCovenant/image.aspx?image=M0017430009). I am grateful to Ian Montgomery from PRONI for his help on this and some related points.

25 http://applications.proni.gov.uk/UlsterCovenant/image.aspx?image=W0018840005

26 Those who were domiciled outside Ulster and who signed have not been included in this calculation. The numerator is 447,197 and the denominator (estimated) is 604,827. (Catholic unionist signatories are a possibility but can only have been of marginal significance, not least in view of the kinds of venues being used and the association with Protestant church services.)

27 'Lunatics sign "The Covenant"' – report in the *Ulster Guardian*, 5 October 1912.

28 A correspondent to the *Ulster Guardian* claimed that workers felt obliged to sign the Covenant because of pressure from a factory owner and fear of losing their jobs (Letters, 28 September 1912) and the issue of 'coercion' was raised again in its columns on the 5 October 1912. See also the *Irish News'* editorials of the 28 September and 1 October 1912.

29 *Ulster Guardian*, 5 October 1912.

30 *Irish Times*, 30 September 1912.

31 Diane Urquhart, *Women in Ulster Politics, 1890–1940* (Dublin, 2000), p. 62. This demonstration of woman power should also be seen as forming part of the build-up to the wider anti-Home Rule campaign of 1912 that culminated in the signing of the Ulster Covenant.

32 See the website of the Centre for the Study of Historic Irish Houses and Estates: http://historicirishhouses.ie/research/postdoctoral-research-projects/1841-irish-testimonial-lord-morpeth [accessed 9 December 2013].

33 Dorothy Thompson, *The Chartists* (Hounslow, 1984).

34 The lists of signatures held by PRONI come from the archives of the Ulster Unionist Council.

35 Liam Kennedy, Lucia Pozzi and Matteo Manfredini, 'Marriage, Fertility, Social Class and Religion in an Irish Industrial City: Belfast 1911', *Popolazione e Storia*, 11 (2010), pp. 83–110.

36 The text of the Covenant and the Declaration at the head of the ordinary signature sheets, however, was in a clearer, more modern font style. Old English was retained for the title words Covenant and Declaration.

37 *A Solemn League and Covenant for Reformation and Defence of Religion, The Honour and Happiness of the King, and the Peace and Safety of the Three Kingdoms of England, Scotland and Ireland*, 1643, as reproduced in Gardiner, *Constitutional Documents*, pp. 267–71.

38 J.J. Lee, *The Modernisation of Irish Society* (Dublin, 1972), p. 135.

39 For a discussion of conditional loyalty see D.W. Miller, *Queen's Rebels: Ulster Loyalism in Historical Perspective* (Dublin, 1978), pp. 1–6, and *passim*.

40 As late as 1766, one rector of the Established Church referred to Presbyterians in his locality as 'Covenanters'. See PRONI T808/15266, p. 22.

41 J.W. Kernohan, a local historian of Presbyterianism, quoted in Andrew Holmes, 'Covenanter Politics: Evangelicalism, Political Liberalism and Ulster Presbyterianism, 1798–1914', *English Historical Review*, 125 (2010), p. 369.

42 Graham Walker, 'The Ulster Covenant as a Reflection of Protestant Ulster', paper presented to the conference 'In Defence of Modernity: the Ulster Solemn League and Covenant, 1912–14', Belfast, 17 January 2014.

43 Source: Gordon Lucy (ed.), *The Ulster Covenant: A Pictorial History of the 1912 Home Rule Crisis* (Belfast, 1989), pp. 45–7.

44 There is also historical depth to the allusion, recalling a Reformation text, *The Confession of Faith of the Kirk of Scotland*, 1580, which was again subscribed to by Scottish puritans in 1638. The opening sentence contains the phrase 'after long and due Examination of our own Consciences' and goes on to protest 'that we are not moved by any worldly respect, but are persuaded only in our Consciences' in adopting the Confession. See S.R. Gardiner, *The Constitutional Documents of the Puritan Revolution, 1625–1660* (Oxford, reprint 1968), pp. 124–36.

45 For an overview of the Ulster economy in the early twentieth century see Liam Kennedy and Philip Ollerenshaw (eds), *Ulster Since 1600: Politics, Economy and Society* (Oxford, 2013), pp. 180–88.

46 Liam Kennedy, *The Modern Industrialisation of Ireland, 1940–88* (Dundalk, 1989), p. 55.

47 A liberal unionist perspective on these issues, which proved hugely controversial at this time, is Horace Plunkett's *Ireland in the New Century* (London, 1905). For notions of progressive and unprogressive elements in Irish society – code words for Protestant and Catholic – see Scholes, *Church of Ireland*, pp. 33–4.

48 See chapter three. William James Pirrie, Ireland's leading industrialist, provisionally backed Home Rule in 1912, though, as has also been indicated, his views on the matter were shared by few of his Ulster peers.

49 *Northern Whig*, 30 September 1912.

50 Fanning, *Fatal Path*, p. 28

51 The *Irish Catholic Directory*, published annually, is a valuable compendium of the scale and variety of clerical interventions in society, as also of the massive infrastructure of churches, schools, convents, monasteries, bishops' palaces, missionary colleges, chaplaincies and asylums. What it does not show is the extent to which the Catholic Church had also become involved in private property ownership through its role as urban landlord.

52 S.J. Connolly, 'Religion and Society, 1600–1914', in Kennedy and Ollerenshaw (eds), *Ulster Since 1600*, p. 88; J. J. Lee, *Ireland, 1912–1985* (Cambridge, 1989), p. 11.

53 John Whyte, *Church and State in Modern Ireland, 1923–1970* (Dublin, 1980), pp. 8–21.

54 R.V. Comerford, *The Fenians in Context: Irish Politics and Society 1848–82* (Dublin, 1998), pp. 214–15. There is some comparison here with Presbyterian and Church of Ireland ministers who struck anti-Home Rule stances to ward off more extreme forms of loyalist protest. *In extremis*, the paramilitary was preferable to the mob.

55 Arthur Griffith, *The Resurrection of Hungary: A Parallel for Ireland* (Dublin, 1918), pp. 100–106. 'The Act of Union was passed to prevent Ireland becoming an Imperial nation' (p. 106).

56 One Tory MP a few years earlier had mentioned self-government in Quebec as a model for a federal Ireland. See Searle, *A New England?* p. 416.

57 The *Irish Catholic Directory*, among other Catholic publications, gave expression to this sentiment.

58 Fanning, *Fatal Path*, pp. 14–26.

59 D.W. Miller, *Queen's Rebels*, p. 97.

60 Scholes, *Church of Ireland*, p. 84.

61 The *Ulster Guardian* (5 October 1912), with some exaggeration, commended 'the heroic stand taken by many Protestant clergymen for conscience sake' in refusing to adopt a covenant the wording of which they could not stand over, singling out for special praise the Rev J.F. M'Neice (a future Church of Ireland bishop and father of the poet and playwright Louis MacNeice) because of the sermon of opposition he preached on Ulster Day itself.

62 *Irish News*, 30 September 1912.

63 Miller, *Queen's Rebels*, p. 101.

64 *Irish Times*, 2 September 1912.

65 A referendum in 1995 on the issue of independence for Quebec resulted in a majority in favour of remaining within the Canadian confederation. A referendum in 2014 on independence for Scotland also failed to secure a majority. However, an unofficial referendum in Catalonia in the same year came out strongly in favour of independence but the results were not recognised by the Spanish government.

66 Urquhart, *Women in Ulster Politics*, p. 23.

67 One might quibble as to whether the Declaration comes under the generic title of the Ulster Solemn League and Covenant. For convenience that is the position taken here, while bearing various distinctions in mind (as explained in the main text).

68 PRONI website on the Ulster Covenant. Not all of the figures quoted on the website seem to be internally consistent (when accessed on the 20 January 2014) but the discrepancies do not affect materially the arguments developed in this chapter.

69 Diane Urquhart (ed.), *The Minutes of the Ulster Women's Unionist Council and Executive Committee, 1911–40* (Dublin, 2001), p. 60. I am grateful to Diane for helpful discussion of this point.

70 Source: Lucy (ed.), *The Ulster Covenant*, p. 48.

71 That Home Rule would be a 'calamity' and 'disastrous' for Ulster is stated in both documents. The identical phrasing suggests not only the close kinship between the Covenant and the Declaration but also the common analysis of the prospect of Home Rule.

72 Diane Urquhart, *Women in Ulster Politics, 1890–1940* (Dublin, 2000), p. 23. Gordon Lucy draws attention to the importance of liberal unionist thought, including Carson's views on a range of social issues, in the campaign against Home Rule. Lucy, 'The Solemn League and Covenant, 1912: Leaders and Supporters', paper presented to the conference 'In Defence of Modernity: the Ulster Solemn League and Covenant, 1912–14', Belfast, 17 January 2014.

73 The Irish Ladies Land League of the early 1880s bears some comparison but this was a minority movement, while the suffragists of Edwardian times, while certainly militant, constituted a minority within a minority.

74 Diane Urquhart (ed.), *The Minutes of the Ulster Women's Unionist Council and Executive Committee, 1911–40* (Dublin, 2001), p. xviii.

75 Urquhart, *Minutes*, p. xvi.

76 Ruth Dudley Edwards, *Patrick Pearse: Triumph of Failure* (London, 1977), p. 177. MacNeill was one of the principal founders of the Irish Volunteers, formed in reaction to the Ulster Volunteers.

Chapter Seven: The Proclamation of the Irish Republic

1   Bertolt Brecht, *Life of Galileo* (translated by John Willett; edited by John Willett and Ralph Manheim; London 1980), p. 254. There are various translations from the German. Willett's rendering is 'unhappy is the land that needs a hero'.

2   Ruth Dudley Edwards, *Patrick Pearse: Triumph of Failure* (London, 1977), p. 277. I very much appreciate the helpful comments of friends and colleagues Marie Coleman, Ruth Dudley Edwards, John Wilson Foster and Sean Farrell Moran on earlier drafts of this chapter. They are, of course, absolved from responsibility for any errors it may contain.

3   Mary E. Daly and Margaret O'Callaghan (eds), *1916 in 1966: Commemorating the Easter Rising* (Dublin, 2007), p. 19. In the summer of 1967, I was a student vacation worker in Montreal, Canada. On my first day I was befriended by a Dubliner who tried unsuccessfully to get me a place in a youth hostel. Sean then offered me some floor space in his rented apartment. The bathroom was adorned with centrepiece spreads from *Playboy* magazine but on the mantelpiece in the living room was a shiny copy, the size of a postcard, of the Easter Proclamation.

4   Niall Whelehan, *The Dynamiters: Irish Nationalism and Political Violence in the Wider World, 1867–1900* (Cambridge, 2012), pp. 163, 188.

5   This rivalry centred on which of the two, Pearse or Clarke, had been the prime mover in the creation of the nascent republic. See Edwards, *Patrick Pearse*, p. 333 and Charles Townshend, *Easter 1916: The Irish Rebellion* (London, 2005), p. 161.

6   John O'Leary, *Recollections of Fenians and Fenianism* (London, 1896, volume 1. Introduction by Marcus Bourke, 1969), pp. 121–2. In terms of this piece of political theology the Proclamation announces 'not so much separation, as a mystically pre-existing independence … Ireland always had been, and now *declares herself to be*, independent.' De Paor, *On the Easter Proclamation and Other Declarations*, (Dublin, 1997), p. 22.

7   A detailed account may be found in C.D. Greaves, *Life and Times of James Connolly* (London, 1972), pp. 47–53, 109–111, 237.

8   De Paor, *On the Easter Proclamation*, pp. 27–8.

9   PRONI, *Robert Emmet: The Insurrection of July 1803* (with commentary by Geraldine Hume and Anthony Malcomson, Belfast 1996). This contains the full text of Emmet's verbose proclamation.

10 In the event of victory, a Provisional civil government would take over the running of the country. Those nominated to this make-believe junta were Alderman Tom Kelly (Sinn Féin member of Dublin City Council, Arthur Griffith (the founder of Sinn Féin), William O'Brien (trade union activist), Mrs Sheehy-Skeffington (suffragette), and Seán T. O'Kelly of Sinn Féin. With one exception these were men, largely Dublin-based, and none came from the mainstream Irish nationalist party. See Edwards, *Patrick Pearse*, p. 276.

11 A satirical play on the text of the Ulster Covenant, published in the *Irish News*, 27 September 1912, ended with the heading: 'The Men and Women of All Ireland'.

12 Edwards, *Patrick Pearse*, pp. 126–8; Elaine Sisson, *Pearse's Patriots: St Enda's and the Cult of Boyhood* (Cork, 2005). For a pioneering psycho-analytic approach to the study of Pearse see Sean F. Moran, *Patrick Pearse and the Politics of Redemption: The Mind of the Easter Rising, 1916* (Washington, 1994).

13 Like most nationalist tropes this was not peculiar to Ireland. Benedict Anderson observes that 'the silence of the dead was no obstacle to the exhumation of their deepest desires'. Benedict Anderson, *Imagined Communities* (2nd edition, London, 1991), p. 198.

14 Daniele Conversi, *Ethnonationalism in the Contemporary* World (London, 2002).

15 Elie Kedourie, *Nationalism* (4th expanded edition, Oxford, 1994); Ernest Gellner, *Nations and Nationalism* (Oxford, 1983).

16 Kedourie, *Nationalism*, p. 1. For a more historically nuanced reading see Anderson, *Imagined Communities* (1991).

17 Some modernist accounts skip over the New World and the case of the United States of America, which rather inconveniently takes one back to the 1770s.

18 Richard English, *Irish Freedom: The History of Nationalism in Ireland* (London, 2006), *passim*.

19 A.D. Smith, *Ethno-Symbolism and Nationalism: A Cultural Approach* (London, 2009).

20 English, *Irish Freedom*, especially chapter seven.

21 Ibid., p. 504.

22 M.J. Kelly, *The Fenian Ideal and Irish Nationalism, 1882–1916* (Woodbridge, 2006).

23 See for instance Irene Boada, *Women Write Back: Irish and Catalan Short Stories in Colonial Context* (Dublin, 2002). The tradition lives on. *Mother Ireland* is also the title of a non-fiction book (London, 1976) by the writer Edna O'Brien.

24 Ironically, in view of the subject matter of this chapter, a major exception may be found in the gendered reference to Ulster in the text of the Declaration signed by women on Ulster Day, 1912.

25 In a curious passage relating to one of W.B. Yeats' great poems on the Easter Rising a literary critic sympathetic to Pearse's ideas, Declan Kiberd, complains that Yeats, in dignifying the rebels in 'Easter 1916', may have 'unwittingly trivialised their gesture and have done this in a time-honoured colonialist way. The rebels, being children were not full moral agents…' Colonised people, Kiberd informs his readers, are often portrayed as children by the coloniser. True enough, as indeed was the practice of Irish missionary priests among others, but the child motif was Pearse and Connolly's own choice. Possibly Kiberd hadn't the Proclamation to hand at the time or maybe ill-fitting literary theory sometimes gets in the way of attentive reading. There is, as it happens, no mention of children in 'Easter 1916' but with day-dreaming between the lines, sure anything's possible. W.B. Yeats, *The Collected Poems of W.B. Yeats* (London, 1952), pp. 202–3 and Declan Kiberd, *Inventing Ireland: The Literature of the Modern Nation* (London, 1995), p. 114.

26 On the confusions surrounding the flying of flags see De Paor, *Easter Proclamation*, pp. 48–9. Sean O'Casey, who liked his flags, made good theatrical play of the various flags of the Rising in the *The Plough and the Stars* (1926).

27 Ibid, p. 49

28 R.G. Lowery, 'Sean O'Casey', in James McGuire *et al.*, *Dictionary of Irish Biography, From the Earliest Times to the Year 2002* (Cambridge, 2009).

29 Fearghal McGarry, *The Rising: Ireland: Easter 1916* (Oxford, 2010), p. 130.

30 Only one member of the ICA, Constance Markievicz, was listed formally as a member prior to 1916. Women members of the ICA trained separately and typically they performed traditionally-ascribed roles such as cooking and first aid. I am grateful to Fearghal McGarry for sharing with me his knowledge of gender differences within the ICA.

31 On these see Margaret Ward, *Unmanageable Revolutionaries: Women and Irish Nationalism* (London, 1983).

32 Perhaps one in eight of those playing some role or other was a woman. For pen portraits of the more prominent women in the Rising, including Constance Markievicz, Winnie Carney, Dr Kathleen Lynn, Madeleine ffrench Mullen and Margaret Skinnider, see the entries in the *Dictionary of Irish Biography* (2009).

33 According to the census enumerator's return, Michael Lahiff, aged twenty-three in 1911, was stationed at Kevin Street, not far from St Stephen's Green. Lahiff was originally from County Clare and was a Catholic whose languages were Irish as well as English. He was probably a single man at the time of his killing. The gravestone inscription in Glasnevin

cemetery records that Michael Lahiff 'died on the 24th April 1916 from wounds received whilst gallantly doing his duty as a member of the Dublin Metropolitan Police'. See: http://www.census.nationalarchives.ie/pages/1911/Dublin/Wood_Quay__part_of_/ Kevin_Street__Police_Barracks/80883/ and also http://irishmedals.org/gpage35.html.

34   W.B. Yeats, *Collected Poems of W.B. Yeats* (London, 1968), pp. 202–203.

35   There is no direct evidence on this, though the suggestion has persisted down the years. The fact that the identity of the executioner is not revealed in testimonies of the Rising, despite its public nature, might suggest a conspiracy of silence round what some of the volunteers had come to see as a disreputable or callous act.

36   De Paor, *Easter Proclamation*, p. 45. Another version has it that Constance Markievicz exulted as Lahiff fell to the ground: 'I shot him! I shot him!' See McGarry, *The Rising*, p. 137.

37   These figures are from McGarry, *Rising*, p. 188.

38   Ibid., p. 188.

39   The notion that 'Ireland' had carefully waited for the right moment is a piece of blarney on several levels, serving to conceal the lack of a popular mandate and the blundering and confused approach to the Rising (which paradoxically helped mislead Dublin Castle and so turned out to favour the insurrectionists).

40   Quoted in Brian Barton, *The Secret Court Martial Records of the Easter Rising* (Port Stroud, 2010), p. 150.

41   McGarry, *Rising,* p. 120

42   *Collected Works of Pádraic H. Pearse: Political Writings and Speeches* (Dublin, 1918), pp. 216–17.

43   Ibid., p. 217.

44   The amended constitution of the IRB was reproduced as an appendix to Bulmer Hobson's *Ireland Yesterday and Tomorrow* (Tralee, 1968), p. 103.

45   For the various conspiracies forming the backdrop to the Rising see F.S.L. Lyons, 'The Revolution in Train', in W.E. Vaughan (ed.), *A New History of Ireland: VI* (Oxford, 2000), pp. 189–206.

46   K.A. Miller, *Emigrants and Exiles: Ireland and the Irish Exodus to North America* (Oxford, 1985). Small numbers of political activists, as in the case of the Young Irelanders for example, were indeed exiled but these represented a droplet within the flood of Irish emigrants abroad. It is true that 'push' factors predominated during the Great Famine. But two points: Famine emigrants represented a small proportion of Irish emigrants in the last two centuries, popular images notwithstanding, and even among Famine emigrants the understandable motive was bettering their position elsewhere.

47   Following the outbreak of the First World War various republican emissaries had beaten a path to Germany to secure arms and, if possible, a German invasion of Ireland. A German arms shipment, on board the *Aud* and destined for the insurgents, had been intercepted at sea just before the rising itself. By then earlier possibilities such as the landing of no less than 25,000 German soldiers, with 50,000 extra guns for collaborators, had evaporated. See Reinhard Doerries, *Prelude to the Easter Rising: Sir Roger Casement in Imperial Germany* (London, 2000), pp. 19–20, 72–3.

48   The banner draped across the front of Liberty Hall soon after the outbreak of the First World War read: 'We Serve Neither King nor Kaiser but Ireland'. Yet Connolly for one was prepared to risk a possible catastrophe: to collaborate in the invasion of Ireland with one of the most authoritarian and militaristic powers in Europe. Late in the game of European imperialism, Germany had already demonstrated brutish resolve in extending its territorial possessions. What the Irish peoples, nationalist and unionist alike, might have thought of the prospect of becoming a German dependency seems to have lain

lightly on the shoulders of the plotters. Some even countenanced the idea of a German prince as head of an Irish state. Fortunately for Connolly's reputation both as a socialist and as a patriot, the German invasion and the collaborationist dilemmas this would have opened up, never materialised.

49 John Horne and Alan Kramer, *German Atrocities, 1914: A History of Denial* (Yale, 2001), p. 15. The latest scholarship now suggests that Allied propagandist exaggeration was limited, not least because the reality of German occupation was sufficiently awful to require little by way of embellishment.

50 Horne and Kramer, *German Atrocities, passim.*

51 Another huge policy blunder came, two years later, with plans to extend conscription to Ireland.

52 *Irish Independent*, 4 May 1916.

53 De Paor, *Easter Proclamation*, p. 29.

54 Quoted in Townshend, *Easter 1916*, p. 157.

55 De Paor, *Easter Proclamation*, p. 62.

56 Mary Daly, *Industrial Development and Irish National Identity, 1922–1939* (Syracuse, 1992), pp. 81–9.

57 Among a small number of exceptions was the land redistribution policy of the Irish Land Commission. See M.A.G. Ó Tuathaigh, 'The Land Question: Politics and Irish Society, 1922–1960', in P.J. Drudy (ed.), *Ireland: Land, Politics and People* (Cambridge, 1982), pp. 167–89.

58 The section on private property in the Irish Constitution, adopted in 1937, makes clear that the state 'guarantees to pass no law attempting to abolish the right of private ownership or the general right to transfer, bequeath, and inherit property'. See http://www.irishstatutebook.ie/en/constitution/index.html#article43

59 Anderson, *Imagined Communities* (1991 and 2006).

60 The imagery is borrowed from Robert Emmet's Proclamation of 1803. Emmet counted five unspecified rebellions over a period of six hundred years of Anglo-Irish history.

61 Though not spelled out, the conventional wisdom is that the Proclamation is referring to rebellions in 1641, 1798, 1803, 1848, 1867 and 1916.

62 Richard English, *Irish Freedom: The History of Nationalism in Ireland* (London, 2006).

63 *Collected Works of Pádraic H. Pearse: Political Writings and Speeches* (Dublin, 1918), p. 224.

64 Alone among the conspirators, James Connolly had put his name before various electorates, in local rather than national contests. He stood unsuccessfully not only in his native Edinburgh but also in Belfast and Dublin (Greaves, *James Connolly*, pp. 47–53, 109–111, 237).

65 There were intra-nationalist and intra-unionist divisions as well. Such divisions were felt most keenly perhaps within Irish nationalism. Some supporters of the Irish parliamentary party were content to accept a Home Rule parliament but others aspired, if at all possible, to something closer to the separatist ideal, even though opposed to military means to bring about such an outcome.

66 See, for example, the words of Sean MacDiarmada quoted in Barton, *Easter Rising*, p. 318: 'I'll be shot and it will be a bad day for Ireland that I am not.'

67 The dead hand of Emmet is apparent once again: 'Whoever refuses to march to whatever part of the country he is ordered, is guilty of disobedience to the government, which alone is competent to decide in what place his services are necessary, and which desires him to recollect, that in whatever part of Ireland he is fighting, he is still fighting for its freedom.' PRONI, *Robert Emmet: The Insurrection of July 1803* (with commentary by Geraldine Hume and Anthony Malcomson, Belfast 1996). The IRB had provision for the

execution of members deemed to be guilty of treason ('any wilful act or word' calculated to betray the cause of Irish independence). See Hobson, *Ireland*, pp. 105–6.

68 Dáil and Seanad debates, now online and easily consulted, are studded with references to the children of the nation, meant sometimes literally, sometimes metaphorically. Of the many examples see the deliberations of the Joint Committee on the Constitutional Amendment on Children in September 2008 at http://oireachtasdebates.oireachtas.ie/Debates%20 Authoring/DebatesWebPack.nsf/committeetakes/CCJ2008090900004?opendocument [accessed 6 January 2013].

69 R.V. Comerford, *Ireland: Inventing the Nation* (London, 2003), pp. 101–111.

70 Thus, for example, Neal Gallagher, an RIC constable living at 55 Columbia Street in the Shankill area of Belfast was, according to the 1911 Census of Ireland, both an Irish speaker and a Catholic. Gallagher was a native of Donegal, as were quite a number of RIC men, and the presumption is that most favoured Home Rule.

71 On the importance of struggle in helping define an ethno-national identity see English, *Irish Freedom*, pp. 454–64.

72 D.H. Akenson puts the point succinctly: '… the Partition of Ireland was just an outward and visible sign of the partition of the Irish people, one sort from the other, that long had existed in their hearts and minds.' Akenson, *Small Differences*, p. 147.

73 See http://www.france.fr/en/institutions-and-values/history-womens-right-vote.

74 PRONI, *Robert Emmet* (copy of the Proclamation reproduced therein).

75 All was not lost! A fragment of the painting, measuring 5 cm by 12 cm, fetched a price of Euro 300 at Whyte's auction in Dublin (as reported by Michael Parsons, *Irish Times*, 21 September 2013).

76 McGarry, *Rising*, pp. 139, 187

77 McGarry makes a strong case for the generally honourable behaviour on the part of the rebels by contrast with the less restrained violence that characterised the IRA campaign of a few years later. See Fearghal McGarry, 'Violence and the Easter Rising', in David Fitzpatrick (ed.), *Terror in Ireland* (Dublin, 2012), pp. 39–57.

78 The words of Benito Mussolini (1883–1945). See John Whittam, *Fascist Italy* (Manchester, 1995), p. 156

79 In excess of 200,000, perhaps 210,000 Irishmen enlisted on the side of Britain and Ireland during the course of the First World War. Tim Bowman, private communication, 28 November 2013.

80 Mary Brigid Pearse, Pat's sister, speaks of Pat's 'big adventure' in Easter 1916, while he himself had written of a love of 'perilous adventure'. Mary Brigid Pearse (ed.), *The Home Life of Pádraig Pearse* (Cork, 1979), pp. 8–9. See also the *Collected Works of Pádraic H. Pearse: Political Writings and Speeches* (Dublin, 1918), p. 94.

81 Betrayal of the leader by the people was also a prominent theme in the Parnellite politics of the late nineteenth century, as John Wilson Foster reminded me, and later found tragicomic expression in the work of James Joyce.

82 Accounts of the young Cúchulainn, to give a favourite example, read like a portrait of the psychopathic warrior as a young man. He is to be found eviscerating opponents, impaling their severed heads on gates, and claiming the 'friendship of thighs' with mother and daughter. See 'The Training of Cúchulainn' (electronic edition compiled by Beatrix Färber and Miriam Trojer) in the Corpus of Electronic Texts (CELT), University College Cork: http://www.ucc.ie/celt/published/T301038/index.html

83 Pearse's sexuality is discussed sensitively in Elaine Sisson, *Pearse's Patriots: St Enda's and the Cult of Boyhood* (Cork, 2005) and in Moran, *Politics of Redemption, passim*. It is hard to escape the impression that St Enda's School, with Pearse as founder-headmaster was

a strange institution even by the standards of its time. The young boys in his charge wore kilts to perform military drilling and were observed in nude bathing; Pearse also took one, sometimes two boys with him to his holiday cottage in the west of Ireland. Nowadays, because of the paedophilic undertones, it might be regarded as a bit creepy, not unlike some English public schools of the Edwardian era with which, ironically, it bears some comparison.

84   *Collected Works*, p. 194.

85   See *Enciclopedia Italiana* to which in 1932 Mussolini contributed an explanation of what fascism meant. The emphasis was on war, holiness and heroism.

86   D.P. Moran, *The Philosophy of Irish Ireland* (edited by Patrick Maume, Dublin, 2006).

87   *Na Scríbhinní Liteartha le Pádraig Mac Piarais: Scríbhinní i nGaeilge* (*bailithe is curtha in eagar ag* Séamas Ó Buachalla, Corcaigh, 1979), l. 30. *Mise Éire* is also the title of a collection of music, both stirring and bombastic, by the noted composer Seán Ó Riada.

88   Great is my glory, I who bore the hardy Cúchulainn.

89   In a sense, Cúchulainn's bloodthirsty deeds make him a not inappropriate role model for the more gung-ho among these civilian warriors.

90   Such anxieties are also present in Pearse's stirring speech at the graveside of Wolfe Tone at Bodenstown in June 1913. Pledging to follow in the footsteps of Tone, Pearse warned: 'Let us not pledge ourselves unless we mean to keep our pledge…' Shame, he suggests, follows fear – the fear of compromise and loss of purity. 'We must account ourselves base', he avows, 'as long as we endure the evil thing against which he [Tone] testified with his blood'. Pearse, *Collected Works: Political Writings*, pp. 53–63.

91   Sean O'Casey, *Three Dublin Plays: The Shadow of a Gunman; Juno and the Paycock; The Plough and the Stars* (London, 1998).

92   This can be confirmed for the Northern Ireland conflict by a look at the cold statistical tables at the back of David McKittrick *et al.*, *Lost Lives: The Stories of the Men, Women and Children Who Died as a Result of the Northern Ireland Troubles* (Edinburgh, 2007).

Chapter Eight: Texting Terror: 1912 and 1916

1   From the belligerent sermon of the Church of Ireland bishop of Down, Connor and Dromore preached at St Anne's Cathedral, on Ulster Day, 28 September 1912. D'Arcy did pray also for 'deliverance from the horrors of Civil War'. This would be ensured by communal solidarity, he complacently assumed. See reports in the *Northern Whig*, *Irish Times*, *Irish Independent*, 30 September 1912.

2   *Collected Works of Pádraic H. Pearse: Political Writings and Speeches* (Dublin, 1918), p. 216.

3   *Belfast News-Letter* (hereafter *BNL*), 19 September 1912; Timothy Bowman, *Carson's Army: the Ulster Volunteer Force, 1910–22* (Manchester, 2007), p. 24.

4   *Irish News*, 19 September 1912. By contrast, for the unionist *BNL* of the same day this was 'a memorable demonstration' and a 'magnificent display', heralding the 'coming of Ulster Day'.

5   *BNL*, 19 September 1912.

6   The concept is developed more fully here but it was deployed also in Liam Kennedy, K.A. Miller and Brian Gurrin, 'Minorities, Majorities and Demographic Power: The Protestant and Catholic Communities of Tipperary since 1660', in Sean Farrell and Michael de Nie (eds), *Power and Popular Culture in Modern Ireland: Essays in Honour of James S. Donnelly, Jr.* (Dublin, 2010), pp. 67–92. On demographic size as a dimension of political power see Joe Ruane and Jennifer Todd, *The Dynamics of Conflict in Northern Ireland: Power, Conflict and Emancipation* (Cambridge, 1996).

7 Calculated from W.E. Vaughan and A.J. Fitzpatrick, *Irish Historical Statistics: Population 1821–1971* (Dublin, 1978).

8 Counting all Protestants in Ireland moves this ratio upwards but only to 26 per cent of all the peoples of Ireland in 1911. Thus we have what is sometimes referred to as a double-minority problem. Catholics and nationalists constituted a minority in the north-east of Ireland but a majority on the whole island. Protestants and unionists formed a majority in the north east but a minority on the whole island. The consequences were the worst of both worlds with mutual suspicion and insecurity characterising both ethnic groups. For a magisterial overview of interpretations of the conflict see John Whyte, *Interpreting Northern Ireland* (Oxford, 1990).

9 Fergus O'Ferrall, *Catholic Emancipation: Daniel O'Connell and the Birth of Irish Democracy 1820–30* (Dublin, 1985).

10 Alan F. Parkinson, *Friends in High Places: Ulster's Resistance to Home Rule, 1912–14* (Belfast, 2012), pp. 161–74.

11 *BNL*, 1 October 1912.

12 The deportation of thousands of Belgian workers – 'assembled in freight cars, and carried off to unknown parts, like a herd of slaves' – was documented by Desire Mercier, the courageous Catholic archbishop of Malines, Belgium. See Henry L. Dubly, *The Life of Cardinal Mercier, Primate of Belgium* (translated from the French by Herbert Wilson, London, 1928), pp. 215–18.

13 As it happens, at the time of writing a wall mural was being unveiled in the Ardoyne area of Belfast. It featured an IRA man (the late Martin Meehan who died in 2007) in military garb, armed with a rifle and taking aim. A copy of the Proclamation formed the backdrop, as if the text had authored and authorised military action. See *Irish News*, 7 November 2013.

14 In Fenian theology, however, the Irish Republic pre-dated the Rising and merely awaited its unveiling.

15 Alvin Jackson, 'Unionist Myths, 1912–1985', *Past and Present*, 136 (1992), p. 164.

16 *Belfast Telegraph*, 29 September 1962.

17 *BNL*, 23 June 1921.

18 R.F. Foster, *Modern Ireland 1600–1972* (London, 1989), pp. 474–6.

19 Calculated from the biographical information contained in Brian Barton, *The Secret Court Martial Records of the Easter Rising* (Stroud, Gloucestershire, 2010).

20 Margaret Ward, *Unmanageable Revolutionaries: Women and Irish Nationalism* (London, 1983).

21 An enormously difficult question to answer and best left to the cultural historians.

22 See Crawford, *Friends in High Places*, especially the chapter on 'Community Resistance'.

23 http://www.proni.gov.uk/index/search_the_archives/ulster_covenant/ulster_day.htm. [Accessed 28 November 2013].

24 Fearghal McGarry, *The Rising: Ireland: Easter 1916* (Oxford, 2010). McGarry discusses the smaller mobilisations outside Dublin; the centrepiece is the Dublin rising.

25 An awkward question is the extent to which the signatories were aware of and accepting of the possibility of violent resistance in the event of Home Rule being imposed on the North. It is also the case that nationalist Ireland's ridiculing of Ulster Day as a test of unionist resolve made a resort to arms that bit more likely.

26 Crawford, *Friends in High Places*, p. 73.

27 Ruth Dudley Edwards, *Patrick Pearse: The Triumph of Failure* (London, 1977), p. 276.

28 John Bew, *The Glory of Being Britons: Civic Unionism in Nineteenth-Century Belfast* (Dublin, 2009).

29 A phrase from the Irish national anthem, Amhrán na bFhiann, meaning (stepping into) the breach or gap of danger.

30   Was Pearse a patriot? The hallmark of modern patriotism is love of people, as expressed in concern for their wellbeing. Presumably the appropriate starting point is that each individual within the national grouping is the best judge of her or his own welfare. It is hard to see how those possessed of a messianic mind-set – the self-appointed few – had acquired the right to presume and over-ride the wishes of others. The determinants of each person's welfare might be material, political, cultural and even spiritual. Pearse was certainly an ultra-nationalist with an uncompromising vision of the 'nation' and its 'destiny'. He could, at moments, be solicitous of individual death, as was apparent during Easter Week, but the thrust of his ideology from the outbreak of the First World War to his death a few years later was to treat people as inputs into his own imaginative scheme for the re-vitalisation of nations. This was the indifference of the ideologue, not the benevolence of the patriot.

31   Ruth Dudley Edwards, *Patrick Pearse: The Triumph of Failure* (London, 1977), p. 276.

32   The phrase 'Small Differences' is borrowed from a classic work by D.H. Akenson, *Small Differences: Irish Catholics and Irish Protestants, 1815–1922: An International Perspective* (Montreal, 1991). See especially chapter six which explains how differences between Catholics and Protestants in nineteenth-century Ireland were deliberately magnified, not by outsiders, but by deliberate campaigns on the part of each.

33   Mary E. Daly and Margaret O'Callaghan (eds), *1916 in 1966: Commemorating the Easter Rising* (Dublin, 2007), p. 19.

34   Marshall McLuhan, *Understanding Media: The Extension of Man* (New York, 1966).

35   In calculating relative frequency it may be noted that close variants of a word are treated as synonyms. Thus 'man', 'men', 'manhood' are treated as one, and similarly 'citizen' and 'citizenship' for instance.

36   Strictly speaking, the Covenant is entered into by men only. While bearing this distinction in mind it is both convenient and sensible to read the Declaration as a variant of the same project.

37   This assumption, in effect a form of geographical predestination that overrode popular will, was widely and uncritically accepted. Arthur Griffith, the founder of Sinn Féin was sure that 'the frontier of Ireland has been fixed by nature'. See Griffith, *The Resurrection of Hungary: A Parallel for Ireland* (Dublin, 1918), p. 70.

38   There are eight mentions of a Republic if one includes words from the title of the document (adding in 'Poblacht' as well but bearing in mind the qualification that there is no precise term in the Irish language for a republic).

39   During the Dáil Éireann debate (Wednesday 4 December 2013) on the report of the Smithwick Tribunal which found instances of collusion between members of the Garda and the Provisional IRA, leading to the killing of two senior RUC officers in South Armagh. See http://oireachtasdebates.oireachtas.ie/Debatesper cent20Authoring/ DebatesWebPack.nsf/takes/dail2013120400019?opendocument [accessed 21 December 2013]. Ironically, Sinn Féin was not party to the 1916 Rising.

40   http://www.ucc.ie/celt/published/E900009/index.html [accessed 29 October 2013]. I am grateful to my colleague Marie Coleman for drawing this to my attention.

41   Mary E. Daly and Margaret O'Callaghan (eds), *1916 in 1966* (Dublin, 2007).

42   Personal observation during an anti-EEC demonstration in Patrick Street, Cork, during the referendum campaign of 1972.

43   The sense of anger and shame at the prospect of foreign control of the Irish public finances almost certainly owes something to the value placed on national sovereignty following the birth of the Irish state. For an analysis of the financial and banking crisis see Donal Donovan and Antoin Murphy, *The Fall of the Celtic Tiger: Ireland and the Euro Debt Crisis* (Oxford, 2013).

44 See *Irish Times*, 15 January 2001. A few years later a freshly discovered copy sold at Sotheby's in London for £70,000, indicating price inflation in this thin market for 1916 memorabilia (*Irish Times*, 12 December 2003). This surge in value accelerated, and a later copy made the astonishing price of almost 400,000 Euros (*Irish Times*, 8 March 2006). On 15 July 2009 the same paper announced that a copy of the Proclamation had failed to sell, and the following year it carried the wry observation 'It looks like 1916 prices have stopped rising' (*Irish Times*, 27 March 2010).

45 A colleague of mine purchased a colour-printed testimonial signed at Belfast City Hall on 'Ulster Day' by Robert Clements Porter. The price at an antique shop in Donegall Pass, Belfast in 2013 was a mere £20.

46 John Wilson Foster, *Irish Novels, 1890–1940: New Bearings in Culture and Fiction* (Oxford, 2008), p. 220.

47 John Wilson Foster, 'Yeats and the Easter Rising', *Canadian Journal of Irish Studies*, 11 (June, 1985), pp. 21–34.

48 Gordon Lucy, *The Ulster Covenant: An Illustrated History of the 1912 Home Rule Crisis* (Newtownards, 2012), p. 7.

49 *BNL*, 22 September 1962.

50 *BNL*, 29 September 1962.

51 George Dickson, 'The Lost Counties', *BNL*, 28 September 1962. A map of the partitioned province of Ulster accompanied the article.

52 Liam Kennedy and Philip Ollerenshaw (eds), *Ulster Since 1600: Politics, Economy and Society* (Oxford, 2013), especially chapters eleven and twelve.

53 D.W. Miller, *Queen's Rebels: Ulster Loyalism in Historical Perspective* (Dublin, 1978), p. 156.

54 *Belfast Telegraph*, 22 September 2012.

55 *The Telegraph*, 29 September 2012. For a video recording of some of the day's events see: http://www.telegraph.co.uk/news/uknews/northernireland/9575713/Unionist-parade-to-mark-Ulster-Covenant-centenary-begins-peacefully-in-Belfast.html [accessed 6 January 2014].

56 Diane Urquhart, *The Ladies of Londonderry: Women and Political Patronage* (London, 2007), p. 105.

57 Edwards, *Patrick Pearse*, p. 179.

58 De Paor, *Easter Proclamation*, p. 76.

59 The British government had 'winked at Ulster breaking the law … wait and see. Well, we waited and now see the result, viz. rebellion and loss of life'. Quoted in Barton, *Records of the Easter Rising*, p. 60.

60 On the career of William O'Brien see Patrick Maume, *The Long Gestation: Irish Nationalist Life 1891–1918* (Dublin, 1999).

61 Was Carson a Lundy? Not in the conventional sense but in so far as he led his forces in a manner that was largely subversive of his original anti-Home Rule aspirations, and in so far as he vastly empowered the most militant of his nationalist opponents, he may be said to have fatally weakened the unionist defence of Ireland as a part of the United Kingdom. Objectively, if not subjectively, Carson was counterproductive as a leader of the Irish and Ulster unionist causes.

62 Vincent Comerford, 'Deference, Accommodation and Conflict in Irish Confessional Relations' (unpublished paper, NUI, Maynooth, 2014).

63 Barton, *Secret Court Martial Records*, pp. 236–7.

64 David W Miller, *Church, State and Nation in Ireland, 1898–1921* (Dublin, 1973), pp. 388–9.

65 Foster, *Modern Ireland*, p. 476.

66　Ed Moloney, *A Secret History of the IRA* (London, 2002).

67　The writer and journalist Eoghan Harris has coined the expressive phrase the 'Recurring IRA'.

68　McGarry, *The Rising*, p. 126.

69　The variance in and the complexities of southern unionist opinion find glittering expression in Elizabeth Bowen's novel, *The Last September* (London, 1998).

70　*Belfast Telegraph*, 12 October 2012, with further clarification on the website of the Methodist Church. See http://www.irishmethodist.org/news/13-october-2012/belfast-synod-letter-belfast-telegraph-re-ulster-covenant-statement [accessed 7 January 2014].

71　Akenson, *Small Differences*, especially chapter five ('Keeping Separate') and also Akenson, *Education and Enmity: The Control of Schooling in Northern Ireland, 1920–1950* (Newton Abbott, 1973).

72　To speak of two major ethnic blocs is something of a simplification, though it broadly makes sense for the twentieth century. Prior to that one needs to bear more fully in mind the distinctive Presbyterian presence in Ulster in terms of politics, religion, culture and world view. This implies a tripartite rather than a binary model of ethnic difference.

73　Dennis Kennedy, *The Widening Gulf: Northern Attitudes to the Independent Irish State, 1919–49* (Belfast, 1988), pp. 141–9, 234–40. See also B.M. Walker, *A Political History of the Two Irelands: From Partition to Peace* (Basingstoke, 2012). The process indicated above was by no means linear, though, and there were counter forces from the beginning. These, in fact, seemed to be in the ascendance by the mid-1960s, that is, before the steeply downward spiral of the later 1960s.

Chapter Nine: Was there an Irish War of Independence?

1　I am grateful to Jim Donnelly and Tim McMahon for a range of constructive criticisms and owe much to Paul Devlin for excellent research assistance. My remarkable colleague Patrick Maume had a considerable influence on the development of the chapter. Yet I cannot claim that any of these shares in full or even in large part my representation of what are still contentious matters. ['Was there an Irish War of Independence?' was originally published in a collection of essays edited by Bruce Stewart under the title *Hearts and Minds: Irish Culture and Society under the Act of Union* back in 2002. The text is substantially unchanged apart from a small number of alterations, including the occasional stylistic change. I would also like to acknowledge helpfully-critical comments at the Monaco conference, 2001 (where an early version was presented) from Anthony Cronin, Luke Gibbons and Bruce Stewart.]

2　Mary Brigid Pearse (ed.), *The Home Life of Padraig Pearse* (Cork, 1979), p. 10.

3　Ernie O'Malley, *On Another Man's Wound* (Dublin, 1979), p. 46.

4　Ibid., p. 153. The barracks survived the attack, and is today an attractive private residence set in a hollow among the Hollyford hills.

5　*An tÓglach: The Official Organ of the Irish Volunteers*, 2, 24 (1 March 1921).

6　Asked in old age if the RIC men had had an opportunity to fire their carbines, Breen answered bluntly: 'No. They did not get a chance to fire.' Quoted in Jim Maher, 'Dan Breen looks back 50 years from 1967', *Tipperary Historical Journal* 1998, p. 106. He also accepted that his group had no authority from the GHQ staff of the Volunteers, or from anyone else for the ambush. In his memoir, *My Fight for Irish Freedom* (Dublin, 1989), revised and enlarged edition, Breen states (pp. 33–4) that the constables were called upon to surrender but responded by holding their rifles at the ready.

7   This is in the second edition of *My Fight for Irish Freedom* (Dublin, 1924), p. 39. In the revised edition (1989) this judgement loses some of its specificity (p. 34). Breen speaks of Irish policemen generally, including the two at Soloheadbeg, as a 'pack of deserters, spies and hirelings'. This may be contrasted with the opinion at the time of the parish priest of Tipperary town, who described the victims, both Catholic, as 'martyrs to duty' *(Tipperary Star,* 1 February 1919).

8   *Tipperary Star,* 1 February 1919.

9   Sinn Féin Publicity Department, *The Good Old IRA: Tan War Operations* (Dublin, 1985), pp. 1–3. The terms the 'Tan War' and the 'Black and Tan War' may also be found in Gerry Adams, *The Politics of Irish Freedom* (Dingle, 1986), p. 50. There is an anomaly here in that the campaign of political violence had started a year before the deployment of the so-called Black and Tans.

10   Ernie O'Malley, *Another Man's Wound* (1979), p. 342.

11   Anthony Cronin has suggested to me the likelihood that the phrase had been invented by the *Irish Press* newspaper in the late 1930s. Growing up in Enniscorthy in the 1930s, he recalls the most commonly used term was the 'Troubles'.

12   Breen, *My Fight for Irish Freedom* (1989), p. 40.

13   *Tipperary Star,* 1 February 1919.

14   Ibid.

15   *An tÓglach,* 11, 1 (February 1919).

16   Peter Hart, 'The Geography of Revolution in Ireland, 1917–1923', *Past and Present,* 155, May 1997, pp. 142–76.

17   *An tÓglach,* 24, 2 (March 1921). The following month under an editorial headed 'The War for Freedom', the journal railed against the treachery of young men emigrating from Ireland and hoped that 'the Volunteers in other parts who have hitherto been backward will wake up to their duty and throw themselves with energy and enthusiasm into the guerrilla offensive'.

18   Commandant General Tom Barry, *Guerrilla Days in Ireland* (Dublin, 1981), p. 60.

19   See chapter five on the Young Ireland 'rising'. The term guerrilla war or 'small war' originated with resistance by irregulars to Napoleon's incursions into Spain (1808–12), but the tactics are much older.

20   Barry, *Guerrilla Days in Ireland* (1981), pp. 113–14. On the vulnerability of Protestants and unionists in West Cork see Peter Hart, *The IRA and Its Enemies: Violence and Community in Cork 1916–1923* (Oxford, 1998).

21   This Orange slogan is a reference to the short-cropped hair of Catholic rebels during the 1798 rising in Leinster.

22   On an alleged plot linking Sinn Féin and the German authorities in 1918 see Michael Laffan, *The Resurrection of Ireland: The Sinn Féin Party, 1916–1923* (Cambridge, 1999), pp. 142–6.

23   Allied propaganda exaggerated German atrocities, particularly those alleging sexual transgression (for which there was a public appetite), but there seems little doubt that the German army of occupation engaged in massive reprisals against Belgian civilians in the early months of the war; later on it systematically plundered Belgian factories and engaged in large-scale, forced deportations of young men to Germany. See E.H. Kossman, *The Low Countries, 1780–1940* (Oxford, 1978), pp. 522–34. On the selective inflation of German abuses see Trevor Wilson, 'Lord Bryce's Investigation into Alleged German Atrocities in Belgium, 1914–15', in *Journal of Contemporary History,* 3, 14 (1979), pp. 369–83. [However, more recent research tends to re-emphasise the view of dreadful atrocities committed by the German troops.]

24 *Irish News,* 20 April 1921.

25 *Belfast Telegraph,* 19 June 1922.

26 W. Alison Phillips, *The Revolution in Ireland, 1906–1923* (London, 1923). The copy in the library of Queen's University, Belfast carries in the margins a lively debate between anonymous authors, expressing support for or outrage at Phillips's avowedly unionist account. The opening graffito is 'British Liar'. Historical debate is conducted in many different ways, and on many different surfaces, from toilet walls to gable ends. [One might add for the more recent period other media such as Wikipedia entries, tweets and blogs.]

27 Richard Abbott, *Police Casualties in Ireland, 1919–22* (Cork, 2000).

28 *Belfast News-Letter (BNL),* 11 July 1921.

29 Breen, *My Fight for Irish Freedom* (1989), p. 93.

30 For a brief discussion of chivalry in wartime, the 'rules of war' and the 'ethics of war', as seen from the vantage point of an IRA officer, see Liam Deasy, *Towards Ireland Free* (edited by John E. Chisholm, Dublin, 1973), pp. 291–2.

31 Roger Scruton, *A Dictionary of Political Thought* (London, 1982), p. 489. A looser definition is employed in Julius Gould and William L. Kolb (eds), *A Dictionary of the Social Sciences* (London, 1964), to the effect that war is 'the violent clash of organised social units' (p. 703), though it does beg the question of what is meant by a social unit.

32 David Fitzpatrick, *Politics and Irish Life 1913–1921: Provincial Experiences of War and Revolution* (Cork, 1998); Peter Hart, *The IRA and Its Enemies* (1998); Paul Bew, 'Moderate Nationalism and the Irish Revolution, 1916–1923', *Historical Journal,* 92 (1999), pp. 729–49.

33 I am drawing on local oral tradition at this point and also on conversations with the village's once-resident American social anthropologist, Dr Carol Bloodworth. Any village worth its salt in the 1970s–1980s had its own resident anthropologist, gawking at the locals and being gawked at in turn.

34 He would insist in conversations in the 1980s that the Protestant and Catholic farmers of Templederry, Tipperary (North Riding), the parish in which he was born, got on well together, and by and large he may well have been correct in this assessment.

35 *The Irish Times,* 4 August 1922.

36 David Cumming was a native of Belfast and a Protestant who had worked in the area for several years. A label attached to the body read: 'Convicted Spy: spies and informers beware'. How useful, as an intelligence agent, a Belfast Protestant, speaking presumably with a Belfast accent, might have been in rural Tipperary in 1921 was never explained. See *BNL,* 11 July 1921.

37 Edward Micheau, 'Sectarian Conflict in Monaghan', in David Fitzpatrick (ed.), *Revolution? Ireland 1917–23* (Dublin, Trinity History Workshop 1990), pp. 107–17; Bew, 'Moderate Nationalism' (1999), p. 740; Peter Hart, 'The Protestant Experience of Revolution in Southern Ireland', in Richard English and Graham Walker (eds), *Unionism in Modern Ireland: New Perspectives on Politics and Culture* (Dublin, 1996), chapter five.

38 Henry Patterson, *Class Conflict and Sectarianism* (Belfast, 1980), pp. 101–14.

39 Jonathan Bardon, *A History of Ulster* (Belfast, 1992), pp. 470–74.

40 Ballymacarrett Research Group, *Lagan Enclave: A History of Conflict in the Short Strand, 1886–1997* (Belfast, 1997).

41 A police officer and later independent unionist politician, J.W. Nixon is widely believed to have been involved in the massacre. For a sceptical view of these claims see Lee Reynolds, *D.I. John William Nixon, MBE: From Dismissal to MP* (BA undergraduate dissertation, Queen's University, Belfast, 1995).

42 *Irish News,* 25 March 1922.

43 The identities of those killed in what has come to be known as the Altnaveigh massacre were as follows: Thomas Crozier, Altnaveigh, farmer, aged over sixty years, and his wife, both Presbyterians; John Heslip, farmer, Lisdrumliska, and his eldest son Robert, aged nineteen, both Presbyterians; James Lockhart, aged twenty-three, only son of Mr William Lockhart, farmer, Lisdrumliska, Unitarian; Joseph Gray, aged twenty, farmer's son, Lisdrumliska. The death toll could have been higher still: four other Protestants shot during the same night of terror recovered from their wounds. Such was the bloody intimacy of the conflict that some of the assassins were known to their victims. This information is based on accounts in the *Belfast Telegraph,* 17 June 1922, *Irish News,* 19 June 1922 and the *Weekly Northern Whig,* 24 June 1922. The *Irish News* suggested these might have been reprisal murders for the killing of two Catholics, Patrick Cregan, a farmer, and Thomas Crawley, an auctioneer, a few days before.

44 Bardon, *History of Ulster* (1992), p. 492.

45 A good historical and sociological account of Protestant sectarianism in Ulster may be found in John Brewer (with Gareth Higgins), *Anti-Catholicism in Northern Ireland, 1600–1998: The Mote and the Beam* (London, 1998). A comparable work on Catholic sectarianism has yet to be written.

46 Ginnell was born in Delvin, County Westmeath where large grazier farms, employing little labour, predominated. As it happens, and around the same period, Delvin was also the setting for Brinsley MacNamara's dark novel of Irish rural life *The Valley of the Squinting Windows* (Dublin, 1918).

47 Paul Bew, *Conflict and Conciliation in Ireland, 1890–1910: Parnellites and Radical Agrarians* (Oxford, 1987), pp. 213–16; *Irish Nationality,* 9 March 1918; *Parliamentary Debates,* Fifth Series (104, 1918), 1172, 1329.

48 Michael McInerney, *Peadar O'Donnell: Irish Social Rebel* (Dublin, 1974), pp. 32–42. For the official Sinn Féin position see the comments of Richard Mulcahy, Chief of Staff of the Irish Volunteers as noted in Maryann Gialanella Valiulis, *Portrait of a Revolutionary: General Mulcahy and the Founding of the Irish Free State* (Dublin, 1992), pp. 93–5.

49 McInerney, *Peadar O'Donnell* (1974), p. 42.

50 David Johnson, *The Interwar Economy in Ireland* (Dublin, 1985), pp. 3–5.

51 I am grateful to Patrick Maume who impressed on me the importance of the local elections of 1920.

52 *The Watchword,* 31 January 1920.

53 Emmet O'Connor, *A Labour History of Ireland, 1824–1960* (Dublin, 1922), pp. 99–113.

54 Ibid., p. 107.

55 O'Malley, *Another Man's Wound* (1979), p. 144. There were of course exceptions, of whom Liam Mellows is one of the best known. Less well known perhaps is Dan Breen's definition of himself, at least in later life, as a 'strong socialist'. See Jim Maher, 'Dan Breen', p. 110.

56 Desmond Ryan, *Sean Treacy and the 3rd Tipperary Brigade* (Tralee, 1945), p. 45.

57 Ibid, pp. 26–7.

58 Quoted in Francis J. Costello, *Enduring the Most: the Life and Death of Terence MacSwiney* (Tralee, 1995), p. 20. In addition to Treacy and MacSwiney, other revolutionaries whose fathers had either died or abandoned them in their early years included Eamon de Valera, Michael Collins and Dan Breen. The psychological implications of absent fathers on the subsequent development of these children might be explored further.

59 Florence O'Donoghue, *No Other Law* (Dublin, 1954), p. 5.

60 There are many biographies of Collins, varying on the whole from the hagiographic to the largely uncritical. Few manage to distort the politics of the period more effectively

– excising both the constitutional nationalist and the Irish unionist traditions – than the Hollywood film representation, directed by Neil Jordan, titled *Michael Collins* (though the portrayal of Collins and his death squad has considerable merit).

61 J. Anthony Gaughan, *Austin Stack: Portrait of a Separatist* (Dublin, 1977), p. 18.

62 This is to paraphrase sentiments found in various memoirs, including Barry, *Guerrilla Days in Ireland*, pp. 9, 60; Breen, *My Fight for Irish Freedom*, pp. 22–4, 34.

63 The text of the Proclamation is reproduced in full in chapter seven of this book.

64 O'Donoghue, *No Other Law*, p. 9. As *An tÓglach* (15 May 1919) put it: 'Since the Irish Volunteers established the Irish Republic in Easter Week, 1916, they have always recognised that an open state of war exists between them and the Army of England, and all their activities have been based on an acceptance of that principle.'

65 This was at Ileigh graveyard, Borrisoleigh, Co. Tipperary, on the occasion of the unveiling of a monument to the memory of Russell, Bourke and O'Shea, three IRA men from my own area of Borrisoleigh, captured by Free State troops and executed while in custody on the 15 January 1923. They had been fighting in defence of the 'Republic' – engaging in a seasonal robbery of the mail car on the road from Nenagh to Thurles, the day before Christmas Eve 1922 – during what was otherwise known as the civil war. See *The Irish Times*, 28 December 1922, 16 January 1923, and also Padraic O'Farrell, *Who's Who in the Irish War of Independence and Civil War, 1916–1923* (Dublin, 1997).

66 It is the term used, for instance, in *The Oxford Companion to Irish History*, edited by S.J. Connolly (Oxford, 1999), pp. 15–16. It is also used by R.F. Foster but subjected to critical discussion in his masterful account of modern Irish history, *Modern Ireland, 1600–1972* (London, 1988), pp. 494–9.

67 Barry, *Guerrilla Days in Ireland*, pp. 6–8, 80, 113–14.

68 *Freeman's Journal*, 2 December, 1918.

69 *Freeman's Journal*, 9 December 1918. Unionist women seem to have been subsumed in this total.

70 McInerney, *Peadar O'Donnell*, p. 40.

71 An introductory whiff of the Irish-Ireland spirit may be had from Patrick Maume's *D.P. Moran* (Dublin, 1995).

72 Breen, *Irish Freedom* (1989), p. 93.

73 Speech by Joe Devlin, MP for West Belfast, *Freeman's Journal*, 9 December, 1918. Reading the speech in its entirety, there must be more than a suspicion that Devlin did not believe his own propaganda, so one wonders what his hearers made of the argument.

74 Michael Laffan, *The Resurrection of Ireland* (1999), p. 244. For the text of the oath, see Bill Hammond, *Soldier of the Rearguard: The Story of Matt Flood and the Active Service Column* (Fermoy, 1977), p. 8.

75 Laffan, *Resurrection of Ireland*, p. 245; Valiulis, *Portrait of a Revolutionary*, pp. 38–40.

76 'O, holy mackerel, do you know what they're calling us, "Bloody Sinn Féiners"' (quoted in Breen, *Irish Freedom*, p. 122).

77 The unionist historian, W.A. Phillips, who worked in Dublin during the period, was of the view that many nationalists were also forced into submission. Phillips, *Revolution*, pp. 173–82.

78 Breen, *Freedom* (1989), pp. 63, 102–03; O'Malley, *Another Man's Wound*, p. 332; Barry, *Guerrilla Days*, pp. 8. 60.

79 Quoted in *Portrait of a Revolutionary*, p. 39.

80 Ryan, *Sean Treacy*, pp. 55–6. In all probability this was the key to the Soloheadbeg killings.

81   ETA (Euskadi Ta Askatasuna), the Basque terrorist group, evolved a remarkably similar strategy during the closing years of Franco's regime in Spain based on what it termed a spiral of action-repression-action.

82   A detailed analysis of the Ulster results may be found in Alec Wilson, *PR Urban Elections in Ulster, 1920* (London, 1972).

83   This needs qualification. Irish historians have tended to assume that the results published in the daily newspapers at the time, for example, those in *The Irish Times* on the 20 January 1920, and based on figures supplied by the Proportional Representation Society, were complete. In fact these were incomplete results but as broad brush strokes are revealing enough.

84   Norman Davies, *Europe: A History* (Oxford, 1996), *passim.*

85   Thomas Bartlett and Keith Jeffery (eds), *A Military History of Ireland* (Cambridge, 1996), pp. 388–9.

86   David A. Wilson, 'Michael Collins' (unpublished paper, University of Toronto, Dept. of Celtic Studies 2000).

87   The interpenetration of Protestant unionist and Catholic nationalist society on the island of Ireland made it an untidy act of secession, but only in the northern counties. In the territory of the Irish Free State only one in ten people was Protestant and this small ethnic bloc was chipped away. But in Northern Ireland a large resentful Catholic minority was now placed under the control of an Ulster Unionist majority, with unpredictable implications for the future.

88   D. George Boyce, *Nineteenth-Century Ireland: The Search for Stability* (Dublin, 1990), pp. 234–9.

89   *Irish News and Belfast Morning News*, Monday 11 July, 1921; *BNL,* 11 July1921.

90   *Irish News,* 12 July, 1921.

91   *BNL*, 15 July 1921.

92   This might be compared with the killing a year earlier of the prominent liberal unionist, Major G.B. O'Connor JP, of Rochestown, Co. Cork *(BNL,* 12 July 1921). 'When the raiders knocked at his door Mrs O'Connor answered them [...]. The major was taken out in his night attire and nothing more was seen of him until his body was found yesterday morning midway between his residence and Rochestown Railway Station with wounds over the heart and in his head. He was over 70 years of age.'

93   See Peter Hart's brilliant study, *The IRA and Its Enemies* (1998), p. 273.

94   Ibid., pp. 276–7.

95   Kathleen Keyes McDonnell, *There is a Bridge at Bandon: A Personal Account of the Irish War of Independence* (Cork: Mercier Press 1972), pp. 10, 168. Her own family and family businesses had suffered during the troubles, which may help explain her bitterness.

96   The killing of ex-servicemen is well treated in Jane Leonard, '"Getting Them at Last": The IRA and Ex-Servicemen', in David Fitzpatrick (ed.), *Revolution?*, pp. 118–29.

97   *The Irish Times*, 4 August 1922.

98   In 1911 some 27 per cent of the population was Protestant, with an even greater concentration in north Monaghan. The proportion was still over 20 per cent in 1926. W.E. Vaughan and A.J. Fitzpatrick, *Irish Historical Statistics: Population, 1821–1971* (Dublin, 1978), pp. 65,72.

99   Micheau, 'Sectarian Conflict', p. 113. This paragraph is based on Leonard's account ('Getting Them at Last').

100 David S. Johnson, 'The Belfast Boycott, 1920–22', in J.M. Goldstrom and L.A. Clarkson (eds), *Irish Population, Economy and Society* (Oxford, 1981), pp. 287–307.

101 Micheau, 'Sectarian Conflict', p. 115.

102   *Weekly Northern Whig,* 24 June 1922.

103   Eamon Phoenix, *Northern Nationalism: Nationalist Politics, Partition and the Catholic Minority in Northern Ireland, 1890–1940* (Belfast, 1994), p. 242.

104   Bardon, *History of Ulster,* p. 494.

105   Kurt Bowen, *Protestants in a Catholic State: Ireland's Privileged Minority* (Dublin, 1983), p. 24.

106   O'Malley, *Another Man's Wound,* p. 332. Lynch was the leader of the anti-Treaty IRA, or irregulars, during the Irish Civil War.

107   Ibid., p. 332.

108   Breen, *Irish Freedom* p. 17. This passage is not included in the revised edition of the book.

109   The words were spoken by Eamon de Valera in a speech at Thurles in March 1922, quoted in John A. Murphy, *Ireland in the Twentieth Century* (Dublin, 1975), p. 50.

110   D.G. Boyce, 'Introduction' to D.G. Boyce (ed.), *The Revolution in Ireland, 1879–1923* (Dublin, 1988).

111   This disadvantaged the bulk of the people as less than 15 per cent of the Irish population was able to speak *as Gaeilge* in 1911.

112   A quick guide to the language of vituperation – part of the underbelly of the Irish cultural revival – may be found in Patrick Maume, *D.P. Moran* (Dundalk, 1995).

113   Ibid., p. 22.

114   The constable was Michael Lahiff. A number of writers have attributed this inglorious killing to the Countess Markievicz but this is disputed by Diana Norman in her biography *Terrible Beauty: A Life of Constance Markievicz, 1868–1927* (London, 1988), pp. 138–40.

115   Stephen Gwynn, *The Irish Situation* (London, 1921), p. 73.

116   D. George Boyce, *Nineteenth-Century Ireland: The Search for Stability* (Dublin, 1990), pp. 237–43.

117   According to Dan Breen, who took part in a march by the Irish Volunteers through Limerick city on 23 May 1915: 'We were sorely tempted to open fire on the hostile crowd that pelted us with garbage as we paraded through the streets.' Breen, *Irish Freedom,* p. 14.

118   *BNL,* 12 July 1921.

119   In an unpublished paper, 'Cain and Abel: A Study of the Societal Dynamics of an Ethnic Conflict' (Dublin, 1999) the psychoanalyst, Mitch Elliott, has developed a persuasive analysis of the parallels between sibling rivalry and civil and communal warfare.

120   Laffan, *Resurrection* (1999), p. 416.

121   See *The Irish Times,* 28 September 1922; report of the coroner's enquiry in *The Irish Times,* 30 September 1922.

122   O'Malley, *Another Man's Wound* (1979), p. 59. Fanaticism rather than chivalry seems, however, to have been his dominant characteristic by 1921, no doubt developed under the duress of the fighting and the torture he had experienced at the hands of British soldiers. An elegantly written account of O'Malley's life may be found in Richard English, *Ernie O'Malley: IRA Intellectual* (Oxford, 1998).

123   Another phrase used at the time was to 'rub them out'. Robert Kee, *Ireland: A History* (London, 1980).

124   Richard Abbott, *Police Casualties in Ireland, 1919–22* (Cork, 2000).

125   Conor Brady, 'Ireland's Silent Assassinations', *The Irish Times,* 2 September 2000.

126   Based on the account in Ulick O'Connor, *The Troubles* (London, 1996), pp. 183–4.

127   See Eamon Phoenix, *Northern Nationalism,* pp. 219, 242–3.

128   Paul Bew, 'Moderate Nationalism', p.736. See also Murphy, *Ireland in the Twentieth Century,* pp. 5–6, 19–20.

129   There is an unexpected acknowledgement of this point in Sinn Féin's *The Good Old IRA* (1985), p. 7.

130   Speech at Carndonagh, Co. Donegal; *Irish Independent,* 13 December 1918.

131   'The North Began' is the title of a famous article by Eoin MacNeill in which he advocated the setting up of an Irish Volunteer Force in imitation of the UVF. See F.S.L. Lyons, *Ireland Since the Famine* (London, 1973), pp. 320–21.

132   *Irish Nationality,* 7 December 1918.

133   Liam Kennedy, 'Michael Collins', *Sunday Times,* 26 December 1999.

134   Bew, 'Moderate Nationalism', pp. 747–8.

135   Arthur Mitchell, *Revolutionary Government in Ireland, Dáil Éireann, 1919–22* (Dublin, 1995).

136   Bew, 'Moderate Nationalism' (1999), pp. 737, 743.

137   Quoted by Valiulis, *Portrait of a Revolutionary*, p. 39.

138   Personal diary, entry for 5 October, 2000.

139   F.S.L. Lyons, *Ireland Since the Famine* (1973), p. 15.

140   D.S. Johnson and Liam Kennedy, 'The Union of Ireland and Britain, 1800–1921', in George Boyce and Alan O'Day (eds), *The Making of Modern Irish History: Revisionism and the Revisionist Controversy* (London: Routledge 1996).

Bibliography

Manuscripts

Franciscan Account Books, Broad Lane, Cork (held at the Franciscan Library, Killiney, Co. Dublin).

Slattery Papers, National Library of Ireland, P 6004.

Parliamentary Debates and Papers

Parliamentary Debates, third series

Census of Ireland, 1901: Area, Houses, and Population (British Parliamentary Papers, 124, 1902).

Census of Ireland, 1911: Area, Houses, and Population (BPP, 115, 1912–13).

Commission on Emigration and Other Population Problems (Dublin, 1954).

Detailed Annual Report of the Registrar General for Saorstát Éireann (various years, Dublin).

Poor Inquiry (Ireland) (BPP, 30–35, 1836).

Report by the Committee on Irish Finance (BPP, 34, 1912–13).

Report on Recruiting in Ireland (BPP, 39, 1914–16).

Report Upon the Conditions of Work in Flax Mills and Linen Factories (BPP, 18, 1893–94).

Reports from the Assistant Handloom Weavers' Commissioners on the West Riding and Ireland (BPP, 23, 1840).

Saorstát Éireann, *Census of Population 1926: General Report* (Dublin, 1934).

Newspapers and Periodicals

An Phobhlacht

An tÓglach

Belfast News-Letter

Cork Constitution

Cork Examiner

Economist

Freeman's Journal

Guardian

Irish Catholic Directory (annual)

Irish Echo
Irish Independent
Irish Nationality
Irish Press
Irish Times
Nenagh News
New York Times
Northern Whig
Shamrock
Sunday Independent
Times
Tipperary Star
Ukrainian Weekly Section
Ulster Guardian
United Ireland
Washington Post
Weekly Northern Whig

Contemporary Works

A Solemn League and Covenant for Reformation and Defence of Religion, the Honour and Happiness of the King, and the Peace and Safety of the Three Kingdoms of England, Scotland and Ireland, 1643, as reproduced in S.R. Gardiner, *The Constitutional Documents of the Puritan Revolution, 1625–1660* (Oxford, reprint 1968).

Barry, Tom, *Guerrilla Days in Ireland* (Dublin, 1981).

Blackwood F.T. (Marquess of Dufferin and Ava), *Narrative of a Journey from Oxford to Skibbereen during the Year of the Irish Famine* (Oxford, 1847).

Breen, Dan, *My Fight for Irish Freedom* (revised and enlarged edition, Dublin, 1989).

Breen, Dan, *My Fight for Irish Freedom* (second edition, Dublin, 1924).

Butt, Isaac, *Land Tenure in Ireland, a Plea for the Celtic Race* (Dublin, 1866).

Carleton, William, *Traits and Stories of the Irish Peasantry* (two volumes, New York, 1862).

Connolly, James, *Labour in Irish History* (Dublin, 1973).

Crawford, F.H., *Guns for Ulster* (Belfast, 1947).

Cusack, M.F., *Speeches and Public Letters of the Liberator* (Dublin, 1875).

Davitt, Michael, *The Fall of Feudalism in Ireland: Or the Story of the Land League Revolution* (London, 1904).

Deasy, Liam, *Towards Ireland Free* (edited by John E. Chisholm, Dublin, 1973).

Dorian, Hugh, *Outer Edge of Ulster: A Memoir of Social Life in Nineteenth-Century Donegal* (edited by Breandán Mac Suibhne and David Dickson, Dublin, 2000).

Engels, Frederick, *The Condition of the Working Class in England in 1844* (London, 1950).

Giraldus Cambrensis, *The History and Topography of Ireland* (translated by J.J. O'Meara, Mountrath, Ireland, 1982).

Godley, A.D. (ed.), *The Poetical Works of Thomas Moore* (London, 1910).

Griffith, Arthur, *The Resurrection of Hungary* (Dublin, 1918).

Hitler, Adolf, *Mein Kampf* (translated by Ralph Manheim, London, 1969, reprint 2009).

Lavelle, Patrick, *The Irish Landlord since the Revolution* (Dublin, 1870).

Lemkin, Raphael, *Axis Rule in Occupied Europe* (Washington, 1944).

Lewis, Helen, *A Time to Speak* (Belfast, 1992).

MacNamara, Brinsley, *The Clanking of Chains* (Dublin, 1920).

MacNamara, Brinsley, *The Valley of the Squinting Windows* (New York, 1919).

Martin, R.M., *Ireland Before and After the Union* (London, 1843).

McDonnell, Kathleen Keyes, *There is a Bridge at Bandon: A Personal Account of the Irish War of Independence* (Cork, 1972).

McGee, Thomas D'Arcy, *A Popular History of Ireland from the Earliest Period to the Emancipation of the Catholics* (Glasgow, 1860).

Mitchel, John, *The Last Conquest of Ireland (Perhaps)* (London, n.d.).

Moran, D.P., *The Philosophy of Irish Ireland* (edited by Patrick Maume, Dublin, 2006).

Na Scríbhinní Liteartha le Pádraig Mac Piarais: Scríbhinní i nGaeilge (bailithe & curtha in eagar ag Séamas Ó Buachalla, Corcaigh, 1979).

Noakes, Jeremy and Geoffrey Pridham (eds), *Documents on Nazism, 1919–1945,* (London, 1974).

Novena Prayer Book (Down and Connor, 1975).

Ó Tuama Seán and Thomas Kinsella (eds), *An Duanaire, 1600–1900: Poems of the Dispossessed* (Dublin, 1990).

O'Brien, William, *Dingle: Its Pauperism and Proselytism. The Operation of Proselytism Exposed, and its Results Exhibited. In a Series of Letters* (Dublin, 1852).

O'Casey, Sean, *Three Dublin Plays: The Shadow of a Gunman; Juno and the Paycock; The Plough and the Stars* (London, 1998).

O'Donoghue, Florence, *No Other Law* (Dublin, 1954).

O'Hanlon, W.M., *Walks among the Poor of Belfast, and Suggestions for their Improvement* (Dublin, 1853).

O'Leary, John, *Recollections of Fenians and Fenianism* (London, 1896, 1. Introduction by Marcus Bourke, 1969).

O'Malley, Ernie, *On Another Man's Wound* (Dublin, 1979).

Pearse, P.H., *Collected Works of Pádraic H. Pearse: Political Writings and Speeches* (Dublin, 1918).

Phillips, W. Alison, *The Revolution in Ireland, 1906–1923* (London, 1923).

Plunkett, Horace, *Ireland in the New Century* (London, 1904).

Robert Emmet: The Insurrection of July 1803 (with commentary by Geraldine Hume and Anthony Malcomson, Belfast, 1996).

Ryan, Desmond, *Sean Treacy and the 3rd Tipperary Brigade* (Tralee, 1945).

Synge, J.M., *Four Plays and the Aran Islands* (edited with an introduction by Robin Skelton, Oxford, 1962).

'The Confession of Faith of the Kirk of Scotland, 1580', in Gardiner, *Constitutional Documents* (1968).

The Irish Journals of Elizabeth Smith, 1840–1850 (edited by David Thompson and Moyra McGusty, Oxford, 1980).

The Minutes of the Ulster Women's Unionist Council and Executive Committee, 1911–40 (edited by

Diane Urquhart, Dublin, 2001).

Trevelyan, Charles E., *The Irish Crisis* (London, 1848).

Tuke, James Hack, *A Visit to Connaught in the Autumn of 1847: A Letter Addressed to the Central Relief Committee of the Society of Friends, Dublin*. Second Edition: *With Notes of a Subsequent Visit to Erris* (York, 1848).

Veblen, Thorsten, *The Place of Science in Modern Civilization and Other Essays* (New York, 1919).

Wiggins, John, *The 'Monster' Misery of Ireland: A Practical Treatise on the Relation of Landlord and Tenant* (London, 1844).

Yeats, W.B., *The Collected Poems of W.B. Yeats* (London, 1952).

Later Works

Books

Abbott, Richard, *Police Casualties in Ireland, 1919–22* (Cork, 2000).

Adams, Gerry, *The Politics of Irish Freedom* (Dingle, 1986).

Adamson, Ian, *Cruithin: The Ancient Kindred* (Newtownards, 1974).

Adamson, Ian, David Hume and David McDowell, *Cuchulainn, The Lost Legend* (Belfast, 1995).

Akenson, D.H., *Education and Enmity: The Control of Schooling in Northern Ireland, 1920–1950* (Newton Abbott, 1973).

Akenson, D.H., *Small Differences: Irish Catholics and Irish Protestants, 1815–1922: An International Perspective* (Montreal, 1988).

Akenson, D.H., *The Irish Diaspora: A Primer* (Toronto, 1993).

Akenson, D.H., *Ireland, Sweden and the Great European Migration, 1815–1914* (Liverpool, 2011).

Anderson, Benedict, *Imagined Communities: Reflections on the Origin and Spread of Nationalism* (London, 2006).

Anderson, Michael, *Population Change in North-Western Europe, 1750–1850* (London, 1988).

Aston, Trevor (ed.), *Crisis in Europe, 1560–1600* (London, 1965).

Ballymacarrett Research Group, *Lagan Enclave: A History of Conflict in the Short Strand, 1886–1997* (Belfast, 1997).

Bardon, Jonathan, *A History of Ulster* (Belfast, 1992).

Bartlett, Thomas, *The Fall and Rise of the Irish Nation: The Catholic Question, 1690–1830* (Dublin, 1992).

Bartlett, Thomas and Keith Jeffery (eds), *A Military History of Ireland* (Cambridge, 1996).

Barton, Brian, *The Secret Court Martial Records of the Easter Rising* (Port Stroud, 2010).

Bergen, Doris, *War and Genocide: A Concise History of the Holocaust* (Plymouth, UK, 2009).

Bernstein, Iver, *The New York City Draft Riots: Their Significance for American Society and Politics in the Age of the Civil War* (New York, 1990).

Bew, John, *The Glory of Being Britons: Civic Unionism in Nineteenth-Century Belfast* (Dublin, 2009).

Bew, Paul, *Conflict and Conciliation in Ireland, 1890–1910: Parnellites and Radical Agrarians* (Oxford, 1987).

Bew, Paul, *Ireland: The Politics of Enmity, 1789–2006* (Oxford, 2007).

Bielenberg, Andy, *Cork's Industrial Revolution, 1780–1880* (Cork, 1991).

Boada Montagut, Irene, *Women Write Back: Contemporary Irish and Catalan Short Stories in Colonial Context* (Dublin, 2002).

Boff, Leonardo, *Cry of the Earth, Cry of the Poor* (New York, 1997).

Bourke, Joanna, *Husbandry to Housewifery: Women, Economic Change, and Housework in Ireland, 1890–1914* (Oxford, 1993).

Bowen, Elizabeth, *The Last September* (London, 1998).

Bowen, Kurt, *Protestants in a Catholic State: Ireland's Privileged Minority* (Dublin, 1983).

Bowman, Timothy, *Carson's Army: The Ulster Volunteer Force, 1910–22* (Manchester, 2007).

Boyce, D. George (ed.), *The Revolution in Ireland, 1879–1923* (Dublin, 1988).

Boyce, D. George, *Nationalism in Ireland* (London, 1982).

Boyce, D. George, *Nineteenth-Century Ireland: The Search for Stability* (Dublin, 1990).

Boyle, Francis A., *United Ireland, Human Rights and International Law* (Atlanta, 2012).

Brady, Ciaran (ed.), *Interpreting Irish History: The Debate on Historical Revisionism, 1938–1994* (Dublin, 1994).

Brewer, John and Gareth Higgins, *Anti-Catholicism in Northern Ireland, 1600–1998: The Mote and the Beam* (London, 1998).

Browning, Christopher R., *The Origins of the Final Solution: The Evolution of Nazi Jewish Policy, September 1939–March 1942* (Lincoln, Nebraska, 2004).

Browning, Christopher R., *The Path to Genocide: Essays on Launching the Final Solution* (Cambridge, 1992).

Buckland, Patrick, *Ulster Unionism and the Origins of Northern Ireland, 1886–1922* (volume 2 of *Irish Unionism,* Dublin, 1973).

Burrows, Edwin and Mike Wallace, *Gotham: A History of New York City to 1898* (Oxford, 1999).

Clark, Samuel, *Social Origins of the Land War* (Princeton, 1979).

Collins, Brenda and Philip Ollerenshaw (eds), *The European Linen Industry in Historical Perspective* (Oxford, 2003).

Comerford, R.V., *The Fenians in Context: Irish Politics and Society 1848–82* (Dublin, 1998).

Connell, K.H., *The Population History of Ireland, 1750–1845* (Oxford, 1950).

Connell, K.H., *Irish Peasant Society: Four Historical Essays* (Oxford, 1968).

Connolly, S.J., *Priests and People in Pre-Famine Ireland, 1780–1845* (Dublin, 1982).

Connolly, S.J., *Religion and Society in Nineteenth-Century Ireland* (Dundalk, 1985).

Connolly, S.J., *Religion, Law, and Power: The Making of Protestant Ireland, 1660–1760* (Oxford, 1992).

Connolly, S.J., *The Oxford Companion to Irish History* (Oxford, 1999).

Connolly, S.J., *Belfast 400: People, Place and History* (Liverpool, 2012).

Conversi, Daniele, *Ethnonationalism in the Contemporary World* (London, 2002).

Coogan, Tim Pat, *The Famine Plot: England's Role in Ireland's Greatest Tragedy* (New York, 2012).

Cosgrove, Art (ed.), *A New History of Ireland. II. Medieval Ireland 1169–1534* (Oxford, 1987).

Costello, Francis J., *Enduring the Most: The Life and Death of Terence MacSwiney* (Tralee, 1995).

Crosby, A.W., *Ecological Imperialism* (Cambridge, 1994).

Crowley, John, William J. Smyth and Mike Murphy (eds), *Atlas of the Great Irish Famine, 1845–52* (Cork, 2012).

Cullen, L.M., *An Economic History of Ireland since 1660* (London, 1972).

Daly, Mary E., *Dublin: The Deposed Capital: A Social and Economic History, 1860–1914* (Cork, 1984).

Daly, Mary E., *Industrial Development and Irish National Identity, 1922–1939* (Syracuse, 1992).

Daly, Mary E., *Women and Work in Ireland* (Dundalk, 1997).

Daly, Mary E. and Margaret O'Callaghan (eds), *1916 in 1966: Commemorating the Easter Rising* (Dublin, 2007).

David, Paul A., *Technical Choice, Innovation and Economic Growth: Essays on American and British Experience in the Nineteenth Century* (London, 1975).

Davies, Norman, *Europe: A History* (Oxford, 1996).

De Paor, Liam, *On the Easter Proclamation and Other Declarations* (Dublin, 1997).

Delaney, Enda, *The Curse of Reason: The Great Irish Famine* (Dublin, 2012).

Dickson, David, *Artic Ireland* (Belfast, 1997).

Dickson, R.J., *Ulster Emigration to Colonial America, 1718–1775* (London, 1966).

Doerries, Reinhard, *Prelude to the Easter Rising: Sir Roger Casement in Imperial Germany* (London, 2000).

Donnelly, J.S. Jr., *The Land and the People of Nineteenth-Century Cork: The Rural Economy and the Land Question* (London, 1975).

Donnelly, J.S. Jr., *The Great Irish Potato Famine* (London, 2001).

Donnelly, J.S. Jr., *Captain Rock: The Irish Agrarian Rebellion of 1821–1824* (Madison, 2009).

Donovan, Donal and Antoin Murphy, *The Fall of the Celtic Tiger: Ireland and the Euro Debt Crisis* (Oxford, 2013).

Dooley, T.P., *Irishmen or English Soldiers?* (Liverpool, 1995).

Dudgeon, Jeffrey, *Roger Casement: The Black Diaries: With a Study of his Background, Sexuality, and Irish Political Life* (Belfast, 2002).

Edwards, R. Dudley and T. Desmond Williams (eds), *The Great Famine: Studies in Irish History 1845–52* (Dublin, 1956).

Edwards, Ruth Dudley, *Patrick Pearse: Triumph of Failure* (London, 1977).

Edwards, Ruth Dudley, *The Pursuit of Reason: The Economist, 1843–1993* (London, 1993).

Elliott, Marianne, *The Catholics of Ulster: A History* (London, 2000).

Elliott, Marianne, *Wolfe Tone* (Liverpool, 2012).

Enciclopedia Italiana (Rome, 1948).

English, Richard, *Irish Freedom: The History of Nationalism in Ireland* (London, 2006).

Eurostat, *Statistiques Demographiques* (Luxembourg, 1994).

Fanning, Ronan, *The Irish Department of Finance, 1922–58* (Dublin, 1978).

Fanning, Ronan, *Fatal Path: British Government and Irish Revolution, 1910–1922* (London, 2013).

Ferro, Marc, *The Great War, 1914–18* (New York, 1973).

Finkelstein, Norman G., *The Holocaust Industry: Reflections on the Exploitation of Jewish Suffering* (London, 2003).

Fitzpatrick, David, *Irish Emigration 1801–1921* (Dublin, 1990).

Fitzpatrick, David, *Politics and Irish Life 1913–1921: Provincial Experiences of War and Revolution* (Cork, 1998).

Flora, Peter, *et al.*, *State, Economy, and Society in Western Europe, 1815–1975* (London, 1983).

Floud, Roderick and D. N. McCloskey (eds), *The Economic History of Britain since 1700, 1, 1700–1860* (London, 1994).

Foster, John Wilson, *Irish Novels, 1890–1940: New Bearings in Culture and Fiction* (Oxford, 2008).

Foster, John Wilson, *Between Shadows: Modern Irish Writing and Culture* (Dublin, 2009).

Foster, R.F., *Modern Ireland, 1600–1972* (London, 1989).

Foster, R.F., *Luck and the Irish* (London, 2007).

Gallagher, Thomas, *Paddy's Lament: Ireland 1846–1847: Prelude to Hatred* (Dublin, 1985).

Gaughan, J. Anthony, *Austin Stack: Portrait of a Separatist* (Dublin, 1977).

Gellner, Ernest, *Nations and Nationalism* (Oxford, 1983).

Gilbert, Martin, *The Holocaust: The Jewish Tragedy* (London, 1987).

Goldhagen, Daniel, *Hitler's Willing Executioners: Ordinary Germans and the Holocaust* (London, 1996).

Grace, Daniel, *The Great Famine in Nenagh Poor Law Union, Co. Tipperary* (Nenagh, Co. Tipperary, 2000).

Graham, B.J. and L.J. Proudfoot (eds), *An Historical Geography of Ireland* (London, 1993).

Gray, Peter, *Famine, Land and Politics: British Government and Irish Society, 1843–1850* (Dublin, 1998).

Green, E.R.R., *The Lagan Valley: A Local History of the Industrial Revolution* (London, 1949).

Grell, O.P., J.I. Israel and Nicholas Tyacke (eds), *From Persecution to Toleration: The Glorious Revolution and Religion in England* (Oxford, 1991).

Gribbon, Sybil, *Edwardian Belfast: A Social Profile* (Belfast, 1982).

Griffith, Kenneth and Timothy O'Grady, *Curious Journeys: An Oral History of Ireland's Unfinished Revolution* (London, 1982).

Guinnane, Timothy, *The Vanishing Irish: Households, Migration, and the Rural Economy in Ireland, 1850–1914* (Princeton, 1997).

Haines, Robin, *Charles Trevelyan and the Great Irish Famine* (Dublin, 2003).

Hales, E.E., *The Catholic Church in the Modern World: A Survey from the French Revolution to the Present* (London, 1958).

Hammond, Bill, *Soldier of the Rearguard: The Story of Matt Flood and the Active Service Column* (Fermoy, 1977).

Hart, Peter, *The IRA and Its Enemies: Violence and Community in Cork 1916–1923* (Oxford, 1998).

Haugen, Einar, J.D. McClure and Derick Thomson (eds), *Minority Languages Today* (Edinburgh, 1990).

Hayes McCoy, G.A. (ed.), *The Irish at War* (Cork, 1969).

Hechter, Michael, *Internal Colonialism: The Celtic Fringe in British National Development, 1536–1966* (London, 1975).

Hepburn, A.C., *A Past Apart: Studies in the History of Catholic Belfast, 1850–1950* (1996).

Hicks, John, *A Theory of Economic History* (Oxford, 1969).

Hilberg, Raul, *The Destruction of the European Jews* (Chicago, 1961).

Hindley, Reg, *The Death of the Irish Language: A Qualified Obituary* (London, 1990).

Hobsbawm, Eric and Terence Ranger (eds), *The Invention of Tradition* (Cambridge, 1983).

Hopkinson, Michael, *Green against Green: The Irish Civil War* (Dublin, 1988).

Hoppen K.T., *Ireland since 1800: Conflict and Conformity* (Dublin, 1989).

Horne, John and Alan Kramer, *German Atrocities, 1914: A History of Denial* (Yale, 2001).

Hroch, Miroslav, *Social Preconditions of National Revival in Europe: A Comparative Analysis of the Social Composition of Patriotic Groups among the Smaller European Nations* (translated by Ben Fowkes, Cambridge, 1985).

Huggett, F.E., *The Land Question and European Society* (London, 1975).

Hutchings, Raymond, *Soviet Economic Development* (Oxford, 1971).

Irish Communist Organisation, *The Economics of Partition* (Belfast, 1969).

Israel, J.I., *The Dutch Republic: Its Rise, Greatness, and Fall 1477–1806* (Oxford, 1995).

Jackson, T.H., *The Whole Matter; The Poetic Evolution of Thomas Kinsella* (Dublin, 1995).

Jacobsen, Hans-Adolf and A.L. Smith (eds), *World War II: Policy and Strategy* (Santa Barbara, 1979).

Johnson, David, *The Interwar Economy in Ireland* (Dundalk, 1985).

Kamen, Henry, *The Rise of Toleration* (London, 1967).

Kedourie, Elie, *Nationalism* (4th expanded edition, Oxford, 1994).

Kee, Robert, *Ireland: A History* (London, 1980).

Kee, Robert, *The Most Distressful Country* (London, 1989).

Kelly, M.J., *The Fenian Ideal and Irish Nationalism, 1882–1916* (Woodbridge, 2006).

Kennedy K.A., Thomas Giblin and Deirdre McHugh, *The Economic Development of Ireland in the Twentieth Century* (London, 1988).

Kennedy, Dennis, *The Widening Gulf: Northern Attitudes to the Independent Irish State, 1919–49* (Belfast, 1988).

Kennedy, Liam, *The Modern Industrialisation of Ireland, 1940–88* (Dundalk, 1989).

Kennedy, Liam, *Colonialism, Religion and Nationalism in Ireland* (Belfast, 1996).

Kennedy, Liam and Philip Ollerenshaw (eds), *An Economic History of Ulster, 1820–1939* (Manchester, 1985).

Kennedy, Liam and Philip Ollerenshaw (eds), *Ulster Since 1600: Politics, Economy and Society* (Oxford, 2013).

Kennedy, Liam and Peter Solar *Irish Agriculture: A Price History, from the Mid-Eighteenth Century to the Eve of the First World War* (Dublin, 2007).

Kennedy, Liam, *et al.*, *Mapping the Great Irish Famine: A Survey of the Famine Decades* (Dublin, 1999).

Kennedy, R.E., *The Irish: Emigration, Marriage and Fertility* (Berkeley, 1973).

Kerr, Dónal, *The Catholic Church and the Famine* (Dublin, 1996).

Kinealy, Christine and Gerard MacAtasney, *The Hidden Famine: Poverty, Hunger, and Sectarianism in Belfast 1840–50* (London, 2000).

Kinealy, Christine, *The Great Irish Famine: Impact, Ideology and Rebellion* (London, 2002).

Kossman, E.H., *The Low Countries, 1780–1940* (Oxford, 1978).

Laffan, Michael, *The Resurrection of Ireland: The Sinn Féin Party, 1916–1923* (Cambridge, 1999).

Lang, D.M., *The Armenians: A People in Exile* (London, 1981).

Larkin, Emmet, *The Historical Dimensions of Irish Catholicism* (New York, 1976).

Lawson, Tom, *Debates on the Holocaust* (Manchester, 2010).

Lee, Joseph, *Ireland: 1912–1985* (Cambridge, 1989).

Lee, Joseph, *The Modernisation of Irish Society, 1848–1918* (Dublin, 1972).

Lemkin, Raphael, *Totally Unofficial: The Autobiography of Raphael Lemkin* (Yale, New Haven, 2013).

Lengel, Edward, *The Irish Through British Eyes: Perceptions of Ireland in the Famine Era* (Westport, CT, USA, 2002).

Levi, Carlo, *Christ Stopped at Eboli* (London, 1984).

Levi, Primo, *The Drowned and the Saved* (New York, 1989).

Levi, Primo, *If This Is a Man; and the Truce* (London, 1987).

Longley, Edna, *From Cathleen to Anorexia: The Breakdown of Irelands* (Dublin, 1990).

Lucy, Gordon, *The Ulster Covenant: An Illustrated History of the 1912 Home Rule Crisis* (Newtownards, 1989).

Lynch, John, *An Unlikely Success Story: The Belfast Shipbuilding Industry 1880–1935* (Belfast, 2001).

Lyons, F.S.L., *Ireland Since the Famine* (London, 1973).

MacConghail, Muiris, *The Blaskets: People and Literature* (Dublin, 1994).

Mark-Fitzgerald, Emily, *Commemorating the Irish Famine: Memory and the Monument* (Liverpool, 2013).

Matthews, Alan, *EC Trade Policy and the Third World: An Irish Perspective* (Dublin, 1991).

Mayersen, Deborah, *On the Path to Genocide: Armenia and Rwanda Reexamined* (New York, 2014).

Maume, Patrick, *D.P. Moran* (Dublin: Historical Association of Ireland 1995).

Maume, Patrick, *The Long Gestation, Irish Nationalist Life 1891–1918* (Dublin, 1999).

Mawdsley, Evan, *The Russian Civil War* (London, 1987).

McGarry John and Brendan O'Leary, *The Future of Northern Ireland* (Oxford, 1990).

McGarry, Fearghal, *The Rising: Ireland: Easter 1916* (Oxford, 2010).

McGimpsey, Chris, *Bombs on Belfast* (Belfast, 1983).

McGuinness, Frank, *Observe the Sons of Ulster Marching towards the Somme* (London, 1986).

McGuire, James and James Quinn (eds), *Dictionary of Irish Biography, from the earliest times to the year 2002* (Cambridge, 2009).

McInerney, Michael, *Peadar O'Donnell: Irish Social Rebel* (Dublin, 1974).

McKittrick, David, Seamus Kelters, Brian Feeney and Chris Thornton, *Lost Lives: The Stories of the Men, Women and Children who Died as a result of the Northern Ireland Troubles* (Edinburgh, 2007).

McLuhan, Marshall, *Understanding Media: The Extensions of Man* (New York, 1966).

McPherson, James, *Battle Cry of Freedom: The American Civil War* (London, 1990).

Miller, D.W., *Queen's Rebels: Ulster Loyalism in Historical Perspective* (Dublin, 1978).

Miller, K.A., *Emigrants and Exiles: Ireland and the Irish Exodus to North America* (Oxford, 1985).

Miller K.A. and Paul Wagner, *Out of Ireland: The Story of Irish Emigration* (New York, 1994).

Miller K.A., Arnold Schrier, Bruce Bolling and David Doyle, *Irish Immigrants in the Land of Canaan: Letters and Memoirs from Colonial America, 1675–1815* (Oxford, 2003).

Mitchell, Arthur, *Revolutionary Government in Ireland, Dáil Éireann, 1919–22* (Dublin,1995).

Mitchell, B.R., *European Historical Statistics, 1750–1970* (London, 1988).

Mokyr, Joel, *Why Ireland Starved: A Quantitative and Analytical History of the Irish Economy, 1800–1850* (London, 1983).

Moody, T.W., *Davitt and the Irish Revolution, 1846–82* (Oxford, 1981).

Moody, T.W., F.X. Martin and F.J. Byrne (eds), *A New History of Ireland. III. Early Modern Ireland 1534–1691* (Oxford, 1978).

Myrdal, Gunnar, *Asian Drama: An Inquiry into the Poverty of Nations* (New York, 1968).

Nicholls, Kenneth, *Gaelic and Gaelicised Ireland in the Middle Ages* (Dublin, 1972).

Noack, Christian, Lindsay Janssen and Vincent Comerford (eds), *Holodomor and Gorta Mór* (London, 2012).

Nolan, K.B. and T.D. Williams (eds), *Ireland in the War Years and After, 1939–51* (Dublin, 1969).

Norman, Diana, *Terrible Beauty: A Life of Constance Markievicz, 1868–1927* (London, 1988).

Nove, Alec, *An Economic History of the USSR* (London, 1978).

O'Brien, Edna, *Mother Ireland* (London, 1976).

O'Brien, Edna, *A Fanatic Heart: Selected Stories* (New York, 1984).

O'Brien, Flann, *The Poor Mouth (An Béal Bocht), A Bad Story about the Hard Life* (London, 1993).

O'Connor, Emmet, *A Labour History of Ireland, 1824–1960* (Dublin, 1992).

O'Connor, Ulick, *The Troubles* (London, 1996).

Ó Cuiv, Brian (ed.), *A View of the Irish Language* (Dublin, 1969).

O'Farrell, Padraic, *Who's Who in the Irish War of Independence and Civil War, 1916–1923* (Dublin, 1997).

O'Ferrall, Fergus, *Daniel O'Connell* (Dublin, 1998).

Ó Gráda, Cormac, *Ireland Before and After the Great Famine: Explorations in Economic History 1800–1925* (Manchester, 1993).

Ó Gráda, Cormac, *Ireland: A New Economic History 1780–1939* (Oxford, 1994).

Ó Gráda, Cormac, *A Rocky Road: The Irish Economy since the 1920s* (Manchester, 1997).

Ó Gráda, Cormac, *Black '47 and Beyond: The Great Irish Famine in History, Economy, and Memory* (Princeton, 1999).

Ó Gráda, Cormac, *Ireland's Great Famine: Interdisciplinary Perspectives* (Dublin, 2006).

Ó Gráda, Cormac, *Famine: A Short History* (Princeton, 2009).

O'Hara, Phillip A. (ed.), *Encyclopaedia of Political Economy* (London, 1999).

O'Leary, Don, *Irish Catholicism and Science: From 'Godless Colleges' to the 'Celtic Tiger'* (Cork, 2012).

Ó Tuathaigh, Gearóid, *Ireland before the Famine, 1798–1848* (Dublin, 2007).

Ofer, Dalia and Lenore Weitzman (eds), *Women in the Holocaust* (New Haven, 1998).

Parker, Geoffrey and Lesley Smith, *The General Crisis of the Seventeenth Century* (London, 1978).

Parker, Stewart, *Northern Star, Heavenly Bodies, Pentecost: Three Plays for Ireland* (Birmingham, 1989).

Parkinson Alan F., *Friends in High Places: Ulster's Resistance to Home Rule, 1912–14* (Belfast, 2012).

Patterson, Henry, *Class Conflict and Sectarianism* (Belfast, 1980).

Peacock, H.L., *A History of Modern Europe, 1789–1939* (London, 1961).

Pearse, Mary Brigid (ed.), *The Home Life of Pádraig Pearse* (Cork, 1979).

Phoenix, Eamon, *Northern Nationalism: Nationalist Politics, Partition and the Catholic Minority in Northern Ireland, 1890–1940* (Belfast, 1994).

Porter-Szucs, Brian, *Poland in the Modern World: Beyond Martyrdom* (Chichester, 2014).

Power, Samantha, *'A Problem from Hell': America and the Age of Genocide* (London, 2003).

Preston, Paul, *The Spanish Holocaust: Inquisition and Extermination in Twentieth-Century Spain* (London, 2011).

Prunier, Gérard, *The Rwanda Crisis: History of a Genocide* (London, 1997).

Purdue, Olwen (ed.), *Belfast: The Emerging City, 1850–1914* (Dublin, 2013).

Ramm, Agatha, *Europe in the Twentieth Century, 1905–1970* (London, 1984).

Read, Jan, *The Catalans* (London, 1978).

Robinson, Philip, *The Plantation of Ulster: British Settlement in an Irish Landscape, 1600–1670* (Dublin, 1984).

Roddy, Sarah, *Population, Providence, and Empire: The Churches and Emigration from Nineteenth-Century Ireland* (Manchester, 2014).

Rosenbaum, Alan S. (ed.), *Is the Holocaust Unique? Perspectives on Comparative Genocide* (Colorado, 1996).

Rosenfeld, Alvin, *The End of the Holocaust* (Bloomington, 2011).

Rowthorn, Bob and Naomi Wayne, *Northern Ireland: The Political Economy of Conflict* (London, 1988).

Ruane, Joseph and Jennifer Todd, *The Dynamics of Conflict in Northern Ireland: Power, Conflict and Emancipation* (Cambridge, 1996).

Scally, Robert J., *The End of Hidden Ireland: Rebellion, Famine, and Emigration* (Oxford, 1995).

Scholes, Andrew, *The Church of Ireland and the Third Home Rule Bill* (Dublin, 2010).

Shee, William, *The Irish Church, its History and Statistics* (London, 1863).

Shukman, Harold, *The Blackwell Encyclopaedia of the Russian Revolution* (London, 1988).

Sinn Féin Publicity Department, *The Good Old IRA: Tan War Operations* (Dublin, Sinn Féin 1985).

Sisson, Elaine, *Pearse's Patriots: St Enda's and the Cult of Boyhood* (Cork, 2005).

Smith, A.D., *Ethno-Symbolism and Nationalism: A Cultural Approach* (London, 2009).

Smith, H.L. (ed.), *War and Social Change: British Society in the Second World War* (Manchester, 1986).

Solow, Barbara, *The Land Question and the Irish Economy, 1870–1903* (Cambridge, Mass. 1971).

Sontag, Susan, *Regarding the Pain of Others* (London, 2003).

Stephens, Meic, *Linguistic Minorities in Western Europe* (Llandysul, Wales, 1976).

Stewart, A.T.Q., *The Narrow Ground: The Roots of Conflict in Ulster* (London, 1977).

Taylor, A.J.P., *The First World War* (London, 1972).

Thomas, Hugh, *The Spanish Civil War* (first ed., New York, 1961; and second ed., 1990).

Thompson, Dorothy, *The Chartists* (Hounslow, 1984).

Tóibín, Colm, *The Irish Famine* (London, 1999).

Townshend, Charles, *Easter 1916: The Irish Rebellion* (London, 2005).

Ulster Scots Community Network, *Understanding the Ulster Covenant* (Belfast, no date, probably 2011 or 2012).

Urquhart, Diane, *Women in Ulster Politics, 1890–1940* (Dublin, 2000).

Urquhart, Diane, *The Ladies of Londonderry: Women and Political Patronage* (London, 2007).

Valent, Paul, *Child Survivors of the Holocaust* (New York, 2002).

Valiulis, Maryann Gialanella, *Portrait of a Revolutionary: General Richard Mulcahy and the Founding of the Irish Free State* (Dublin, 1992).

Vaughan, W.E. and A.J. Fitzpatrick, *Irish Historical Statistics: Population 1821–1971* (Dublin, 1978).

Vaughan, W.E., *Landlords and Tenants in Mid-Victorian Ireland* (Oxford, 1994).

Walker, B.M., *A Political History of the Two Irelands: From Partition to Peace* (Basingstoke, 2012).

Walker, Christopher A., *Armenia: The Survival of a Nation* (London, 1990).

Ward, Margaret, *Unmanageable Revolutionaries: Women and Irish Nationalism* (London, 1983).

Weber, Eugen, *Peasants into Frenchmen: The Modernisation of Rural France, 1870–1914* (London, 1979).

Whelan, Irene, *The Bible War in Ireland: The 'Second Reformation' and the Polarization of Protestant–Catholic Relations, 1800–40* (Madison, 2005).

Whelehan, Niall, *The Dynamiters: Irish Nationalism and Political Violence in the Wider World, 1867–1900* (Cambridge, 2012).

Whittam, John, *Fascist Italy* (Manchester, 1995).

Whyte, John, *Church and State in Modern Ireland, 1923–1970* (Dublin, 1980).

Whyte, John, *Interpreting Northern Ireland* (Oxford, 1991).

Wilson, David A., *Thomas D'Arcy McGee. 1. Passion, Reason and Politics, 1825–1857*, (Montreal and Kingston, 2008).

Wilson, David A., *United Irishmen, United States: Immigrant Radicals in the Early Republic* (Dublin, 1998).

Winch, Donald, *Malthus* (Oxford, 1987).

Wright, Patrick, *On Living in an Old Country: The National Past in Contemporary Britain* (London, 1985).

Later Works

Articles and Essays

Akenson, D.H., 'A Midrash on "Galut", "Exile" and "Diaspora" Rhetoric', in E.M. Crawford (ed.), *The Hungry Stream: Essays on Emigration and Famine* (Belfast, 1997), pp. 5–15.

Allen, Robert C., 'The High Wage Economy and the Industrial Revolution: A Restatement', *Economic History Review*, 68 (2015), pp. 1–22.

Archdeacon, Thomas J., 'The Irish Famine in American School Curricula', *Éire-Ireland* (2002), pp. 139–44.

Bew, Paul, 'Moderate Nationalism and the Irish Revolution, 1916–1923', *Historical Journal, 92* (1999), pp. 729–49.

Bliss, Alan, 'The English Language in Early Modern Ireland', in T.W. Moody, F.X. Martin and F.J. Byrne (eds), *A New History of Ireland. III. Early Modern Ireland, 1534–1691* (Oxford, 1978), pp. 546–60.

Bock, Gisela, 'Ordinary Women in Nazi Germany: Perpetrators, Victims, Followers and Bystanders', in Dalia Ofer and Lenore Weitzman (eds), *Women in the Holocaust* (New Haven, 1998), pp. 85–100.

Bourke, P.M.A., 'The Irish Grain Trade, 1839–48', *Irish Historical Studies*, 20 (1976), pp. 156–67.

Bowler, Peter, 'Race Theory and the Irish', in Seán Ó Síocháin (ed.), *Social Thought on Ireland in the Nineteenth Century* (Dublin, 2009), pp. 135–46.

Bradshaw, Brendan, 'Nationalism and Historical Scholarship in Modern Ireland', *Irish Historical Studies*, 26 (1989), pp. 329–51.

Brownlow, Graham, 'The Political Economy of the Ulster Crisis: Historiography, Social Capability and Globalisation', in D. George Boyce and Alan O' Day (eds), *The Ulster Crisis, 1885–1922* (London, 2005), pp. 27–46.

Burke, M.J., 'The Politics and Poetics of Nationalist Historiography: Matthew Carey and the *Vindiciae Hibernicae'*, in Joep Leerssen (ed.), *Forging in the Smithy* (Amsterdam, 1995), pp. 190–94.

Cantore, Nicole, Jane Kennan, Sheila Page, *CAP Reform and Development* (London, 2011).

Collins, Brenda, 'Proto-Industrialisation and Pre-Famine Migration', *Social History*, 7 (1982), pp. 127–46.

Cullen, L.M. and T.C. Smout, 'Economic Growth in Scotland and Ireland', in L.M. Cullen and T.C. Smout (eds), *Comparative Aspects of Scottish and Irish Economic and Social History, 1600–1900* (Edinburgh, 1977), pp. 3–18.

Cullen, L.M., 'The Irish Economy in the Eighteenth Century', in L.M. Cullen (ed.), *The Formation of the Irish Economy* (Cork, 1972), pp. 9–21.

Cullen, L.M., T.C. Smout and Alex Gibson, 'Wages and Comparative Development in Ireland and Scotland, 1565–1780', in Rosalind Mitchison and Peter Roebuck (eds), *Economy and Society in Scotland and Ireland, 1500–1939* (Edinburgh, 1988), pp. 105–16.

Director, Aaron, 'The Parity of the Economic Market Place', *Journal of Law and Economics*, 7 (1964), pp. 1–10.

Donnelly, J.S. Jr., 'Irish Agrarian Rebellion: The Whiteboys of 1769–76', *Proceedings of the Royal Irish Academy*, 83, C (1983), pp. 293–331.

Donnelly, J.S. Jr., 'Pastorini and Captain Rock: Millenarianism and Sectarianism in the Rockite Movement of 1821–4', in Samuel Clark and J.S. Donnelly Jr. (eds), *Irish Peasants: Violence and Political Unrest, 1780–1914* (Madison, 1983), pp.134–5.

Donnelly, J.S. Jr., 'Mass Eviction and the Great Famine', in Cathal Póirtéir (ed.), *The Great Irish Famine* (Cork, 1995), pp. 155 73.

Donnelly, J.S. Jr., 'The Construction of the Memory of the Famine in Ireland and the Irish Diaspora, 1850–1900', *Éire-Ireland*, 31 (1996), pp. 26–61.

Feinstein, Charles H., 'Pessimism Perpetuated: Real Wages and the Standard of Living in Britain during and after the Industrial Revolution', *Journal of Economic History*, 58 (September, 1998), pp. 625–58.

FitzGerald, Garret, 'Estimates for Baronies of Minimum Level of Irish-Speaking among Successive Decennial Cohorts: 1771–1781 to 1861–1871', *Proceedings of the Royal Irish Academy,* 84, C, 3, pp. 117–55.

Fitzpatrick, David, 'Militarism in Ireland, 1900–1922', in Thomas Bartlett and Keith Jeffery (eds), *A Military History of Ireland* (Cambridge, 1996), pp. 379–406.

Fleischmann, Ruth, '"The Blood Our Fathers Spilt": Rhetoric and Poetry', in T.A. Westendorp and Jane Mallinson (eds), *Politics and the Rhetoric of Poetry* (Amsterdam, 1995), pp. 65–75.

Foster John, Wilson, 'Yeats and the Easter Rising', *Canadian Journal of Irish Studies*, 11 (June, 1985), pp. 21–34.

Froggatt, Peter, 'The Response of the Medical Profession to the Famine', in E.M. Crawford (ed.), *Famine: The Irish Experience* (Edinburgh, 1989), pp. 134–56.

Geary, Frank, 'The Act of Union, British-Irish Trade, and Pre-Famine Deindustrialisation', *Economic History Review,* 48 (1995), pp. 68–88.

Goldstrom, J.M., 'The Industrialisation of the North East', in L.M. Cullen (ed.), *The Formation of the Irish Economy* (1972), pp. 101–112.

Gray, Peter, 'Memory and the Commemoration of the Great Irish Famine', in Peter Gray and Kendrick Oliver (eds), *The Memory of Catastrophe* (Manchester, 2004), pp. 46–64.

Guinnane, T.W. and Cormac Ó Gráda, 'Mortality in the North Dublin Union during the Great Famine', *Economic History Review*, 55, 3 (2002), pp. 487–506.

Hart, Peter, 'The Geography of Revolution in Ireland, 1917–1923', *Past and Present,* 155, (May 1997), pp. 142–76.

Hart, Peter, 'The Protestant Experience of Revolution in Southern Ireland', in Richard English and Graham Walker (eds), *Unionism in Modern Ireland: New Perspectives on Politics and Culture* (Dublin, 1996), pp. 81–98.

Holmes, Andrew, 'Covenanter Politics: Evangelicalism, Political Liberalism and Ulster Presbyterianism, 1798–1914', *English Historical Review*, 125, 513 (2010), pp. 340–69.

Ignatieff, Michael, 'The Unsung Hero Who Coined the Term "Genocide"', *New Republic*, 21 September 2013.

Jackson, Alvin, 'Unionist Myths, 1912–1985', *Past and Present*, 136 (1992), pp. 164–85.

Jackson, Jim, 'Famine Diary: The Making of a Best Seller', *Irish Review*, 11 (1991–2), pp. 1–8.

Johnson, David S. and Liam Kennedy, 'National Income in Ireland on the Eve of the Great Famine', paper read to the Historical National Accounts Group for Ireland, Dublin, January 1995.

Johnson, David S., 'The Belfast Boycott, 1920–22', in J.M. Goldstrom and L.A. Clarkson (eds), *Irish Population, Economy and Society* (Oxford, 1981), pp. 287–307.

Johnson, David. S. and Liam Kennedy, 'The Two Economies in Ireland in the Twentieth Century', in J.R. Hill (ed.), *A New History of Ireland. VII. Ireland 1921–1984* (Oxford, 2003), pp. 452–86.

Johnson, David. S. and Liam Kennedy, 'The Union of Ireland and Britain, 1801–1921', in George Boyce and Alan O' Day (eds), *The Making of Modern Irish History: Revisionism and the Revisionist Controversy* (London, 1996), pp. 34–70.

Kennedy, Liam, 'The Roman Catholic Church and Economic Growth in Nineteenth-Century Ireland', *Economic and Social Review*, 10 (1978), pp. 45–59.

Kennedy, Liam, 'Farmers, Traders and Agricultural Politics in Pre-Independence Ireland', in S. Clark and J.S. Donnelly Jr. (eds), *Irish Peasants: Violence and Political Unrest, 1780–1914* (Madison, Wisconsin, 1983).

Kennedy, Liam, 'The Economic Thought of the Nation's Lost Leader: Charles Stewart Parnell', in George Boyce and Alan O' Day (eds), *Parnell in Perspective* (London, 1991), pp. 171–200.

Kennedy, Liam, 'Was there an Irish War of Independence?', in Bruce Stewart (ed.), *Hearts and Minds: Irish Culture and Society under the Act of Union* (Gerrard's Cross, Buckinghamshire, 2002), pp. 188–229.

Kennedy, Liam, 'The Cost of Living in Ireland, 1698–1998', in David Dickson and Cormac Ó Gráda (eds), *Refiguring Ireland* (Dublin, 2003), pp. 249–76.

Kennedy, Liam and Martin Dowling, 'Prices and Wages in Ireland, 1700–1850', *Irish Economic and Social History*, 24 (1997), pp. 62–104.

Kennedy, Liam, K.A. Miller and Brian Gurrin, 'Minorities, Majorities and Demographic Power: The Protestant and Catholic Communities of Tipperary since 1660', in Sean Farrell and Michael de Nie (eds), *Power and Popular Culture in Modern Ireland: Essays in Honour of James S. Donnelly, Jr.* (Dublin, 2010) pp. 67–92.

Kennedy, Liam, K.A.Miller and Brian Gurrin, 'The Protestant Population of Ireland since the Seventeenth Century: Numbers, Proportions and Conjectures', in Joseph Ruane and Patrick Cabanel (eds), *Religion et Violence: Protestants et Catholiques en France et en Irelande, 16ᵉ-21ᵉ siècle* (Université de Rennes, Rennes, forthcoming (perhaps)).

Kennedy, Liam, K.A. Miller, Brian Gurrin and Gareth Davies, 'The Planter and the Gael: Explorations in Irish Ethnic History', in Karin White and Julie Costello (eds), *The Imaginary of the Stranger: Encountering the Other* (Letterkenny, 2012), pp. 13–26.

Kennedy, Liam, Lucia Pozzi and Matteo Manfredini, 'Marriage, Fertility, Social Class and Religion in an Irish Industrial City: Belfast 1911', *Popolazione e Storia*, 11,2 (2010), pp. 83–110.

Knightly, Joseph, 'The Godfrey Estate during the Great Famine', *Kerry Archaeological and Historical Society*, 3 (2nd series, 2003), pp. 125–33.

Leonard, Jane, '"Getting Them at Last": The IRA and Ex-Servicemen', in David Fitzpatrick (ed.), *Revolution?* (1990), pp. 118–29.

Mac Suibhne, Breandán, 'A Jig in the Poorhouse', *Dublin Review of Books*, 31 (April 2013).

MacRaild, Donald, 'Irish Immigration and the "Condition of England" Question: The Roots of an Historiographical Tradition', *Immigrants and Minorities*, 14 (1995), pp. 67–85.

MacRaild, Donald, '"No Irish Need Apply": The Origins and Persistence of a Prejudice', *Labour History Review*, 78, 3 (2013), pp. 269–99.

Maher, Jim, 'Dan Breen looks back 50 years from 1967', *Tipperary Historical Journal* (1998), pp. 105–111.

Meaney, Gerardine, 'Sex and Nation: Women in Irish Culture and Politics', in Ailbhe Smyth (ed.), *Irish Women's Studies Reader* (Dublin, 1993), pp. 230–44.

Mullin, James V., 'The New Jersey Famine Curriculum: A Report', *Éire-Ireland* (2002), pp. 127–8.

Murphy, Maureen and Alan Singer, 'New York State's Great Irish Famine Curriculum: A Report', *Éire-Ireland*, (2002), pp. 108–118.

Myrdal, Gunnar, 'Institutional Economics', *Journal of Economic Issues*, 12 (December 1978), pp. 771–83.

Nadal, Jordi, 'Spain 1830–1914', in Carlo Cipolla (ed.), *The Fontana Economic History of Europe* (London, 1973), pp. 553–68.

North, D.C. and P.R. Thomas, 'The Rise and Fall of the Manorial System: A Theoretical Model', *Journal of Economic History*, 31, 4 (1971), pp. 777–803.

Ó Cuiv, Brian, 'Irish Language and Literature', in T.W. Moody and W.E. Vaughan (eds), *A New History of Ireland. IV. Eighteenth-Century Ireland, 1691–1800* (Oxford, 1986), pp. 374–423.

Ó Gráda, Cormac, 'The Great Famine and Other Famines', in Ó Gráda (ed.), *Famine 150* (Dublin, 1997), pp. 129–31.

O'Rourke, Kevin, 'Emigration and Living Standards in Ireland since the Famine', *Journal of Population Economics*, 8 (1995), pp. 407–21.

Ó Tuathaigh, M.A.G., 'The Land Question: Politics and Irish Society, 1922–1960', in P.J. Drudy (ed.), *Ireland: Land, Politics and People* (Cambridge, 1982), pp. 167–89.

Ollerenshaw, Philip, 'Industry', in Liam Kennedy and Philip Ollerenshaw (eds), *An Economic History of Ulster, 1820–1938* (Manchester, 1985), pp. 62–108.

Patterson, Henry, 'The Decline of the Collaborators: The Ulster Unionist Labour Association and Post-War Unionist Politics', in Francis Devine, Fintan Lane and Niamh Puirséil (eds), *Essays in Irish Labour History: A Festschrift for Elizabeth and John W. Boyle* (Dublin, 2008), pp. 238–56.

Póirtéir, Cathal, 'Folk Memory and the Famine', in Cathal Póirtéir (ed.), *The Great Irish Famine* (Cork, 1985), pp. 219–231.

Quinn, James, 'John Mitchel and the Rejection of the Nineteenth Century', *Éire-Ireland*, Fall/Winter 2003, pp. 90–108.

Roberts, Paul E., 'Caravats and Shanavests: Whiteboyism and Faction Fighting in East Munster, 1802–11', in Samuel Clark and James S. Donnelly, Jr. (eds), *Irish Peasants: Violence and Political Unrest, 1780–1914* (Madison, 1983), pp. 64–101.

Ruane, Joseph and Jennifer Todd, 'The Roots of Intense Ethnic Conflict May Not In Fact Be Ethnic: Categories, Communities and Path Dependence', *European Journal of Sociology*, 45 (2004), pp. 209–232.

Serbyn, Roman, 'Lemkin on Genocide of Nations', *Journal of International Criminal Justice*, 7 (2009), pp. 123–130.

Simpson, Glenn, 'William Pirrie, the Titanic and Home Rule', *History Ireland*, 20 (2012).

Smyth, Ailbhe, 'Ireland', in Claire Buck (ed.), *Bloomsbury Guide to Women's Literature* (London, 1992), pp. 36–41.

Smyth, W.J., 'The Story of the Great Irish Famine, 1845–52: A Geographical Perspective', in John Crowley, William J. Smyth and Mike Murphy (eds), *Atlas of the Great Irish Famine* (Cork, 2012), pp. 4–12.

Solar, Peter, 'The Great Famine was No Ordinary Subsistence Crisis', in E.M. Crawford (ed.), *Famine: The Irish Experience* (Edinburgh, 1989), pp. 112–31.

Stark, Tom and Frank Geary, 'Examining Ireland's Post-Famine Economic Growth Performance', *Economic Journal*, 112 (2002), pp. 919–35.

Thompson, E.P., 'The Moral Economy of the English Crowd in the Eighteenth Century', *Past and Present*, 50, 1 (1971), pp. 76–136.

Walker, B.M., 'Villain, Victim or Prophet? William Gregory and the Great Famine', *Irish Historical Studies*, 38 (2013), pp. 579–99.

Whyte, John, 'How much Discrimination was there under the Unionist Regime, 1921–1968?', in Tom Gallagher and James O'Connell, (eds), *Contemporary Irish Studies* (Manchester, 1983), pp. 1–35.

Wilson, Trevor, 'Lord Bryce's Investigation into Alleged German Atrocities in Belgium, 1914–15', *Journal of Contemporary History,* 3, 14 (1979), pp. 369–83.

CDs

Matt Molloy, Paul Brady, Tommy Peoples (CD, Green Linnet, Danbury, USA, 1985).

Online Websites

Centre for the Study of Historic Irish Houses and Estates, http://historicirishhouses.ie/research/postdoctoral-research-projects/1841-irish-testimonial-lord-morpeth [accessed 9 December 2013].

Corpus of Electronic Texts (CELT), University College Cork, http://www.ucc.ie/celt/published/T301038/index.html [accessed 3 March 2014].

http://www.flickr.com/photos/gerryward/919237617/ [accessed 21 March 2014].

Holocaust Encyclopedia, United States Holocaust Memorial Museum, http://www.ushmm.org/wlc/en/article.php?ModuleId=10007050 [accessed 10 April 2014].

http://www.irishmemorial.org/ [accessed 14 April 2014].

Jacobs, Joseph, 'Anglo-Israelism', http://www.jewishencyclopedia.com/ [accessed 17 May 2012].

Jewish Virtual Library, https://www.jewishvirtuallibrary.org/jsource/Holocaust/killedtable.html [accessed 10 April 2014].

http://www.measuringworth.com/ukcompare/ [accessed 5 May, 2014].

National Archives of Ireland, http://www.census.nationalarchives.ie [accessed regularly 2013–2015].

Organisation for Economic Co-operation and Development (OECD),

http://www.compareyourcountry.org/chart.php?cr=21andlg=enandproject=odaandpage=1 [accessed 18 April 2014].

Joint Committee on the Constitutional Amendment on Children in September 2008, http://oireachtasdebates.oireachtas.ie/Debates%20Authoring/DebatesWebPack.nsf/committeetakes/CCJ2008090900004?opendocument [accessed 6 January 2013].

Public Records Office of Northern Ireland (PRONI), Ulster Covenant, 1912, (http://applications.proni.gov.uk/UlsterCovenant/image.aspx?image=M0017430009). (http://applications.proni.gov.uk/UlsterCovenant/image.aspx?image=W0018840005 [accessed 14 April 2013].).

Serbyn, Roman, 'The Holodomor: Reflections on the Ukrainian Genocide', 16th Annual J.B. Rudnyckyj Distinguished Lecture, http://umanitoba.ca/libraries/units/archives/media/Lecture_XVI_Serbyn.pdf [accessed 21 March 2014].

United Nations Convention on the Prevention and Punishment of the Crime of Genocide, http://www.un.org/en/ga/search/view_doc.asp?symbol=A/RES/260%28III%29 [accessed 3 April 2011].

Unpublished

Comerford, Vincent, 'Deference, Accommodation and Conflict in Irish Confessional Relations' (unpublished paper, National University of Ireland, Maynooth, 2014).

Kennedy, Liam, 'Did Industrialisation Matter? Nationalist and Unionist Conflict in Ireland', paper presented to the International conference on Politics and Demography (London School of Economics, September 2006).

Kennedy, Liam, 'Writing Irish History in the Shadow of the Troubles in Northern Ireland' (Institute of Irish Studies, Queen's University, Belfast, 2015).

Lucy, Gordon, 'The Solemn League and Covenant, 1912: Leaders and Supporters', paper presented to the conference 'In Defence of Modernity: the Ulster Solemn League and Covenant, 1912–14' (Belfast, 17 January 2014).

Murphy, Clare, 'The Social Basis of Irish Nationalism, 1867–1879' (unpublished Ph.D. thesis, Queen's University, Belfast, 1993).

Read, Charles, '"Laissez-faire": The Irish Famine and British Financial Crisis', paper presented to the annual conference of the Irish Economic and Social History Society (Galway, November 2013).

Reilly, Ciarán, 'Culpability and the Great Famine', paper presented to the annual conference of the Irish Economic and Social History Society (Galway, November 2013).

Reynolds, Lee, *D.I. John William Nixon, MBE: From Dismissal to MP* (B.A. dissertation, Queen's University, Belfast, 1995).

Walker, Graham, 'The Ulster Covenant as a Reflection of Protestant Ulster', paper presented to the conference 'In Defence of Modernity: The Ulster Solemn League and Covenant, 1912–14' (Belfast, 17 January 2014).

Index

Note: Page locators for tables appear in bold.

Adams, Gerry, 178, 260n9
Address to the Inhabitants of the Countries subject to the British Crown, 13
Agar-Robartes, Thomas, 246n1
age profile of Easter 1916 revolutionaries, 172
agricultural prices in the 1820s, 69–70
agricultural protectionism, 121, 245n101 (*see also* protectionism as economic policy)
Aiken, Frank, 196 (*see also* Altnaveigh massacre, the)
Akenson, Donald H., 34, 60–1, 104, 254n72
Algerian war for independence, 19
All-for-Ireland League, the, 183
Altnaveigh massacre, the, 196, 207, 262n43
American civil war, the, 22, 220n34, 222n61
American Declaration of Independence, the, 148, 161, 162
American War of Independence, the, 189–90
Ancient Order of Hibernians, the, 183
Anglican establishment in Ireland, the, 39
Anglo-Irish Treaty, the, 7, 203–4
Anglo-Irish war as label for the war of independence, 200, 201, 203, 212
anti-Catholicism in British political culture, 136–7, 138
anti-clerical measures across Europe, 32–3
anti-Semitic pogroms, 21 (*see also* Nazi treatment of Jews)
anti-Semitism in Ireland, 223n94
anti-Treaty IRA, the, 7, 21, 195, 199, 203, 210
appeal of nationalism, the, 3
apportioning blame and responsibility for the Famine, 112–13, 238n81
Archdeacon, Thomas, 123

Armenian massacres by Turkey, 108–9, 110
Arnott, Lady, 200
Asquith, H.H., 136–7
assassinations of ex-servicemen of the First World War, 206
Axis Rule in Occupied Europe (book), 109

B Specials, the, 211, 213
Barbour, John Milne, 72–3, 74, 136, 141
Barry, Tom, 189, 191, 200
Belfast and industry, 59, 63
Belfast News-Letter (*BNL* - newspaper), 128, 140, 180, 181, 246n8
benefits of the Act of Union, 57, 61, 64, 72–3
Bew, Paul, 212
Birmingham, George, 130
Birrell, Augustine, 157
'Black and Tan' war as label for the 'war of independence', 189, 260n9
Black and Tans, the, 193, 207
Blair, Tony, 103, 122
blood sacrifice, notion of the, 155, 158, 161, 163, 168, 175, 199, 226n149
Bloody Sunday, November 1920, 194
Blueshirts, the, 20
Bonaparte, Napoleon, 20
Bonar Law, Andrew, 127, 186, 200
Book of Invasions, The (Leabhar Gabhála Éireann) (book), 43
Boyce, George, 208
Boyle, Prof. Francis, 108, 117
Bradshaw, Brendan, 14
Breen, Dan, 188, 200–1, 208, 215, 259n6, 260n7, 262n55, 262n58, 265n117
Breton language, the, 29

British policy before the Famine, 83–4
British policy during the Famine, 81, 84–5, 86–8, 94, 95–6, 97–8, 103, 112, 118
British readiness for concessions, 214–15
Brookeborough, Lord, 171
Browning, Christopher, 91
Bruce, Edward, 43
'Bulgarian Atrocities', the, 12
Burke, Edmund, 112
business cycle, the, 58–9
Butt, Isaac, 12
Buttimer, James, 206

Canadian confederation, the, 138, 249n65
Carroll, Kitty, 192–3
Carson, Sir Edward, 135, 142, 143, 170, 175; and the Covenant, 128–9, 130, 169; political legacy of, 183, 258n61
Casement, Sir Roger, 165
Castledawson affair, the, 128
Catalan language and culture, 28–9, 234n102
Cathleen ni Houlihan, 36
Catholic Church, the, 33, 114–15, 137, 138, 248n51
Catholic Church in France, the, 31
Catholic Emancipation, 69–70, 232n72
Catholic middle class, the, 56, 63, 69, 70, 113
Catholic pogroms in Belfast, 195–6, 205
Catholic workers in the north, 75–6
Catholicism in eighteenth-century Ireland, 31
Cavanagh, Michael, 164
Ceannt, Eamonn, 147, 184
Charles I, King, 134
Chartist movement, the, 132
'children of the nation', 18, 149–50, 152–3, 161, 163, 165, 254n68; and the call to sacrifice, 164, 165, 175; as infantilising language, 156, 162; and lack of inclusiveness, 155–6, 166; as misunderstood phrase, 162, 176
Christianity, 43–4
Church of Ireland, the, 63, 115–16, 134, 141, 246n7
Civil War, the, 20, 21–2, 195, 199, 203, 209–10, 263n65
civil war conflicts, 20–2, 220n34, 222n61
civil war patterns from 1913 to 1923, 204–10, 213, 215
civilian deaths in the 1916 Rising, 154–5

claim to sovereignty through the generations, 159–60, 179
Clancy, Peadar, 211
Clarendon, Lord, 86, 117
Clark, Sir George, 181
Clarke, Tom, 147, 155, 172
clerical opposition to university colleges, 115
Cole, John, 210
collectivisation programme in Russia, 22
Colley, Alfred, 210
Collins, Michael, 189, 198, 210, 214, 262n58, 262n60
commemorations of the Easter Rising, 179, 184–5
commemorative activities on the Famine, 116–17, 119–21, 122–3, 243n69, 243n70
Commission on Financial Relations between Britain and Ireland, 141
communal violence in Ulster, 21, 128, 132; during the 'war of independence', 195–6, 205, 207, 211, 214, 262n43
concepts relating to the conflicts in Ireland, 1919-23, 189–91, 190, 199–200, 210–13, 215–16, 219n13, 260n9
Confession of Faith of the Kirk of Scotland, The, 248n44
Connell, K.H., 13
Connolly, James, 86, 106, 240n9, 252n48, 253n64; and the Easter Rising, 147, 148, 158, 161, 172; and the Proclamation, 150, 158; on women, 36, 150, 225n141
conscription, possibility of, 172, 184, 192, 202
conscription and the 1916 Proclamation, 161
Conservative Party, the, 140, 185, 205
constitutional crisis from the Third Home Rule Bill, 127, 185–6
contrast between Famine curricula in New York and New Jersey, 107–8
Control of Manufactures Acts, the, 158
Convention on the Prevention and Punishment of the Crime of Genocide, 109–10, 117
conversions across religious lines, 45–8, **48,** 51–2
Coogan, Tim Pat, 117
Cooke, Rev. Henry, 59
Cork Examiner (newspaper), 89, 93
County Cork during the 'war' 1919-22, 194, 205–6

covenant, notion of a, 133–4
Craig, James, 76, 129, 130, 136, 143, 175
Craig, William, 181
Crawford, Maj. Frederick Hugh, 129
creation myths for nationalists and unionists,
171, 186, 256n13 (*see also* Cúchulainn;
gendered representations of nationhood)
Crowley, Joseph, 107
Cruithin, the, 42
Cúchulainn, 36, 254n82, 255n89
Cullen, Paul, Cardinal, 30–1
cultural mix resulting from Norman
settlement, 43
cultural wars and notions of Irishness, 208–9
Cumann na mBan, 154, 173
Cumming, David, 195, 261n36

Dáil Éireann, 179
Danish land tenure, 22
Davitt, Michael, 71, 235n26
de Paor, Liam, 119, 154, 158
de Valera, Eamon, 102, 154, 159, 203, 262n58
Dead Republic, The (book), 180
death rates in Irish and mainland European
conflicts, comparison of, 18–22
death rates in World War I, **18**
death rates of the Famine, 92–3, 237n58;
'excess' deaths, 92, 234n1
Declaration, the, 142, 143–4, 177, 249n67,
251n24
declarations and proclamations, comparison
of, 148
decline of the Irish language, 27, 28, 30,
224n99, 232n80
defence of the 'Republic', 7, 189, **190,
199–200, 212
Democratic Programme of the first Dáil, the,
179
demographic implications of industrialisation
in Ulster, 76, 77
demographic power of Ulster Unionists,
169–70
Devlin, Joe, 201, 263n73
devolved assemblies, 141
differences between the 1916 Proclamation
and the Solemn League and Covenant,
172–8, **178**
Dillon, Bridget, 209
discrimination against Catholics and
Presbyterians, 83

doctrine of succession in republican theology,
179, 184–5
Doherty Gaelic sept, the, 46–7
dominance of men in the Easter 1916
Rising, 173
Donnelly, Jr., James, 102
Dorian, Hugh, 114
Doyle, Avril, 119–20
Doyle, Roddy, 180
Draft Riots of New York, 100–1, 239n91
Drummond, Thomas, 83

'Easter 1916' (poem), 154, 180, 251n25
Easter Rising, the, 146, 153, 155–6,
172, 173–4, 180, 183, 247n20;
casualty rates, 154–5, 164–5, 221n44;
commemorations of, 179, 184–5;
executions of leaders and punitive
measures, 157–8, 184, 252n35;
opportunistic timing of, 155–6, 170–1,
252n39 (*see also* Proclamation of the Irish
Republic, the)
ecology of Ireland, the, 15–16
economic equity for Catholics, 61–3
economic grievances in the nineteenth
century, 67
economic progress and nationalism, 54–6,
55, 62, 63–77
economic sovereignty, 179, 257n43
Economist, The (magazine), 239n105
Edict of Nantes, the, 30, 47
Edwards, Ruth Dudley, 1, 216
Emigrants and Exiles (book), 13
emigration, 59–60, 115, 223n84, 252n46; as
economic phenomenon, 25–6, 62, 63; of
Irish women, 26, 35, 223n84
Emmet, Robert, 148, 164, 253n60, 253n67
End of Hidden Ireland, The (book), 82
Engels, Frederick, 84, 235n17
English, Richard, 151
equality and the 1916 Proclamation, 161–2
ETA (Euskadi Ta Askatasuna), 264n81
'ethnic autism,' 102, 239n97
ethnic blending of diverse groups from the
seventeenth century, 45–8, 52, 133–4
ethnic composition of Irish America, 122,
124
ethnic influences on U.S. school curricula,
106–8
ethnic minorities of both Irish states, 8

ethno-religious divide, the, 48–50, **49,** 70, 74, 113–14, 160; conversions across denominations, 45–8, **48**; between North and South, 76, 183, 185, 213; in Ulster, 45, 70, 75, 162–3, 195–6 (*see also* partition; sectarian attacks on southern Protestants; sectarian violence in Ulster)

ethno-symbolic approach to national identity, 151–2

European famines, 82, 110, 111, 239n102

European romanticism and Irish nationalism, 37 (*see also* gendered representations of nationhood)

European Union, the, 245n101

'excess deaths' during the Famine, 92, 234n1

faction fighting, 85

'Faith of our Fathers' (hymn), 30

Falk laws of Germany, the, 31–2

Famine, the, 4–5, 24, 57, 62, 68, 103, 113–16, 164, 218n8; apportioning blame and responsibility for, 112–13, 238n81; British policy during, 81, 84–5, 86–8, 94, 95–6, 97, 98, 103, 112, 118; death rates, 92–3, 234n1, 237n58; as genocide, 5, 14, 82, 105–6, 108, 109, 111–12, 117–18, 119–20, 123–4, 244n78; and the Holocaust, 5, 14, 82–3, 88–98, 99, 100, 103–4, 105–6, 107, 221n55; as nationalist ideological weapon, 102, 119, 123; relief efforts, 96–7, 115, 118, 231n38, 238n71, 238n75, 239n105

Famine Plot, The (book), 117

famine refugees in Britain, 84–6

Fanning, Ronan, 139

feminisation of the persona of Ireland, the (*see* gendered representations of nationhood)

Fenians, the, 159

Field, The (play), 114

fiftieth anniversary of the Solemn League and Covenant, 180–1

Finkelstein, Norman, 102

Finnish struggles for independence, 19

First World War, the, 17–18, **18,** 146, 155, 164, 203, 218n11, 221n42; German atrocities during, 157, 171, 253n49, 260n23

Fitzpatrick, John, 206

flags flown during the Easter Rising, 153

FLN *(Le Front de Libération Nationale),* 19

food exports during the Famine, 117, 118

foreign ownership of Irish resources, 158–9

Franco, General Francisco, 20

freedom of exit for Irish emigrants, 25–6

freedom of religious worship, 33

French, Lord Sir John, 193, 200–1

French Revolution, the, 20, 29, 31

Fry, Rev. William, 60

GAA (Gaelic Athletic Association), the, 208

Gaelic League, the, 208

Gallagher, Thomas, 14

Gangs of New York (film), 100

Gellner, Ernest, 53, 151

gender issues: for the 1916 Proclamation, 150, 154, 163, 173; for signing the Solemn League and Covenant, 130, 132–3, 142–4, 172–3

gendered representations of nationhood, 36, 152–3, 155, 166, 174–5

general election (December 1918), 6, 179, 185, 192, 201, 212

general election (June 1922), 203

genetic make-up of the peoples of Ireland, 2–3; myth of pure original ethnic stock, 42, 52

genocide: agreeing the definition of, 108–11, 241n25; and the Famine, 5, 14, 82, 105–6, 108, 109, 111–12, 117–18, 119–20, 123–4, 244n78

German arms shipments, 158, 252n47

German atrocities in the First World War, 157, 171, 253n49, 260n23

German church-state relations, 31–2

German colonial rule in Namibia, 110

German plot of 1918, the, 192

Ginnell, Lawrence, 196, 262n46

Gladstone, William, 12, 67

Gonne MacBride, Maud, 200

Gray, Peter, 86, 122

Great Dublin Lockout, the, 137

Green Flag, The (book), 13

Gregory, Sir William, 87, 117; and the Gregory Clause, 113

grievances from earlier periods and senses of victimhood, 38; the Famine as ideological weapon, 102, 119, 123 (*see also* Irish sense of victimhood)

Griffith, Arthur, 30, 67, 138, 244n84, 257n37

Griffith, Kenneth, 14
Grosse Isle Famine memorial, 118
guerrilla tactics of the IRA, 188, 193–4, 260n19
guilt amongst Holocaust and Famine survivors, 99–100, 104, 120–1
Guinnane, Timothy, 122, 245n106
gunrunning operations in Ulster, 129, 139
Gwynn, Stephen, 209

Hannon, Tom, 211
Harland, Edward, 45
Harper's Weekly (magazine), 101
Harris, Eoghan, 259n67
Hart, Peter, 206
Harty, John, Archbishop, 191
Hewitt, John, 42, 52, 227n2
Hibernicised Old English, the, 37
Hitler, Adolf, 89, 236n44
Hollyford RIC barracks ambush, 187–8
Holocaust, the, 82, 101–2, 109; comparisons with the Famine, 5, 14, 82–3, 88–98, 99, 100, 103–4, 105–6, 107, 221n55
Holodomor (Ukrainian famine), the, 110, 111
Home Rule, 64, 65, 71, 72, 145, 170, 185; and the Third Home Rule Bill, 127, 136, 137, 139–40, 246n7 (*see also* Unionist opposition to Home Rule)
Hoppen, Theodore, 11
House of Lords veto, the, 127
Hungarian national revival, the, 29–30
hunger in Africa, 121
Hyde, Douglas, 163

ICA (Irish Citizen Army), 153, 154, 214, 251n30, 252n48
identity of the Irish, 151–2, 200, 208–9, 213–14
ideological exploitation of the Famine, 102, 119, 123
Ignatieff, Michael, 109
immigration and industrialisation, 45
income per head of population, 24–5
increasing use of the English language, 66, 69, 231n43
industrial revolution in England, the, 56, 58
industrialisation in Ulster, 4, 45, 63, 64, 71–2, 135–6, 175; demographic implications of, 76, 77; due to Protestant immigrants, 45; and the textile industry, 58–9, 107

infant mortality rates, **34,** 34–5
Iníona na hÉireann, 154
insularity of Irish culture, the, 39
insulation of Ireland from war, 17, 18, 19–20
intentionality of the British towards deaths in the Famine, 95–6, 103
interdependence between the North and South economies, absence of, 135–6
IPP (Irish Parliamentary Party), the, 137, 183, 191, 201, 202, 214
IRA (Irish Republican Army), the, 187, 192, 197, 201–2, 203, 214; and the anti-Treaty IRA, 7, 21, 195, 199, 203, 210; attacks on civilians and Protestants, 7, 194–5, 196, 205–7, 211, 219n15, 264n92; guerrilla tactics of, 188, 193–4, 260n19; regionalisation of activity, 191, 210; and the Soloheadbeg ambush, 188, 191, 193, 215, 259n6, 260n7 (*see also* Provisional IRA, the)
IRB (Irish Republican Brotherhood), the, 154, 155, 156, 165, 183, 201, 253n67
Irish America and the Famine, 105–8, 117, 122–4, 244n78
Irish Catholic Directory, 248n51
Irish contributions to foreign wars, 16–17, 18, 164; in the British armed forces, 155, 164, 191, 203, 254n79
Irish Convention, the, 184, 214
Irish Famine Curriculum in U.S. public schools, 105–7, 122
Irish Free State, the, 67, 216–17
Irish Independent (newspaper), 193–4, 239n96
Irish Ladies Land League, the, 249n73
Irish News (newspaper), 130, 140, 162, 262n43
Irish prejudices and phobias, 85
Irish racism in the United States, 101, 123, 223n92
Irish sense of victimhood, 1–2, 11–15, 36–41, 123–4, 156, 226n146
Irish service in the British armed forces, 155, 164, 191, 203, 254n79
Irish Times, The (newspaper), 131
Irish Volunteers, the, 182–3, 192, 204, 209, 214, 263n64
Islamist terror attacks on the Twin Towers, 174
Israel, 102
ITGWU (Irish Transport and General Workers Union), the, 197

Jackson, Alvin, 171
Jackson, Andrew, 123
Jackson, Thomas, 14
Jacobite poetry, 37
James I, King, 44
Jeanie Johnston (ship), 116, 243n70
Jewish immigration, 45
Jews in Nazi Germany, treatment of, 84,
    88–9, 91–2, 93–4, 95, 108, 237n57
John XXIII, Pope, 33
Joseph, Emperor Franz, 32
Journal of International Criminal Justice, 111

Kedourie, Elie, 151
Kee, Robert, 13–14
Kelly, Dr. Denis, Bishop, 72, 73
Kennedy, R.E., 35
Kerr, John, 106
Kettle, Tom, 68
Keyes McDonnell, Kathleen, 206
Kiberd, Declan, 251n25
Kinealy, Christine, 116, 117
Kipling, Rudyard, 180
'Knocklong Soviet,' the, 197
Kristallnacht, 84

labelling of wars as defences of the
    'Republic,' 7, 189, **190**, 199–200, 212
Lahiff, Constable Michael, 154, 164, 251n33,
    265n114
laissez faire economics, 86–8, 94, 98, 103, 106,
    114
Land League, the, 208
land reforms, 64, 197
land tenure system, the, 12, 22–3, 222n70
Land War, the, 62, 70–1, 102
landlords and the Famine, 87, 97, 112–13,
    118
landowner-peasant relations in Europe, 22–3
language and perception of Protestant
    identity, 50–1
Larkin, Jim, 86, 161, 198
Leader, the (newspaper), 200, 208
Lee, Joseph, 7, 134, 227n156
legacy of the 1913-23 conflicts, 216–17
Lemkin, Prof. Raphael, 5, 108–9, 111–12,
    120
Lengel, Edward, 85–6
length of time of English oppression, the,
    37–8

Levi, Primo, 99, 120
Lewis, Helen, 94, 99
liberal influence in Britain on the use of
    force in Ireland, 212–13
Liberal Party, the, 127, 139–40, 185, 205
life expectancy of Irish women, 35
Limerick Trades Council, 197–8
linguistic intolerance in Europe, 28–30
linkage between suffering and subsequent
    behaviour, 100–1
literacy rates, 34
living standards, 23–5, 56–7, 61, 63
Lloyd George, David, 73, 214–15
local elections (January 1920), 202–3, 212,
    264n83
Londonderry, Lady Theresa, 14, 182
Lynch, Liam, 199, 207
Lyons, F.S.L., 216

Mac Suibhne, Breandán, 99–100
MacDiarmada, Sean, 147, 253n66
MacDonagh, Thomas, 147, 148, 158
MacHale, John, Archbishop, 115
MacNeill, Eoin, 145
MacSwiney, Terence, 198, 262n58
malaria, 220n28
Markievicz, Constance, 154, 251n30, 265n114
marriage across ethnic and religious lines,
    45–7
mass evictions during the Famine, 118
mass slaughter and industrialisation, 93
Maxwell, Sir John, 183, 184
McDonnell, James, 188
McEneny, John J., 106
McGimpsey Gaelic sept, the, 46
McIldoon Gaelic sept, the, 46
McKee, Dick, 211
McLuhan, Marshall, 176
McMahon, John, 195–6
Mein Kampf (book), 88, 236n44
Methodist Church of Ireland, the, 185
migrations across religious and ethnic divides,
    2–3
militant separatists and aims of the Irish
    Republic, 198–9
Miller, David, 140
Miller, K.A., 13, 65
mindscape, notion of, 246n113
minority languages in France and Spain,
    28–9, 224n106

Mise Éire (poem), 166
misunderstandings in popular culture about
    the Famine, 118
Mitchel, John, 12, 95–6, 123, 245n112
mixed marriages, 132, 137
M'Kean, Rev. Dr., 136, 137
modernisation in the nineteenth century, 66
modernism and nationalism, 151–2
Mokyr, Joel, 116–17
Monaghan during the war of independence,
    206–7
monetary value of copies of the
    Proclamation and Covenant, 179–80,
    258n44, 258n45
'Monster' Misery of Ireland, The (book), 12
Moore, Thomas, 13
Moore, William, 141
MOPE (Most Oppressed People Ever)
    acronym, 1, 36, 226n145 (*see also* Irish
    sense of victimhood)
Moran, D.P., 165–6, 208
Morpeth, Lord, 132
Mulcahy, Richard, 202, 215
Mullin, James V., 105, 107
Munster Plantation, the, 44
Murphy, Prof. Maureen, 107
Murray, Dr. Daniel, Archbishop, 115
Mussolini, Benito, 164
Myrdal, Gunnar, 76
myths of pure ethnic stock in Ireland, 42,
    43, 52

national flag, the, 153
nationalism, 37, 151–2, 165–6; as a
    backlash against industrial progress,
    53–4; and unionism, 3–4, 7–8, 73–4,
    162–3
nationalist mobilisation through civil
    organisation and the first Dáil, 214, 215
nationalist thinking on the North, 140,
    162–3, 183, 256n25 (*see also* partition)
nature of Ireland's incorporation into the
    United Kingdom, 185–6, 212–13
nature of the freedom being fought for by
    nationalists, 154, 253n65
Nazi treatment of Jews, 84, 88–9, 91–2, 93–4,
    95, 108, 236n44, 237n57
Ne Temere papal decree on mixed marriages,
    132, 137
New Irish, the, 42

New Jersey Holocaust Education
    Commission, 105, 108
New York Times (newspaper), 111
Norman and Anglo-Norman invasions, the,
    43
Nuremberg Laws, the, 84

O'Brien, Edna, 228n21
O'Brien, William, 183
O'Casey, Sean, 153, 167, 180
O'Connell, Daniel, 13, 16, 32, 56, 69, 70,
    139, 170
O'Connell, Patrick, 188
O'Doherty, Sir Cahir, 46
O'Donnell, Peadar, 197, 200
O'Donoghue, Florence, 198
O'Malley, Ernie, 7, 13, 187–8, 189, 201, 207,
    210–11, 265n122
online availability of Ulster Covenant
    signatures, 181–2
openness of Ireland to invasions, 42, 43
Orange Order, the, 70, 85, 162, 181
original Gaelic ethnic group, notion of, 42,
    43
origins of the Irish mind-set of victimhood,
    37–8
O'Shea, Joe, 185
Ostmen, the, 43
overseas aid by Ireland, 121–2

Parnell, Charles Stewart, 12, 71, 231n57
partition, 4, 7–8, 38, 163, 183, 200,
    214, 254n72; 1916 Proclamation as
    foundational document for, 156, 184; as
    secession, 204, 212, 264n87
Path to Genocide, The (book), 91
Pearse, Mary Brigid, 146–7, 187, 254n80
Pearse, Patrick, 156, 160, 182, 257n30,
    25590; and the 1916 Proclamation, 146,
    147, 148; blood sacrifice as national
    purification, 155, 158, 168, 175, 226n149;
    conflicted sexuality of, 150, 165;
    mythmaking of, 153, 165, 166; unhealthy
    preoccupation with children, 162, 165,
    254n83
Peel, Sir Robert, 83, 86
Penal Laws, the, 30–1, 38, 47, 82, 107
People's Petition, the, 132
petitions and signature-collecting, 132
Philadelphia Famine Monument, the, 117

Phoblacht, An (newspaper), 119
Pirrie, Lord William James, 233n94, 248n48
Pius IX, Pope, 32, 115
plantations as form of English conquest, 44
Planter stock, 42, 52, 227n2
Plunkett, Joseph, 147, 158, 172
Poland and victimhood, 2
policing of the Solemn League and
    Covenant, 130–1
poor-law system, the, 13, 57–8, 88, 89–90,
    96–7, 103, 229n12
population census (1851), 63
population census (1911), 46
Population History of Ireland, The (book), 13
population of Ireland, the, 103; of Protestants,
    169–70, 256n8, 264n98
potato crop and food supply, the, 57
poverty in Ireland before the Famine, 83–4,
    103
Power, Samantha, 110
power structures from the seventeenth
    century onward, 65–6, 71
precedent for violence set by the Easter
    Rising, 164
prerogatives of the welfare of Ireland, 144
Presbyterianism in Ireland, 134, 228n25,
    232n78, 259n72
press portrayal of the Irish in the nineteenth
    century, 84, 90, 101
private donations to developing countries,
    121
private property and the Irish social system,
    159, 253n58
Proclamation of the Irish Republic, the,
    6, 18, 146–50, 159, 186, 199, 250n6;
    compared with the Solemn League and
    Covenant, 168–78, **178**; critique of,
    150–1, 152–4, 157, 158, 160–2, 163–5,
    166–7; as foundational document for
    partition, 156, 184; monetary value of
    copies, 179–80, 258n44, 258n45
PRONI (Public Record Office of Northern
    Ireland), 130, 181, 249n68
protectionism as economic policy, 72–3, 121,
    233n87, 245n101
Protestant immigration from Europe, 45
Protestant population, the, 169–70, 256n8,
    264n98; role in the independent Irish
    state, 207–8, 209
Protestant Reformation, the, 44

Provisional Government, the, 148–9, 163,
    171, 174, 175, 250n10
Provisional IRA, the, 119, 185, 257n39 (*see
    also* IRA (Irish Republican Army), the)
psychological implications of absent fathers,
    262n58
public desire for a violent struggle, lack of,
    201, 202, 203, 214
punitive measures against the Easter Rising
    leaders, 157–8, 184, 252n35

Quebec referendum for independence,
    249n65

racialist attitudes to the Irish, 84–6, 87,
    235n15, 235n17, 235n27 (*see also* Irish
    racism in the United States)
racialist consciousness across Europe, 208–9
reaction of Irish society to the Holocaust,
    102
realities of the Irish Free State, 67
rebellion of 1641, the, 159
Red Hand of Ulster, The (book), 130
redemption of Ireland through violence,
    211–12 (*see also* blood sacrifice, notion
    of the)
Redmond, John, 127, 137, 138, 145, 183, 209
reforms as moderating influence on
    constitutional nationalism, 231n52
regionalisation of IRA activity in the war of
    independence, 191, 210
relations between economics and politics,
    64–5
relations between the IRA and Sinn Féin,
    194
release of wartime photographs of Nazi
    concentration camps in the Irish press,
    101–2
relief measures during the Famine, 96–7, 118,
    231n38, 238n71, 238n75, 239n105
religion as the driver of Unionist opposition
    to Home Rule, 73, 74
religious freedom, 31, 225n129
religious persecution in Europe, 31–3, 47
rental incomes to landlords, 97
Repeal movement, the, 113, 139
republican theologies, 211–12; doctrines
    of generational succession, 179, 184–5;
    notion of blood sacrifice, 155, 158, 161,
    163, 168, 175, 199, 226n149

Resurrection of Hungary, The (book), 30
RIC (Royal Irish Constabulary), the, 187, 195, 211
Rice, Prof. Charles, 108
rigging of the June 1922 general election, 203
Robinson, Mary, 120, 122
Robinson, Peter, 182
Robinson, Seamus, 188
Roche, Sir Boyle, 1, 218n1
Rockite insurrection, the, 70, 225n133
role of emotion in the popular memory of the Famine, 4–5
role of Protestants in an Irish republic, 207–8, 209
Ross, Martin, 180
royalism and the Irish psyche, 138, 152, 160
Russell, Lord John, 81, 86, 87, 112, 117
Russian civil war, the, 20
Russian land struggles, 22–3
Russian Revolution, the, 25
Rwandan mass killings, 93, 110

Scottish Covenanters, the, 134, 139
Scottish economic standards, 23–4
Scottish influence in north-east Ireland, 43, 44–5
sea passage of Irish emigrants, 26
secession through partition, 204, 212, 264n87
Second World War, the, 18, 21, 108
sectarian attacks on southern Protestants, 194–5, 196, 205–7, 211, 219n15, 264n92
sectarian violence in Ulster, 195–6, 205, 207, 211, 214, 262n43
self-accusation, notion of, 120
Serbia and victimhood, 2
Serbyn, Prof. Roman, 111
sesquicentenary commemorations of the Famine, 116
seventeenth-century Ireland, 14–15
Shadow of a Gunman (play), 167
shipbuilding in Ulster, 45, 63, 71 (*see also* Pirrie, Lord William James)
Sinclair, Thomas, 141, 142
Sinn Féin, 119, 184, 189, 211, 214, 215; and the 1918 general election, 6, 179, 192, 199, 201; and the 1920 local elections, 202–3, 212; absence of public mandate for violence or war, 201, 202–3, 212; attitude to social agitation, 197, 198, 201

Slattery, Michael, Archbishop, 115
slave trade, the, 108
slavery, 12, 123, 245n112
Small Differences (book), 61
small-farmer militancy, 196–7
Smith, A.D., 151
Smith, Elizabeth, 112
Smithwick Tribunal, the, 257n39
Smyth, Col. G.F., 195
social class interpretation of the Famine, 114–16
social inequalities, 63
social militancy and class warfare, 196–8, 211
socio-economic differences between Catholics and Protestants, 60–1, 63, 228n18, 228n21 (*see also* stratification of social occupations by religious affiliation)
socio-economic status of original British Protestant families of different religions, comparison of, **49**, 49–50
Solar, Peter, 103
Solemn League and Covenant, the, 5–6, 128–35, 139–41, 145, 246n7, 247n26, 247n28; comparison with the 1916 Proclamation, 168–78, **178**; legacy of, 179–82, 186
Soloheadbeg ambush, the, 188, 191, 193, 215, 259n6, 260n7
Sontag, Susan, 100, 102
southern economy after the Famine, the, 62, 63–4, 72
Southern Unionism, 192, 200, 202
Spanish civil war, the, 20–1
Spanish Inquisition, the, 47
split in the Irish Volunteers, 209, 213
Stack, Austin, 198
State of the Irish Poor in Great Britain (book), 84
state structures as an influence on Gaelic, 27, 28, 30
stratification of social occupations by religious affiliation, 60–1, 65–6 (*see also* socio-economic differences between Catholics and Protestants)
Stuart monarchy, the, 134, 159
survival of native languages, **27**, 27–30
Sweeney, James Pius, 82

tenant farmer-labourer relations, 113–14, 118, 197
terror against civilians by the IRA, 7

textile industry, the, 58–9, 107
textual analysis of the Easter Proclamation
    and the Solemn League and Covenant,
    176–8, **178,** 247n36, 257n35
Third Home Rule Bill, the, 127, 136, 137,
    139–40, 246n7
Times, The (newspaper), 81, 87, 88, 90, 236n42
Tipperary Star (newspaper), 191
tÓglach, An (journal), 191, 260n17
Tóibín, Colm, 114
Tone, Theobald Wolfe, 226n152
Treacy, Sean, 188, 198, 202, 215, 262n60
Trevelyan, Charles Edward, 86, 87–8, 98, 112,
    117, 238n75
Trevor, William, 228n21
Trotsky, Leon, 25
'Troubles' as a phrase, the, 215–16, 260n11
'Troubles' of Northern Ireland, 181, 184
Tuke, James Hack, 89–90, 95
Twisleton, Edward, 86, 98

Ukrainian Weekly (newspaper), 111
Ulster as an imaginative construct, 133
Ulster Covenant Jubilee Committee, 180
Ulster Guardian (newspaper), 131, 247n28,
    249n61
Ulster Plantation, the, 44–5, 46
Ulster Unionism, 43, 67–8, 71–2, 77; and
    anti-Catholicism, 137, 138–9; attitude to
    the 'Troubles', 192, 193
Ulster Unionist Council, the, 127–8, 174
Ulster Women's Unionist Council, 132
Ulysses (book), 156
Union, the, 58, 62, 67, 113, 189, 216, 217;
    benefits of, 57, 61, 64, 72–3, 203
Unionist opposition to Home Rule, 5–6, 64,
    127, 134, 145, 249n71; for economic and
    trade reasons, 72–3, 74, 136; nationalist
    underestimation of, 140, 162–3, 183,
    256n25; religion as the driver, 73, 74,
    138; through demographic strength, 4,
    76, 77, 169–70 (*see also* Solemn League
    and Covenant, the)
Unionist population of Ulster, 169–70

United Ireland, A (book), 117
United Irishmen, the, 148, 159, 244n92
United Irishmen rebellion of 1798, the, 17,
    32, 46, 162, 225n133, 260n21
United Nations, the, 109, 121
United States public school curricula and the
    Famine, 105–8, 122, 240n14
UVF (Ulster Volunteer Force), the, 7, 76, 145,
    182, 204, 246n7; arming of, 139, 183,
    196; prerequisites for joining, 131
UWUC (Ulster Women's Unionist Council),
    142, 144, 182

Vanguard movement, the, 181
Victoria, Queen, 118, 164
Viking raids, 43–4
violence in twentieth-century Ulster, 45
violence levels in a colonial conflict, 212–13

'war of independence', the, 6–7, 187–96,
    198–9, 200–1, 205–7, 226n153; absence
    of wide support for violence, 201, 202,
    203, 214; comparative analysis of, 18–19,
    21; labelled as the Anglo-Irish war, 200,
    201, 203, 212; retrospective concepts of,
    189–91, **190,** 199–200, 210–13, 215–16,
    219n13, 260n9
warfare in Europe, 14, 17–18, **18**
wartime censorship, 102, 239n95, 239n96
Welsh language, the, 28
whiskey taxes, 67
Why Ireland Starved (book), 116–17
Wilson, Sammy, 243n69
Wolff, Gustav, 45
women in Ireland, 33–6, 63, 64, 142–4,
    251n30, 251n32 (*see also* gender issues)
Wood, Charles, 86, 98, 112, 117
Woodham-Smith, Cecil, 117
workhouses (*see* poor-law system, the)

Yeats, W.B., 154, 163, 180, 251n25
Yellow Lane executions, the, 210
Young Irelanders, the, 12–13, 113, 242n48,
    252n46

Printed in Great Britain
by Amazon

55844257R00182